Cover photo: Mansion on Turtle Creek, Dallas, Texas

I stay at the Huntington because it is quiet and elegant like home. I know all the people and there are no ladies in the lobby with purple hairdos.

—Alistair Cooke

Thank you, Pamela for your unerring good taste for quality and for your talent in telling us about it.

—Peter Balas, President
International Hotel Association

It is indeed very good and full of fascinating addresses for people who travel as much as we do.

—Duchess of Bedford

*The switchboard operator knows your name, the people at the desk say welcome back when you come through the door, and they try to give you your favorite room if you've stayed there a long time, and its fine to have dinner in the dining room if you're there alone. My favorite is the Hotel Bel Air because that's where I spent my honeymoon. . . . We all **know** small hotels are sexy because they **are** small and intimate.*

—Helen Gurley Brown

The elegant ones make staying in hotels a little more bearable. The elegant ones don't seem like hotels at all.

—Philip Glass

All the best for a sure success.

—Valentino

. . . devoted to pleasing the most discriminating. The photos put you on the scene while the text and side notes offer explicit answers.

—Los Angeles Times

Elegant Small Hotels makes a seductive volume for window shopping.... Handsomely illustrated. Hotels that provide the atmosphere of a fine residence: beauty in design, color and furnishings, fresh flower, luxurious toiletries and linens. Other considerations are select business and physical fitness facilities, excellence of cuisine and concierge services.
—Chicago Sun Times

They were chosen, both for their elegant decor and because they possess an ambience like that of a fine residence.
—Washington Post

If elegant small hotels are your thing—and whose aren't they?—check out **Elegant Small Hotels**. *. . . Details 168 such establishments, complete with celeb comment on many of them.*
—Elle

The entries for each hotel include rates, service and facilities available, as well as a short description of the **style and mood** *of the establishment.*
—San Francisco Chronicle

Every great hotel in this guide is unique...handsome photographs.
—Hideaways International

What I love about managing a fine, elegant small hotel is the same that makes me choose these houses for staying: Elegance and efficiency, smallness and smoothness, accuracy and actuality and that personal touch I like so much to feel.
—Count Johannes Walderdorff

My schedule is so hectic that when I can steal a few days for myself, they are very precious to me. I always choose small, out-of-the-way places, which give me and my family privacy, while providing excellent service and luxury accommodations.
—Donna Karan

Congratulations Pamela! Looks *good. Ch... ...ll best regards.*

A sweet collection of great hotels.
—Gavin McLeod

My enjoyment of the elegant small hotel lies in its uniquely personalized service. This smaller scope also affects my role as designer, for I am allowed the freedom to draw upon my residential design knowledge. This approach would be impossible in a larger establishment.
—Valerian Rybar

It's a great adventure to read.
—Roger Horchow

Breaking the rules was the challenge: to create charm by giving up overdone effects, pompous details, nostalgic fake Louis'...to attract attention with almost invisible details; these little things grow on you during your stay...and cast a spell.
—Andree Putman

Let me tell you that we are proud to collaborate with you, and it will be a pleasure to welcome you in France.
—Pierre Cardin

One of the rewards of designing small high quality hotels is that they often are the culmination of a greater sense of interest from the owner and the operator, and therefore provide us, the designer, with a more personalized direction. It also offers us an opportunity to promote the specialized field of hotel design to a higher level of professionalism and excellence. This in turn influences the level of sophistication and appreciation of the general public who previously experienced this design only in high and residential work.
—James Northcutt

A small hotel is your home away from home.
—Caroline Hunt Schoelkopf

There is less chance of running into people you know, so there is more time for the actual purpose of being there.

—Bill Graham

The author and Peter Duchin, who wrote the introduction, make a very persuasive case for staying at small elegant hotels ... these hotels lived up to the author's description. Fortunately the author covers a range of rates from affordable ($50) to expensive ($300) and more.

—St. Louis Post-Dispatch

Pamela Lanier offers up a wish-book for the most luxurious small hotels (less than 200 rooms) in America.

—Dallas, Texas News

... unique places with exquisitely appointed rooms, interesting architecture, luxurious ambiance and excellent food and service. "Small" translates into fewer than 200 rooms.

—Cincinnati Enquirer

"Small" is fewer than 200 guestrooms, "elegant" refers to decor as well as attitude...In a book which differs from the usual guides.

—Midwest Book Review

A collection of 168 fine hotels is described ... A page is devoted to each hotel, with a description of the accommodations and facilities plus information on dining rates, credit cards, and other items of interest.

—Chicago Sunday Sun-Standard

...inviting descriptions of each hotel, along with detailed lists of the services offered.

—Milwaukee Journal

From the Huntington in San Francisco to the Pierre in New York, these hotels cater to a choosy clientele devoted to their particular charms and personal services, seductively described here.

—Banana Republic Travel Bookstore

Services, facilities and amenities nation-wide...Available in retail outlets.

—Travel Age West

...detailed information about 108 small hotels in the U.S.

—San Francisco Examiner

If you are looking for exquisitely appointed guest rooms in a small hotel, inspired architecture, luxurious ambiance and extraordinary personal service then this is the book for you.

—Book Passage

Each hotel is described in detail with a side listing that includes everything...this is an excellent guide for the traveler who is looking for European style tradition in the U.S.

—The Armchair Traveler

A valuable source for the discriminating traveller seeking a luxurious lodging in the European tradition. . . . In addition to exquisite decor, they offer an elegance of atmosphere, accomplished only through the meticulous attention to detail so rare in contemporary life.

—Innsider

America's finest!...An abundance of places to stay; that rival any European hotel in warmth, charm and service.

—The Horchow Collection

Biggest is not always best.... If you can afford to be choosy.

—Dallas Magazine

If you've enjoyed the charming personalized hotels of Europe, you will love Pamela Lanier's selection of ... outstanding hotels here at home. The information and photographs will allow the discerning traveller to choose from among the best....

—Traveller's Bookstore

Elegant small hotels have always fascinated me. This connoisseur's guide describes the atmosphere and individual style of 108 selected hotels.... Detailed listings of all services, facilities and amenities.
—Travel Briefs—Station WLOO, Chicago

... as a resource on elegant, somewhat smaller hotels, this is a good one. Good descriptions, photographs, and all practical data are included.
—Going Places

It happens I always stay at a fine small hotel when given the choice. I'm familiar with quite a few of your selections and must commend you upon the realistic assessments you provide.
—Tom Shane

Dignified and classy.
—Publish

Lanier Publishing has facilitated the planting of nine trees for every tree used in the production of this book.

ELEGANT
SMALL HOTELS™

A CONNOISSEUR'S GUIDE

PAMELA LANIER

The interactive version of this book
may be found on the Internet
(www.travelguides.com)
Also: America Online and CompuServe.

A *Lanier* Guide
▲

Other books from Lanier Travel guides

Family Travel—The Complete Guide
Elegant Hotels of the Pacific Rim
Condo Vacations — The Complete Guide
All-Suite Hotel Guide — The Definitive Directory
Golf Courses — The Complete Guide
Golf Resorts — The Complete Guide
Golf Resorts International
Complete Guide to Bed & Breakfast Inns & Guesthouses in the United States & Canada
22 Days in Alaska
Cinnamon Mornings and Raspberry Teas

Cover photograph: The Mansion on Turtle Creek, used by permission.
Design by Mary Shapiro
Production Coordinators: J.C. Wright, John Richards, Hal Hershey

Editor: Mariposa Valdes
Assistant Editor: Sally Carpenter

Library of Congress Cataloging-in-Publication Data
Lanier, Pamela
      Elegant small hotels: a connoisseurs's guide/Pamela Lanier.
          p.   cm.—(A Lanier guide)
      ISBN 1-58008-023-5
      1. Hotels, taverns, etc.—United States—Guidebooks.   2. United
States—Guidebooks.   I. Title.   II. Series.
Library of Congress Cataloging in Publication data is on file with the publisher.

First Edition September 1986
Thirteenth Edition September 1998

Published by Lanier Publishing International, Ltd.
Drawer D
Petaluma, CA 94953

American Hotel
& Motel Association
ALLIED MEMBER

Distributed to the trade by Ten Speed Press
P.O. Box 7123
Berkeley, CA 94707

Printed in Canada on recycled paper

This book is lovingly dedicated to the memory of John Muir. Very special thanks to
Sarah Morse, Lauren Childress, Marianne Barth, Venetia Young, Mary Kreuger, Jay
Clark, Katherine Bertolucci, Mary Ellen Callahan, Marjorie Silverman, Harriet
Choice, Jeremy Dove, Frank Waldrop, Sartain Lanier, Carol Delattre, Lorraine Strain,
Ann Chandler, Judy Johnson, Mary Shapiro, and the staff of Ten Speed Press.

"There's a small hotel,
with a wishing well,
I wish that we were there
together . . ."
—Rodgers and Hart

CONTENTS

INTRODUCTION

. . . And then there was the time that my band (eight men and one woman) and myself travelled all day changing planes twice to get from New York to a small town in the West where we had to play that night. It had been *that* kind of travelling day—replete with rudeness, abruptness, computer mixups and a complete lack of attention or care for the individual. So somehow it didn't really surprise us when we found upon reaching our ultimate destination that all our instruments and other bags had been mis-routed and sent to Kalamazoo, Chattanooga or some other strange Indian-sounding city. This meant that only those of us who had carried our clothes on board (something I've learned to do) had anything to wear that evening and only me on piano (it doesn't travel with us, thank God) and the trumpet player (who had carried his instrument with him) had anything to play that night—a most unlikely duet! What to do? One could rage uselessly at the cipher in back of the airlines desk, or one could attempt to be cunning.

Opting for the second alternative, I remembered that we were staying in an elegant small hotel which had a reputation for service and attention to the individual; so with fading hope I called the hotel. I was immediately switched to a polite concierge whom I belabored with our seemingly insoluble problem. He listened attentively, asked intelligent questions (a first that day, I'll tell you) and told me to come directly to the hotel and see him there. When we arrived and assembled numbly around his desk, we found that this wonderful man had done the following: he had contacted the local music store which was standing by to hear the specifications of the instruments we needed and would deliver them to the job on time: he had contacted the local evening wear store, which was waiting to hear our sizes and would deliver to the hotel; he had contacted the airlines and traced our bags; he had pre-registered us in our rooms; and finally, he had set up a private room for us in which he had arranged to serve us dinner before we left for the job. Furthermore, it all worked!

Believe me, I need no further inducement to stay in elegant small hotels for the rest of my days. When I travel, which I do a great deal of the time (we played in 41 states in the last three years). I really do appreciate those wonderful qualities that can be found in these hotels: politeness, attentiveness and really an old-fashioned attention to detail and to the needs of the client. Sadly, these qualities are quite lacking in everyday life as we prepare for the 21st century. I'm glad to see, though, that these hotels are returning to a sense of service and style . . . I just hope that with the publication of this book my band and I will be able to get reservations whenever we need them!

—*Peter Duchin*

GUIDE NOTES

This book is sorted by state and within each state, by city or town. Hotels are listed in alphabetical order within each city. Canada, the Caribbean, and Mexico appear at the back of the book

If you are among those discerning travelers who understand that the essence of the good life is quality, this book is designed especially to enhance your travel enjoyment.

To identify the most elegant small hotels in the United States today, we have used the following criteria:

When we say "small," we generally mean fewer than 200 guest rooms; in fact, the typical hotel selected for inclusion in this guide has approximately half that number. We have found that small hotels are best able to offer the high staff-to-guest ratio enabling a genuine concern for each guest's comfort and pleasure.

By "elegant," we mean decor—and also something more. If a hotel is to be one's "home away from home," its atmosphere should be like that of a fine residence. The feeling should be reflected not only in design, color and furnishings, but also in those little touches that *really* matter; fresh flowers, nightly turndown (with a chocolate!), overnight shoeshine, luxurious toiletries and oversized towels . . . all the myriad details that add up to the intangible quality we call elegance.

For us to even consider a particular hotel, it must first have met the foregoing standards. Other factors we have kept in mind, while separating the exceptional from the merely first-class, relate to individual traveler's needs. For example . . .

If you conduct business while traveling, such facilities as secretarial service on call, teleconferencing, telex and computer telecommunications, and perhaps an appropriately-sized meeting or conference room, will be essential.

If you are among the growing number of people to whom physical fitness is a personal must, your hotel should provide in-house facilities such as swimming pool, tennis, spa and massage room, and perhaps weight training equipment. Many of our recommended hotels also arrange guest privileges at prestigious private country clubs and health centers.

If you are among those travelers for whom fine cuisine is a top priority, we agree completely. We have chosen our hotels with excellent dining in mind, and we often include a description of a representative dinner recently served at the hotel. The words "Dress Code" in any listing show that coat and tie are appropriate. We have also indicated when a hotel's dining room is for guests only.

Whether you travel for business, pleasure, or a bit of both, each elegant small hotel described in this guide deserves a special place in your plans and your memories.

This guide encompasses five types of elegant hotel accommodations:

Grand Luxe Hotels: Each of these world-class hotels projects an incomparable aura of tradition and grace. A few of the services provided are superb restaurant and room service, an attentive but very discreet staff with full concierge services, and a sumptuous atmosphere of well-secured luxury. There are only about 3 dozen such hotels in the United States.

City Center Hotels: Designed especially for the business traveler, each of these hotels offer a comfortable, inviting environment where an executive may return each day to lodgings ideally appointed to satisfy business, personal and recreational needs. Special emphasis is placed upon conference facilities and services for executives.

Outstanding Resorts: The quick weekend trip or brief resort holiday is becoming the new vacation style of the ultra-busy. From a wide range of possibilities, we have selected our resort recommendations with regard for their luxurious ambience, excellent cuisine and sporting facilities. Most also offer excellent conference facilities and are perfect for combining recreation and business meetings in beautiful surroundings.

Affordable Elegance: Though one normally expects elegant lodgings to come at higher-than-ordinary rates, we have discovered a select few that offer some of the best of both worlds: comfortable, well-appointed rooms, excellent restaurants and access to sports facilities, with many of the essential amenities associated with Grand Luxe hotels—at surprisingly reasonable prices. Please bear in mind, though, that in the U.S., as elsewhere in the world, the very top quality accommodations carry a correspondingly steep price.

Wonderful Country Inns: Those great small hideaways we all dream about, the perfect place for restoring body and soul (and romance!) cosseted by a caring staff in a gracious and restful ambiance.

For different styles in affordable elegance, please check our most recent editions of *The All-Suite Hotel Guide* and *The Complete Guide to Bed and Breakfasts, Inns and Guesthouses in the United States and Canada*, both by Pamela Lanier.

We have indicated room rates with a code showing the price range of the lowest-priced double-occupancy room:

$=From $50 to 100
$$=From $100 to 150
$$$=From $150 to 225
$$$$=From $225 up

All prices quoted are European Plan; a few resorts offer the American Plan, and some others provide complimentary continental breakfast. Be sure to call and verify exact prices when making your reservation.

We have noted many amenities provided. Other services and sundries are often available. When you call to book reservations, ask whether the hotel offers those you desire.

We have indicated when a hotel will not accept pets, or when pets are accepted only under special conditions. An additional deposit is often required. In establishments that do not permit pets, the concierge can make arrangements with the best local kennel.

Children are accepted when accompanied by their parents except where otherwise noted. There is no additional charge for children under a certain age; the age varies among hotels.

Most hotels have at least some rooms designed to accommodate the handicapped. We have noted the number of rooms so equipped. Hotels with only a few handicapped-accessible rooms should be booked well in advance.

An important key to getting the most out of your Elegant Small Hotel experience is to allow the concierge to assist you whenever possible. The hotels described in this guide are small enough to permit a degree of personal attention rarely encountered in modern life. Accordingly, the function of the concierge is to cater to the individual needs (and whims) of each guest. Rather than attempt a detailed description of services and amenities the concierge can arrange—which would leave no space in this guide for the hotels themselves— we have presented "A Concierge's Day," the viewpoint of one outstanding concierge, on the following page.

Every attempt has been made to be absolutely current. Some information contained in this guide has been provided by the hotels' management, and management policies may change. If you feel that anything in this book is even slightly inaccurate, please inform us so we can put it right in future editions.

We appreciate reader comments, including any hotel we have overlooked which you feel deserves to be included.

—*Pamela Lanier* September 1998

A CONCIERGE'S DAY

"I am absolutely certain we can have the car and driver here in twenty minutes, sir. I only need to know what sort of car and what sort of driver you would prefer. And yes, I expect your day in the wine country will be splendid; the weather is perfect."

The 20-minute wait for the special car and driver to arrive will not be wasted. The concierge first calls ahead for luncheon reservations at a spot that normally requires two weeks' notice. Next, he will call the wineries for any special considerations that might be possible for his guest. After all, everything must be the best. (It will soon become evident that perfect weather is the only thing the concierge has not arranged—the sunshine being courtesy of a somewhat higher power.)

The larger day's work begins for the concierge at this small Nob Hill hotel (the Huntington) in San Francisco with a review of the arriving guest list and of their special requests noted in his log. He opens that delicious document with the same excitement felt by a maestro opening the score of a beautiful symphony.

Appreciating that not everyone who travels in America is yet fully acquainted with the full range of services he can provide, the concierge will promptly call each guest within minutes of arrival to extend a personal introduction and a warm invitation to take full advantage of his skills and resources. To him and his hotel, every guest is a Very Important Person.

The concierge next turns his attention to a couple at his desk, eager to begin a day of sightseeing. Shopping, museum-hopping and general about-towning are the plan, with a lovely lunch along the way. The concierge will not only point them in the right direction, but also enhance their day with helpful hints and local insights.

The couple will return with happy faces and tired feet, to swap a few stories with the concierge and then retire for a nap or workout followed by tea.

Afterward they will consult the concierge once again to plan an evening grand finale to a delight-filled day. Knowledgeable and sensitive to his territory, he can advise them concerning matters of cuisine, attire, entertainment, transportation and adventure; then he will make the necessary arrangements.

You see, living vicariously is the route to concierge heaven. As the concierge plans the guests' daytime and evening activities with them, striving to maximize their pleasure, and as he takes the necessary measures to bring the plan to reality, and as he hears guests tell of their experiences afterwards, he feels something beyond professional pride. He actually enjoys it.

—Jeremy Dove

[*Special thanks to Marjorie Silverman, First Vice President of Les Clefs d'Or, for her help on his project. —P.L.*]

WESTMARK CAPE FOX LODGE

This unique lodge is set amidst the Tongass National Forest with most guestrooms overlooking the beautiful Deer Mountain. The gracious structure is complimented by the area's native Alaskan art, featuring a Totem screen carved by Nathan Jackson at the second floor mezzanine. Facing the front of the Lodge is a Totem circle with six totems carved by Tlingit carver Lee Wallace.

High ceilings, vast window expanses and smooth pine create a natural, elegant setting which invites guests to relax and enjoy the beautiful island of Ketchikan. There are several well-maintained trails to hike, or guests may take the tram from the lobby to historic Creek Street. The library, with its large fireplace and assortment of books, is a delightful spot to linger.

Each large guestroom features either two doubles or one king bed with soft plaid comforters for a restful night's sleep. White pine furniture compliments this cozy atmosphere. All the convenient amenities are included in each room. The suites, tucked up under the eaves of the main lodge on the third floor, give the feeling of being in the tree tops. They offer views of the Tongass Narrows and include a large living area with a couch. Suites are accented by local native art.

The Heen Kahidi Dining Room (which is Tlingit for Creek House) boasts a wall of floor to ceiling windows overlooking downtown, the marina and the Narrows. The dress code is casual but chef Timothy Frank creates a magnificent selection of locally caught Halibut and Salmon entrees. Of course, guests will have an everlasting memory of the Mud Pie dessert. The Heen Kahidi Lounge serves up Blue Glacier Daiquiris as guests enjoy jazz music.

The combination of nature, art and luxury are unparalleled at the Westmark Cape Fox Lodge. Guests are bound to return year after year.

Address: 800 Venetia Way, Ketchikan, AK 99901
Phone: 907-225-8001
Toll-Free: 800-544-0970
Fax: 907-225-8286
Room Rates: $$
Suite Rates: $$$
Credit Cards: Most credit cards accepted
No. of Rooms: 72 **Suites:** 2
Services and Amenities: Car hire, Library, Laundry service, Cable TV, Radio, Suites with whirlpool, Individual heat control, Complimentary toiletries, Most rooms overlook the Tongass Narrows, the town of Ketchikan and Deer Mountain, Convenient & inexpensive airport shuttle
Restrictions: No pets except seeing eye dogs, Up to 2 children in parents' room, 2 rooms equipped for handicapped
Room Service: 7:00 a.m.–11:00 p.m.
Restaurant: Heen Kahidi Dining Room, 7:00 a.m.–11:00 p.m.
Bar: Heen Kahidi Lounge, 11:00 a.m.–11:00 p.m.
Business Facilities: Copiers, Audio-Visual, Fax
Conference Rooms: 3 rooms, capacity 100
Sports Facilities: Numerous hiking trails right outside the Lodge's doors in the Tongass National Forest, Indoor climbing
Location: Downtown, Cape Fox Hill
Attractions: The lodge is located in the middle of the Tongass National Forest and overlooks the town of Ketchikan; Facing the front of the Lodge is a Totem circle with six totems carved by Tlingit carver Lee Wallace; Take a tram to historic Creek Street

THE BOULDERS

The dramatic and innovative architecture of The Boulders blends with the prehistoric boulder formations and harmonizes with the natural beauty of the surrounding Sonoran desert foothills. Navajo rugs and southwestern Indian pottery accent the subtle desert-hued decor.

160 individual casitas and 39 villas are scattered throughout the 1,300-acre resort. Rooms have viga ceilings, horno-style corner fireplaces, private patios, and such special touches as quality toiletries and fluffy bathrobes.

Outdoor sports abound: 36 holes of golf on courses designed by Jay Morrish, 8 plexi-cushion all-weather tennis courts, 3 swimming pools, bicycling, marked hiking trails and nature paths. There is also the Sonoran Spa and Rock Climbing Clinics.

The concierge will gladly arrange a hot air balloon ride, desert jeep trip, or spectacular flying tour of the Grand Canyon. Five dining rooms offer a full range of outstanding cuisine. The Latilla features Grand American Cuisine as well as a diverse and tantalizing main menu and irresistible continental pastries. It also affords a stunning view of waterfalls and the impressive rock formations for which the resort is named. The light and airy Palo Verde features Southwestern cuisine characterized by local ingredients and dramatic presentations. The Boulders Club serves both lunch and dinner. The Cantina del Pedregal features inspired Mexican cuisine. The Bakery Cafe is also available for breakfast, lunch and dinner.

For large groups there are 7,000 square feet of meeting rooms including a 5,600 square foot ballroom. Together, the meeting spaces can accommodate up to 450 persons.

Address: 34631 North Tom Darlington Road, PO Box 2090, Carefree, AZ 85377
Phone: 602-488-9009
Toll-Free: 800-553-1717
Fax: 602-488-4118
Room Rates: $$$
Suite Rates: $$$$
Credit Cards: Visa, MC, DC, AmEx
No. of Rooms: 160 **Suites:** 39
Services and Amenities: Valet service, Car rental available, Parking, Gift shop, Tennis & golf pro shop, Baby-sitting, Laundry service, Card/game area, Cable TV, 2-line telephone, CD Player, Hair dryer, Robes, Complimentary newspaper & toiletries, Complimentary tea & coffee
Restrictions: Handicapped-equipped facilities
Concierge: 7:30 a.m.–7:00 p.m.
Room Service: 6:30 a.m.–10:00 p.m.
Restaurant: Latilla Restaurant, 7:00 a.m.–9:30 p.m., Sunday Brunch, Palo Verde, lunch & dinner, Boulders Club, lunch & dinner, Cantina del Pedregal, lunch & dinner, The Bakery Cafe, breakfast, lunch & dinner
Bar: Discovery Lounge
Business Facilities: Full service business center
Conference Rooms: 11 rooms, capacity 450, 7,000 sq. ft.
Sports Facilities: 8 tennis courts, 36 holes of golf, 3 pools, Sonoran Spa, Biking, Hiking/Nature path, Rock Climbing Clinics, Hot air ballooning
Location: 15 miles north of Scottsdale, 33 miles northeast of Phoenix
Attractions: El Pedregal, Art galleries, Heard Museum North, Specialty shops, Restaurants, Day trips to Sedona/Oak Creek Canyon, Fly or tour Grand Canyon, Jeep tours, In January: Boulder Fest

SOUTHWEST INN AT EAGLE MOUNTAIN

Guests at the stunning architecturally designed Southwest Inn at Eagle Mountain enjoy dramatic daytime views of Red Mountain and 50 miles of desert terrain and nighttime city light views from their private deck or patio. This brand new Santa Fe adobe-style resort is located on a 6-acre site bordering the Eagle Mountain Golf Course just outside of Scottsdale.

Bold southwest prints, high ceilings and custom designed southwest decor grace each room, along with a kiva fireplace and 25-inch cable TV. Baths have their own telephones, robes, Jacuzzis, and complimentary toiletries. Every guest room has a work center with 2 phone lines and computer and modem setup, and separate outside phone numbers for guests' private fax and answering machines. Guests can also use the Inn's voice mail system.

The lobby is a Navajo style kiva building with a stone floor, six-foot skylight, and stained glass doors.

Amenities include Eagle Mountain's 18-hole championship golf course, a large pool, outdoor spa and a conference center designed for meetings of up to 60 people. The continental breakfast features fresh baked bagels with a variety of cream cheeses, muffins, fruits, juices, coffee and tea.

The Inn is close to Scottsdale, Frank Lloyd Wright's Taliessen home, and beautiful lakes and desert terrain.

Those who are committed to walking lightly on the land will appreciate the care that went into the environmental aspects of the facility, with recycling, water conservation, and protection of the native landscape a top priority.

Address: 9800 North Summer Hill Boulevard, Fountain Hills, AZ 85268
Phone: 602-816-3000
Toll-Free: 888-GO-SWINN
Fax: 602-816-3050
E-mail: info@southwestinn.com
Web site: http://www.southwestinn.com
Room Rates: $
Suite Rates: $$$
Credit Cards: Visa, MC, AmEx
No. of Rooms: 42 **Suites:** 11
Services and Amenities: Parking, Gift shop, Fireplaces, Balconies, Cable TV, VCR, Telephone, Radio, Complimentary newspaper, hand lotion, shampoo, conditioner, shower cap, sunscreen, Complimentary breakfast
Restrictions: No pets allowed, 2 rooms handicapped-equipped, Children under 12 free in parent's room
Concierge: 10:00 a.m.–9:00 p.m.
Restaurant: Club House, Lunch until 1:00 p.m.
Business Facilities: Message center, Copier, Audio-Visual, Teleconferencing, Fax, Modems, Every room has a work center
Conference Rooms: 3 rooms, capacity 20, 20, 60
Sports Facilities: Outdoor swimming pool, Whirlpool, Massage, Weight training, Exercise equipment, Nearby Eagle Mountain Golf Club
Location: Fountain Hills, East suburb of Scottsdale
Attractions: Eagle Mountain Golf Club, Scottsdale ¼ mile away, "Out of Africa" 5 miles, Taliessen (Frank Lloyd Wright's winter home) 5 miles, Lakes 10 miles

ROYAL PALMS HOTEL & CASITAS

Possibly one of the most photographed locations in Phoenix, the original Mediterranean villa-style mansion of the Royal Palms was built in 1929 as the home of world traveler and financier Delos Cooke. Expanded and reopened as an inn in 1948, The Royal Palms became the winter destination of such celebrities as Groucho Marx and Helena Rubenstein. Royal Palms, now under new ownership, Destination Hotels and Resorts, consists of 116 beautifully appointed casitas and guest rooms set in lush gardens, where many of the original exotic palms, shrubs, flowers and cactus were planted by the Cooke family. Antiques and artifacts from Cooke's world travels also abound.

The casitas have master bedroom suites and individual patios. All guest rooms feature king-sized beds, 25-inch color televisions and mini bars. Baths are indulgent with separate shower, luxurious bathtubs, pedestal sinks and a selection of deluxe toiletries.

Guests enjoy full-scale fitness facilities, a swimming pool with poolside cabanas, and nearby championship golf facilities. Over 27,000 square feet of distinctive function areas, including two salons, two boardrooms, a library, meeting room, outdoor patio and numerous lawns and gardens serve business needs, weddings and other events. Complete catering and audio-visual services are available.

Dinner at T. Cook's, located in the mansion and set against a spectacular view of Camelback Mountain, features the Mediterranean style cuisine of chef Michael Hoobler.

Fashionable shopping, art galleries, world-famous golf courses and fine restaurants are all within minutes of the hotel. Concierge staff is available to arrange theater and sporting event tickets, transportation, massages and a host of additional services and special requests.

Address: 5200 East Camelback Road, Phoenix, AZ 85018
Phone: 602-840-3610
Toll-Free: 800-672-6011
Fax: 602-840-6927
Room Rates: $$$
Credit Cards: Most credit cards accepted
No. of Rooms: 116
Services and Amenities: Valet parking, Same-day laundry, Dry Cleaning and pressing, Barber & beauty shop, Card/game area, Library, Cellular telephones, 25-inch color TV, Refrigerator, Complimentary toiletries and shoeshine
Restrictions: 2 rooms handicapped-equipped, Pets on leashes please
Room Service: 6:30 a.m.–9:00 p.m.
Restaurant: T Cook's, breakfast, lunch and dinner
Bar: Mirage Lounge, noon to midnight
Business Facilities: Audio-Visual, Copier, Catering
Conference Rooms: 2 salons, 2 boardrooms, 1 meeting room
Sports Facilities: Swimming pool, Tennis court, Fitness center, Golf at nearby championship facilities
Location: Eight miles from downtown, Ten miles from Black Canyon, Residential area
Attractions: One mile from Scottsdale (Fashion Square), Four miles from Biltmore Fashion Park, Five miles from Borgata

APPLE ORCHARD INN

Nestled in the heart of Sedona, sitting on the site of the historic Jordan Apple Orchard, is the Apple Orchard Inn. Their unparalleled location allows easy access to uptown galleries and shops while at the same time providing a secluded setting on nearly 2 acres of wooded grounds. The Inn boasts spectacular views and wonderful hiking to some of Sedona's most magnificent red rocks. Guests will enjoy an experience of first-class elegant accommodations carefully crafted and created in a blend of the Old West and the Southwest.

One of the most popular and captivating rooms is "The Victorian" which features 19th century antique furnishings and sets the mood for a romantic and special getaway. The lower level room is plush and charming, designed with low lights and mood-setting romance in mind. The decor of the room is complimented by faux-painted walls, hand-painted roses, and silk floral arrangements. The room is accessible through a private gated patio and features a quiet bath with private whirlpool tub/shower. Special amenities include: turndown service on the king-size beds with chocolates; fireplaces in select rooms; over 110 complimentary videos; masseuse on call; and cultural anthropologist as your private tour guide.

A full three-course gourmet breakfast is served each morning on the dining patio with gorgeous red rock views. The chefs, John Paul and Susan Etlinger, fashion creative menus to satisfy a vast variety of tastes. A favorite breakfast includes custard french toast topped with red raspberries served with bacon, fresh fruit, homemade blueberry muffins, juice and Sedona's own fresh roasted coffee.

Address: 656 Jordan Road, Sedona, AZ 86336
Phone: 520-282-5328
Toll-Free: 800-663-6968
Fax: 520-204-0044
E-mail: appleorc@sedona.net
Web site: http://www.appleorchardbb.com
Room Rates: $$
Credit Cards: Visa, MC, AmEx
No. of Rooms: 7
Services and Amenities: Gift shop, Library, Laundry, Fireplaces in some rooms, Five patios, Cable TV with HBO, VCR, Telephone, Radio, Individual heat/air-conditioning control, Robes, Jacuzzi tub, Mini-refrigerator with complimentary juice & sodas, Complimentary toiletries
Restrictions: No pets allowed, One room with handicapped access, Smoke-free environment, Children over 10 welcome
Concierge: Innkeeper
Restaurant: Home-cooked three course breakfast prepared by chef, Dining patio with red rock views
Business Facilities: Copiers, Fax
Sports Facilities: Massage, Hiking, Private tour guide (cultural anthropologist), Skiing—45 minutes
Location: "Uptown" Sedona, 15 miles from I-17
Attractions: Sedona Jazz & Art Festival, Jeep tours & excursions, Airplane & helicopter tours, Parks, Museum, Hot air ballooning, Horseback riding, Bicycling, Hiking, Golfing, Great shopping

CANYON VILLA B&B INN

The Sedona area is easily one of the most beautiful places on earth, where awe-inspiring towers of spectacular red sandstone dazzle the eye against a brilliant blue sky. It is here, amidst the natural splendor of this dramatic landscape, that innkeepers Chuck and Marion Yadon built Canyon Villa. Tall windows in the living room area take full advantage of this amazing panorama. The feeling is grand and homey; the living room features high ceilings, large fireplace, comfortable furnishings, original art and sculptures, antiques, and piano.

Down to the last detail, the Inn has been designed with maximum comfort and privacy in mind. Each of the individually decorated 11 guestrooms, featuring themes from Santa Fe to Oriental to Victorian, boast arched French doors opening onto a private patio or balcony with unrestricted views of Sedona's famous red rocks. The furnishings are elegant and comfortable, the ambiance quiet and refined.

You'll awaken to the delicious aroma of homemade rolls or muffins and freshly brewed coffee. Fresh fruit, juices, pumpkin pancakes, waffles, french toast or one of Marion's special egg dishes, such as her Mushroom-Artichoke Oven Omelette, will start your day. The dining room, with its crackling fireplace, soft upholstered tapestry chairs, and crystal, linen and china table settings, is a welcome spot. In the late afternoon, guests gather around the pool (weather permitting) for appetizers and beverages. A poolside fireplace takes the chill off for those who want to enjoy the magnificent Sedona starry nights.

During the day, the beautiful landscape can be enjoyed by guided jeep tours, hot air balloons, great hiking and helicopters. Nearby Indian ruins are accessible. Sedona is a major art center, with many fascinating galleries.

Address: 125 Canyon Circle Drive, Sedona, AZ 86351
Phone: 520-284-1226
Toll-Free: 800-453-1166
Fax: 520-284-2114
E-mail: canvilla@sedona.net
Web site: http://www.arizonaguide.com/canyonvilla
Room Rates: $$
Credit Cards: Visa, MC
No. of Rooms: 11
Services and Amenities: Card and game area, Library, Fireplaces, Balconies or patios, Cable TV, Radio, Individual heat and air-conditioning control, Whirlpool bath, Complimentary toiletries, Complimentary breakfast
Restrictions: No pets, 1 room with handicapped access, Additional charge for children, 2-night minimum on weekends
Concierge: 8:00 a.m.–7:00 p.m.
Restaurant: Elegant dining room
Sports Facilities: Outdoor heated swimming pool, Whirlpool bath in rooms, Golf, Skiing, Tennis nearby
Location: Residential suburb of village of Oak Creek
Attractions: Outstanding landscape seen by guided jeep tours, Hot air balloons, Helicopter rides, Indian ruins, Hiking, Major art center—Numerous galleries

SOUTHWEST INN AT SEDONA

Set on an acre in the heart of "Red Rock Country," the Southwest Inn at Sedona is near the ancient Anasazi and Sinagua Indian ruins, with their mystical pictograph and petroglyph sites, in an area known as the adventure capital of Arizona. A completely non-smoking inn, it offers an array of spacious rooms and suites, and a staff that takes pride in offering particularly warm personal service.

The Inn's award-winning decor is the ultimate in Santa Fe style, with nine-foot ceilings, fireplaces, lodgepole furniture, southwest fabrics and wall decor. Among the many thoughtful appointments are in-room coffee makers, refrigerators, and hair dryers. After peaceful nights, guests awaken to the splendor of breathtaking red-rock vistas from each room's deck or patio.

A complimentary sumptuous continental breakfast of freshly baked muffins, bagels, fruit, juices, teas and coffees is served daily in the breakfast room, which is flooded with natural light and open to the spectacular views. Weather permitting, guests may choose to breakfast on the outdoor viewing deck, or on their own deck or patio.

Concierge service is provided to arrange reservations at a wide selection of nearby restaurants, many of which are within walking distance, and to help guests plan their days. In addition to the numerous restaurants and shopping opportunities, guests can explore ancient ruins, learn the ways of Native Americans, play golf, and enjoy horseback riding, hiking, and the many other outdoor activities and tours available. Guests of the Southwest Inn at Sedona have the option to pay a small fee for privileges at the nearby Sedona Racquet Club, which is a complete health club with tennis courts.

The Inn's year-round pool and spa provide a place for those who choose to simply soak or sun poolside, and for others, relaxation after more strenuous activities.

True to its reputation for being "The" place to stay in Sedona, the Inn was awarded the AAA Four Diamond award for its attention to detail.

Address: 3250 West Highway 89A, Sedona, AZ 86336
Phone: 520-282-3344
Toll-Free: 800-483-7422
Fax: 520-282-0267
E-mail: info@swinn.com
Web site: http://www.swinn.com
Room Rates: $
Suite Rates: $$
Credit Cards: Visa, MC, AmEx
No. of Rooms: 28 **Suites:** 4
Services and Amenities: Complimentary continental breakfast and newspaper, 25" cable TV with VCR, Refrigerators, Coffee makers, Telephones with free local and 800 calls, Fireplaces, Patios or decks with views, Whirlpool baths, Turndown service, Complimentary toiletries
Restrictions: No pets allowed, 2 rooms with handicapped access
Concierge: 8:00 a.m.–9:00 p.m.
Restaurant: Complimentary deluxe continental breakfast served daily in the Breakfast Room
Business Facilities: Computer modem hookups, Copier, Fax
Conference Rooms: 1 room, capacity 35
Sports Facilities: Year round outdoor swimming pool and spa, Optional Sedona Racquet Club privileges for $15/day, 1 hour to skiing, Hiking, Biking
Location: 3½ miles west of uptown Sedona, 2 hours to Grand Canyon
Attractions: Ancient Native American ruins, Sedona's restaurants, theatres and galleries, 10 minutes to Oak Creek Canyon, Ballooning, Jeep and other tours

HACIENDA DEL SOL

The timeless splendor and unmatched tranquility of the Arizona Sonoran desert is yours at Hacienda del Sol. Set on 34 secluded acres of the majestic Santa Catalina mountains, the Hacienda is only a short drive from downtown Tucson. Panoramic views of city lights, majestic mountains and inspiring sunsets surround this desert oasis. Individually decorated rooms and casitas reflecting a Mexican-Spanish tradition have been carefully updated since its 1929 debut to preserve a sense of comfort and service.

The staff at the Hacienda is genuinely interested in helping you make the most of your stay. The Hacienda offers many on-site activities: pool, hot tub, tennis, massage, horseback riding, guided desert walks with the naturalist and Western barbecues. Championship golf is nearby and tee times are gladly arranged.

Enjoy world class cuisine from the Americas as you watch the sun paint the mountains on the outside terrace or dine at the chef's table in the display kitchen. Sample unique regional cooking prepared from the freshest ingredients along with fine wines selected by our sommelier. Complete the evening relaxing in the intimate courtyard under the starlit sky.

A part of Tucson's history, once a private gateway for many Hollywood stars, the Hacienda Del Sol is still the best stay in Tucson.

Address: 5601 North Hacienda del Sol Road, Tucson, AZ 85718
Phone: 520-299-1501
Toll-Free: 800-728-6514
Fax: 520-299-5554
Web site: http://www.haciendadelsol.com
Room Rates: $
Credit Cards: AmEx, Visa, MC
No. of Rooms: 30 **Suites:** 8
Services and Amenities: Car hire, Parking, Baby-sitting service, Massage, Library, Non-smoking rooms, Television, Individual heat and cooling controls, Many rooms with fireplaces, patios and wet bars
Restrictions: Pets accepted with deposit, Children welcome, Special handicapped access rooms
Room Service: Limited
Restaurant: The Grill, 7:00 a.m.–10:00 p.m.
Bar: The Bar, 12:00 p.m.–until the last coyote leaves
Business Facilities: Full-scale conference facilities
Conference Rooms: 2 rooms, capacity 150
Sports Facilities: Outdoor heated pool, Hot tub, Tennis court, Horseback riding, Nature walks, Golf arranged
Location: Catalina Mountain foothills, 25 miles from airport, 15 miles from downtown
Attractions: 34 acres of lush desert with much wildlife, Bird watching, Panoramic views of city and mountains, World Class Golf nearby, Sabino Canyon, Old Tucson movie studio, Kitt Peak Observatory, Accent on privacy

THE 1886 CRESCENT HOTEL

High above mist filled valleys of the fabled Ozark Mountains, wealthy midwesterners built one of America's grandest resorts, the legendary Crescent Hotel. Since May of 1886, The Crescent has been the summer place of the wealthy. Today, guests are still flocking to The Crescent for the luxurious accommodations as well as numerous activities such as golf, fishing, scenic rivers, Civil War battlefields, antiquing, and the wondrous natural beauty of the Ozarks.

Elegant 19th century architectural heritage is preserved at The Crescent. The five story brownstone was built in the style of America's castles. The owners want guests to share the feeling of the renaissance. Hand-carved marble fireplaces grace the tower rooms where 14-foot ceilings are complimented by plush carpet and period furnishings. Tall windows reveal the Ozark panorama.

Guestrooms and suites showcase fresh Victorian era colors and stencil designs, antique furnishings, crown moldings and hardwood floors. In the bathrooms, period tubs and sinks blend with new ceramic tile floors in green and white. The Penthouse suite sits on the highest point in the county with a 15-mile view. Jacuzzi tub and Victorian designs make guests feel wholly private and romantically inclined.

The Crystal Dining Room is a two-story grand Victorian room which once served as the grand ballroom and now welcomes diners with deep walnut walls and 15-foot windows. Chef Johnny Curet offers guests such delights as Shrimp Portofino. Dress code with evening wear and coat are requested. The Top of the Crescent lounge offers guests a quiet place to unwind with piano entertainment from 5:00 p.m. until closing.

This one-of-a-kind Victorian castle, perched high on Crescent Mountain, serves as an upscale destination for travelers everywhere.

Address: 75 Prospect Avenue, Eureka Springs, AR 72632
Phone: 501-253-9766
Toll-Free: 800-643-4972
Fax: 501-253-5296
E-mail: basinprk@ipa.net
Web site: http://www.crescent-hotel.com
Room Rates: $
Suite Rates: $$
Credit Cards: Visa, MC, AmEx, DS
No. of Rooms: 68 **Suites:** 8
Services and Amenities: Gift shop, Card/game area, TV lounge, Laundry service, Four balconies, Cable TV, VCR available (fee), Telephone, Radio, Wet bar, Individual heat & air-conditioning control, Whirlpool bath, Complimentary toiletries, Spa facility on premises
Restrictions: 3 rooms equipped for handicapped, Small pets only, Children free with adults
Concierge: 8:00 a.m.–5:00 p.m.
Room Service: 7:00 a.m.–5:00 p.m.
Restaurant: Crystal Dining Room, 7:00 a.m.–9:00 p.m., Chef Johnny Curet, Evening coat requested
Bar: Top of Crescent, 5:00 p.m.–close
Business Facilities: E-mail, Copiers, Audio-Visual, Fax
Conference Rooms: 2 rooms, capacity 300
Sports Facilities: Spa facility on premises, Outdoor swimming pool, Whirlpool, Massage, Aerobics, Weight training, Shuffleboard, Hiking trails
Location: Crescent Park, Victorian Village
Attractions: Heart of the Ozarks, Home of the great Passion Play, Daytrip to three major lakes, Branson, Missouri and Fayetteville, Arkansas

SUMMIT HOTEL RODEO DRIVE

At the center of the most famous shopping district in the world, the Summit Hotel Rodeo Drive offers a wonderful experience in the exciting community known as Beverly Hills. An aura of taste and quality begins with the exquisite lobby. Light muted tones blending with subtle touches of gilded furnishings and a lavish floral display are highlighted by a silk hand-painted chandelier.

The Summit Hotel's elegant guestrooms feature rich hues of forest green and burgundy with European style decor including French armoires, and are complemented by additional amenities. Some rooms have views of Rodeo Drive, and the rooftop penthouse suites offer private sundecks. Warmth and hospitality are reflected in the tea and fruit service upon guests' arrival. In the evening, turndown service is offered.

The excitement of the world-famous Cafe Rodeo is enhanced by the chef's incredible, eclectic recipes. Traditional and trendy cocktails along with late-night menu selections are available at the Cafe Rodeo Bar.

The Cafe Rodeo staff also offers outstanding catering service, including Kosher catering, for business and social gatherings.

Guests may take the complimentary shuttle to the hotel's sister hotel, the Summit Bel-Air, for an invigorating swim in the outdoor heated pool, or a quick workout in the exercise facility. A tennis professional and tennis court is available. The resident tennis pro is a willing partner for a scheduled game.

Shopping, entertainment, airports and many attractions in the Los Angeles area are conveniently close by.

The Summit Chauffeur Service is yours for the asking. It will make your arrival easy at LAX. Assistance with luggage and private executive car are provided for transportation between the airport to the hotel and return.

This is the only hotel on Rodeo Drive.

Address: 360 North Rodeo Drive, Beverly Hills, CA 90210
Phone: 310-273-0300
Toll-Free: 800-HOTEL-411
Fax: 310-859-8730
Room Rates: $$$
Suite Rates: $$$$
Credit Cards: Most credit cards accepted
No. of Rooms: 86 **Suites:** 5
Services and Amenities: Valet service, Parking, Car hire, Laundry service, TV lounge, Baby-sitting service, Cable TV and VCR, 2-line phones with voicemail, Robes, Some rooms have views, Sundecks, Robes, Complimentary newspaper and toiletries
Restrictions: No pets allowed, No charge for children with adult
Concierge: Daily business hours
Room Service: 24 hours
Restaurant: Cafe Rodeo, 7:00 a.m.–10:30 p.m.
Bar: Cafe Rodeo
Business Facilities: Message center, Audio-Visual, Teleconferencing, Modems, Secretarial service, Copiers, Fax
Conference Rooms: Indoor & outdoor settings, capacity 350, Catering available
Sports Facilities: Golf nearby, Complimentary shuttle access to tennis, Outdoor swimming pool, Exercise facility at Summit Hotel Bel-Air
Location: Rodeo Drive shopping district, 10 miles to LAX
Attractions: Famous Rodeo Drive shops: Tiffany's, Chanel, Gucci, Cartier and more, Fine art galleries, Numerous restaurants

SONOMA COAST VILLA

Terraced grounds, terra-cotta stucco, red tiled roofs, and an expansive veranda give this elegant small hotel a Mediterranean flair. Set on sixty beautifully manicured acres, the discerning traveller will find relaxation and comfort in Sonoma's infamous wine country. The landscaped courtyards, gardens, and buildings flow together creating the perfect setting for weddings, corporate retreats or any special event. According to Bon Appetit Magazine, "…The Sonoma Coast Villa is an intimate escape from the City…A mere hour's drive from the Golden Gate Bridge."

Each room is elegantly appointed with rich slate floors, Italian fabrics, authentic Spanish furniture, and romantic fireplaces. Bathrooms are adorned with slate floors, marble sinks, walk-in showers, and luxurious whirlpool tubs. After a relaxing whirlpool, guests may indulge themselves with a message in their room or merely lounge around the pool area or library with a good book. Most rooms have a private balcony with tranquil views.

An extended continental breakfast is included each morning at the Villa's intimate country dining room. Sample some of Sonoma's finest wines. Taste their delicious Mediterranean Tapas and feast on coastal salmon. For dessert, indulge in their renowned profitaoles with chocolate sauce. The Villa's outstanding culinary talent defines the best of Sonoma County's abundance from dinner parties to wedding receptions and banquets.

Set amongst pasture lands along Coastal Highway One, the Villa is conveniently located a stone's throw away from various vineyards, an 18-hole Golf course, Northern California beaches and Redwoods, fishing, antique shops, and numerous gourmet restaurants. At Sonoma Coast Villa guests have the choice of constant exploration or luxurious relaxation.

Address: 16702 Coast Highway One, Bodega, CA 94922
Phone: 707-876-9818
Toll-Free: 888-404-2255
Fax: 707-876-9856
E-mail: reservations@scvilla.com
Web site: http://www.scvilla.com
Room Rates: $$
Credit Cards: Visa, Mastercard, American Ex.
No. of Rooms: 12
Services and Amenities: Card/game area, Library, Fireplaces, Numerous balconies and decks, Dance floor, TV, VCP, 3 Phones, Individual heat control, Complimentary toiletries and newspaper, Breakfast, Afternoon tea
Restrictions: No handicapped access, No pets, Minimum stay weekend—2 nights, Children discouraged
Concierge: 24 hours
Restaurant: Exclusive dining room—Serving breakfast & dinner
Business Facilities: Fax, Modems
Conference Rooms: 2 rooms, capacity 8-50
Sports Facilities: Outdoor swimming pool, Whirlpool, Putting green, Indoor Spa, Pool table
Location: 1.5 hours from SFO, Easy access from Hwy. One
Attractions: Wine tasting, 18-hole Panoramic Golf course, Whale watching, Northern California Beaches and Redwoods, Antique shops, Gourmet restaurants

INN AT DEPOT HILL

Originally constructed in 1901, this stately turn-of-the-century railroad depot has been lovingly transformed into a sophisticated seaside inn with all of the amenities of a top-flight European hostelry. Located near a sandy beach along the Monterey Bay, the Inn overlooks the jewel-box village of Capitola-by-the-Sea, a charming cluster of shops, restaurants and galleries.

Each guest room at the Inn has been painstakingly decorated to evoke a singular time, place, and state of mind. Guests may choose from a variety of distinctive suites and rooms which have been lovingly decorated to create the ultimate getaway retreat. The Railroad Baron Suite, for example, boasts a large indoor soaking tub, domed ceiling, red/gold fabrics, and luxurious amenities. The Portofino Room, modeled after an Italian Coastal Villa, is lavishly appointed with a large canopy bed, private patio, and outdoor whirlpool tub. Rooms feature fireplaces, private entrances and gardens, state of the art video and audio equipment, private white marble baths, two person shower, and such amenities as bathrobes and hair dryers.

Guests can also enjoy the Inn at Depot Hill's garden, parlor and dining room. The garden, landscaped in the classical mode, is full of roses, azaleas, ferns and colorful trumpet vines surrounding a reflecting pond. A herringbone brick patio and pergola are the perfect setting for a morning cup of coffee or afternoon tea. The dining room features a clever trompe l'oeil, a scene that creates the illusion of the dining car of a train. Sumptuous breakfast dishes such as Cinnamon Apple Strudel, Raspberry Cream Crepes and Peach Stuffed French Toast are complimented by the ambiance of the room.

Known for their first class service and accommodations, the Inn at Depot Hill is a secret getaway retreat that shouldn't be missed.

Address: 250 Monterey Avenue, Capitola-by-the-Sea, CA 95010
Phone: 831-462-3376
Toll-Free: 800-572-2632
Fax: 831-462-3697
E-mail: lodging@innatdepothill.com
Web site: http://www.innatdepothill.com
Room Rates: $$$
Suite Rates: $$$
Credit Cards: Most credit cards accepted
No. of Rooms: 12 **Suites:** 6
Services and Amenities: On-site parking, Library, Fireplaces, Balconies, Cable TV/VCR, Telephones, Audio cassette player, Radio, Complimentary toiletries, newspaper and in-room refreshments
Restrictions: 1 room with handicapped access, No pets allowed
Concierge: 8:00 a.m.–10:00 p.m.
Room Service: 8:00 a.m.–10:00 p.m.
Restaurant: Breakfast served in rooms, dining area, or patio
Bar: Tea, wine, hors d'oeuvres
Business Facilities: Fax, Modems
Conference Rooms: 1 room, capacity 10
Sports Facilities: Whirlpool, Sailing nearby
Location: Monterey Bay Coast
Attractions: Walking distance to beach, numerous restaurants, shops, and art galleries; Situated between Golf Courses; 15-20 minutes south of Santa Cruz Beach Boardwalk and Steam Railroad

LA PLAYA HOTEL

The "grand lady of Carmel-by-the-Sea," as local residents have known this Mediterranean-style villa since artist Chris Jorgensen built it for his bride in 1904, is now grander than ever. A resort since the 1920s, La Playa was acquired in 1983 by the Cope family (owners of San Francisco's incomparable Huntington), who have done extensive restoration and renovation to make it Carmel's only full-service resort.

The subtly exquisite decor accents pale pastel walls and upholstery with custom hand-loomed area rugs, paintings by contemporary artists, and the Cope family's extensive collection of California antiques and heirlooms. Rooms afford views of the garden, the ocean, or residential Carmel. Handcrafted furnishings incorporate La Playa's mermaid motif in hues of soft rose and blue. The baths have marble floors and inlaid decorative tile. La Playa's five guest cottages offer the luxuries of a private vacation home. Complete with kitchens, wet bars, fireplaces, terraces, and patios, La Playa's cottages are ideal for a private getaway or family outing.

The Terrace Grill's gorgeous terrace is a perfect spot to watch the sunset. The wood-paneled interior of the restaurant provides a cozy dining atmosphere. An extensive California wine list and a fine collection of old ports and sherries set the stage for tempting cuisine. If you can pull yourself away from La Playa's lush formal gardens and heated swimming pool, there are myriad recreational options in the area, including Pebble Beach, Spyglass, and Carmel Valley Country Club golf courses. The boutique shops and galleries of Carmel Village are just four blocks from the hotel.

For the meeting-minded, a conference coordinator is on the premises and complete business facilities are available.

Address: Camino Real & Eighth, PO Box 900, Carmel-by-the-Sea, CA 93921
Phone: 408-624-6476
Toll-Free: 800-582-8900
Fax: 408-624-7966
Web site: http://www.infohut.com/laplayahotel
Room Rates: $$
Suite Rates: $$$$
Credit Cards: Visa, MC, AmEx, DC
No. of Rooms: 75 **Suites:** 7
Services and Amenities: Valet service, Off-street parking, Baby-sitting service (available on request), Color TV, Radio, Hair dryer, Iron & ironing board, Shampoo, Conditioner, Hand lotion, Bath gel
Restrictions: No pets allowed, Handicapped access to 3 rooms
Concierge: 9:00 a.m.–5:00 p.m.
Room Service: 7:00 a.m.–11:00 p.m.
Restaurant: Terrace Grill Restaurant, 7:00 a.m.–10:30 a.m., 11:30 a.m.–2:00 p.m., 5:00 p.m.–10:00 p.m.
Bar: Terrace Grill Lounge, 10:00 a.m.–midnight
Business Facilities: Message center, Secretarial service, Translators, Copiers, Audio-Visual
Conference Rooms: 5 rooms, capacity 10-150
Sports Facilities: Heated outdoor swimming pool
Location: Residential Carmel
Attractions: 2 blocks to beach, Shopping, 17 Mile Drive, Pt. Lobos, Carmel Mission, Monterey Bay Aquarium, 11 nearby golf courses

QUAIL LODGE RESORT & GOLF CLUB

A new chapter has begun for Quail Lodge Resort & Golf Club as the latest addition to the renowned Peninsula Group, which owns award-winning hotels in Beverly Hills, New York and throughout Asia. Guests can look forward to a harmonious blend of legendary Peninsula elegance and uncompromising standards with the warmth, comfort and hospitality they've come to expect from Quail Lodge.

Situated on the Central California Coast just minutes from Carmel-by-the-Sea, Quail Lodge is located beyond the fog on the sunny side of Carmel. Guests enjoy the best of both worlds: cool ocean breezes and lots of sunshine.

The Resort is nestled on 850 acres of lush fairways, oak-studded meadows and sparkling lakes. In addition to its natural beauty, guests enjoy such pleasures as a championship 18-hole golf course, 4 tennis courts, 2 swimming pools and miles of hiking and jogging trails. A special enticement is the casually elegant Covey Restaurant, which features award-winning Euro-California cuisine inspired by the abundance of fresh ingredients from the Central Valley. The Covey also features one of the finest collections of Central California wines on the Monterey Peninsula.

Quail Lodge's handsomely appointed guest rooms and suites offer a multitude of comfortable amenities. Each room features a private deck or patio overlooking one of the Resort's ten lakes, the golf course or lush gardens. The Executive Villa Suites represents the ultimate in luxurious accommodations.

Shopping is a highlight in Carmel's chic boutiques. Guests may also like to visit Steinbeck's Cannery Row, the Monterey Bay Aquarium or famous 17-Mile Drive.

Address: 8205 Valley Greens Drive, Carmel, CA 93923
Phone: 408-624-1581
Toll-Free: 800-538-9516
Fax: 408-624-3726
E-mail: qul@peninsula.com
Web site: http://www.peninsula.com
Room Rates: $$$$
Suite Rates: $$$$
Credit Cards: Most credit cards accepted
No. of Rooms: 86 **Suites:** 14
Services and Amenities: Parking, Airport transfers available, Laundry service, Baby-sitting service, Resort & gift shop, Library, AM/FM radio, Cable television, In-room movies, Hair dryer, Bathrobes, Refrigerator & fully stocked mini-bar, Complimentary bottle of wine & newspaper
Restrictions: Pets allowed by prior arrangement
Room Service: 7:00 a.m.–10:00 p.m.
Restaurant: The Covey, 6:30–10:00 p.m., Dress code; Country Club Dining Room, 7:00 a.m.–2:30 p.m.
Bar: The Covey Lounge, 5:00 p.m.–Midnight; Country Club Lounge, 7:00 a.m.–7:00 p.m.
Business Facilities: Message center, Secretarial service, Translators, Copiers, Audio-Visual
Conference Rooms: 7 rooms, capacity 15–300
Sports Facilities: Outdoor swimming pool, Tennis courts, Access to Carmel Valley Racquet Club, Croquet, Golf, Hiking, Full health spa adjacent
Location: Carmel Valley, 4 miles to Pacific Ocean/Hwy. 1, 12 miles Monterey Airport
Attractions: Wildlife Refuge, 17 Mile Drive in Pebble Beach, Big Sur, Monterey Jazz Festival, Monterey Bay Aquarium

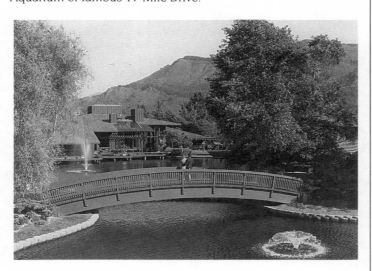

Westmark Cape Fox Lodge, *Ketchikan, Alaska.* PAGE 1

Quail Lodge Resort & Golf Club, *Carmel, California.* PAGE 14

THE HIGHLANDS INN

Sunset over the Pacific, viewed from the historic Main Lodge, is spectacular. Waves crash on rocky crags 200 feet below, evening breezes whisper among Monterey pines, and whales break the surface of an ocean sparkling orange and indigo. The panorama has made the Highlands Inn a favorite writers' and artists' hideaway for over 75 years.

The Main Lodge was entirely renovated in 1985. The lobby area features deep leather settees, two granite fireplaces and a grand piano.

New cottage-like suites and townhouses, as well as three open air spas, are secluded along flowering walkways on the Inn's forested hillsides. Recently refurbished rooms feature natural wool custom carpets, wool-covered furniture, woodburning fireplaces and vista decks.

The celebrated glass-walled Pacific's Edge restaurant, with sweeping ocean vistas, offers contemporary California/French gourmet cuisine. The menu draws from the bounty of the region, changing with the seasons. A special Prix Fix menu presents chef Cal Stamenov's latest innovations each evening. Diners complement fine food with California wines and select European vintages that comprise the award-winning wine list. An inviting alternative to the Pacific's Edge is the Inn's California Market, a cozy, casual restaurant where patrons may dine indoors or al fresco from morning to late at night.

The delights of the Monterey-Carmel area are close at hand and the concierge will be happy to assist in planning sporting activities, entertainment and sightseeing tours. Many guests, however, spend romantic days here without leaving the inn's own fabulous grounds.

Address: P.O. Box 1700, Carmel, CA 93921
Phone: 408-624-3801
Toll-Free: 800-682-4811
Fax: 408-626-1574
E-mail: highlands-inn.com
Room Rates: $$$$
Suite Rates: $$$$
Credit Cards: Most credit cards accepted
No. of Rooms: 142 **Suites:** 103
Services and Amenities: Valet service, Garage and parking, Car hire off-site, Gift shop in California Market, Baby-sitting service, Laundry, Cable TV, VCRs in all rooms, Radio, Telephone, Robes, Spa bath, Binoculars, Complimentary newspaper and toiletries
Restrictions: No pets allowed, 6 rooms with handicapped access
Concierge: 10:00 a.m.–6:00 p.m.
Room Service: 7:00 a.m.–10:00 p.m.
Restaurant: Pacific's Edge, 11:30 a.m.–10:00 p.m., California Market, 7:00 a.m.–11:00 p.m.
Bar: Sunset Lounge, 11:00 a.m.– closing time
Business Facilities: Message center, Secretarial service, Translators, Copiers, Audio-Visual, Telex, Fax
Conference Rooms: 6 rooms, capacity 110
Sports Facilities: Swimming pool
Location: Carmel Highlands
Attractions: Monterey wine country tours, Point Lobos State Reserve, Pebble Beach, 17 Mile Drive, Monterey Bay Aquarium, Cannery Row, Laguna Seca Raceway, Monterey Jazz Festival

JOHN GARDINER'S TENNIS RANCH

This 25-acre ranch was the first tennis camp in the world, started in 1957 by tennis teacher John Gardiner, who was convinced that people would take a vacation where the main activity was playing tennis. He was right, and nearly four decades later, his remains a popular and exclusive tennis resort.

The Ranch, known for its beautiful landscaping and botanical gardens, enjoys a climate of warm days and cool nights. Guest rooms are located in cottages of varying sizes just steps away from the courts. The airy, yet cozy accommodations, all have private patios and fireplaces, and are provided with complimentary fruit, beverages, coffees and teas.

Varied use of nutritious fresh ingredients insures memorable, well-balanced meals to satisfy the diet conscious, the gourmet, and the hungriest tennis enthusiast at the Ranch. Popular specialties are lamb dishes and souffles, complemented by a plentiful selection of local fruits and vegetables, and Pacific seafood. The breakfast buffet is served in the glass-roofed garden room, and lunch is a selection of hot and cold entrees served poolside. Dinner is formal, begins with drinks and hors d'oeuvres in the elegant clubhouse, then moves to the dining room.

The Tennis Ranch has fourteen championship tennis courts, one for each guest room, two training aid courts, two swimming pools, jacuzzi spas, and saunas. Guests are requested to wear the traditional predominately white on courts. At your request, a professional tennis staff member can arrange matches, organize tournaments, or be the fourth in a set of doubles. Customized group clinics, mixed doubles strategy, and private lessons can be structured along any format you desire. Win, lose or tie breaker, you feel like a winner when you visit John Gardiner's Tennis Ranch.

Address: 114 Carmel Valley Road, PO Box 228, Carmel Valley, CA 93924
Phone: 408-659-2207
Toll-Free: 800-453-6225
Fax: 408-659-2492
E-mail: tennis@JGTR
Web site: http://www.jgtr.com
Room Rates: $$$$
Suite Rates: $$$$
Credit Cards: Visa, MC, AmEx
No. of Rooms: 14 **Suites:** 6
Services and Amenities:
Complimentary Airport Shuttle, Parking, Gift shop, Full service Pro Shop, Fireplaces, Cable TV, Telephone, Individual heat & air-conditioning, Complimentary newspaper, toiletries; health bars, fruits, juices & beverages served on breaks during clinics
Restrictions: No pets allowed, Summer boarding camp for children 8-16 offered
Concierge: 8:30 a.m.–4:30 p.m.
Restaurant: Meals served in the Clubhouse, 7:30 a.m.–11:00 p.m.
Bar: Cocktails in the Clubhouse living room, 7:00 p.m.–8:00 p.m.
Business Facilities: Message center, Fax, Copiers
Sports Facilities: 14 tennis courts, 2 outdoor swimming pools, Whirlpool, Sauna, Massage
Location: 11 miles from Hwy. 1, 17 miles from Monterey Peninsula Airport
Attractions: Within 20 miles, Monterey Bay Aquarium, Pt. Lobos, Carmel-by-the-Sea, Pebble Beach, Steinbeck's Cannery Row, Big Sur, Historical Monterey

FURNACE CREEK INN

The historic 4-diamond Furnace Creek Inn offers an inviting oasis surrounded by the towering mountains and chiseled canyons of Death Valley National Park. The mission-style luxury hotel, now over 70 years old, presents magnificent views of the area from the snow-capped Panamint Mountains to the salt beds of the desert floor. Constructed of adobe bricks, native stone, and tile roofs, the unique architecture of the 66 room hotel has attracted the famous and not-so-famous for decades.

The resort's 18-hole golf course, opened in 1931, was the first grass course built in the California desert and remains the world's lowest golf course today. It has recently been re-designed by Perry Dye. The swimming pool is fed by a natural warm-spring, uses no chemicals, and the water averages 85F year round. The gardens create a true oasis of grass, flowers, and date palm trees accentuated by flowing streams.

A recent restoration has focused on the classic look of the 1930's. The refurbished guest rooms offer balconies, stone terraces and some spa tubs. Meetings, weddings, and social events are welcome in the special Oasis area.

Enjoy golf, tennis, horseback riding, hiking, a massage, or just relaxing by the pool. Afternoon Tea is served daily. The Inn Dining room, which still suggests jackets for gentlemen, provides breathtaking views of the sun setting over the Panamint Mountains. The sky is crystal clear and star gazing is encouraged from the rock decks surrounding the Inn.

Address: P.O. Box 1, Death Valley, CA 92328
Phone: 760-786-2345
Fax: 760-786-2423
Web site: http://www.furnacecreekresort.com
Room Rates: $$$$
Suite Rates: $$$$
Credit Cards: AmEx, Visa, MC, DC
No. of Rooms: 66 **Suites:** 2
Services and Amenities: Free parking, Gift shop, Baby-sitting service, Check cashing service, Balconies & decks, Ceiling fans, Massage available, Daily turndown service, In-room refrigerators, Iron & ironing boards, Hair dryers, Robes
Restrictions: No pets allowed, Crib & Rollaway charge $15.00, Extra person charge (above 2 persons) $15.00
Room Service: 7:00 a.m.–9:00 p.m.
Restaurant: Inn Dining Room, 7:00 a.m.–2:30 p.m., 5:30 p.m.–9:30 p.m., Wrangler Steakhouse, breakfast & luncheon buffet, 49'er Cafe, 6:30 a.m.–9:00 p.m., Sunday Brunch, Afternoon Tea, Pool Bar
Bar: Lobby Lounge, 3:00 p.m.–closing, Corkscrew Saloon, 12 noon to midnight
Business Facilities: Copiers, Audio-Visual, Fax
Conference Rooms: 6 rooms, capacity 150
Sports Facilities: 18-hole Golf course, 2 natural spring-fed pools, Basketball court, Six tennis courts, Horseback riding, Carriage rides, Hay rides
Location: Hwy 190, Death Valley
Attractions: Death Valley National Park, Borax Museum, Adjacent to Visitor's Center

THE GOLDEN DOOR

The world's smallest luxury spa resort in the most distinguished Japanese-style building outside Japan, The Golden Door offers coordinated programs to invigorate the body, mind and spirit. Though primarily a women's retreat, it invites men 5 weeks a year and 4 weeks are co-ed.

The low, graceful complex, patterned after Japan's ancient *honjin* inns, is reached by a 140-foot wooden footbridge. 327 acres of grounds contain a thousand feet of walkways and three courtyards. Each guest room has a wooden ceiling, jalousie windows with *shoji* screens, a traditional *tokonoma* shrine, a private garden view and a moon viewing deck.

Each guest is provided with a complete set of spa clothing daily, or as needed, including bath robe and Japanese yukata.

Vigorous programs are individually designed for each guest. A typical morning may include a sunrise walk, breakfast in bed, pool exercise, body contouring, steam bath and herbal wrap. The afternoon schedule may include facial and hair treatments, tennis, a twilight walk-jog and meditation. Evening is the time for lectures, flower arranging, prayer arrows and cooking classes.

The Golden Door's low calorie gourmet cuisine is world-famous. Most of the produce served by the kitchen is grown on the premises. How Chef Michel Stroot creates such natural-food masterpieces as a 300-calorie dinner of tabbouleh salad with fresh cranberries, Chinese stir-fry vegetables with jumbo prawns, and tangerine ice, is a secret he loves to share.

Address: 777 Deer Springs Road, San Marcos; PO Box 463077, Escondido, CA 92046-3077
Phone: 760-744-5777
Toll-Free: 800-424-0777
Fax: 760-471-2393
Room Rates: $$$$ (weekly)
Credit Cards: AmEx, Visa, MC
No. of Rooms: 39
Services and Amenities: Valet service, Car hire, Gift shop, Library, Laundry service, Complimentary shoeshine & newspaper, Audio cassette player, Radio, Hair dryer, Makeup lights, Complimentary skin care products, Each guest is provided with a complete set of spa clothing daily
Restrictions: No pets allowed, Not appropriate for children under 17
Room Service: 6:00 a.m.–11:00 p.m.
Restaurant: In-house kitchen facility, 7:00–8:00 a.m., 1:00–2:00 p.m., 7:00–8:00 p.m.
Sports Facilities: One asphalt tennis court, One concrete tennis court, Full-scale luxury spa, Two swimming pools
Location: Rural area; Guests are requested to remain on premises during their stay
Attractions: Always temperate in climate with mountain breezes

THE CARTER HOUSE ~ HOTEL CARTER

Built in 1986, the Hotel Carter is modeled after Eureka's Old Town Cairo Hotel. The Carter House is a renovated 1880s Victorian residence. The lobby of the brand-new Victorian Hotel Carter features unshaded windows, ceramic urns, oriental rugs, and antique pine furniture imported from England. Each afternoon, guests enjoy complimentary wine and appetizers before a crackling fire in the lobby's marble fireplace.

Rooms are decorated in a salmon and ivory color scheme with bleached pine antiques. Original contemporary artwork and fresh flowers add a tasteful touch. The queen-size beds with comforters and overstuffed lounge chairs are reminiscent of a Victorian bed and breakfast, but these accommodations have all the modern conveniences: desks, telephones, clock-radios, and cable TV in the armoires. Spacious modern bathrooms are done in black and white tile. Many have whirlpool baths.

At the Hotel Carter's Restaurant 301, tables are formal, with white linens, fresh flowers, and crystal candlestick holders. Live music enhances the romantic ambiance and a large selection of fine regional wines if available. A typical five-course dinner might begin with cabbage leaf stuffed with smoked salmon and cream cheese, followed by homemade soup and a refreshing sorbet. The entree might be rock Cornish game hen with sage sauce, or seasonal fresh fish. All are served with fresh vegetables and sprigs of herbs and edible flowers, many grown in the hotel's own gardens. For the finale, try one of the Hotel Carter's award-winning desserts.

The Hotel Carter is located at the gateway to Eureka's Old Town, with its charming brick-and flower-lined streets, art galleries, antique shops, and boutiques. It is also only two blocks from Humboldt Bay and the Marina. Before sitting out in the morning to explore, be sure to savor the homemade muffins and tarts offered with the complimentary continental breakfast.

Address: 301 "L" Street, Eureka, CA 95501
Phone: 707-444-8062
Toll-Free: 800-404-1390
Fax: 707-444-8067
E-mail: carter52@carterhouse.com
Web site: http://www.carterhouse.com
Room Rates: $$
Suite Rates: $$$
Credit Cards: Most credit cards accepted
No. of Rooms: 32 **Suites:** 12
Services and Amenities: Valet, Laundry service, Baby-sitting service with prior arrangement, Wine & Gift Shop, Breakfast included, Cable TV, Radio, Whirlpool baths, Sewing Kit, Complimentary toiletries, Complimentary wine & hors d'oeuvres in evening, cookies & tea for turndown
Restrictions: No pets allowed, 22 rooms equipped for handicapped
Concierge: 7:00 a.m.–6:00 p.m.
Restaurant: Restaurant 301, 6:00–9:00 p.m. (until 9:30 p.m. on Friday-Saturday)
Bar: Full cocktail service
Business Facilities: Message center, Copiers, Small conferences
Conference Rooms: 2 rooms, capacity 35
Sports Facilities: Privileges to Adorni Center (fee)
Location: Northern border of Old Town, Quiet residential-commercial-artist's quarters
Attractions: Fort Humboldt, Sequoia Park and Zoo, Old Town Eureka, Humboldt Bay harbor cruises, Lost Coast, Humboldt Redwoods State Park

GINGERBREAD MANSION INN

Originally settled by Scandinavians and Portuguese, the entire village of Ferndale is a State Historical Landmark, known for its well-preserved Victorian homes and Main Street boutiques, art galleries, cafes and museums. The Gingerbread Mansion Inn, a unique combination of Queen Anne and Eastlake styles elaborately trimmed with ornate gingerbread and painted in striking yellow and peach tones, is one of Northern California's most photographed homes. Built in 1899, the building was restored as a bed and breakfast inn by Innkeeper Ken Torbert in 1983.

Many of the rooms have plush floral carpets, rich Victorian wallpapers and Battenburg lace comforters. Three of the four suites have new fireplaces. The award-winning Empire Suite features a dramatic twelve-foot foyer with checkerboarded dark and light marble, a king bed, twelve-foot ionic columns, and two fireplaces.

Included is afternoon high tea with cake, pastries and assorted home-baked items served in one of four Victorian parlors, an early morning tray of coffee or tea served in your room, and many little extras, such as bubble bath, bathrobes and bedside chocolates. All guests enjoy a full breakfast of homemade delights, such as Gingerbread Mansion Baked Eggs Benedict, in the Renaissance Revival dining room adorned with dramatic art nouveau glass and damask wallpapers in gold and cream. Ken's collection of green cameo depression glass is used daily for breakfast.

From the formal English gardens to the full afternoon tea with twelve selections, the Gingerbread is an experience not to be missed by lovers of the Victorian era in its full glory.

Address: P.O. Box 40, 400 Berding Street, Ferndale CA 95536
Phone: 707-786-4000
Toll-Free: 800-952-4136
Fax: 707-786-4381
E-mail: kenn@humboldt1.com
Web site: http://www.gingerbread-mansion.com
Room Rates: $$
Suite Rates: $$$$
Credit Cards: Visa, MC, AmEx
No. of Rooms: 10 **Suites:** 3
Services and Amenities: Garage and parking, Gift shop, Card/Game area, Library, Fireplaces in 7 rooms, Some telephones, Radio, Robes, Complimentary toiletries, Complimentary breakfast and afternoon tea
Restrictions: No pets allowed, No handicapped facilities
Concierge: 8:30 a.m.–9:00 p.m.
Room Service: 8:00 a.m.– 9:00 p.m.
Restaurant: Gingerbread Mansion Dining Room for breakfast only
Business Facilities: Message center, Limited fax and copying
Location: Victorian Village of Ferndale
Attractions: Antiques, Boutiques, Victorians of Ferndale Village, 5 miles to Pacific Coast beaches, 20 miles to giant redwoods

NORTH COAST COUNTRY INN

For those who cherish the renewing power of California's wild and beautiful North Coast, the North Coast Country Inn is a haven to be returned to again and again.

The rustic but luxurious redwood buildings, nestled into a forested hillside with views of the ocean, have been restored and expanded and a new wing constructed. Each of the 6 spacious suites has bed-sitting, dining and kitchenette areas, a wood-burning fireplace, wet bar, private bathroom and deck. Innkeepers Loren and Nancy Flanagan have lovingly furnished each room with their own antiques, handmade quilts and handcrafted four-poster beds, where guests are lulled to sleep by the wind in the pines and the distant call of sea lions.

Breakfast is served in the "common room" with its white wood paneling, tile floor and pine furniture. White tablecloths and china lend a touch of formality. Evenings feature sherry and snacks by the fire.

Guests may stroll among the flowers and fruit trees in the lower gardens or wander up the hill to a romantic redwood gazebo and sitting deck in a grassy glen surrounded by towering pine trees. Or they may soak in the secluded outdoor hot tub set into a two-level deck among the pines.

Browsing is encouraged in the inn's office, which the Flanagans have converted into a tiny antique shope filled with treasures they have collected themselves. It is the only antique shop on this part of the coast.

Address: 34591 South Highway 1, Gualala, CA 95445
Phone: 707-884-4537
Toll-Free: 800-959-4537
Room Rates: $$$
Credit Cards: Visa, MC, AmEx
No. of Rooms: 6
Services and Amenities: Parking, Gift shop, TV lounge, Card and game area, Library, Complimentary breakfast, Complimentary evening sherry and snacks
Restrictions: No pets allowed, No children please, No smoking in rooms, No rooms equipped for handicapped
Conference Rooms: Common room, seats 12-16
Sports Facilities: Hot tub, Nearby 18-hole golf course, Tennis, Kayaking, Fishing, Horseback riding, Hiking, Beachcombing, Massage
Location: North Coast, 120 miles from San Francisco airport
Attractions: Pristine beaches, Sea lions, Whale watching, Point Arena Lighthouse, Art galleries, Fort Ross historic site, Anderson Valley wine country, Many restaurants and parks nearby

HEALDSBURG INN ON THE PLAZA

The Healdsburg Inn On The Plaza is the ultimate quiet place in the center of town where history and hospitality meet. This historic Wells Fargo Building of 1900 now accommodates guests amidst an elegant, modern setting. The solarium and roof garden provide a charming common area for guests to meet for coffee, tea and cakes every afternoon and a full breakfast in the morning.

A grand staircase in the gallery leads guest to their suites amidst vaulted skylights and warm sunlight. Each suite is furnished in American antiques and decorated in warm shades of peach, rose and coral. All rooms include queen or king-size beds, private bathrooms (some with tubs for two), central air and heat, TV/VCRs, room telephones, fluffy towels and guest's very own rubber duckie.

Guests' dining experience in the Solarium is complimented by classical flute or guitar. An extensive breakfast buffet is served including such dishes as quiche, apple crisp, fresh bran muffins, seasonal fruit, murder-by-chocolate cake, and other sumptuous dishes. An elegant, traditional tea service is available including freshly baked scones, tea sandwiches, and desserts.

Area attractions include the beautiful Plaza Park shopping with gazebo and fountain, golf courses, river rafting, bicycle rental, antiquing, and wine tasting.

The Inn provides the best features of both a Bed & Breakfast and hotel. With attention to detail and guest comfort, as well as a 24 hour staff, guests feel pampered and stress-free minutes after they arrive.

Address: 110 Matheson Street, Healdsburg, CA 95448
Phone: 707-433-6991
Toll-Free: 800-431-8663
Fax: 707-433-7510
Web site: http://www.healdsburginn.com
Room Rates: $$
Credit Cards: Visa, Mastercard
No. of Rooms: 10
Services and Amenities: Gift shop, Card/Game area, Library, Fireplaces, Balconies, Carble TV/VCR, Movie library, Audio cassette player, Radio, Guest Refrigerator, Central heat and air-conditioning, Wine hour, Complimentary toiletries and newspaper
Restrictions: 1 room with handicapped access, No pets allowed, Limited space to accomodate children
Concierge: 8 a.m.–10 p.m.
Restaurant: Breakfast Service, 7:30 a.m.–10:00 a.m in Solarium
Bar: Tea, 2:30 p.m.–4:30 p.m.
Business Facilities: Copiers, Fax, Modems
Sports Facilities: Jacuzzi in one room, Massage next door, Golf nearby, River rafting, Bicycling, Wine tasting, and Antiquing in surrounding area
Location: Downtown Healdsburg
Attractions: Plaza Park Shopping across the street, Set admist fountains and antique street lights

THE BED AND BREAKFAST INN AT LA JOLLA

Once the home of John Philip Sousa, the Bed and Breakfast at La Jolla is one of the finest examples of Irving Gill's "Cubist" style of architecture and is listed as a historic site on the San Diego Registry. The original gardens were planned by renowned horticulturist Kate Sessions.

CBA—"Can Be Arranged"—is the phrase that best describes La Jolla's commitment to European-style personalized service and hospitality.

A block from the beach, the inn offers deluxe accommodations in fifteen charmingly appointed bedrooms. Each room's decor, antiques and art feature a unique theme, from the nautically flavored Pacific View Room to the elegant Holiday Room with its canopied four-poster, antique armoire and grand fireplace. Fresh fruit, sherry, flowers and terry robes await guests. Some rooms provide refrigerators, fireplaces and ocean views; and all rooms provide hair dryers. Phones and bed turn down upon request.

Wine and cheese are served in the dining room from 4:00 to 6:00 p.m. A complimentary gourmet breakfast may be enjoyed in the dining room or the lush garden. Guests may also order a picnic basket to take to the beach or park. La Jolla Village's fabulous restaurants, art galleries, antique stores and designer shops are two blocks away.

Address: 7753 Draper Avenue, La Jolla, CA 92037
Phone: 619-456-2066
Toll-Free: 800-582-2466
Fax: 619-456-1510
Web site: http://www.innlajolla.com
Room Rates: $$
Suite Rates: $$$$
Credit Cards: MC, Visa, AmEx
No. of Rooms: 15 **Suites:** 2
Services and Amenities: Garage and parking, Car hire, Beauty Shop, House doctor, Baby-sitting service, TV lounge, Some fireplaces and balconies, Cable TV and VCR in library and penthouse, Robe, Shampoo, Soap, Complimentary full breakfast and newspaper
Restrictions: No pets allowed, 1 room with handicapped access, Children ages 12 and up only
Concierge: On staff
Business Facilities: Fax
Conference Rooms: Library, Dining room, Holiday suite, Capacity 12-20
Sports Facilities: Public tennis courts, Fitness center & Clinic nearby, Snorkeling, Scuba diving & Wind sailing 1 block away, Massage by request
Location: La Jolla Village by the Sea
Attractions: Villages restaurants, Art galleries, Museum, Antique stores, Designer shops, Golf, Stephen Birch Aquarium, UCSD, Sea World, Other main attractions

BEVERLY PLAZA HOTEL

Situated in Los Angeles' most fashionable, exciting and friendly neighborhood, bordering Beverly Hills and West Hollywood, is the Beverly Plaza Hotel. Fashioned in the true style of a "Boutique" Hotel, attention is paid to the smallest of details with extensive amenities and personalized services.

Ninety-eight oversized guest rooms have either light oak or mahogany furniture, each with a sitting area, gourmet honor bar, two telephones, writing desk and cotton robe. Complimentary amenities include daily newspaper, nightly turndown service, featuring Joseph Schmidt® Truffles, fresh fruit and gourmet coffee each day in the lobby, complimentary transportation within a five-mile radius, natural soaps and shampoos, linen and terry in all guest rooms.

Located within the Beverly Plaza Hotel, Cava Cafe & Tapas Bar is one of L.A.'s most celebrated restaurants and jazz supperclubs. Famed chef Toribio Prado's creative cuisine draws a guest list that includes behind-the-scenes industry professionals and many recognizable faces of Hollywood.

Twenty-four hour room service including delivery from Jerry's Famous Deli and uniquely designed meeting and banquet spaces provide an alternative to the traditional hotel scenario. An Executive Boardroom features ergonomic seating, VCR, facsimile, multi-line speaker telephone and private dining.

The "Spa @ the Plaza" with a fitness center featuring top quality Maxicam equipment Precor Treadmill, Lifestep & Lifecycle and saunas. Massage, personal training, Dermalogical® skin care, outdoor garden swimming pool and whirlpool with alfresco poolside dining service complete the spa environment.

This unique boutique hotel leaves guests with a lasting impression of intimacy, quality service and casual yet elegant ambiance unlike any other L.A. hotel experience.

Address: 8384 West Third Street at Orlando, Los Angeles, CA 90048
Phone: 213-658-6600
Toll-Free: 800-62-HOTEL
Fax: 213-653-3464
E-mail: info@beverlyplazahotel.com
Web site: http://www.beverlyplazahotel.com
Room Rates: $$$
Credit Cards: Most credit cards accepted
No. of Rooms: 98
Services and Amenities: Valet parking, Gourmet mini-bar, Daily coffee/fruit, Free taxi-5 mile radius, House doctor, Baby-sitting available, Satellite TV with in-room movies, Radio, 2 Telephones, Daily newspaper, Turndown w/Joseph Schmidt® chocolates, Special packages available
Restrictions: No pets allowed, 4 rooms equipped for handicaped access, Children under 12 stay free with parents
Concierge: 24 hours
Room Service: 24 hours
Restaurant: Cava Cafe & Tapas bar, 6:30 a.m.–11:00 p.m. (until midnight on Friday & Saturday)
Bar: Cocktails from 8:00 p.m.–1:00 a.m., Supperclub "upstairs @ Cava"
Business Facilities: Voice Mail, Secretarial services, Audio-Visual, Executive Boardroom
Conference Rooms: 3 rooms, capacity 10-200 including private Boardroom
Sports Facilities: Fitness Center, Outdoor swimming pool, Whirlpool, Sauna, Massage, Weight training, Skin Care, Nearby: Golf, Tennis, Rollerblading
Location: City/residential, Westside, 9 miles to LAX, 3 miles to freeways
Attractions: Fabulous dining and shopping within walking distance, Farmers Market, Sunset, Melrose, Studios, Beverly Center, Restaurant Row all within close proximity, Borders West Hollywood and Beverly Hills

FOUR SEASONS HOTEL AT BEVERLY HILLS

The Four Seasons Hotel at Beverly Hills is a 16-story residential tower in soft shades of beige. Jade green balcony railings frame white french doors to the guest rooms. All is surrounded by lush foliage and flowers.

Public rooms have lofty ceilings, marble floors and are richly decorated with European art and antiques reminiscent of a European manor house. Some guest rooms and suites are in shades of warm rose, beige and cream; others in cool, restful gray-blue. The majority of the guest rooms have king-sized beds, two televisions (one in the bath), an armoire, mini-bar, three telephones with two-lines and the usual bathroom amenities.

In the dining room, gray and yellow walls complement charcoal banquettes with silk chairs, white table cloths and Limoges china. A dinner specialty is grilled veal chop and for dessert, a luscious, flourless chocolate tart. A pianist plays nightly and on Friday and Saturday evenings a trio entertains. Afternoon tea is served in The Window Lounge Bar.

A number of complimentary services are available: limousine service for business travelers on Monday through Friday from 7:30 a.m. to 9:30 a.m. for transportation to the Wilshire Corridor; limousine service to Rodeo Drive on Monday through Saturday leaving every hour on the half-hour; personal VCRs and facsimile machines are available for delivery to guest rooms through the concierge's desk; coffee is offered in the Library from 5:00 a.m. to 8:00 a.m.

Address: 300 South Doheny Drive, Los Angeles, CA 90048
Phone: 310-273-2222
Toll-Free: 800-332-3442
Fax: 310-859-3824
Room Rates: $$$$
Suite Rates: $$$$
Credit Cards: Most credit cards accepted
No. of Rooms: 285 **Suites:** 106
Services and Amenities: Valet, Garage & parking, Car hire, Laundry, Baby-sitting, Currency exchange, House doctor, Library, Private balconies, Cable TV, Radio, Mini bar, Robes, Hair dryer, Complimentary toiletries & shoeshine
Restrictions: 10 rooms are handicapped-equipped, Children under 18 are free with parents
Concierge: 24 hours
Room Service: 24 hours
Restaurant: Gardens, 7:00 a.m.–10:30 p.m.
Bar: Windows Lounge, 11:00 a.m.–1:00 a.m.
Business Facilities: Message center, Copiers, Audio-Visual, Telex, Translators
Conference Rooms: 10 rooms, capacity 560
Sports Facilities: Outdoor swimming pool, Whirlpool, Massage, Weight training, Exercise equipment
Location: Beverly Hills residential
Attractions: Rodeo Drive, Universal Studios, Disneyland, L.A. County Museum of Art

HOTEL BEL-AIR

Where else can you be surrounded by fountains and courtyards, beside waterfalls that tumble into a lake that hosts a family of white swans—a short drive from Rodeo Drive? Nestled in an eleven-and-a-half acre estate garden, where redwoods, pampas grass, orchids, lilies and roses blend to create a fabulous color array.

The Bel-Air is a most private, secluded and unhurried Shangri La. Accommodations are in mission-style buildings and bungalows. Each spacious guest room or suite is individually decorated, reflecting different styles. The atmosphere is opulent, luxurious and quintessentially comfortable. Wood-burning fireplaces, bay windows with window seats, and terra cotta tiled floors are featured throughout. The lush baths and separate vanity areas gleam with marble and brass fixtures.

The Hotel Bel-Air restaurant is renowned for its California-inspired cuisine. Original art enhances walls upholstered in peachy beige; strikingly beautiful carpeting in a moss green and beige floral pattern unifies the whole. Tables are set with the finest crystal, china and silver.

Our recent dinner experience at the Bel-Air began with Bel-Air's house smoked salmon potato galettes, caviar and sour cream. Of the 5 salads available we chose the Caesar with shaved parmesan which was delicious. For an entree the grilled swordfish with snowpea-cashew springrolls and roasted garlic-sweet pepper was our favorite. Weather permitting (and it usually is), al fresco dining is available on the bougainvillea draped terrace overlooking the hotel gardens and Swan Lake.

The wood-panelled bar has a baby grand piano, fireplace, and fresh flowers. Howard Hughes used the Bel-Air's bar as an informal "office," and the aura of intimacy remains.

Address: 701 Stone Canyon Road, Los Angeles, CA 90077
Phone: 310-472-1211
Toll-Free: 800-648-4097
Fax: 310-476-5890
Room Rates: $$$$
Suite Rates: $$$$
Credit Cards: Most credit cards accepted
No. of Rooms: 92 **Suites:** 39
Services and Amenities: Valet service, Car hire, Parking available, Currency exchange, Laundry service, Complimentary shoeshine, Baby-sitting service, House doctor on request, Cable TV, Radio, Telephone, Robes, Complimentary specially packaged toiletries, Welcome amenities
Restrictions: No pets allowed, Handicapped access to 2 rooms
Concierge: 24 hours
Room Service: 24 hours
Restaurant: Hotel Bel-Air Restaurant, 7:00 a.m.– 10:30 a.m., 11:30 a.m.–2:00 p.m., 6:00 p.m.–10:30 p.m., Dress Code
Bar: Hotel Bel-Air Bar, 10:00 a.m.–2:00 a.m.
Business Facilities: Services available upon request
Sports Facilities: Outdoor swimming pool, Golf arranged
Location: 45 minutes from downtown, 30 min. from airport
Attractions: 1 mile from Rodeo Drive, Close to Century City, Westwood and Beverly Hills

THE SUMMIT HOTEL BEL-AIR

Set on seven acres, just below the new Getty Museum, this unique and inviting resort, with its wealth of conveniences, offers the perfect atmosphere for a wonderful vacation or business stay.

Each of the hotel's 162 spacious, comfortable rooms and suites is meticulously appointed and is equipped with a refrigerator, 2-line phone, satellite television and marble bathroom.

Guests can refresh themselves with an invigorating swim in the outdoor heated pool or workout in the exercise facility. The Summit Retreat offers a wealth of services to rejuvenate the spirit, from facials and body wraps, to massages and much more. A Tennis Pro is available by appointment for private court sessions.

Chef Reiner Schmidt prepares exquisite cuisine for Cafe Bel-Air, accented by fine wines, appetizers and decadent desserts. Specially-themed events and cuisine are featured throughout the year as dining alternatives. The Oasis Bar and garden patio provides the perfect place to enjoy cocktails or to meet with friends.

Catering and meeting facilities are available for business or social gatherings accommodating up to 400 people. Kosher catering is also available.

For a trouble-free arrival at LAX, one of the hotel's private executive cars can meet guests and chauffeur them to the Summit Hotel Bel-Air or the Summit Rodeo Drive. Complimentary shuttle service is also provided from the Summit Bel-Air to the Summit Hotel Rodeo Drive, located on the world-famous Rodeo Drive.

The Summit Hotel Bel-Air offers casual elegance, warm personal service and convenient access to the airport, business centers, shopping, entertainment, and the many Los Angeles metropolitan area attractions.

Address: 11461 Sunset Boulevard, Bel-Air, CA 90049
Phone: 310-476-6571
Toll-Free: 800-HOTEL-411
Fax: 310-471-6310
Room Rates: $$$
Suite Rates: $$$$
Credit Cards: Most credit cards accepted
No. of Rooms: 111 **Suites:** 52
Services and Amenities:
Complimentary shuttle service, Tennis pro, Beauty salon, Gift shop, Voicemail, Remote control color TV with satellite channels, Pay per view movies, Hair dryers, Coffeemakers, Mini-bar, Refrigerators, Robes, Complimentary newspaper & afternoon coffee/tea
Restrictions: No pets allowed, Non-smoking and handicapped rooms available
Concierge: 7:00 a.m.–11:00 p.m.
Room Service: 6:00 a.m.–11:30 p.m.
Restaurant: Cafe Bel-Air, 5:00 a.m.–11:30 p.m., plus Sunday Champagne Brunch
Bar: Oasis, 11:00 a.m.–midnight, Complimentary hors d'oeuvres weekdays 5:00–7:00 p.m.
Business Facilities: Message center, 24 hour fax/photocopy service, In-room 2-line phones w/ computer modem, Secretary
Conference Rooms: 8 rooms, capacity 400, Off-site & kosher catering available
Sports Facilities: Heated outdoor swimming pool, Hilltop tennis court, Exercise facility
Location: 8 miles north of LAX, 15 miles from Hollywood Burbank Airport
Attractions: UCLA/Westwood, Santa Monica, Century City, Beverly Hills, Hollywood, Local beaches, Visit our newest neighbor The Getty Center Museum

WESTWOOD MARQUIS

This ultra-elegant all-suite hotel is located in residential Westwood Village, within walking distance of fashionable boutiques, restaurants, theatres and the UCLA campus. Handsome magnolias frame your approach to the Westwood Marquis, and the hotel gardens offer winding pathways, grassy knolls, flowering shrubs and shade trees for tranquil contemplation in the heart of the city. Here, privacy is of primary importance.

Each suite is individual in design and decor. All share the European style grand hotel ambiance, accented by fine furniture, paintings, art objects and live plants. Bedrooms have king, queen or twin beds and color television. The living room has a sofa, easy chairs and desk. The dining room is separate. The penthouse floor now offers 20 newly decorated suites with splendid views including palatial Bel-Air estates, the Santa Monica Mountains, the city and the ocean.

The Dynasty Room, the hotel's dining salon, serves Continental/Nouvelle cuisine, most recently the "Menu Minceur" designed for health-conscious clientele. The room is named not for a television series but rather for its display of T'ang Dynasty porcelains from the "Magnificence of China" exhibition.

The Garden Terrace restaurant is best known for its Sunday brunch, which Los Angeles restaurant critics have called, "...the finest brunch I have ever been to in the world," and, "...the buffet brunch against which all buffet brunches have to be judged."

Each day guests of the hotel can enjoy a relaxed afternoon tea in the lounge or evening cocktails accompanied by grand piano performances. Men's and Women's health spa facilities offer saunas, steam baths and Jacuzzis. An exercise room features Universal equipment and a Life Cycle. Massages, facials and personal trainer are available by appointment.

Throughout, the Westwood Marquis creates a garden resort feel in the midst of the city.

Address: 930 Hilgard Avenue, Los Angeles, CA 90024
Phone: 310-208-8765
Toll-Free: 800-421-2317
Fax: 310-824-0355
Suite Rates: $$$
Credit Cards: Most credit cards accepted
No. of Suites: 258
Services and Amenities: Valet parking, Limousine & car rental, Foreign currency exchange, Floral shop, Doctor & baby-sitting service on call, Refrigerators in suites, Cable TV, Radio, 3 telephones in suites, Hair dryers, Complimentary shoeshine, newspapers, robes, & toiletries
Concierge: 7:00 a.m.–11:00 p.m.
Room Service: 24 hours
Restaurant: Garden Terrace (breakfast & lunch), Dynasty Room
Bar: 10:00 a.m.–2:00 a.m.
Business Facilities: Message center, Secretarial service, Translators, Copiers, Audio-Visual, Fax
Conference Rooms: 6 rooms, capacity 10-150
Sports Facilities: Health spas for ladies & gentlemen with Sauna, Whirlpool, Massage, Complete exercise facility, 2 outdoor heated swimming pools
Location: West Los Angeles, Westwood Village
Attractions: Close to Rodeo Drive, Beverly Hills, Santa Monica/Venice beaches, J. Paul Getty Museum, Universal Studios, Walk to Westwood Village

MALIBU BEACH INN

Of all the beaches along the coast of California, perhaps the best known is Malibu, due to its association with Hollywood luminaries. Once a community exclusively of homes and shops, since 1989 it has been home to the Malibu Beach Inn, the first hotel to be built there in 40 years.

The influence of California mission style architecture is evident in the inn's light pink textured stucco exterior, Mexican tile roof, and guestroom decor.

Each guestroom has its own private balcony from which to view the ever-changing ocean, fascinating coastal strip and Malibu pier. Baths are decorated with hand-painted tiles and some have jacuzzi tubs overlooking the beach. Each has a refrigerator stocked with snacks and beverages, a spirits locker, a wet bar, television, VCR, safe, coffeemaker and most have a fireplace.

A complimentary breakfast is served to guests each morning in the comfortable lobby. There is also a video library available to guests, and a gift shop featuring a truly outstanding collection of Native American jewelry.

The many nearby restaurants are unique, innovative and informal, mirroring the casual but elegant Malibu lifestyle.

Water sports abound, such as swimming, snorkeling, surfing and wind surfing. Other sports available are tennis, golf, horseback riding and deep sea fishing. The hotel has an on-call masseuse and a top-flight health club is nearby. Other attractions include the Santa Monica Mountains National Recreation Area, Malibu Creek State Park, Pepperdine University, boutique shopping, Malibu Lagoon Museum and Bird Park. All of these are only 5 minutes away. The J. Paul Getty Museum is 10 minutes and the Malibu Creek State Park is 15 minutes away.

Address: 22878 Pacific Coast Highway, Malibu, CA 90265
Phone: 310-456-6444
Toll-Free: 800-4-MALIBU
Fax: 310-456-1499
E-mail: reservations@malibubeachinn
Room Rates: $$
Suite Rates: $$$$
Credit Cards: Most credit cards accepted
No. of Rooms: 47 **Suites:** 3
Services and Amenities: Gift shop, 24 hour room service, Laundry service, House doctor, Baby-sitting service, Private balconies, Fireplaces, Radio, Wet bar, VCR, Terry cloth robes, Complimentary newspaper and toiletries, Complimentary breakfast
Restrictions: No pets allowed, One child per room, 2 rooms handicapped-equipped, Maximum 3 persons per room
Concierge: 24 hours
Room Service: 24 hours
Business Facilities: Copiers, Audio-Visual
Conference Rooms: 1 room, capacity 22
Sports Facilities: Massage, Weight training, 18-hole golf, Sailing, Riding, Tennis courts, Fishing, Surfing
Attractions: Boutique shopping, Malibu Lagoon Museum, J. Paul Getty Museum, Universal Studios (30 minutes), Beverly Hills (30 minutes)

MARINA DEL REY HOTEL

The Marina del Rey Hotel is perched at the tip of one of the Marina del Rey peninsulas. The abundance of water surrounding the Hotel and its remote feeling place guests in an atmosphere akin to a private island paradise, while the Hotel's gardens bordering the sea produce a lush, tropical-like romantic haven. Most rooms have patios or balconies with sweeping views of the harbor, offering guests spectacular displays of sunsets and the dazzling harbor lights.

The Hotel's outdoor gazebo, which overlooks the Marina, has become a favorite of celebrities for garden weddings. The Hotel's Waterfront Room, surrounded by picture windows, allows as many as 250 reception guests to enjoy a breathtaking view as they celebrate the happy event.

Two restaurants, naturally with nautical themes, are on the premises. The Crystal Seahorse specializes in fresh seafood and fine dining, while the Dockside Cafe serves breakfast and lunch in a casual atmosphere. Both restaurants offer complete water views.

A heated swimming pool, putting green, jogging trails, bicycles, windsurfing or good old fishing await those seeking outdoor recreation.

Many travellers using LAX think this hotel, with 24-hour complimentary transportation to and from the airport, is an "Oasis by the Sea."

Address: 13534 Bali Way, Marina del Rey, CA 90292
Phone: 310-301-1000
Toll-Free: 800-882-4000
Fax: 310-301-8167
Room Rates: $$$
Suite Rates: $$$$
Credit Cards: Most credit cards accepted
No. of Rooms: 157 **Suites:** 3
Services and Amenities:
Complimentary transportation service from LAX, Valet service, Baby-sitting service, Cable TV, Radio, Complimentary toiletries
Restrictions: No pets allowed, Handicapped access to 2 rooms
Room Service: 6:00 a.m.–11:00 p.m.
Restaurant: Waterfront Bar & Grille, 6:00 a.m.–11:00 p.m.
Bar: Waterfront Bar, 11:00 a.m.–2:00 a.m.
Business Facilities: Copiers, Audio-Visual, Teleconferencing, Fax
Conference Rooms: 8 rooms, capacity 18-450
Sports Facilities: Heated outdoor swimming pool, Guest privileges to L.A. Fitness Center
Location: In the heart of Marina del Rey, 5 miles—L.A.X., 10 miles—downtown L.A.
Attractions: One-half mile from Fisherman's Village (30 specialty shops), One mile from a beautiful stretch of Pacific Ocean and pier

MONTEREY HOTEL

A historic "European" style hotel built in 1904 in downtown Monterey, The Monterey Hotel had a complete renovation in 1996. New marble floors, custom carpet, hand-carved teak and mahogany furniture, designer linens and Victorian decorative accents create romantic rooms and historic Victorian charm.

The Monterey Sports Center is within walking distance of the hotel. In addition, within a few miles are the Monterey Bay Aquarium, Fisherman's Wharf and Cannery Row with its many restaurants, shopping and sights to see. Also some of the world's finest golf courses are within 20 minutes of the hotel.

An ornate gilt, brass and beveled glass cage elevator delivers guests up to their rooms. Guestrooms are filled with antique Victorian furnishings in rose tones. All 45 guestrooms and suites have been lavishly restored with hand-carved furnishings, marble baths, ceiling fans and plantation shutters. The romantic Fireplace Suite features an oversized marble tub for two, king bed, quaint sitting room with fireplace, wet bar, TV, queen sofa sleeper and ocean views.

Guests begin each morning with a complimentary deluxe continental breakfast of selected coffees and teas, a variety of baked goods, fresh fruit and juices. After a busy day of sightseeing or shopping, enjoy an assortment of refreshments presented each evening in the garden rooms.

Just one block from the Conference Center, the Hotel is a convenient location for the business traveler. Business amenities include two-line phones with data ports and voice mail, intimate conference facilites and professional assistance in planning meetings or seminars. The comfortable Executive Board Room is an excellent environment for board meetings, staff retreats, client negotiations or small seminars.

The friendly staff pay every attention to guests by providing personal service with a smile. Guests are bound to experience the graciousness of the Victorian heritage.

Address: 406 Alvarado Street, Monterey, CA 93940
Phone: 408-375-3184
Toll-Free: 800-727-0960
Fax: 408-373-2899
Web site: http://www.montereyhotel.com
Room Rates: $$
Suite Rates: $$$
Credit Cards: Most credit cards accepted
No. of Rooms: 45 **Suites:** 6
Services and Amenities: Valet service, Laundry service, Baby-sitting service, Card/Game Area, Fireplaces, Cable TV with HBO, Radio, Wet bar, Individual heat control, Robes in suites, Complimentary breakfast, newspaper and toiletries
Restrictions: 1 room with handicapped access, No pets allowed, Minimum 2 night stay on weekends
Concierge: 7:00 a.m.–11:00 p.m.
Restaurant: Continental breakfast included in room rate, 7:00 a.m.–11:00 a.m.
Business Facilities: Fax, Copiers
Conference Rooms: 1 room, capacity 10
Sports Facilities: Monterey Sports Center one block from hotel, World famous golf courses 20 minutes from hotel, Massage
Location: Monterey Peninsula, Historic Downtown
Attractions: Monterey Bay Aquarium, Fisherman's Wharf, Cannery Row

CHURCHILL MANOR BED & BREAKFAST

This grand 3-story mansion was built in 1889 and is on the National Historic Registry. Surrounded by an extensive covered veranda and flanked by large white columns, the building rests amid an acre of beautiful trees, expansive lawns and lush gardens. Through the manor's massive, beveled glass doors, one steps back in time to a less hurried way of life. The first floor boasts four large parlors, each with magnificent carved redwood moldings and fireplaces, and a solarium with an original mosaic-laid floor of over 60,000 marble tiles.

The entire mansion is furnished with fine European antiques, oriental rugs, brass and crystal chandeliers, and a grand piano in the music room. All 10 guestrooms are individually and uniquely decorated. "Edward's Room" (the largest), is Edward Churchill's original master bedroom and features a French, king-size bed with matching nightstands, a dressing table, and a gorgeous triple-mirrored armoire. It also boasts beautiful gold-laced bathroom and fireplace tiles, a giant claw-footed tub/shower and a pedestal sink.

Included in the room rate is a delicious full breakfast featuring homemade muffins, nut breads, croissants, a generous fruit platter, and daily egg entrees. Breakfast is served either in the sunny marble-floored solarium overlooking the garden or outside on the verandas. Each evening there is a two hour Napa Valley varietal wine and cheese reception, and each afternoon fresh-baked cookies, coffee and tea are available for snacking. Croquet and tandem bicycles are available to guests to enhance the Victorian charm of a stay at Churchill Manor.

Churchill Manor is an ideal place for a romantic wedding or reception for any festive occasion. The inn hosts weddings each year with in-house catering, equipment and coordination. Hot air ballooning, the Napa Valley Wine Train, mud baths in nearby spas, fabulous gourmet restaurants, shopping, tennis, and golf are among the many recreational activities available.

Address: 485 Brown Street, Napa, CA 94559
Phone: 707-253-7733
Fax: 707-253-8836
Room Rates: $
Credit Cards: Visa, MC, AmEx, DS
No. of Rooms: 10
Services and Amenities: Packages available, TV lounge, Card/game area with VCR/movies, Music room with grand piano, Sunroom, Veranda, 5 rooms with fireplaces, 4 rooms with antique bathtubs, Private baths, Radio, Telephones, Complimentary full breakfast, snacks, wine/cheese
Restrictions: No pets allowed, 1 handicapped-equipped room, 2 night minimum on Saturday, Children under 12 only
Concierge: 9:00 a.m.–9:00 p.m.
Restaurant: Breakfast only, 8:30 a.m.–10:00 a.m.
Bar: Main parlor for evening wine and cheese
Business Facilities: Complete wedding and catering services
Conference Rooms: For up to 45 persons
Sports Facilities: Croquet, Tandem bicycles, Nearby health club privileges, 4 golf courses
Location: Old Town Napa
Attractions: Napa Valley wineries, Hot air ballooning, Mud baths, Art galleries, Gourmet restaurants, Shopping, Horseback riding, Napa Valley Wine Train

LA RESIDENCE COUNTRY INN

Embodying the distinctly French ambiance of the vineyards, architecture and climate of Napa Valley's acclaimed Carneros region, La Residence is set amid oaks and pines and surrounded by world-famous vineyards.

The 20 rooms and suites of the newly remodeled Mansion and recently built French Barn are lovingly decorated in French country style with European antiques and designer prints in individual color themes. French doors, European bed linens, sunken baths for two, private verandas or patios, and fireplaces are among the pleasures of La Residence. The residence buildings, outdoor pool and jacuzzi spa are surrounded by two acres of gardens and heritage oaks.

When they are not busy baking fresh bread for breakfast, innkeepers David Jackson and Craig Claussen eagerly assist in planning activities such as wine tours, bicycle tours past wildflowers and wineries, and site-seeing excursions, all beginning at the inn's doorstep.

The innkeepers are also your hosts for evening wine and cheese sampling on the veranda—or by the fire in cool weather—and for breakfast at antique pine tables for two, with piano accompaniment. For dinner, the acclaimed Bistro Don Giovanni is a short stroll away, and other fine restaurants, antiques and art galleries are nearby.

Address: 4066 St. Helena Highway, Napa, CA 94558
Phone: 707-253-0337
Fax: 707-253-0382
Room Rates: $$$
Suite Rates: $$$
Credit Cards: Visa, MC, AmEx, Diners
No. of Rooms: 20 **Suites:** 4
Services and Amenities: Baby-sitting service by arrangement, Telephones, CD player, Radio, Most rooms have fireplaces, Complimentary toiletries, Complimentary breakfast, afternoon wine and hors d'oeuvres
Restrictions: No pets allowed, 1 room handicapped-equipped
Concierge: 12:00 noon-8:00 p.m.
Room Service: 8:00 a.m.–8:00 p.m.
Business Facilities: Message center, Audio-Visual, Teleconferencing, Fax
Conference Rooms: 1 room, capacity 15
Sports Facilities: Swimming pool, Spa, Massage by appointment, Nearby golf, tennis, horseback riding
Location: Napa Valley vineyards
Attractions: World-famous Napa Valley vineyards and restaurants, Wine tasting tours, Shopping, Antiques, Art galleries, Biking, and Driving the beautiful Napa Valley

OJAI VALLEY INN & SPA

Used as the setting for the mythical Shangri-La in the 1937 movie, *Lost Horizon*, the Ojai Valley Inn & Spa still resembles paradise. On 220 acres surrounded by the Topa Topa mountains of the Los Padres National Forest, it was built in Spanish hacienda style as a golf resort with the aura of a private estate. That atmosphere was preserved in a recent restoration and expansion.

Soft earth tones pervade the decor of the spacious guest rooms and suites, all with the ambiance and thoughtful amenities of a fine country home. Most accommodations have private patios or balconies from which to enjoy "The Pink Moment," a natural phenomenon which bathes the valley and its mountains in a rosy hue at dusk.

The Topa Center conference facility stands at the end of an oak-shaded drive with a plaza of flowers gracing its entrance. From the ballroom windows and terraces guests view the mountains as they were seen in *Lost Horizon*. Equipped with its own kitchen, the Center can accommodate every catering need from theme parties to formal dinners for 400.

The Inn's 18-hole, par 70 golf course, is one of the most beautiful in the United States. Its tennis complex includes eight courts, four of which are illuminated, a clubhouse, pro shop and snack bar. The Ranch & Stables at the Inn offer a complete horseback riding program, including Western riding lessons. Two heated swimming pools, guided hiking, nearby fishing and fitness center offer additional opportunities for exercise. Golf, tennis, and fitness packages are available.

Known for excellent California Coastal Harvest Cuisine including choices naturally low in calories, cholesterol and sodium, the Inn offers a wide variety of indoor and terrace dining options.

By advance arrangement, airport limousine service to the Ojai Valley Inn is available from Santa Barbara, 30 miles to the northwest, and from Los Angeles, about 73 miles southeast of the Inn. Once settled in this paradise, a guest doesn't need a car.

Address: Country Club Road, Ojai, CA 93023
Phone: 805-646-5511
Toll-Free: 800-422-6524
Fax: 805-646-7969
E-mail: info@ojairesort.com
Web site: http://www.ojairesort.com
Room Rates: $$$
Suite Rates: $$$$
Credit Cards: Most credit cards accepted
No. of Rooms: 182 **Suites:** 24
Services and Amenities: Valet, Laundry, Baby-sitting, House doctor, Gift shops, TV lounge, Library, Cable TV, In-room movies, Radio, Climate control, Mini-bar, Coffee, Robes, Complimentary toiletries & newspaper, Non-smoking rooms, Golf, tennis & fitness packages available
Restrictions: 8 rooms handicapped-equipped, Children at no extra charge if sharing room with parents
Concierge: 8:00 a.m.–8:30 p.m.
Room Service: 24 hours
Restaurant: Vista Dining, breakfast daily, Sunday Brunch, 11:30 a.m.–2:00 p.m. (piano music), Oak Cafe, informal dining, Maravilla, formal dining, Acorn Cafe at Spa Ojai, Splashes, poolside lunches & beverages
Bar: The Club Bar, 11:00 a.m.–11:00 p.m. daily
Business Facilities: Message center, Audio-Visual, Teleconferencing
Conference Rooms: 14 rooms, capacity 500
Attractions: Annual: Wine Festival, Shakespeare Festival, Tennis tournament, Music Festival; Also near wineries and the ocean

POINT REYES SEASHORE LODGE

Point Reyes Seashore Lodge, 35 miles north of San Francisco at the gateway to one of America's most beautiful national seashores, was built in 1988 in turn-of-the-century country lodge style.

Its lobby, library, and game room feature generous use of native wood. An 1880s billiards table and stone fireplace contribute to the ambience of an old western lodge.

The guest rooms, decorated in pastels, have queen-size beds, brass reading lamps on the bedside tables, armoires, and sitting areas with floor lamps. Many have fireplaces and most have whirlpool tubs with shoji screens and tranquil views of the pastoral surroundings and Mount Wittenberg.

There are three suites, all having wet bars, refrigerators, and bedroom lofts with European feather beds. History buffs and romantics should try the Sir Francis Drake Suite, named for the famous 16th century English navigator who explored this area of the Pacific coast. Its Victorian furnishings, two-story bay window, tile fireplace, and artifacts of Drake and Queen Elizabeth I might just provide the inspiration necessary before one's own exploration of the area.

This exploration could include hiking, biking, or horseback riding the park trails down to the shore. There one might enjoy whale-watching, birdwatching, tidepooling, or beachcombing.

By car the Lodge is 15 minutes from the San Geronimo Golf Course, through the giant redwoods.

The Lodge serves a complimentary expanded continental breakfast. Opportunities for lunch and dinner at approximately 10 good restaurants in the area appease the explorer's appetite.

Before or after the day's adventure, modern-day queens and their knights can obtain bottles of wine, champagne, or lighter beverages at the desk.

Casa Olema Retreat, a separate house with an 8-person Spa adjoining the Lodge, is available for conferences and weddings. It adjoins an additional one acre of lawn and garden on the creek.

Address: 10021 Coastal Highway 1, P.O. Box 39, Olema, CA 94950
Phone: 415-663-9000
Toll-Free: 800-404-LODG
Fax: 415-663-9030
Room Rates: $
Suite Rates: $$$
Credit Cards: Visa, MC, AmEx, Discover
No. of Rooms: 18 **Suites:** 4
Services and Amenities: Parking, Baby-sitting available upon pre-arrangement, Library, Game area, Gift shop, Telephone, Radio, Breakfast served in suites, Mini-bar & wet bar in suites, Many rooms have Jacuzzi tubs, balconies & fireplace, Complimentary toiletries
Restrictions: No pets allowed, 1 room handicapped-equipped
Concierge: 7:00 a.m.–11:00 p.m.
Business Facilities: Conference facilities, Fax, Copier, Audio-Visual equipment
Conference Rooms: 1 room, capacity 25
Sports Facilities: 70,000 acres of National Park behind property
Location: 35 miles north of San Francisco, Next to Point Reyes National Seashore
Attractions: Hiking, Biking, Sailing, Horseback riding, Whale watching, Point Reyes National Seashore

THE MARTINE INN

This gracious palace was built in 1899 high atop the cliffs of Pacific Grove overlooking the rocky coastline of Monterey Bay. The Martines and their staff attempt to create for you the ease and grace of being a guest of the very wealthy 100 years ago. Innkeepers and veteran antique collectors, Marion and Don Martine, have carefully filled this Victorian-turned-Mediterranean mansion with their extensive collections of pewter and sterling silver, vintage automobiles and early California art.

The inn's twenty guest rooms are filled with an impressive sampling of furniture designs including American Victorian and lyrical deco styling. The Edith Head Room, for example, contains a nine-piece 1920's walnut bedroom suite which once graced the costume designer's home, and the McClatchy Room has a massive Eastlake inlaid walnut and mahogany suite. Some rooms have spectacular views of waves crashing against the rocks and/or wood-burning fireplaces. In the morning guests awake to a newspaper placed outside their door and a full breakfast served on Old Sheffield silver, Victorian-style china, crystal and lace.

Possible activities may include reading in the library, sunbathing in the courtyard, whale-watching from the parlor or sitting rooms, playing pool in the game room or lounging in the spa. Guests who choose to venture outside may stroll 4 blocks to the Monterey Bay Aquarium and Cannery Row, or walk, jog or bike along the 7-mile coastal recreational trail. Guests may relax at the end of the day with wine and hors d'oeuvres served each evening in the parlor.

Address: 255 Ocean View Boulevard, Pacific Grove, CA 93950
Phone: 408-373-3388
Toll-Free: 800-852-5588
Fax: 408-373-3896
Web site: http://www.martineinn.com
Room Rates: $$$
Suite Rates: $$$$
Credit Cards: Visa, MC, AmEx, Discover
No. of Rooms: 19 **Suites:** 3
Services and Amenities: Full breakfast included, Offstreet parking, Vintage auto display, TV lounge, Card/game area, Library, Billiard room, Baby-sitting service, Some fireplaces, Jacuzzi, Robes, Complimentary newspaper and toiletries
Restrictions: No pets (will arrange boarding), 1 room equipped for handicapped, 2-night minimum with Saturday
Concierge: 8:00 a.m.–11:00 p.m.
Room Service: 8:00 a.m.–9:30 p.m.
Restaurant: The Parlor, 8:30 a.m.–10:00 a.m. for breakfast, 6:00–8:00 p.m. for wine hour
Business Facilities: Message center, Copier, Audio-Visual, Teleconferencing, Translators on request
Conference Rooms: 6 rooms, capacity 6–25
Sports Facilities: Whirlpool, Massage, Aerobics & weight training nearby, Golf at Pebble Beach (5 minutes), Sailing on the Bay, Tennis nearby
Location: Butterfly Town U.S.A. (Monarchs), Nearest airport is Monterey
Attractions: Whale and Sea Otter watching, Aquarium, Cannery Row, Antique shopping, 17 Mile Drive, Carmel

THE WILLOWS HISTORIC PALM SPRINGS INN

Built in 1927 embraced by Mount San Jacinto, the striking architecture of this Mediterranean Villa set against the hillside creates a dramatic effect. Mahogany beams, frescoed ceilings and the mountain waterfall that spills into a pool just outside the stone-floored dining room delights visitors and creates a memorable atmosphere.

The Willows has been meticulously restored to its former grandeur, refinement and elegance. Each room is beautifully appointed with antique furniture, sumptuous linens, luxurious private baths, hand-made tiles, stone fireplaces, hardwood floors, private garden patios, and mountain and garden vistas. Rooms are decorated individually so that each room has its own unique character. The Loft Room, for example, is charmingly complemented by vaulted ceiling, Italian burled walnut antique furnishings, a two-person claw foot tub in the bathroom, as well as a fireplace which is enhanced by cascading water outside the windows. These romantic rooms conjure up images of times past and times to be had.

Each nights stay at The Willows is followed by an extensive gourmet breakfast which will tempt even the most discerning palate. Specialty dishes include cilantro rolled omelets served with fresh avocado and salsa, pumpkin waffles topped with apple-cider syrup, caramelized poached pears, sides of chicken apple sausage and praline bacon, an assortment of pastries, and more. The Willows also serves afternoon hors d'oeuvres and wine to celebrate yet another leisurely day.

For the curious guest, The Willows boasts a magical hillside garden which leads to secluded lookouts where one may contemplate the "sun-bleached land, the pale mysterious desert" or the star splashed night sky above the still mountains.

The Willows beckons visitors to its superb setting and tranquil atmosphere.

Address: 412 W. Tahquitz Canyon Way, Palm Springs, CA 92262
Phone: 760-320-0771
Fax: 760-320-0780
E-mail: innkeeper@thewillowspalmsprings.com
Web site: http://www.thewillowspalmsprings.com
Room Rates: $$$$
Credit Cards: Most credit cards accepted
No. of Rooms: 8
Services and Amenities: Valet service, Garage & parking, Car hire, Laundry, Gift shop, House doctor available, Baby-sitting available, Card/Game Area, Fireplaces, Balconies, Cable TV/VCR, Telephones, Audio-cassette player, Radio, Wet bar, Complimentary toiletries & newspaper
Restrictions: 1 room with handicapped access, Children over 16 years welcome, No pets allowed
Concierge: 24 hours
Room Service: 11:00 a.m.–11:00 p.m
Restaurant: Le Vallauris, operated by Paul Bruggermans
Business Facilities: Voicemail, E-mail, Copiers, Audio-Visual, Fax
Conference Rooms: 1 room, capacity 20
Sports Facilities: Outdoor swimming pool, Whirlpool, Massage
Location: Historic old village, 2 blocks from downtown
Attractions: A short walk to the Desert Museum, restaurants, shopping and theatres

VILLA ROYALE

Open beam ceilings, tile floors, massive wood fireplace mantels and lace-canopied beds are among the features guests may find in their quarters at the Villa Royale. Here you will enjoy the atmosphere of a real international country inn, decorated in colors, textures and art collected from all over Europe and Morocco.

Overall, the resort is a series of interior courtyards framed with bougainvillea and shade trees. Asymmetrical gardens with potted flowers, brick paths and bubbling fountains create the intimate atmosphere of a Mediterranean villa.

Rooms, each different, have telephones and cable TV. Many have fireplaces and kitchens. The main gathering area features stucco walls with natural wood trim, French doors, fireplace and brick flooring. There is an outdoor living area with a fireplace and comfortable rattan chairs. Guests may enjoy 2 pools and a brick-terraced hot tub set among palm trees and desert flowers. A complimentary breakfast is served.

So romantic is the Villa Royale's Europa Inn restaurant that in the words of the *Desert Sun*, "One thinks of stolen kisses." Highly recommended are the deviled crab fritters, salmon in parchment, and baked apple with pecan sauce. Dine indoors in the Northern Italian ambiance of coral walls, brick floor, fireplace and flowered tablecloths, or outdoors under the soft desert sky. It's an experience you won't forget.

Tennis, golf and horseback riding are a few minutes from the Villa Royale, and Palm Canyon with its shops and romantic night life is within walking distance.

Address: 1620 Indian Trail, Palm Springs, CA 92264
Phone: 760-327-2314
Toll-Free: 800-245-2314
Fax: 760-322-3794
E-mail: info@villaroyale.com
Web site: http://www.villaroyale.com
Room Rates: $
Suite Rates: $$$
Credit Cards: AmEx, Visa, MC, DC, Disc.
No. of Rooms: 33 **Suites:** 10
Services and Amenities: Concierge services, Bellmen, Cable TV, Bathrobes, Toiletries, Professional masseuses on call, Complimentary newspaper/ continental breakfast poolside/ health club priviledges
Restrictions: No pets allowed, No rooms handicapped-equipped
Room Service: 5:30–10:00 p.m.
Restaurant: Europa, Tuesday—Sunday, 5:30—10:00 p.m.
Bar: Same as restaurant
Business Facilities: Copiers, Fax
Sports Facilities: 2 Outdoor swimming pools, Whirlpool, Massage
Location: Deepwell
Attractions: Palm Springs Aerial Tram, Horseback riding, Desert Museum, Desert jeep tours, Golfing, Tennis, Shopping

GARDEN COURT HOTEL

Mediterranean architecture and a warm, comfortable environment characterize downtown Palo Alto's only luxury hotel. The Garden Court Hotel's colorful, European villa-like ambiance features a large, open-air courtyard, complete with classical columns, arches, potted plants, blooming flowers and resplendent bougainvillea. Decorated by famed interior designer, Nan Rosenblatt, all 62 tastefully appointed guest rooms, each adorned in soft, timeless pastels, feature spacious tiled balconies and all of the comforts of home. Warm service and thoughtful amenities are valued trademarks of the Garden Court Hotel. Upon arrival, an attending valet will escort you to the intimate lobby with burning fireplace. The traveler's needs are always anticipated with a choice of complimentary morning newspaper, in-room high speed Internet access, in-room office supplies, complimentary shoeshine, on-site fitness center and terry cloth bathrobes. Every morning gourmet coffee and fresh fruit baskets are provided on each individual floor.

Dining at the Garden Court is as worldly as the surroundings. The Bay Area's popular Italian bistro, Il Fornaio Cuccina Italiana is adjacent to the hotel and serves breakfast, lunch and dinner seven days a week. Homemade pastas, wood-fired rotisserie, crisp-crusted pizzas and a full selection of fresh roasted seafood can be savored in the "see and be seen" dining room or in the romantic al fresco dining courtyard.

For important business meetings or memorable social gatherings—from rehearsal dinners to weddings, reunions to anniversaries—the Garden Court Hotel has everything you will need to host the perfect event. Luxurious banquet rooms, fully equipped with audio-visual and communication facilities, can accommodate up to 250 guests and feature adjoining spacious decks and large arched windows that were designed to bring the outdoors inside. With an attentive, experienced service staff and cuisine prepared by Il Fornaio, catering at the Garden Court Hotel is unequaled.

Whether it be the location, the friendly service or the comforting, residential-like atmosphere, a visit to the Garden Court Hotel will keep you returning time and time again.

Address: 520 Cowper Street, Palo Alto, CA 94301
Phone: 650-322-9000
Toll-Free: 800-824-9028
Fax: 650-324-3609
E-mail: ahotel@gardencourt.com
Web site: http://www.gardencourt.com
Room Rates: $$$$
Suite Rates: $$$$
Credit Cards: Most credit cards accepted
No. of Rooms: 49 **Suites:** 13
Services and Amenities: Valet, Laundry, Baby-sitting, Cable TV, VCR, Radio, Mini bar, Computers available, High speed Internet access, Dual phone lines, In-room office supplies, Terry cloth robes, Nightly turndown service, Complimentary shuttle/shoeshine/newspapers/coffee/fruit
Restrictions: 3 rooms ADA compliance, No pets please
Concierge: 24 hours
Room Service: 24 hours
Restaurant: Il Fornaio Restaurant, 7:00 a.m.–11:00 p.m. every day, weekend brunch 9:00 a.m.–2:00 p.m.
Bar: 7:00 a.m. to midnight
Business Facilities: Audio-Visual, Copiers, Teleconferencing, Fax, Computer, ISDN, T-1 internet access
Conference Rooms: 8 flexible and attractive rooms, capacity 10-230
Sports Facilities: On-site fitness center
Location: Downtown, Nearest airports are San Francisco International and San Jose
Attractions: Stanford University and Medical Hospital, Stanford Shopping Center, Silicon Valley and many upscale shops and dining venues on University Avenue

LODGE AT PEBBLE BEACH

In all of golf, there is nothing quite like Pebble Beach. Regarded as one of the top five courses in the world, it has hosted both the PGA Championship and the U.S. Open. Pebble Beach Golf Links is open to lodge guests on a preferential basis. You may also elect to play Spyglass Hill, designed by Robert Trent Jones and rated in the Top 40 American golf courses by *Golf Digest*, or Del Monte, the first golf course west of the Mississippi, virtually unchanged since it opened in 1897.

Quality specialty shops line the colorful breezeway facing the lodge. The architecture is California traditional, circa 1919. Meticulously landscaped gardens and grounds create a special feeling of casual stateliness. Clusters of flowers, trees, and walks blend naturally with the graceful lines of the lodge exterior.

While 11 rooms are in the main building, 150 are in 12 separate low-rise buildings with expansive views of the ocean and the gardens. Most guest rooms have wood-burning fireplaces, balconies, and wet bars. The furniture is overstuffed and the elegance is understated.

The award-winning restaurant, Club XIX, serves contemporary French cuisine inspired by acclaimed chef, Hubert Keller. Fresh salmon baked in a tender corn pancake, topped with golden caviar, herb crusted lamb rack on roasted shallots and black olive jus are just a few of the offerings Chef Keller has created.

In addition to the golf courses and the new Tennis Pavilion at Spanish Bay, guests enjoy full privileges at the Beach and Tennis Club, with its 14 hard-surface tennis courts, outdoor swimming pool, and full health spa. Riding is available at the nearby Pebble Beach Equestrian Center. Hikers and joggers have a choice of five trails, from the 3.5-mile Indian Village Trail to the 9-mile Shore Course Trail.

Address: Seventeen Mile Drive, Pebble Beach, CA 93953
Phone: 408-624-3811
Toll-Free: 800-654-9300
Fax: 408-624-6357
Web site: http://www.pebble-beach.com
Room Rates: $$$$
Suite Rates: $$$$
Credit Cards: Most credit cards accepted
No. of Rooms: 161 **Suites:** 6
Services and Amenities: Valet service, Garage and parking, Car hire, House doctor, Baby-sitting service, Barber shop, Beauty shop, Game area, Remote control cable TV, Honor bar, Robes, Telephone in bath, Complimentary toiletries and newspaper
Restrictions: Handicapped access to 7 rooms
Concierge: 6:00 a.m.–10:00 p.m.
Room Service: 6:00 a.m.–Midnight
Restaurant: The Cypress Room, 7:00 a.m.–10:00 p.m., Club XIX, lunch and dinner, The Gallery, breakfast and lunch, The Tap Room, lunch and dinner
Bar: Terrace Lounge/Tap Room, 11:00 a.m.–1:00 a.m.
Business Facilities: Message center, Secretarial service, Translators, Copiers, Audio-Visual, Teleconferencing
Conference Rooms: 10 rooms, capacity 25–400, Tents available
Sports Facilities: 4 golf courses, Tennis Pavilion, 14 tennis courts, Riding, Hiking, Bicycling, Full health spa, Outdoor pool, Access to beach
Location: 17 Mile Drive
Attractions: Monterey Aquarium, Cannery Row, Carmel, Highway One, Scenic drive to Big Sur

THE INN AT RANCHO SANTA FE

The Inn at Rancho Santa Fe, 25 miles from San Diego, is one of those discreet spots to which a loyal and devoted clientele returns year after year. Amid towering eucalyptus and citrus groves, The Inn offers pure serenity.

Most accommodations are in cottages scattered about the property. Each cottage room has been individually decorated and nearly all have secluded porches or sun decks. Rooms with fireplaces and kitchens, and interconnecting suites for larger groups, are available.

The Inn offers fine dining in a variety of settings. The Library is filled with books and firelight. The Vintage Room, a replica of an early California taproom, opens onto a patio where guests dine and dance under the stars on summer weekend evenings. The Garden Room, all lattices and flowers, affords a sweeping view across The Inn's emerald lawns and pool. The cuisine is fine classic American. The 20-acre beautifully landscaped grounds bloom almost continuously. Guests enjoy not only The Inn's heated pool and three tennis courts, but also golfing privileges at the famous Rancho Santa Fe Golf Club. For ocean swimming, The Inn has a beach cottage with showering and dressing facilities at nearby Del Mar Beach. Within an hour's drive are San Diego's Zoo and Sea World, the old gold mining town of Julian, and perhaps a quick step across the border into colorful Mexico.

Address: 5951 Linea del Cielo, Rancho Santa Fe, CA 92067
Phone: 619-756-1131
Fax: 619-759-1604
Room Rates: $$
Credit Cards: Most credit cards accepted
No. of Rooms: 91
Services and Amenities: Valet service for laundry and drycleaning, Air-conditioning, Color television
Restrictions: Pets allowed
Room Service: During meal hours
Restaurant: Garden Room and Vintage Room 7:00 a.m.– 9:00 p.m., dress code
Bar: Vintage Room, 11:00 a.m.– 11:00 p.m.
Business Facilities: Audio-Visual
Conference Rooms: 2 rooms, capacity 25-100
Sports Facilities: 3 hard-surface tennis courts, Croquet, Exercise room, 18-hole golf course nearby, Swimming pool
Location: 25 miles from San Diego, Nearest airport is San Diego
Attractions: Sea World, San Diego Zoo, Wild Animal Park, San Diego Symphony, La Jolla Museum of Modern Art

RANCHO CAYMUS INN

Rancho Caymus Inn, located in the village of Rutherford in the heart of the Napa Valley, was built in Spanish-Hacienda style, designed to capture the rustic spirit of Early California. The Early California atmosphere is created by the use of hand thrown stoneware basins set in black walnut countertops, hewn beams, stained-glass windows, wrought iron lamps and handwoven bedspreads.

The inn affords both the seclusion of its walled gardens and the close proximity to the quaint towns of Yountville and St. Helena. There are 5 different styles of suites to choose from, some with fireplaces, some with kitchens, some with cabin-like big beamed ceilings and hand-carved beds.

All choices of room include a "Hacienda Breakfast" served in the dining room or the garden courtyard. In fact, there is a choice of outdoor and indoor dining for all meals, served by the Rancho Grill. The menu at the Grill has a variety of garden fresh salads, pastas and grilled items, as well as daily specials with a full selection of local wines.

This is the perfect place to stay for winetasters! There are approximately 30 wineries within 5 minutes of the inn. For those who do not want to go winetasting there are lovely shops in nearby towns. For the more adventuresome, hot air balloon flights are available, leaving from the steps of the inn. Many other outdoor activities can also be arranged.

Address: 1140 Rutherford Road, Rutherford, CA 94573
Phone: 707-963-1777
Toll-Free: 800-845-1777
Fax: 707-963-5387
Room Rates: $$
Suite Rates: $$$$
Credit Cards: Visa, MC, AmEx
No. of Rooms: 26 **Suites:** 5
Services and Amenities:
Complimentary breakfast, Some rooms with: Kitchens, Fireplaces and Balconies; All rooms with: TV, Radio, Wet bar, Individual climate control, Robes, Whirlpool bath, Complimentary toiletries
Restrictions: No pets allowed, 2 rooms with handicapped access
Concierge: 10:00 a.m.–7:00 p.m.
Room Service: 7:30 a.m.–10:00 p.m.
Restaurant: The Garden Grill, 8:00 a.m.–3:00 p.m.
Conference Rooms: 1 room, capacity 40
Sports Facilities: Nearby tennis and golf
Location: Downtown
Attractions: Walking distance to several wineries

HOTEL VINTAGE COURT

The historic Hotel Vintage Court is a 1912 Victorian building located on lower Nob Hill, merely two blocks from Union Square and the famed gates of Chinatown. Less than half a block from the famous Cable Car line, the hotel neighbors the French Quarter and the Financial District—the perfect address for business or pleasure. This European AAA 3 Diamond hotel, reminiscent of an inviting Napa Valley Inn with its intimate setting, provides a high degree of personalized service by a friendly, knowledgeable, and multi-lingual staff.

The lobby serves as a warm and inviting living room with comfortable sofa seating and a large fireplace. Guests can freely make use of the 24 hour gourmet coffee and tea service as well as the inviting bowl of fresh apples. The hotel hosts, often in conjunction with local California wineries, a wine reception in this stylish, relaxing setting every evening.

The 107 spacious and elegant guest rooms feature a writing desk, honor bar, remote control television with cable, direct dial telephone with voice mail and data port, hair dryer, iron and ironing board, coffee maker and complimentary coffee. The decor is elegant and comfortable in beautiful shades of rich jade and rose. In addition to these amenities, the Penthouse Suite features a Jacuzzi bathtub, wood burning fireplace, an original stained glass ceiling, breathtaking views over the City, and complimentary deluxe continental breakfast.

For meeting or business needs, the hotel provides a Private Reserve Boardroom featuring natural light and city views with an oak conference table and executive boardroom chairs. Audio-Visual equipment as well as catering services are available. The hotel provides complimentary limousine service to and from the Financial District.

Breakfast is served either by room service or in the internationally acclaimed restaurant Masa's. The four star award winning restaurant offers the best in French nouvelle cuisine, one of the most extensive fine wine collections on the West Coast, a full bar, and a private dining room. The friendly hotel staff is able to arrange preferred reservations for hotel guests.

Address: 650 Bush Street, San Francisco, CA 94108
Phone: 415-392-4666
Toll-Free: 800-654-1100
Fax: 415-433-4065
Web site: http://www.vintagecourt.com
Room Rates: $$
Suite Rates: $$$$
Credit Cards: AmEx, Visa, MC, DC, Disc.
No. of Rooms: 107 **Suites:** 1
Services and Amenities: Valet service, Garage/parking, Individual heat & air-conditioning control, Cable TV, Radio, Direct dial telephone with voice mail & data port, Hair dryers, Fully stocked refrigerator & honor bar, Complimentary toiletries, Complimentary wine in the evening
Restrictions: No pets allowed
Concierge: Available
Room Service: 4:00 p.m.–11:00 p.m.
Restaurant: Masa's, reservations required, Tuesday-Saturday, 6:00 p.m.–9:00 p.m., Dress code
Business Facilities: Catering service, Copiers, Projection screen, Flip chart and AV equipment available
Conference Rooms: 1 room, capacity 12-25
Location: On the Nob Hill side of Union Square, Nearest airport—San Francisco Int'l
Attractions: ½ block to Cable Cars, Near the famed gates of Chinatown, Steps away from Union Square, In the heart of San Francisco's finest shopping, Neighboring San Francisco's French Quarter, Walking distance to many bistros, cafes, and restaurants

HUNTINGTON HOTEL - NOB HILL

Known for a long-standing tradition of high standards, and gracious service, the prestigious Huntington Hotel, located atop Nob Hill, has been a favorite among visiting dignitaries, nobility, celebrities and discriminating travelers throughout its existence.

Built originally as a residence hotel in 1924, this was the first brick and steel high-rise west of the Mississippi. At its inception, a guarded secret among the most elite, the family-owned and operated Huntington remains somewhat of a best-kept secret today.

As the doorman admits guests to the intimate lobby, they are presented with an understated luxury that is difficult to find in more contemporary lodgings. The spacious, comfortable rooms, each individually decorated by top designers, have a rare, one-of-a-kind feel that is both luxurious and residential. Guests such as Placido Domingo, Luciano Pavarotti, Robert Redford and Paloma Picasso regularly request their own personal favorites of the 40 elegant suites.

Named for the four railroad tycoons of the 19th century—C.P. Huntington, Charles Crocker, Leland Stanford and Mark Hopkins—The Big Four Restaurant proves a perfect showcase for its impressive collection of original artifacts, historical photographs, memorabilia appointed with lead glass mirrors and rich, forest green banquettes. One step into The Big Four will transport guests to another era of California's wild past.

The finest in innovative and contemporary American cuisine is prepared by Executive Chef Gloria Ciccarone-Nehls, named "1995 Hotel Chef of the Year." Try the crabcakes, David Letterman's favorite, or start with the venison chili, as wild game is one of the chef's specialties. Then savor a roast maple leaf duckling or pepper-crusted beef tenderloin, followed by a luscious Creme Brulee. The cozy bar is a San Francisco favorite.

Address: 1075 California Street, San Francisco, CA 94108
Phone: 415-474-5400
Toll-Free: 800-227-4683
Fax: 415-673-2505
Room Rates: $$$$
Suite Rates: $$$$
Credit Cards: Most credit cards accepted
No. of Rooms: 140 **Suites:** 30
Services and Amenities: Valet, Garage and parking, Car hire, Chauffeured limo, Laundry service, House doctor, Baby-sitting service, Individual heat and air-conditioning controls, Radio, Cable TV/VCR's, Audio cassette players, Complimentary shoeshine and newspaper
Restrictions: No pets allowed
Concierge: Available
Room Service: Available
Restaurant: The Big Four, 7:00 a.m.–10:30 p.m., Weekend breakfast, 7:00 a.m.–11:00 a.m., Dress code
Bar: The Big Four Bar, 11:30 a.m.– midnight
Business Facilities: Message and secretarial service, Copiers, Audio-Visual, Teleconferencing, Fax
Conference Rooms: 4 rooms, capacity 65
Sports Facilities: Massage upon request, Privileges to Club One at Nob Hill (one block away)
Location: Nob Hill near Grace Cathedral, Huntington Park & the Pacific Union Club
Attractions: Financial district, Fisherman's Wharf, Pier 39 and Union Square are just blocks away on Cable Car line

MANDARIN ORIENTAL, SAN FRANCISCO

Towering high above the San Francisco skyline, Mandarin Oriental occupies the top 11 floors of the city's third-tallest building, giving every guest room spectacular sweeping views. Luxurious amenities and warm atmosphere with attention to detail fill 158 spacious guest rooms and suites. Among the hotel's accolades are Best Hotel in San Francisco by *Institutional Investor* magazine and 10th Best U.S. City Hotel by *Andrew Harper's Hideaway Report*.

Ideally situated in the heart of downtown and one-half block from the California Street cable car line, all of the city's activities are minutes from the hotel. For a gourmet dining experience with uncompromising service, guests may enjoy the award-winning Silks restaurant serving California cuisine with Asian accents. A perfect beginning or end to the evening awaits in the newly renovated Mandarin Lounge for cocktails and piano music.

The hotel offers distinctive meeting and banquet space, all with windows and unique designs for any business meeting or social event. An extensive state-of-the-art Business Center is available with a private conference room, computer work station and secretarial services. A new fitness center with state-of-the art equipment including Cybex, Paramount, Stairmaster and LifeFitness is available for guest use.

Mandarin Oriental, San Francisco is part of the Hong Kong-based Mandarin Oriental Hotel Group, whose other locations include nine Asian cities and Honolulu, Hawaii.

Address: 222 Sansome Street, San Francisco, CA 94104-2792
Phone: 415-276-9888
Toll-Free: 800-622-0404
Fax: 415-433-0289
E-mail: mosfo@aol.com
Room Rates: $$$$
Suite Rates: $$$$
Credit Cards: Most credit cards accepted
No. of Rooms: 154 **Suites:** 4
Services and Amenities: Valet and garage parking, Car hire, International currency exchange, Complimentary shoeshine and newspaper, Baby-sitting service, Laundry, Iron/ironing board, Cable TV with on-command video, Radio, Mini-bars, Robes, Hair dryer, Fine English toiletries
Restrictions: Handicapped accessible
Concierge: 7:00 a.m.–10:00 p.m.
Room Service: 24 hours
Restaurant: Silks
Bar: The Mandarin Lounge
Business Facilities: Business Center with secretarial service, Copiers, Audio-Visual rental
Conference Rooms: 5 rooms
Location: Downtown, Nearest airport is San Francisco
Attractions: Near cable car line, Chinatown, Embarcadero Center, Union Square shopping, Museums and theaters, Wine country tours available through the concierge

MONTICELLO INN

Just two blocks from Union Square, this handsome renovation has journeyed back in time to emerge as a colonial-style inn, combining charm with sophistication. The interior was meticulously planned, and the decor is characterized by first- rate Chippendale reproductions, beautifully coordinated fabrics, cozy fireplaces, and an air of graciousness with service by an attentive staff.

Guest rooms are bright and cheerful, following Early American themes and colors, and light sleepers will appreciate the soundproofed windows and walls. The pièce de résistance is the Jefferson Grand Suite, with two spacious rooms, a good-sized wood-burning fireplace, and a Jacuzzi tub. Added touches such as ample lighting over writing desks, plants, and long telephone cords are appreciated by tourists and business travelers alike. Rather than large public areas, the inn has a personable library where complimentary continental breakfast and evening wine service are offered. Those headed for the financial district can arrange with the concierge to be driven by limousine.

The Monticello's exciting new Puccini & Pinetti Italian Grill & American Bar serves up good food at reasonable prices in a casual atmosphere that out-of-town visitors as well as people who live and work in the area may enjoy. Murals in brilliant hues add to the casual appeal, accentuated by live music in the evenings. Under chef Dan Schretter, entrees such as Chicken Marsalla, Pork Loin with White Beans, and Grilled Salmon or Skirt Steak are complemented with a selection of California wines. Portions are generous, but diners might want to save room for the 80-proof tiramisu.

The Monticello is convenient to theaters, Union Square, cable cars, and BART.

Address: 127 Ellis Street, San Francisco, CA 94102
Phone: 415-392-8800
Toll-Free: 800-669-7777
Fax: 415-398-2650
E-mail: montinn@aol.com
Web site: http://www.monticelloinn.com
Room Rates: $$
Suite Rates: $$$
Credit Cards: Most credit cards accepted
No. of Rooms: 91 **Suites:** 32
Services and Amenities: Valet parking, Garage, House doctor, Laundry service, Library, Game area, Non-smoking floor, TV, Radio, Honor bar and refrigerator, Complimentary toiletries, Complimentary continental breakfast and Wine service
Restrictions: No pets allowed, 4 rooms with handicapped access
Concierge: 24 hours
Room Service: 5:00 p.m.–10:00 p.m.
Restaurant: Puccini & Pinetti Italian Grill & American Bar, 11:30 a.m.–10:00 p.m., Sunday 5:00 p.m.–11:00 p.m.
Bar: 11:30 a.m.–Midnight
Business Facilities: Message center, Complete business service center one block away
Location: Downtown/Union Square, Nearest airport is San Francisco International
Attractions: Moscone Convention Center, Theater district, Opera, Symphony, Ballet, Cable cars, Union Square shopping, BART

Furnace Creek Inn, Death Valley, California. PAGE 17

John Gardiner's Tennis Ranch, Carmel Valley, California. PAGE 16

North Coast Country Inn, Gualala, California. PAGE 21

Beverly Plaza Hotel, Los Angeles, California. PAGE 24

STANYAN PARK HOTEL

This elegantly restored Victorian Hotel will take you back to a bygone era of style, grace and comfort. The 36 romantic rooms and suites, many with views of Golden Gate Park, are done in a variety of period decor in muted shades of peach and green. Each room has color TV, direct-dial telephone and private bath.

Stanyan Park Hotel is within walking distance of Golden Gate Park with its Asian Art and DeYoung Museums, Museum of Natural History, Aquarium, Hall of Flowers, Japanese Tea Garden, and bicycling and horseback riding. The University of California Medical Center, St. Mary's Hospital and the University of San Francisco are within 6 blocks. (Evening shuttle service is available to UC Medical Center.) San Francisco attractions such as Golden Gate Bridge, Chinatown, Pier 39, Ocean Beach and Fisherman's Wharf are an easy drive away.

Receptions, meetings, parties and weddings can also be arranged at Stanyan Park Hotel. Owner John Brockelhurst and staff pride themselves on their attention to the individual needs of all guests. In the heart of busy San Francisco, the Stanyan Park Hotel is a beautiful and quiet getaway.

Address: 750 Stanyan Street, San Francisco, CA 94117
Phone: 415-751-1000
Fax: 415-668-5454
E-mail: info@stanyanpark.com
Web site: http://www.stanyanpark.com
Room Rates: $
Suite Rates: $$
Credit Cards: AmEx, MC, Visa, Disc., DC
No. of Rooms: 30 **Suites:** 6
Services and Amenities: Valet service, Cable TV, Telephones, Clock Radio, Hair dryer, Complimentary toiletries, Complimentary breakfast, Tea Service 4:00–6:00 p.m.
Restrictions: No pets allowed, 2 rooms are handicapped-equipped, Non-smoking hotel
Concierge: Front desk
Business Facilities: Copiers, Fax
Location: Near Golden Gate Park, 10 miles from SF Airport, 2 miles from downtown SF
Attractions: Golden Gate Park, UC Medical Center, St. Mary's Hospital, Haight-Ashbury

THE DONATELLO

Italian design, craftsmanship, cuisine and staff are perfectly integrated at the Donatello a remarkable hotel in the heart of San Francisco's fashionable shopping and theatre district. The Italian sculptor Donatello was a major figure in 15th-Century Renaissance art, and the hotel bearing his name reflects classic European spirit.

The interiors, designed by Andrew Delfino, blend travertine, Italian marble, Venetian glass and European antiques. The spacious guest rooms are luxuriously decorated in soft pastels and designer prints, with Ming and Biedermeier furnishings. In the marble-clad baths you will find fine soaps and full-length terry cloth robes. Our favorite suite has a bedroom done in cream color with dark details, with a fine corner view. The living room has walls covered in Fortuny fabrics, couches in pale rose, and an impressive marble entryway.

Zingari Ristorante has been a success since the day it opened. Its two dining rooms are done in luxurious fabrics with Veronese marble floors. The atmosphere, while elegant and formal, maintains an intimate ambiance and charm.

An all time favorite dinner at the ristorante includes creamy risotto with truffles and wild mushrooms, followed by mussels sauteed in garlic white wine and black pepper. The next course includes a butter fly cut of tender filet mignon, sauteed in Gorgonzola sauce, accompanied by roasted potatoes and sauteed spinach. Dessert consists of dark chocolate fondant in a light orange-scented custard, delicious with Moscato Rosa. This feast would have impressed even the Medici. Besides daily special dinners such as this, there is an extensive a la carte menu.

Sophisticated travelers from the U.S. and abroad have fallen in love with *la dolce far niente* at the Donatello. You will too.

Address: 501 Post Street, San Francisco, CA 94102
Phone: 415-441-7100
Toll-Free: 800-227-3184
Fax: 415-885-8842
E-mail: sfcadntlo@aol.com
Room Rates: $$$
Suite Rates: $$$$
Credit Cards: Most credit cards accepted
No. of Rooms: 93 **Suites:** 3
Services and Amenities: Valet service, Garage & parking, Car hire, House doctor, Laundry service, Baby-sitting service, Turndown service, TV, Radio, Bath phone, Robes, Fine soaps, Complimentary shoeshine and newspaper
Restrictions: No pets allowed
Concierge: 7:00 a.m.–10:00 p.m.
Room Service: 6:30 a.m.–10:30 p.m.
Restaurant: Zingari Ristorante, 6:30 a.m.–11:00 p.m., Dress Code
Bar: In restaurant, 11:30 a.m.–Midnight
Business Facilities: Secretarial service, Translators, Copiers, Audio-Visual, Telex
Conference Rooms: 4 rooms, capacity 100
Sports Facilities: Full health spa services, Whirlpool, Sauna
Location: Union Square
Attractions: Boutique shopping, Major theater district, Fine dining

THE INN AT UNION SQUARE

Because of its size—30 rooms—the Inn at Union Square is what is known as a boutique hotel. It is also among the first to be a completely non-smoking establishment!

Beginning with the valet parking, special emphasis is placed upon personal service. From the moment they arrive, guests are made to feel favored, rather than like just another room number. The Inn at Union Square is the only hotel in San Francisco that does not accept gratuities from its guests.

Rooms are individually decorated in bright, cheerful colors, and feature goosedown pillows and comforters, and fresh flowers. Polished shoes greet guests at their doors every morning, along with a newspaper. The penthouse has its own fireplace, whirlpool bath and sauna. Room service can deliver an ala carte breakfast to rooms upon request, or guests may be served in the intimate lobby with seating areas that grace each floor. The lobby also has a wet bar. Complimentary tea with sandwiches and cakes are served each afternoon, followed in the evening by wine and hors d'oeuvres.

Should you wish to tour the town, say, to Fisherman's Wharf and on to the Legion of Honor on the edge of Lincoln Park Golf Course, with its unsurpassed view of the Golden Gate and the bridge that spans it, or venture to the wine country, the Concierge will be pleased to arrange it for you.

Within walking distance to the financial district and Union Square with its fascinating shops, the Inn at Union Square is ideally located for the business traveller, theater lover, or one bent on a shopping spree.

Address: 440 Post Street, San Francisco, CA 94102
Phone: 415-397-3510
Toll-Free: 800-AT-THE-INN
Fax: 415-989-0529
E-mail: inn@unionsquare.com
Room Rates: $$$
Suite Rates: $$$
Credit Cards: Visa, MC, AmEx, DC, JCB
No. of Rooms: 24 **Suites:** 6
Services and Amenities: Valet service, Car rental, Laundry service, Cable TV, Phone, Radio, Climate control, Robes, Complimentary toiletries, shoeshine & newspaper, Ala carte breakfast available, No gratuities accepted by staff
Restrictions: No pets allowed, 2 rooms with handicapped access, No-smoking hotel
Concierge: 24 hours
Room Service: 6:30 a.m.–11:00 a.m.
Location: Half block west of Union Square, Nearest airport: San Francisco Intl.
Attractions: Close to shopping and theater district, Sight-seeing tours to Chinatown, Fisherman's Wharf, Ghirardelli Square, The Cannery and Golden Gate Park, Wine country and Cable car tours leave from Union Square

THE PRESCOTT HOTEL

Elegance, convenience and premier location is the desire of the astute traveler, and The Prescott Hotel in downtown cosmopolitan San Francisco has it all, including an acclaimed restaurant supervised by world-renowned executive chef Wolfgang Puck. This historic 1913 brick-faced hotel has been impeccably renovated, opening its doors and guest rooms to an impressed clientele in Spring, 1989. Classically San Franciscan, The Prescott is just a block from famed prestigious Union Square, theatres, stylish shops, restaurants, and the Fisherman's Wharf-bound Powell St. cable car.

Urban elegance marks the lobby, with its inviting fireplace, comfortable seating arrangements of richly-upholstered furniture, and display of California Indian artifacts. Careful attention to detail mark the splendid decor of the hotel's 109 spacious rooms. Comfortable, tasteful appointments are complemented by pecan-hued Empire furniture, including a stocked honor bar, remote control TV and complimentary HBO. Baths offer terry robes, hair dryers and generous toiletries. In its 17 elegant suites, The Prescott has added VCRs, whirlpool bathtubs and double phones. The Presidential suite has the added luxury of a wood-burning fireplace.

Special Prescott courtesies are evening-time wine and hors d'oeuvres in the library, day-long coffee and tea service, same-day laundry service, and complimentary transportation to the financial district, six blocks away. Two floors are reserved for non-smokers. Opened in April, 1989 to lavish reviews, the PosTrio Restaurant is under the aegis of famed executive chef Wolfgang Puck and his equally-inspired co-chefs Anne and David Gingrass. Modern artworks accentuate the contemporary American design, imaginatively opened to three levels and tied together innovatively by ribboned patterns in the carpet, marble floor and handrails. The first-floor bar introduces the guest to this signature restaurant, and there is a garden patio room off the top-level dining area for private gatherings. Hailed as the "chefs' interpretation" of classic San Franciscan cuisine, the menu emphasizes the freshest of local produce and ingredients. Among the rave-winning entrees is grilled eggplant with mozzarella and David's homemade salami.

The new San Franciscan ambience at The Prescott is directed at the guest who desires the finest—at an affordable price.

Address: 545 Post Street, San Francisco, CA 94102
Phone: 415-563-0303
Toll-Free: 800-283-7322
Fax: 415-563-6831
E-mail: sales@prescotthotel.com
Web site: http://www.prescott.com
Room Rates: $$$
Suite Rates: $$$$
Credit Cards: Most credit cards accepted
No. of Rooms: 129 **Suites:** 35
Services and Amenities: Valet service, Library, Individual climate control, Cable TV with complimentary HBO, Radio, Whirlpool in suites, Toiletries, Two non-smoking rooms, Complimentary wine and hors d'oeuvres
Restrictions: Handicapped access to 9 rooms
Concierge: 7:00 a.m.–11:00 p.m.
Room Service: 6:00 a.m.–12:00 a.m.
Restaurant: PosTrio, 7:00 a.m.–10:30 p.m., Dress code
Bar: PosTrio, 11:30 a.m.–12:00 p.m.
Business Facilities: In-room fax, 2-line phones & dataports in room, Voice mail, Copying services
Conference Rooms: 2 rooms, capacity 10-45
Sports Facilities: Guest privileges to Hotel Monaco Health Club & Spa (fee)
Location: Heart of downtown San Francisco, 25 minutes—airport, 1 mile—Hwy. 101
Attractions: 1 block from Union Square and Cable Car to Fisherman's Wharf, Theatres, Elegant shops

VICTORIAN INN ON THE PARK

The Victorian Inn on the Park, a registered historic landmark, also known as the Clunie House, was built in 1897, Queen Victoria's Diamond Jubilee year. Carefully restored with reproductions of original wallpapers and other features, the Inn revives late 19th century elegance. It overlooks Golden Gate Park in an area well known for its noble victorians.

The guestrooms, all with private baths, reflect Victorian San Francisco. Each is uniquely decorated and features its own design in beautiful comforters and down pillows.

Guests are greeted each morning in the oak paneled dining room with a newspaper and a pleasing breakfast of fruit, cheese, juice, coffee, preserves, and warm breads baked daily on the premises. Guests are also invited to gather in the parlor each late afternoon and early evening to relax and enjoy refreshments.

The Inn is conveniently located less than five minutes from the Civic Center and museums, ten minutes to downtown, and so central that most points in the city are no more than fifteen minutes away. It is within a few blocks of the University of California San Francisco Medical Center, St. Mary's Hospital and the University of San Francisco.

Address: 301 Lyon Street, San Francisco, CA 94117
Phone: 415-931-1830
Toll-Free: 800-435-1967
Fax: 415-931-1830
E-mail: vicinn@aol.com
Web site: http://www.citysearch.com/sfo/victorianinn
Room Rates: $$
Suite Rates: $$$
Credit Cards: AmEx, Visa, MC, DC, Disc., JCB
No. of Rooms: 12 **Suites:** 2
Services and Amenities: Romantic Getaway package available, Garage & parking, Car hire, Common Game room, Library, Parlor, Laundry service, Cable TV, Telephones, Radios, Some rooms with fireplaces, Complimentary breakfast, newspaper and toiletries
Restrictions: No pets allowed, Children welcome
Concierge: 7:30 a.m.–11:00 p.m.
Room Service: Nearby restaurants
Restaurant: Breakfast served to guests in Victorian Inn dining room 7:15-10:30 a.m., Chef William Benau
Business Facilities: Fax, Computer jacks
Conference Rooms: 1 room, capacity 12
Sports Facilities: Massage available by prior arrangement; Tennis and Golf nearby
Location: Haight Ashbury adjacent to Golden Gate Park, 12 miles—SFO airport
Attractions: Walk to Japanese Tea Gardens, DeYoung Museum, Easy access to any tourist sight in San Francisco, Wonderful Park events, Perfect for Bay to Breakers Race, San Francisco Marathon and Shakespeare in the Park

APPLE FARM INN

The Apple Farm Inn is an experience in traditional hospitality. Guests enjoy what is remembered as the "good old American" virtues of friendliness, cleanliness, honest value, homemade food and cozy rooms. The inn conveys country Victorian charm, while providing all the modern conveniences and comforts of a luxury hotel.

The sunny, spacious octagon-shaped lobby is decorated with Ralph Lauren wicker furniture. It allows spectacular views of the giant sycamores that grace the quiet banks of the San Luis Creek and the beautiful coastal mountains. Each room features a gas log fireplace and is uniquely appointed with canopy or enamel and brass beds, love seats and wingback chairs.

Service at the Apple Farm Inn is based on the philosophy of warm hospitality. Complimentary wake-up coffee, fresh flowers and plants in every room, three sheet beds, remote control TVs and breakfast in bed with a newspaper are just some of the ways guests are pampered. Homemade food served with country charm describes the fare at the Apple Farm Restaurant. For dinner, American favorites like chicken and dumplings and turkey with dressing are featured. Fish entrees such as broiled orange roughy and baby salmon are also available. All are served with cornbread and honey butter. There are selections for the diet-conscious as well. The breakfast menu is extensive (all fresh-baked, of course). The lunch menu includes old favorites such as hot roast beef sandwiches, turkey pot pies, and freshly prepared salads.

The Apple Farm Gift Shop is an experience unto itself. Housed in an exact replica of a two-story country Victorian house, it offers a wide variety of items including decorative accessories, framed prints, glassware, kitchenware, toys, cards and books. The Apple Farm Brand products are the real draw of the shop—apple butter and spreads in canning jars, gift packages in miniature wooden crates, pressed cider and mulled cider spices—are only some of the items. Also worth a visit is The Old Millhouse. This is an operating grist mill with a 14 foot wheel which harnesses water to power a cider press, grind wheat and make ice cream.

Address: 2015 Monterey Street, San Luis Obispo, CA 93401
Phone: 805-544-2040
Toll-Free: 800-374-3705
Fax: 805-544-1502
Room Rates: $$
Credit Cards: MC, Visa, AmEx, Discover
No. of Rooms: 67
Services and Amenities: Parking, Gift shop, Fireplaces, Balconies (3 rooms), Cable TV, Radio, Robes, All rooms accessible to handicapped, Complimentary toiletries and newspaper
Restrictions: No pets allowed, Children under 18 free with parents
Concierge: Front desk
Room Service: Limited
Restaurant: Apple Farm Restaurant, 7:00 a.m.–9:30 p.m.
Business Facilities: Message center, Copiers, Audio-Visual
Conference Rooms: 1 room, capacity 40
Sports Facilities: Outdoor swimming pool, Whirlpool, Nearby tennis, golf and sailing
Location: Monterey Street near Highway 101, Close to historic downtown
Attractions: Evening carriage rides, Within 10 miles of numerous wineries, 12 miles to fishing village of Morro Bay, 45 miles to Hearst Castle, 2 miles to Performing Arts Center, Millhouse Gift Shop with creekside patio is the perfect spot to relax & enjoy lunch

GARDEN STREET INN

The grace and simplicity of yesteryear prevail at the 1887 Italianate/Queen Anne home, lovingly restored in 1990. Classic decor reflects Victorian charm in the 9 guestrooms and 4 suites appointed with antiques, fireplaces, jacuzzis, and historic, cultural and personal memorabilia.

A homemade full breakfast - family style - is served in the McCaffrey Morning room (which has original stained-glass windows) each morning. Guests also enjoy a wine and cheese hour in the evening. Spacious outside decks and the well-stocked Goldtree Library are perfect settings for reading. The Vose & Sons upright grand piano is circa 1893 and is adorned by family heirlooms. The library has floor-to-ceiling bookcases surrounding a fireplace and Victorian wallcoverings.

Each of the guestrooms and suites has a distinctive personality of its own: "Cocoon" has a multitude of butterfly works of arts; "Our Town" honors Thornton Wilder's classic Play; "Field of Dreams" is decorated with baseball memorabilia collected by the innkeeper's father; and "Amadeus" is covered with prints, posters and works of art saluting Mozart.

If you love antique cars, the "Concours d'Elegance" suite is for you. In addition to its automobile memorabilia, the suite has a cast-iron fireplace, sitting room, in-room sink in the bedroom and a clawfoot tub/shower in the bathroom.

Address: 1212 Garden Street, San Luis Obispo, CA 93401
Phone: 805-545-9802
Fax: 805-545-9403
E-mail: garden@fix.net
Web site: http://www.fix.net/garden
Room Rates: $
Suite Rates: $$
Credit Cards: AmEx, Visa, MC
No. of Rooms: 13 **Suites:** 4
Services and Amenities:
Complimentary breakfast, Garage, Car hire, Laundry, Gift shop, Card/game area, Library, 6 rooms with fireplaces, 4 with balconies/decks, Cassette player, Radio, Individual heat & AC, Robes, Whirlpool bath, Complimentary toiletries & newspaper in library
Restrictions: Minimum stays for holidays & some weekends, No pets, 1 suite equipped for handicapped
Concierge: Innkeepers available
Room Service: Breakfast in suites
Bar: Wine and hors d'oeuvres served in evening, 5:30–7:00 p.m.
Conference Rooms: One suite suitable for conferencing
Sports Facilities: Whirlpool, Massage, Many facilities nearby
Location: Downtown, Nearest airport: San Luis Obispo
Attractions: Trolley to Historical Museum, Art Center, Quaint downtown, Shops, Mozart Festival, Shakespeare Festival

MONTECITO INN

The Montecito Inn is unique among Santa Barbara landmarks. Located two blocks from the beach, the hotel is a product of Hollywood's Golden Era, built in 1928 by silent screen legend Charlie Chaplin as a haven for tinsel town celebrities.

Today's red tile roof and white plaster walls pay homage to the original construction. In the 1950's, a terrace and formal garden were replaced by a driveway leading into an enclosed parking facility. Later a pool, spa and sauna were added at the rear of the building. During this renovation, the wishing well that inspired composer Richard Rodgers to write his memorable love song, "There's a Small Hotel" (1963) was lost. A replica of that "well" now sits in the highly acclaimed Montecito Cafe.

Magnificently restored, the Inn's 53 guestrooms are furnished in a French Provincial style with soft floral cotton prints, armoires, overhead fans and hand-painted tile baths. Seven one-bedroom luxury suites feature spacious Italian marble bathrooms with jacuzzi tubs and custom fireplaces.

The casual, intimate restaurant has a partially open kitchen allowing guests to watch as chef Mark Huston prepares dishes such as goat cheese pancakes with smoked salmon and caviar, daily fresh seafood creations and a "decadent" homemade chocolate mousse cake. Gourmet meals may also be ordered through room service. The warm Cafe Lounge has a baby grand piano and boasts a special appetizer menu, cocktails and fine wines.

Complimentary amenities include a continental breakfast served in the popular cafe, use of the Inn's touring bicycles and free sightseeing trolley passes which tour the world famous Mission, Santa Barbara Zoo, Art Museum, Botanical Gardens, Pier and downtown State Street—a visitor's paradise!

The Montecito Inn is a time machine, offering both the quaint elegance and attentive service of the 1920's and the modern conveniences of the finest contemporary hotels.

Address: 1295 Coast Village Road, Santa Barbara, CA 93108
Phone: 805-969-7854
Toll-Free: 800-843-2017
Fax: 805-969-0623
E-mail: info@montecitoinn.com
Web site: http://www.montecitoinn.com
Room Rates: $$$
Suite Rates: $$$$
Credit Cards: Most credit cards accepted
No. of Rooms: 50 **Suites:** 10
Services and Amenities:
Complimentary Continental Breakfast daily, Valet service, Garage & free parking, Cable TV with free HBO, In-room movies for an additional charge
Restrictions: No pets allowed
Room Service: 7:00 a.m.–10:00 p.m.
Restaurant: Montecito Cafe, Breakfast 7:00 a.m.–10:00 a.m., Lunch 11:30 a.m.–2:30 p.m., Dinner 5:30 p.m.–10:00 p.m.
Bar: Cafe Lounge open nightly, piano entertainment
Business Facilities: Copiers, Audio-Visual, Fax machine
Conference Rooms: Chaplin Meeting Facility, capacity 60
Sports Facilities: Outdoor heated pool, Whirlpool, Sauna, Exercise room, Massage, Hotel bicycles (free), Access to Montecito Country Club for golf
Location: Seaside community of Montecito, 2 blocks from secluded Butterfly Beach
Attractions: Walk to beach & specialty boutiques, Free sightseeing trolley passes to art museum, Botanical gardens, Harbor area, Santa Barbara Mission, Zoo & downtown State Street—a visitor's paradise

SANTA BARBARA INN

The Santa Barbara Inn, with its sprawling tri-level facade painted white with teal awnings faces the ocean and is flanked by palms and flowers in a tropical garden setting.

Lobby decor is cream, teal and rose with marble floor. Guest rooms are over-sized; furniture is light gold tones and soft goods are earth toned with rich sandy shades.

The Santa Cruz Island suite is truly spectacular. It has an over-sized round bedroom, richly appointed parlor and wrap-around deck with a breathtaking view of mountains and ocean. A cream textured wall covering adorns the bath in which there is also a telephone.

The restaurant, Citronelle, is fronted with glass, overlooking the Pacific, and has been praised for its fine California-French cooking. It offers appetizers such as procupine shrimp with frisee salad and ginger dressing, entrees such as Roasted Venison Chop with black pepper sauce and pears, and for dessert (always the high point of the dinner), a chocolate creme brulee. There is also an interesting wine list featuring California and French wines from which to choose. Silver service coffee is served in the lobby. Business facilities can be arranged through the Sales Office. The Montecito Room can be easily converted into a conference room with audio visual equipment.

There is an outdoor swimming pool. Sports such as golf, boating, bicycling, horseback riding and sailing are all available nearby.

Address: 901 East Cabrillo Boulevard, Santa Barbara, CA 93103
Phone: 805-966-2285
Toll-Free: 800-231-0431
Fax: 805-966-6584
Room Rates: $$
Suite Rates: $$$
Credit Cards: Most credit cards accepted
No. of Rooms: 66 **Suites:** 5
Services and Amenities: Valet service & parking, Laundry service, Baby-sitting service, Balconies, Cable TV, Wet bar in suites, Telephone, Complimentary toiletries, coffee & newspaper, Catering & banquet facilities for 100 guests, Turndown service available
Restrictions: No pets allowed, Children free with parents
Concierge: 10:00 a.m.–7:00 p.m.
Room Service: 7:00 a.m.–10:00 p.m.
Restaurant: Michel Richard's Citronelle, 7:00 a.m.–10:00 a.m., Noon-2:30 p.m., 6:00 p.m.–10:00 p.m.
Bar: Citronelle Lounge, 11:00 a.m.–midnight
Business Facilities: Message center, Secretarial center, Copiers, Audio-Visual, Teleconferencing
Conference Rooms: 3 rooms, capacity 230
Sports Facilities: Outdoor swimming pool, Whirlpool, Nearby golf, Tennis, Boating, Sailing, Horseback riding, Fishing, Bicycling
Location: Eastside
Attractions: Santa Barbara Mission, Stroll to Wharf, Antique and specialty shops, Artists display of works along beach each weekend, Whale-watching expeditions, Museums, Galleries

THE UPHAM HOTEL & GARDEN COTTAGES

In 1871, Boston banker Amasa Lincoln sailed to Santa Barbara and built the Victorian hotel of his dreams with redwood timbers, sweeping verandas, and topped with a cupola. Today, completely restored, The Upham Hotel and Garden Cottages is the oldest continuously operating hotel in Southern California.

Situated on an acre of lovely gardens are seven buildings housing fifty guest rooms and suites, some with gas fireplaces highlight the accommodations all of which include private baths, color cable televisions, radios and telephones. Daily amenities include a deluxe continental breakfast buffet, afternoon refreshments of fruit, wine and cheese, and Oreo cookies with milk in the evening.

Louie's Restaurant, adjoining the hotel lobby, is one of Santa Barbara's finest. This restaurant features innovative California cuisines and serves year-round on the veranda. The Upham is located in the heart of downtown within easy walking distance of restaurants, shops, art galleries and museums.

Address: 1404 De La Vina Street, Santa Barbara, CA 93101
Phone: 805-962-0058
Toll-Free: 800-727-0876
Fax: 805-963-2825
Room Rates: $$
Suite Rates: $$$$
Credit Cards: Visa, MC, AmEx, Diners Club
No. of Rooms: 50 **Suites:** 4
Services and Amenities: Valet service, Garage and parking, Laundry service, Cable TV, Complimentary newspaper, toiletries, Continental breakfast and afternoon refreshments
Restrictions: No pets allowed, No handicapped-equipped rooms
Concierge: 7:00 a.m.–11:00 a.m.
Restaurant: Louie's, Lunch 11:30 a.m.–2:30 p.m., Dinner 6:00 p.m.–10:00 p.m.
Business Facilities: Conference rooms, Copiers, Audio-Visual, Fax
Location: Santa Barbara
Attractions: Walking distance from restaurants, shops, art galleries and museums

CHANNEL ROAD INN

Once a privately-owned mansion built in Colonial Revival style, the Channel Road Inn is situated in a choice location that affords wide-range views of the mountains and the sea.

All guest rooms are individually decorated. Beds have down comforters and pillows to give a homey feeling. Suites are spacious with fireplace, refrigerator, couch, pine tables, chairs and an armoire that houses the TV and VCR. Suites also have a fine view of the ocean. A complimentary breakfast is included in your stay prepared by the finalist of the Jones Dairy Farm breakfast cooking contest.

Baths are done in attractive white or pastel tiles. They contain large sinks, a tub for two and windows.

Antique furniture and Chinese oriental rugs decorate the lobby. The library is done in chintz and wicker furniture.

A whirlpool bath is available, as are bicycles for guests who wish to ride the beach bike path.

It is less than a 5-minute walk to beach and shops. The J. Paul Getty Center and the Santa Monica Pier are close by.

Address: 219 West Channel Road, Santa Monica, CA 90402
Phone: 310-459-1920
Fax: 310-454-9920
E-mail: ChannelInn@aol.com
Room Rates: $$
Suite Rates: $$$
Credit Cards: Visa, MC, AmEx
No. of Rooms: 14 **Suites:** 2
Services and Amenities: Parking, Cable TV, VCR, Telephone, Cassette player, Radio, Fireplaces, Down comforters, Robes, Complimentary toiletries, tea/wine/hors d'oeuvres, and breakfast
Restrictions: Children free with parents
Business Facilities: Message center, Secretarial center, Copiers, Fax
Conference Rooms: 1 room
Sports Facilities: Jacuzzi, Bicycles, Beach
Location: Santa Monica, Nearest airport is LAX
Attractions: Shopping, Beach, J.Paul Getty Center, Santa Monica Pier, 10 minutes to Venice Beach

SHUTTERS ON THE BEACH

Guests at Shutters on the Beach will particularly enjoy the informal luxury here, reminiscent of the colorful beach resorts and cottages built in Southern California during the 1920s and '30s. Shutters is the only luxury hotel in L.A. nestled right on the sand. The intimate lobby is warm and inviting, with two large fireplaces, wood floors, and a spacious balcony overlooking the Pacific Ocean.

Guestrooms and suites have the ambience of a grand but unpretentious beach home. Sliding shuttered doors and windows open to the ocean breeze. Furnishings crafted from dark, warm walnut wood contrast with the crisp, white walls and custom-designed armoires, desks and night stands. Tufted lounge chairs, blue and white carpeting in a nautical pattern, and slip covered headboards give a plush, inviting feeling.

One Pico, a specialty 85-seat restaurant with magnificent windows on three sides, offers one of the most panoramic restaurant experiences in Southern California. Modern American cuisine is served with an emphasis on locally grown produce. One of the most popular entrees is the Seabass with Black Beans and Scallions. The Warm Chocolate Pudding Cake for dessert is a great way to end your dinner.

Pedals is a more casual, beach promenade restaurant. With seating both indoors and out, this high-energy California cafe evokes an Italian trattoria feel. The menu features California cafe cuisine with multi-ethnic influences. Adjoining Pedals is Handlebar, a long, flowing bar and lounge from which you may watch people stroll, jog, bicycle, skate swim or tan, while you enjoy a light snack, afternoon cocktail or evening drink overlooking the Pacific.

A fabulous pool and spa, with wonderful views of the Pacific Ocean and beach below, offer plenty of chaise lounges for all-day sunning. A stroll on nearby Santa Monica Pier is always fun, and the beach is just steps away.

Address: One Pico Boulevard, Santa Monica, CA 90405
Phone: 310-458-0030
Toll-Free: 800-334-9000
Fax: 310-458-4589
Room Rates: $$$$
Suite Rates: $$$$
Credit Cards: Most credit cards accepted
No. of Rooms: 186 **Suites:** 12
Services and Amenities: Parking, Valet, Car hire, Gift shop, International currency exchange, House doctor, Laundry, Baby-sitting service, Fireplaces, Balconies, Cable TV/VCR, Radio, Individual heat/air-conditioning control, Robes, Complimentary toiletries, shoeshine & newspaper
Restrictions: Children under 5 free in parents' room, 9 rooms & 1 suite with handicapped access, No pets allowed
Concierge: 24 hours
Room Service: 24 hours
Restaurant: Pedals Cafe, 6:30 a.m.–11:00 p.m.
Bar: Handlebar, 5:00 p.m.–11:00 p.m.
Business Facilities: Message center, Secretarial services, Copiers, Audio-Visual
Conference Rooms: 6 rooms, capacity 300
Sports Facilities: Outdoor swimming pool, Whirlpool, Sauna, Massage, Aerobics, Weight training, Nearby sailing & tennis, Beach activities
Location: Santa Monica Beach
Attractions: Walk to historic Santa Monica Pier, Art galleries, Short drive to shopping

VINTNERS INN

Set in a 45-acre vineyard, the warm glow of terra-cotta walls and tile roofs evoke the mood of southern France, while the California mission detailing reminds you of the Sonoma County wine-making community, redwood forests and Pacific beaches just minutes away.

The European-style Vintners Inn was patterned after a small village in Provence, with four guest buildings encircling the courtyard fountain plaza. The rooms are spacious, with antique French pine furnishings, some with wood-burning fireplaces, balconies or patios and beamed ceilings. The bathrooms feature large, oval, oversized tubs. The main building leads to tile walkways, trellis-covered sun deck and spa. Conference rooms also open to the courtyard. The large and well-trained staff are ready to assist in the success of your meetings or seminars.

John Ash & Co. is the award-winning and nationally-acclaimed restaurant at the Inn and epitomizes wine country dining at its best. Chef Jeffrey Madura's commitment to incorporating all that is fresh and wonderful from Sonoma County's wealth of produce, meats, poultry, and seafood is evident in his ever-changing menu. Begin your meal with Crab Cakes or a Warmed Red Cabbage Salad with Laura Chenel's goat cheese, followed by a main entree of Smoked and Grilled Rack of Lamb on a bed of artichoke risotto. Sonoma Chocolate "Stonehenge" finishes your dinner while you savor another Sonoma county wine, perhaps one which began life on the Sauvignon Blanc vines just off your patio.

Spend your day in the Russian River resort area and wind your way to the seal beaches at the coast. Start with an early morning hot air balloon ride or go antiquing in Sebastopol. Golf one of the local courses, or visit the sprawling orchards and fields by bike. Hike the redwood forests or go boating on Lake Sonoma. You'll be back to Sonoma County and Vintners Inn.

Address: 4350 Barnes Road, Santa Rosa, CA 95403
Phone: 707-575-7350
Toll-Free: 800-421-2584
Fax: 707-575-1426
Web site: http://www.vintnersinn.com
Room Rates: $$$
Suite Rates: $$$
Credit Cards: Visa, MC, AmEx, Diners
No. of Rooms: 44 **Suites:** 5
Services and Amenities: Valet service, Parking, Private baby-sitting service, Library, Gifts available in lobby area, Fireplaces, Balconies, Patios & decks, Cable TV, VCR's for rent, Radio, Individual climate control, Complimentary newspaper & toiletries, Complimentary breakfast
Restrictions: No pets, No checks, 3 rooms handicapped access, Kids under 6 free with adults, 2-day min. for Sat. stay
Concierge: 24 hours
Room Service: Noon—10:00 p.m.
Restaurant: John Ash & Co., 11:30 a.m.–9:00 p.m.
Bar: Vineyard Lounge at John Ash & Co., 11:30 a.m.–10:00 p.m.
Business Facilities: Message center, Secretarial services, Copiers, Audio-Visual, Teleconferencing, Translators upon request
Conference Rooms: 3 rooms, capacity 30
Sports Facilities: Whirlpool, Massage available on-site, Tennis, Aerobics and weight training at nearby Airport Fitness Club, Golf, Hiking, Biking
Location: 5 miles north of Santa Rosa in Sonoma County wine country and Russian River
Attractions: Vineyards, Wineries, 1 mile to Luther Burbank Center for the Arts, Antique shopping, Hot air ballooning with pick-up at hotel, Golf, Tennis, Hiking, Biking

CASA MADRONA HOTEL

Nestled on a hillside overlooking San Francisco Bay is Casa Madrona, Sausalito's most famous hotel. Its original building, constructed in 1885 and known as Victorian House, has 13 accommodations. In 1980 it was entered in the National Register of Historical Places. Since then, 16 accommodations have been added with the construction of New Casa, a New England-style structure built into the hillside and connecting the restored Victorian above to Bridgeway Street below.

Each of Casa Madrona's accommodations has an individual theme. Most rooms have fireplaces and wonderful views of the water. There are ten honeymoon suites, three in Victorian House. The Rose Chalet, located in New Casa, is a honeymoon suite with rose-colored walls, pine furniture, and white accents. It has a fireplace, spacious deck, and bedroom alcove with a dramatic view.

Casa Madrona might be just the place for a small executive retreat or board of directors meeting. The Villa Madrona Suite has two bedrooms, each with a private bath, separated by a living room with a brass fireplace and wet bar. It offers a beautiful harbor view from three decks, and accommodates 22 people in a formal boardroom setting, as many as 50 for cocktails, and can provide elegant lodging for two couples.

All guests are invited to the Victorian House library for a complimentary wine and cheese social hour each evening. Dinner is served in the award-winning restaurant, Mikayla, on a terrace with bay views through retractable glass roof and sliding glass walls that are open in warm weather. Menu options range from Vegetable Risotto, Zucchini twirls, Leek and tomato broth, Chilean Sea Bass wrapped in potato with salmon caviar sauce, to Grilled New York Strip with baked new potatoes and roast garlic sauce.

Address: 801 Bridgeway, Sausalito, CA 94965
Phone: 415-332-0502
Toll-Free: 800-567-9524
Fax: 415-332-2537
Room Rates: $$
Suite Rates: $$$$
Credit Cards: Visa, MC, AmEx
No. of Rooms: 34 **Suites:** 16
Services and Amenities: Valet, Parking, Laundry service, Baby-sitting service, TV lounge, Library, Cable TV, Radio, Individual climate controls, Robes, Complimentary newspaper, toiletries and continental breakfast
Restrictions: No pets allowed, 1 room handicapped-equipped
Concierge: 24 hours
Room Service: 6:00 p.m.–10:00 p.m.
Restaurant: Mikayla, Dinner nightly 6:00 p.m.–10:00 p.m., Lunch Monday-Friday 11:30 a.m.–2:30 p.m., Sunday brunch 10:00 a.m.–2:30 p.m.
Business Facilities: Audio-Visual equipment, Copier, Message center
Conference Rooms: 1 room, capacity 22
Sports Facilities: Private outdoor jacuzzi, Steam room
Location: Sausalito hillside overlooking San Francisco Bay, Nearest airport is SFO
Attractions: Boutique shopping only a few steps away, San Francisco half hour by ferry or 6 miles by car, Muir Woods

THE INN ABOVE TIDE

The Inn Above the Tide, a new three story contemporary structure with elevator service, a gated courtyard and exceptionally beautiful views, is the only hotel in the entire Bay Area that is on the water. Its location in the heart of Sausalito within walking distance of 200 art galleries, boutiques, restaurants, and many hiking trails, is a few steps from the ferry landing and a short ride to San Francisco.

An elegant lobby furnished in bird's eye maple with floors of cream colored marble and black granite leads to the Drawing Room. Overlooking the ferry landing, the Drawing Room accommodates up to fifteen people for small board meetings.

The luxurious guest rooms are decorated in a soft palette of seafoam green and sea blue with custom-designed furniture in washed light birch, and feature elegant baths with oversized tubs. Binoculars are provided so that guests may fully enjoy the unobstructed and ever-changing marine views of the San Francisco Bay, and those of Angel Island, the Tiburon Peninsula, the Bay Bridge, and the San Francisco skyline. Guests are invited to enjoy the courtyard sun deck on the second level.

The contemporary "Vista Suite," with its four-poster king-size bed, offers a breathtaking panoramic view of San Francisco Bay and skyline and includes a wood-burning fireplace, sitting area, deck, wet bar, and marble-tiled bath with Jacuzzi tub and separate shower.

Guests enjoy the Inn's comfortably furnished Drawing Room for complimentary breakfast and for a sunset wine and cheese hour each evening. Breakfast may be served in guest rooms by request. Room service meal delivery is also available from top restaurants in the area via Room Service of Marin.

Nearby activities such as bicycle rental, fishing charters, golfing, hiking, scuba diving and children's playground can be arranged through the Inn. The luxuriously relaxed and elegant interior design and guest-pampering service contribute to a truly memorable stay.

Address: 30 El Portal, Sausalito, CA 94965
Phone: 415-332-9535
Toll-Free: 800-893-8433
Fax: 415-332-6714
E-mail: inntide@ix.netcom.com
Web site: http://www.citysearch.com/sfo/innabovetide
Room Rates: $$$
Suite Rates: $$$$
Credit Cards: Visa, MC, AmEx
No. of Rooms: 30 **Suites:** 2
Services and Amenities: Valet, Laundry service, Baby-sitting service, Cable TV, 2-line telephone & computer dataport, Radio, Honor bar, Mini-bar/refrigerator, Robes, Most rooms have fireplaces & balconies, Some rooms have whirlpool bath, Complimentary toiletries, Cribs available
Restrictions: No pets allowed, No smoking, 2-night minimum stay on weekends, Handicapped access, Children welcome
Concierge: 24 hours
Restaurant: Complimentary breakfast, or sunset wine & cheese delivered to rooms by request, Walking distance to many dining opportunities
Business Facilities: Message center, Copiers, Audio-Visual, Fax, Modem hook-up
Conference Rooms: 1 room, capacity 15
Sports Facilities: Massage by appointment, Public tennis courts nearby, Bicycle rentals, Fishing charters, Golf, Hiking, Scuba diving, Playground
Location: Downtown Sausalito on San Francisco Bay, Next to ferry landing
Attractions: Walking distance to Sausalito's 200 art galleries, boutiques and restaurants, 100 yards from ferry landing for access to San Francisco, Hiking and bicycling trails

THE SEAL BEACH INN & GARDENS

The historic Seal Beach Inn & Gardens, Southern California's original country inn, is nestled in a quiet seaside village, within steps of a pristine ocean beach and sophisticated dining and shopping. Disneyland, Los Angeles, and Orange County's cultural and entertainment centers are all nearby.

The Inn is built in a French Mediterranean style, with a brick courtyard, antique street lamps, flowering planters, ornate French ironwork and a profusion of color year round. Creating a memorable stay reminiscent of the French Riviera, the Inn combines old-world elegance and charm with the amenities so prized by the world class traveler.

The guest accommodations are named after flowers, from Azalea to Zinnia, many of which can be found growing in the Inn's mini gardens. Each of the 23 unique rooms and suites is tastefully ornate in decor with antiques and period furnishings including a four poster bed from John Barrymore's estate, a Civil War era bed, and Victorian or Eastlake beds. Several rooms have fireplace and/or Jacuzzi. All feature european-style down bedding, intimate terrycloth robes and English bath amenities. A freshly baked cookie from the Inn's kitchen welcomes each guest bedside.

A lavish breakfast buffet of Belgian waffles, quiches, and sumptuous fruits, pastries, and gourmet teas and coffees is served to guests either in the Tea Room or on the poolside patio, where roses and flowering plants add further charm to an antique French fountain pouring water from a frescoed lady's pitcher. An evening tea is provided with tea and hors d'oeuvres served in the Inn's Tea Room by a cozy fire in the fireplace. Guests are also invited to enjoy the library stocked with delightful reading materials.

Address: 212 Fifth Street, Seal Beach, CA 90740
Phone: 562-493-2416
Toll-Free: 800-443-3292
Fax: 562-799-0483
E-mail: hideaway@sealbeachinn.com
Room Rates: $$$
Suite Rates: $$$
Credit Cards: Visa, MC, AmEx, Diners, JCB
No. of Rooms: 22 **Suites:** 3
Services and Amenities: Parking, Library, Gift shop, Game area, Cooking facilities, Television, Radio, Wet bar, Refrigerators, Fans, Individual heat control, Complimentary newspapers and toiletries, Complimentary breakfast, Elegant extras
Restrictions: No pets allowed, Children discouraged
Concierge: 7:00 a.m.–11:00 p.m.
Business Facilities: Copiers, Message center
Conference Rooms: 2 rooms, capacity 12 and 25
Sports Facilities: Outdoor swimming pool, Some whirlpools available
Location: Seal Beach Old Town, Nearest airports are Long Beach, LAX, Orange County
Attractions: Within walking distance of beach, Second longest pier in southern California, Superb restaurants and antique shops, Gondola rides, Golf courses nearby

THE ALISAL GUEST RANCH AND RESORT

In a 10,000-acre pastoral setting on California's Central Coast presides The Alisal Guest Ranch and Resort. Year-round beauty envelops the 1946-built retreat which sprawls comfortably in the Santa Ynez Valley. The Ranch's cluster of one-story cottages, with unending views of the countryside and mountains, has become the destination for generations of families who have made vacations here part of their traditions.

Relaxation and comfort, complemented by attentive service, are high priorities at this resort. Each room boasts individuality with wonder-filled views and a wood-burning fireplace, which guests find more intimate than television. TV can be enjoyed in the public rooms when desired. Golf on two championship 18-hole courses, along with tennis, swimming, water activities on the Ranch's own 96-acre spring-fed lake, and superb horseback riding over many trails of this working cattle ranch may fill your days. Touring this beautiful area is yet another treat—scenic parks, horse ranches, and wineries. The town of Solvang is nearby, where two- thirds of the population is of Danish descent, a heritage visible in their shops, good food and windmills.

Business conference facilities are generous, with an array of audio-visual equipment and an accommodating staff.

Red hues highlight the Ranch Room Restaurant, artfully appointed with western antiques and colorful country quilts adjacent to the spacious picture windows. The fireplace crackles invitingly while you select a dinner entrée by Chef Pascal Gode from the menu which changes daily. One of tonight's choices may be Fresh Dungenness Crabcakes with Creole Sauce or Grilled Colorado Lamb Chops with Herbs de Provence and Balsamic Glaze. A featured dessert might be Tulip of Chocolate Mousse with White Chocolate Shavings. Enjoy after-dinner relaxation, conviviality, music and dancing in the Oak Room.

Address: 1054 Alisal Road, Solvang, CA 93463
Phone: 805-688-6411
Toll-Free: 800-425-4725
Fax: 805-688-2510
E-mail: info@alisal.com
Web site: http://www.alisal.com
Room Rates: $$$$
Suite Rates: $$$$
Credit Cards: Visa, MC, AmEx
No. of Rooms: 36 **Suites:** 37
Services and Amenities: Garage and parking, Library for adults, Baby-sitting service, Laundry service, Game area, Playground, Gift shop, Ballroom, Music, Summer wine tastings, Vacation packages, Fireplaces, Wet bar, Cable TV, Complimentary newspaper
Restrictions: 3 rooms with handicapped access, No pets allowed
Restaurant: Ranch Room open 7:30 a.m.–10:00 a.m. and 6:30 p.m.–9:00 p.m (breakfast and dinner included in room rate); Sycamore Room open summers (same dining hours as Ranch Room)
Bar: Oak Room, open evenings (live music nightly)
Business Facilities: Message center, Copiers, Audio-Visual, Fax
Conference Rooms: 5 rooms, capacity 150
Sports Facilities: Outdoor swimming pool/spa, Refurbished Billy Bell-design 18-hole golf course, 7 tennis courts, Fishing, Horseback riding, Boating
Location: Countryside, Solvang 3 mi., Santa Barbara 35 mi.
Attractions: Famed Danish village with shops & restaurants, Danish heritage, 21 wineries, Art galleries, Thoroughbred & Arabian horse ranches

SUTTER CREEK INN

The Sutter Creek Inn is located in the heart of California's Mother Lode, an area in the Sierra foothills steeped in Gold Rush history. Built in 1859, the Greek revival style house was the former residence of California Senator E. C. Voorhies. It was purchased in 1966 from a member of the original family, and was soon opened as the Sutter Creek Inn. Occasionally someone catches an impression of the old senator, who appears to keep a watchful eye on the inn.

Known as The Inn of the Hanging Beds, many of the rooms feature beds hung on chains from the ceilings. The beds, which are easily stabilized, sway slightly, making guests feel as if they are aboard an ocean liner or in a very gentle hammock. A full family style hot breakfast is served every morning around a large table in the old kitchen and is included in the price of the room, as are the afternoon refreshments of beverages and cookies.

The eighteen guest rooms, all with private bath, are uniquely decorated in soft colors. Many rooms have fireplaces, private patios or decks, and several boast secret gardens. Two rooms have a hot tub large enough for two. Tables and chairs, chaises, and hammocks are tucked into the spacious treed grounds.

The front room is a favorite gathering place for pre-breakfast coffee or an evening's card game. Guests may select books from the extensive and eclectic library or browse through the current magazines.

With advance reservations, guests may have an analysis of their handwriting or visit the massage room for a professional rubdown on a heated table.

Address: 75 Main Street, P.O. Box 385, Sutter Creek, CA 95685
Phone: 209-267-5606
Fax: 209-267-9287
E-mail: info@suttercreekinn.com
Web site: http://www.suttercreekinn.com
Room Rates: $
Credit Cards: Visa, MC
No. of Rooms: 18
Services and Amenities: Complimentary full hot breakfast and afternoon refreshments, Card/game area, Library, Cable TV, 10 rooms have fireplaces, Patios, Tubs for two, Massage available by advance reservations, Complimentary newspaper
Restrictions: No pets allowed
Concierge: Innkeeper assistance
Restaurant: Full country breakfast served in Sutter Creek Inn kitchen, 9:00 a.m., Walk to nearby restaurants for dinner
Conference Rooms: 3 rooms, capacity 35
Sports Facilities: Croquet, Swimming pool nearby, 3 golf courses nearby, Tennis courts nearby, 1 hour to skiing
Location: Downtown Sutter Creek, 1 mile Westover Airport, 35 miles Sacramento airport
Attractions: Unique shops and restaurants, Antique shows, Shops and auctions, Live theatre, Amador County Museum, Chawse Indian Grinding Rock State Historic Park, Gold country tours, Wineries, Daffodil Hill for 2 weeks starting March 15th—Fabulous!

PIERPONT INN

The classic Pierpont Inn is owned and operated by the fourth generation of the same family in ownership since 1928. A blend of the original craftsman cottages and the contemporary style of newer rooms, it comprises seven acres with lush gardens overlooking the Pacific Ocean. Spectacular views, award-winning cuisine and personal, friendly service to generations of families have made the Inn popular for romantic getaways and for social events and garden weddings.

The lobby has a feeling of warmth with its inviting fireplace, freshly cut flowers, and craftsman accents. Guests have a choice of 84 rooms, suites and cottages, all unique quarters offering views of the ocean and Channel Island, mountains, or colorful gardens.

The Pierpont Dining Room, with chef Louis Ludwig presiding, serves breakfast, lunch, and dinner in a relaxed atmosphere with ocean views from every table. Abalone is always on the dinner menu, as is the traditional bouillabaisse. The Garden Room bar, features live piano music and serves hors d'oeuvres from 4:30 to 7:00 p.m. every Thursday. Special picnic baskets can be ordered from the kitchen for guests planning an outing at the beach, fishing or hiking.

Banquet areas accommodate from 10 to 125, and the experienced staff is available to help with the detailed planning of special guest functions.

The Ventura area is a sportsman's paradise famous for sunshine and cool breezes. The Pierpont Racquet Club on the premises of the Inn offers tennis, and a golf game can be arranged for you at one of the numerous nearby courses. The Inn is located across from Ventura State Beach a half mile from Ventura Pier. Fishing, hiking, sailing and shopping on historic Main street are just minutes away.

Address: 550 Sanjon Road, Ventura, CA 93001
Phone: 805-643-6144
Toll-Free: 800-285-4667
Fax: 805-641-1501
E-mail: info@pierpontinn.com
Web site: http://www.pierpontinn.com
Room Rates: $$
Suite Rates: $$
Credit Cards: Most credit cards accepted
No. of Rooms: 70 **Suites:** 12
Services and Amenities: Romantic Escape Package available, Valet, Garage & parking, Game room, Cable TV, VCR, Telephones, Radio, Individual heat control, Some rooms have fireplaces & balconies, Complimentary newspaper & toiletries
Restrictions: $50 for pets, Children under 18 free in same room with parents
Concierge: Staff available
Room Service: 7:00 a.m.–9:00 p.m.
Restaurant: Pierpont Dining Room, 7:00 a.m.–9:00 p.m.
Bar: 10:00 a.m.–closing
Business Facilities: Copier, Audio-Visual, Fax, Modems
Conference Rooms: 4 rooms, capacity 20-60
Sports Facilities: Golf nearby, Pierpont Racquet Club on location with tennis, Indoor & outdoor pools, Handball/squash, Whirlpool, Sauna, Massage
Location: 1½ miles from downtown Ventura, 7 miles from Oxnard Airport
Attractions: Walk to Pier, Beaches, Restaurants, Downtown antique shopping, Ventura State Beach, 2 miles from Ventura Harbor, Chamber Music Festival

CAL-A-VIE

An oasis in a secluded valley 40 miles north of San Diego, Cal-a-Vie has one purpose: to revitalize the body, mind and spirit. Here 24 guests relax for a week of individually tailored fitness, nutrition and beauty therapy in rustic elegance amid beautiful natural surroundings.

Each of the 24 guest cottages has been individually decorated to recall the serene luxury of a European country villa: terra cotta roofs, wide wooden plank doors, private terraces with breathtaking views and window boxes full of flowers, and inside, hand-carved furniture covered in floral chintz.

Cal-a-Vie's fitness program, which begins with a personal fitness assessment, is a seven-day regime individually designed to achieve personal goals in stress reduction, relaxation, weight control and toning, and to fit into each guest's lifestyle to produce lasting results. Exercise includes hiking on trails on the inn's 150 acres, aerobic conditioning, body contouring classes, water sports, tennis and personalized workouts on state-of-the-art equipment. Golf is available at an adjacent country club.

Guests are served gourmet cuisine highlighted by herbs and vegetables from Cal-a-Vie's gardens and carefully prepared to make staying slim an enjoyable eating experience. A weekly cooking class in Cal-a-Vie's kitchen is a fun way for guests to learn the techniques used here. The *Cal-a-Vie Gourmet Spa Cookery* cookbook is available through Cal-a-Vie's boutique.

Cal-a-Vie's beauty therapy program for men and women employs European techniques of thalassotherapy, hydrotherapy and aromatherapy to help restore inner balance and serenity. Massage, meditation, tai chi and yoga leave guests feeling relaxed, content and deliciously pampered.

Address: 2249 Somerset Road, Vista, CA 92084
Phone: 760-945-2055
Fax: 760-630-0074
E-mail: calavie@adnc.com
Web site: http://www.cal-a-vie.com
Room Rates: $$$$
Credit Cards: Visa, MC, AmEx
No. of Rooms: 24
Services and Amenities: TV lounge, Boutique, Balconies, Telephones, Radios, Robes, Individual heat and air-conditioning control, Complimentary shampoo, conditioner, body lotion and suntan lotion, All meals included, Complimentary transportation to and from San Diego Airport
Restrictions: Minimum age: 18 years, One room handicapped-equipped, No pets allowed
Business Facilities: Message center, Copiers, Fax
Sports Facilities: Outdoor pool, Whirlpool, Sauna, Massage, Aerobics, Weight training, One har-true tennis court, Privileges at Country Club for golf
Location: Semi-rural Vista/Bonsall area, 40 miles from San Diego
Attractions: Coastal beaches, San Diego Zoo, Wild Animal Park, Seaworld, Botanical Gardens, Palomar Mountain and Observatory, Del Mar Fairgrounds and Racetrack

PARK SUNSET HOTEL

Located on the legendary Sunset Strip in the heart of West Hollywood, the Park Sunset Hotel is surrounded by shops, restaurants and nightspots, and is a departure point to a variety of tours and attractions. Adjacent to Beverly Hills with its world class restaurants and exciting Rodeo Drive shops, it is also minutes away from fashionable Melrose Avenue, Century City, Bel-Air, Santa Monica, Marina del Rey and downtown Los Angeles. The hotel prides itself in its first class service provided by an experienced, multilingual staff.

The recently refurbished lobby and guest rooms are beautifully furnished with the Georgian Collection, creating a cozy and intimate atmosphere with classic elegance and good taste. Many of the rooms have views of downtown Los Angeles, and fully equipped kitchens are available in some of the suites. For the fitness minded, or just for relaxation, an outdoor heated swimming pool and sundeck are also provided.

Park Sunset Hotel has an intimate restaurant serving breakfast, lunch and dinner. Guests can walk to many nearby restaurants such as Spago's, the House of Blues, Sky Bar, and Le Dome, as well as numerous sidewalk cafes, cocktail lounges and nightspots.

An ideal location for business meetings, the Park Sunset is fully equipped for the business traveler, yet affordable for the family.

Address: 8462 Sunset Boulevard, West Hollywood, CA 90069
Phone: 213-654-6470
Toll-Free: 800-821-3660
Fax: 213-654-5918
Room Rates: $
Credit Cards: Most credit cards accepted
No. of Rooms: 84
Services and Amenities: Valet service, Garage and parking, Car hire, Laundry service, Baby-sitting service, Barber/beauty shop, Cable TV, VCR, Radio, In-room voice mail, Complimentary toiletries, Children under 12 are free
Restrictions: No pets allowed, All rooms are handicapped-equipped
Concierge: 7:00 a.m.–11:00 p.m.
Room Service: 7:00 a.m.–11:00 p.m.
Restaurant: Park Sunset Restaurant, 7:00 a.m.–11:00 p.m.
Bar: House of Blues and Sky Bar
Business Facilities: Voice mail, Message center, Copiers, Audio-Visual, Telex, Translators
Conference Rooms: 1 room, capacity 50
Sports Facilities: Skin spa, Outdoor heated swimming pool, Sundeck
Location: Sunset Strip in West Hollywood, 12 miles to LAX
Attractions: Sidewalk cafes, Walking distance to boutique shopping, Universal Studios 10 minutes away, Convenient to all Los Angeles attractions and tours

THE MONDRIAN

Reopened in 1996 under the ownership of Ian Schrager Hotels, the Mondrian has undergone a multi-million-dollar renovation designed by Philippe Starck and personally directed by Ian Shrager. As befits a hostelry in the entertainment capital of the world, the new Mondrian strikes a balance between cutting edge style and simplicity, between illusion and reality.

The new indoor-outdoor lobby is a totally original space composed of distinct areas without formal and restrictive boundaries, creating the feeling of being outdoors at all times and inviting guests to participate in the concept of "Hotel as Theater."

The spacious rooms and suites—all with kitchens, wet bars and floor to ceiling windows—are done in neutral tones with splashes of primary colors in the style of Dutch painter Piet Mondrian. The effect is stylish, witty—and surprisingly comfortable. Guests are welcomed with a basket of fresh fruit, and twice-daily maid service includes evening turndown. Business needs are served by the state-of-the-art technology available in each room: three telephones with teleconference capability; fax machines, portable computers and modem hookups available as needed.

This self-contained "urban resort" also offers a landscaped garden with panoramic views of the city and mountains; a yoga and wellness studio for the integration of body, mind and spirit; a 24-hour state-of-the-art gymnasium and fitness center; a pool designed for meditation and relaxation; and six indoor/outdoor beverage and food areas. There is a hair-styling and skin care salon and an international gift shop.

The Mondrian's full-service hotel facilities are located in the heart of Los Angeles' entertainment and design community.

Address: 8440 Sunset Boulevard, West Hollywood, CA 90069
Phone: 213-650-8999
Toll-Free: 800-525-8029
Fax: 213-654-5215
Room Rates: $$
Suite Rates: $$$$
Credit Cards: Most credit cards accepted
No. of Rooms: 237 **Suites:** 184
Services and Amenities: Gift shop, Valet, Barber/Beauty shop, Garage, Parking, Car hire, Laundry, House Doctor, Baby-sitting, Cable TV, Complimentary newspaper, Robes, Custom-milled soaps & personal care products, Portable phones, Lap tops on request, Kitchen
Restrictions: No handicapped access, No pets allowed
Concierge: 24 hours
Restaurant: Coco Pazzo 7:00 a.m.–11:30 p.m., Lobby Table
Bar: Skybar 11 a.m.–2 a.m.
Business Facilities: Message center, Secretarial service, Copiers, Audio-Visual
Conference Rooms: Grand Salon capacity 100; 3 Boardrooms capacity 30
Sports Facilities: Billiards area, Heated swimming pool & Water salon with underwater surround sound, 24-hour fitness center, Steam rooms, Saunas
Location: West Hollywood
Attractions: Convenient to Beverly Hill, Hollywood, Burbank, downtown Los Angeles business district; Walking distance to night life, restaurants, shopping and theater

SARDY HOUSE

Even when they are crowded in a row as though clinging to each other to keep from falling down, Victorian houses seem to be surrounded by a romantic atmosphere. None more so than Sardy House. Seeing it conjures up visions of an opulent interior; of tables set with snowy white linen and gleaming silver and crystal; soft candle light; lace curtains and fresh flowers, velvet or damask clothing windows. All these visions are reality at Sardy House. Ceilings are high and windows are tall and rather narrow (in Victorian times the outdoors was kept out). Arched top windows are of stained glass. Built in 1892, Sardy House is now 102 years old and has attained the status of a historic landmark.

The color scheme throughout the guest room and suites is mauve and gray. Beds and armoires are of cherrywood. Chairs are wicker, walls are covered with custom wallpaper and brass sconces are used as accents. There are also ceiling fans, while rose-patterned Axminster carpeting covers the floors that are as sturdy as the day Sardy House was built. Laura Ashley fabrics cover the duvets and all beds have feather comforters.

A complimentary full breakfast is served daily. Guests may choose from Eggs Benedict, Omlette du jour or Sardy House's famous blueberry pancakes. Jack's Restaurant offers a gourmet dining experience. House specialties include Roast Rack of Colorado Lamb, Caribou Tenderloin and Crispy Sea Bass. A favorite salad consists of fresh garden greens, garden herbs and raspberry vinaigrette. Soft classical music is piped into the dining room during the dinner hour.

Mobile 4 Star Award, "Outstanding…worth a special trip."

Address: 128 East Main Street, Aspen, CO 81611
Phone: 970-920-2525
Toll-Free: 800-321-3457
Fax: 970-920-4478
E-mail: hotltsard@rof.net
Room Rates: $
Suite Rates: $$$
Credit Cards: AmEx, DC, MC, Visa
No. of Rooms: 14 **Suites:** 6
Services and Amenities: Valet service, Parking, Car hire, Baby-sitting service, Cable TV, VCR in suites, Robes, Whirlpool bath, Complimentary toiletries & newspaper, Complimentary breakfast, Children welcome
Restrictions: No pets allowed
Concierge: 7:00 a.m.–9:00 p.m.
Room Service: 7:30 a.m.–9:30 p.m.
Restaurant: Sardy House, 7:30 a.m.–10:30 a.m., 6:00 p.m.–Midnight
Bar: Jack's Bar, 6:00 p.m.–Midnight
Business Facilities: Message center, Copiers, Audio-Visual, Fax service
Conference Rooms: 1 room, capacity 17
Sports Facilities: Outdoor swimming pool, Whirlpool, Sauna, Skiing six blocks away, Ballooning, Biking
Location: Downtown
Attractions: Walk to Music Festival, Free ski shuttles, Shops, Restaurants, West End, Rio Grande Trail

CASTLE MARNE - A LUXURY URBAN INN

Come fall under the spell of one of Denver's grandest historic mansions. Built in 1889, Castle Marne is considered by many to be the finest example of "America's most eclectic architect," William Lang (designer of Unsinkable Molly Brown's house). Its history glows through the handrubbed woods, the renowned circular stained glass "Peacock Window," and original ornate fireplaces.

Your stay at Castle Marne combines Old World elegance and Victorian charm with modern-day convenience and comfort. Each guest room is a unique experience in pampered luxury. Carefully chosen furnishings bring together authentic period antiques, family heirlooms, and exacting reproductions to create the mood of long-ago charm and romance. The parlor invites you to spend some quiet time nestled with a good book. A romantic interlude, whether a weekend getaway or honeymoon, will be truly unforgettable when spent in one of the luxury suites replete with jetted whirlpool tub.

In the heart of one of Denver's most historic neighborhoods, the inn is just minutes from many fine restaurants, plus the city's finest cultural, shopping and sightseeing attractions.

Awake to the spicy aroma of brewing Marne-blend coffee, and homemade breads and muffins. Linger over a complete gourmet breakfast in the original cherry-paneled Formal Dining Room.

Join other guests at check-in time for Afternoon Tea, served in the Parlor, with freshly baked scones, shortbread, lemon curd, raspberry butter, and a plentitude of sweets and savory treats. Browse in the library, enjoy the game room, work on the jigsaw puzzle or savor the beauty of a Colorado sunset. Relax your mind and spirit, soak up history—or just soak in a hot tub.

Address: 1572 Race Street, Denver, CO 80206
Phone: 303-331-0621
Toll-Free: 800-92-Marne
Fax: 303-331-0623
E-mail: themarne@ix.netcom.com
Web site: http://www.bedandbreakfastinns.org/castle
Room Rates: $
Suite Rates: $$$
Credit Cards: Visa, MC, Discover, AmEx
No. of Rooms: 9 **Suites:** 2
Services and Amenities: Gift shop, Card/game area, Garden, In-room telephones, Radios, Heat control, Some rooms feature air-conditioning, jacuzzis for two, private balconies and private hot tubs for two, Complimentary toiletries and newspaper
Restrictions: No pets allowed, Children over 10 welcome
Concierge: Daily
Restaurant: Formal Dining Room, daily gourmet breakfast; Parlor, complimentary afternoon tea, scones, shortbread, lemon curd, raspberry butter and more; Walking distance to excellent dining
Business Facilities: Fully-equipped guest office with computer, phone and fax, Message center, Copiers, Audio-Visual
Conference Rooms: 1 room, capacity 8
Sports Facilities: Nearby City Park with running paths, tennis courts and public golf course
Location: Downtown Wyman Historic District, 30 minutes to Denver International Airport
Attractions: Denver Zoo, Museum of Natural History, IMAX Theatre, Gates Planetarium, Denver Botanic Gardens, Historic Molly Brown House, Denver Art Museum, U.S. Mint, Colorado History Museum, Cherry Creek Shopping Center, Downtown Denver's 16th Street Mall

THE STRATER HOTEL

Authentic Victorian elegance with a hint of the Wild West characterizes this four-story red brick beauty as it has since this southwestern Colorado landmark first opened its doors over a century ago in 1887. Conveniently located in the heart of downtown Durango, the Strater Hotel has plenty to offer both inside and out. Impressive craftsmanship is a signature of the Strater, which displays a facade of elaborately carved sandstone sills and cornices. Housing the world's largest collection of American Victorian walnut antiques, the Strater faithfully reflects this bygone era of history in comfortable detail.

Walking into the lobby is like taking a trip to yesteryear. One is greeted with an array of antiques including marble-topped tables, ornate mahogany and cherry woodwork, stained and leaded glass, and brass and crystal chandeliers. The guest rooms are all as unique as they are plush, down to every last detail. Custom-made rich velvet draperies, hand-stenciled wallpapers, and ornate bed art compliment the other unique pieces of the period in any given room. Constant renovations make this hotel a class act. Fine dining in-house can be enjoyed in Henry's Restaurant. Meeting and Banquet facilities can cater up to 150. But the true meeting place among guests and locals alike is the Diamond Belle Saloon, which features live honky-tonk piano nightly and saloon girls in traditional costume—traditional, that is, for Old West saloon girls. Guests can also enjoy turn-of-the-century melodrama and vaudeville in the Diamond Circle Theatre during the summer months.

Durango is located in the four-corners region (in the heart of Anasazi-land) and ringed by mountains, offering a nice variety of outdoor activities. The Strater Hotel is centrally located in downtown Durango and surrounded by galleries, factory outlet shops, night spots, and only two blocks from the famous Durango-Silverton Narrow Gauge Train Station, which can take you on an unforgettable day-long excursion into the heart of the rugged San Juan Mountains. Fabulous skiing is available at Purgatory Ski Area just 25 minutes away, and Mesa Verde National Park is less than an hour away. Or try your luck at the Sky Ute Casino, only 20 minutes away. Durango is served by air service from Denver, Phoenix, Albuquerque and Dallas.

Address: 699 Main Avenue, P.O. Drawer E, Durango, CO 81302
Phone: 970-247-4431
Toll-Free: 800-247-4431
Fax: 970-259-2208
E-mail: strater@frontier.net
Room Rates: $
Credit Cards: Visa, MC, DC, CB, AmEx
No. of Rooms: 93
Services and Amenities: Full American breakfast included, Valet service, Free parking, Jacuzzi, Cable TV, Diamond Circle Theatre, Meeting facilities
Restrictions: No pets allowed, Limited handicapped access
Concierge: 8:00 a.m.–8:00 p.m.
Room Service: 7:00 a.m.–9:00 p.m.
Restaurant: Henry's, 7:00 a.m.–11:00 a.m., 5:30 p.m.–9:00 p.m.
Bar: Diamond Belle Saloon, 5:00 p.m.–closing, Pelican's Nest featuring live jazz
Business Facilities: Secretarial service, Copiers, Audio-Visual, Teleconferencing, Pagers, Fax, Meeting rooms
Conference Rooms: 5 rooms, capacity 150
Sports Facilities: Three major golf courses, Skiing, Horseback riding, Rafting, Hiking, Fishing, Ballooning, Kayaking, Mountain biking
Location: Historic downtown Durango, Four Corners area—in the heart of Anasazi land
Attractions: Galleries, Factory outlet shopping, Night spots within walking distance, Sky Ute Casino, Durango/Silverton narrow-gauge train, Mesa Verde National Park, Million Dollar Highway, Purgatory ski area

THE WIT'S END GUEST RANCH & RESORT

The indescribably beautiful Wit's End Guest Ranch and Resort, located in the Vallecito Valley in southwestern Colorado near Durango, has a unique and colorful history dating back to 1859. The ranch's centerpiece is a magnificent 129-year-old three-story fully restored barn that has been turned into a wonderful dining, dancing and social center. Split logs, heavy beams, a massive river stone fireplace and cut glass mirrors from the 1836 Crystal Palace in London define the interior.

Surrounding the lodge and in select locations on the Vallecito River or the Lake are a variety of unique guest cabins ranging from 1–4 bedrooms. All boast knotty pine paneling, stone fireplaces, queen sized beds, fully equipped kitchens and superb Country French and willow porch furnishings and handmade log swings.

Horses owned by the Ranch are offered for a variety of horseback riding, instruction, and trail rides over many wide areas of the adjacent 575,000-acre Weminuche wilderness area, where no motor vehicles or modern day equipment are permitted. Customized pack trips are also organized by the Ranch for guests interested in fishing, photography, gold panning, backpacking and mountain climbing, drop camps, and luxury pack trips.

The kids go off with individual group counselors and have their day filled with planned activities. The kids also have their own recreation building made out of the Old Saloon and fixed up for them with games to play. Full children's program is optional.

After breakfast together in the lodge or on the deck, guests have the option to participate in the various planned activities, play tennis, go for a swim, or to just relax and enjoy the marvelous scenery from a cabin deck. Lunch is served in the lodge to those who stay on the premises. The daily activities end between 4 & 5 p.m., at which time families are re-united and guests return from the dusty trail. Evening dining takes place in the Old Lodge at the Lake Restaurant, D'Creek Cafe is the children's dining area. Fine dining selections please even the most discriminating guests, and a "kids" menu is offered. Ranch cookouts, hayrides, and outside dining around the fire round off a great Ranch week.

Address: 254 CR 500, Durango, CO 81122
Phone: 970-884-4113
Toll-Free: 800-BE MY GUEST
Fax: 970-884-3261
E-mail: weranch@aol.com
Suite Rates: $$$
Credit Cards: Most credit cards accepted
No. of Suites: 39
Services and Amenities: AP-meals included in rates in high seasons, Gift shop, Library, Game area, Laundry service, Robes, In-room TV/VCR, Telephones, Kitchen facilities, Fireplaces, Decks, Complimentary toiletries, Full children's program, Cabins & houses with 1-4 bedrooms each
Restrictions: No pets allowed
Concierge: 8 a.m.–6 or 11 p.m.
Room Service: 7:00 a.m.–10:00 p.m.
Restaurant: Old Lodge at the Lake
Bar: Colorado Tavern, lunch—1:00 a.m.
Business Facilities: Message center, Copiers, Audio-Visual, Fax
Conference Rooms: 3 rooms, capacity 200
Sports Facilities: All included: Heated outdoor pool, Hot tubs, Massage, Croquet, Volleyball, Boating, Fishing, Hayrides, Horseback riding
Location: Vallecito Valley, 23 miles from Durango, 30 miles to La Plata Airport
Attractions: Great shops in Durango, Silverton Train, 1 hour to Mesa Verde, Golf, White Water Rafting, Skiing, and more!

VAILGLO LODGE

The Vailglo Lodge was opened in 1973 by Craig Holzfaster. The lodge is run like a private hotel. The hotel is locked every night when the front desk closes, and every guest is given a key to the front door. It is very much like a Swiss inn with exquisite appointments.

White ash panelling and custom made white ash furniture dominate the decor of this contemporary style resort. The lobby has accents of pink Brazilian Juparana granite on the tabletops and fireplace. Complimentary coffee, tea, and Danish cookies are served all day by the fire, welcoming those who have just arrived or just returned from the slopes.

The hotel is adjacent to the slopes, and is also within walking distance of Vail's gourmet restaurants and famous shopping.

In order to preserve its treasured quietude, Vailglo Lodge does not accept groups. The atmosphere is cozy, intimate, relaxed, and very quiet. The hotel caters to a very select clientele which makes it all the more attractive for the individual or couple seeking a peaceful retreat. The Vailglo is, without question, one of the most unique lodging properties in Vail.

Address: 701 West Lionshead Circle, Vail, CO 81657
Phone: 970-476-5506
Toll-Free: 800-541-8245
Fax: 970-476-3926
Room Rates: $$
Credit Cards: AmEx, Visa, MC, DS
No. of Rooms: 34
Services and Amenities: Valet, Parking, Laundry service, Cable TV, Radio, Individual heat control, In-room safes, Hair dryers, Complimentary toiletries and newspaper
Restrictions: No pets allowed, Children under 6 free with parents
Sports Facilities: Outdoor swimming pool, Whirlpool, Skiing
Location: Downtown, Nearest airport is Denver International
Attractions: Ski-slopes adjacent to hotel, Famous restaurants and shopping within walking distance

INN AT CHESTER

The Inn at Chester is the perfect getaway to escape the ordinary. Serenity abounds in this country inn located on 12 luscious acres in the Connecticut River Valley. An 18th century farmhouse was the inspiration for this 42-room full-service country inn. Each room is individually appointed with Eldred Wheeler reproduction antiques and twentieth century amenities including air conditioning, televisions, and telephones.

There is much to do while staying at the Inn. Downstairs in the Billiard Room you can play billiards, backgammon, or cards, or you can enjoy reading from the library while sitting in front of the fire. For the fitness conscious, revitalize yourself in the exercise room with weights, stationary bikes, a treadmill, and a Nordic ski machine. Get a massage, or melt in the sauna. Partake in tennis, hiking, bocci, croquet, and cycling or just relax in the hammock by the pond. In the winter cross country ski, ice skate, or ski at nearby Powder Ridge.

Dine elegantly, but comfortably in the Post and Beam dining room which serves award winning New American cuisine presented by chef Lorelei Reu-Helfer. A few popular menu choices are the spicy Thai Shrimp served with a pepper and pineapple salsa, the Rack of Lamb roasted with seasonal vegetables enhanced with a provencal sauce, and the Cafe Chocolate, a "crashed" chocolate souffle inside a chocolate lattice served with espresso sauce. Breads and pastries are baked fresh daily on the premises.

Enjoy lively conversation, or listen to live music while imbibing your favorite cocktail at Dunk's Landing, the informal and relaxing tavern, which serves a lighter, but equally delicious menu of dinners and daily specials.

Providing the perfect getaway for any meeting or conference, the unique meeting rooms accommodate from 2 to 35 guests. The Inn at Chester offers professional service and attention to every detail to make your event pleasurable and productive.

Address: 318 West Main Street, Chester, CT 06412
Phone: 860-526-9541
Toll-Free: 800-949-STAY
Fax: 860-526-4387
E-mail: innkeeper@innatchester.com
Web site: http://www.innatchester.com
Room Rates: $$
Suite Rates: $$$
Credit Cards: Visa, MC, AmEx, Diners
No. of Rooms: 42 **Suites:** 2
Services and Amenities: Dinner/Overnight package rates, Art gallery, Library, TV lounge, Baby-sitting service, Laundry service, Billiards/Game room, Vending machines, Massage (by prior arrangement)
Restrictions: Pets allowed, 2 rooms handicapped-equipped
Restaurant: Post & Beam, Lunch & Dinner, 11:30 a.m.–9:00 p.m., Sunday Brunch, 11:30 a.m.–2:30 p.m.
Bar: Dunk's Landing, 11:30 a.m.–midnight
Business Facilities: Message center, Secretarial center, Copiers, Audio-Visual
Conference Rooms: 3 rooms, capacity 45
Sports Facilities: Sauna, Massage, Croquet, Bocci, Billiards, Darts, Biking, Sledding, Skating, 25 minutes to ski lift & golf, 15 minutes to sailing
Location: Connecticut River Valley, Just off Rte. 9, Exit 6, 30 mins. to New Haven
Attractions: Goodspeed Opera House, Gillette's Castle, Essex Steam Train, Antiques and art galleries nearby, Essex Village

THE GRISWOLD INN

New England has no country inn more traditional than The Griswold, known as "The Gris." Its main building, the first three-story frame structure in Connecticut, has been in continuous operation as a hostelry since its construction in 1776. The inn has been under the direction of only six families.

Guestrooms have colonial decor and many of the wooden floors slant with the settling of time. There are no televisions or radios, only piped classical music. Each accommodation does, however, offer such modern amenities as private baths, telephones, and climate control.

A complimentary continental breakfast is served daily in the Steamboat Room. There are four other dining rooms. The Covered Bridge is an abandoned bridge moved from New Hampshire and now famous for its important collection of Currier and Ives steamboat prints. The Gun Room houses a library of firearms dating back to the 15th century. The Library is a book lined dining room with a crackling fireplace. Hearty New England fare, including marvelous fresh seafood, is served in these rooms. The Sunday Hunt Breakfast is a tradition started by the British when they occupied the inn in the War of 1812.

Today's yachtsmen on Long Island Sound often drop in at the Tap Room, built in 1738 as a schoolhouse, and later moved to its present location by a team of oxen. Visitors sit around the Tap Room's pot-bellied stove and enjoy nightly musical entertainment such as piano, banjo, sea chanteys, dixieland or jazz.

Three 18th-century houses are also part of The Griswold Inn. The John Hayden House is ideal for small business groups, family gatherings, and special reunions.

Address: 36 Main Street, Essex, CT 06426
Phone: 860-767-1776
Fax: 860-767-0481
E-mail: griswoldinn@snet.com
Room Rates: $$
Suite Rates: $$
Credit Cards: Visa, MC, AmEx
No. of Rooms: 30 **Suites:** 14
Services and Amenities: TV lounge, Library, Gift shop, Climate control, Complimentary toiletries
Restaurant: Griswold Inn Dining Room, Luncheon Monday-Saturday, approximately 11:30 a.m.–3:00 p.m., Dinner Monday-Sunday, approximately 5:30–10:00 p.m., Sunday Hunt Breakfast, 11:00 a.m.–2:30 p.m.
Bar: Tap Room, 11:00 a.m.–1:00 a.m.
Business Facilities: Audio-Visual equipment, Message center, Copiers, Teleconferencing
Conference Rooms: 2 rooms, capacity 12-75
Sports Facilities: Hiking, Nature preserves
Location: Rural, Nearest airport is Bradly International at Hartford
Attractions: Historic attractions, Museums, Art galleries, Antique shops, Goodspeed Opera House, Ivoryton Playhouse, Essex Steam Train, Riverboat cruises, Premium factory outlet stores, ½ hour from Connecticut College, Coast Guard Academy, Mystic Seaport, Yale

THE HOMESTEAD INN

The Belle Haven neighborhood in Greenwich is famous for being an elite residential area. One of its great attractions is The Homestead Inn, set among three acres of oaks and maples.

The Homestead Inn was built in 1799 by Augustus Mead; in 1859 it was sold and converted into an inn. Architecturally, it was transformed from a colonial farmstead into a Victorian "Italianate Gothic" house, complete with a distinctive belvedere and wraparound porches. In 1978, the Homestead was restored and transformed into an elegant hostelry. Guestrooms are found in both the original home, as well as in converted satellite buildings. Rooms in the former have a more genuine feel, while the newer rooms tend to be more spacious, with modern baths, and better soundproofing.

Theresa Carroll and Master Chef Thomas Henkelmann purchased the inn in September of 1997, and have powdered her nose and received rave reviews from the New York Times among others. The Homestead is also well known for its French restaurant, "Thomas Henkelmann," which has garnered consistent praise from local and national media. Breakfast can be ordered from an impressive array of menu choices.

Many companies find that enjoying the past while planning for the future is accomplished by hosting executive meetings and retreats at the Homestead Inn and restaurant "Thomas Hankelmann."

Address: 420 Field Point Road, Greenwich, CT 06830
Phone: 203-869-7500
Fax: 203-869-7502
Room Rates: $$$
Suite Rates: $$$$
Credit Cards: Most credit cards accepted
No. of Rooms: 23 **Suites:** 6
Services and Amenities: Valet service, Laundry service, Telephone with modem outlets, call waiting and voice mail, Radio, TV, Desk, Air-conditioning, Multiple languages spoken: English, German, French, Spanish, Arabic and Portuguese
Restaurant: La Grange, 7:30–9:30 a.m., 12:00 noon–2:30 p.m. Monday–Friday, 8:00–10:30 a.m. Weekends, Evenings, 3 working fireplaces in the restaurant
Bar: The Chocolate Bar
Business Facilities: Exclusive meeting facility
Conference Rooms: 2 rooms, capacity 24
Sports Facilities: Three acres with garden, Walking, Biking, Large park, Tennis and golf nearby
Location: Greenwich, Nearest airport: Westchester, LAG/JFK
Attractions: Antique and boutique shopping in Greenwich, Local Museums, 40 minutes to New York City and Yale University

INN AT NATIONAL HALL

1998 AAA Five Diamond Award and member of Relais and Chateaux. An historic, Riverside, luxury hotel, The Inn at National Hall invites you to journey into the rich heritage of yesteryear. Decor at the Inn is a delightful mix of whimsy and history. The unique restoration of this circa 1873 Italianate structure includes the skilled hand-stenciling of gifted artisans from throughout the area. Each public room, hallway, and chamber itself is a unique work of art, stenciled thematically from the wonders of nature and fantasies of fairy tale. Handcrafted arched ceilings and cherry panel moldings add to the warmth and intimacy of the Inn's fine interior.

Each guestroom is individually designed, furnished with antiques, original art, lavish fabrics, and king or queen canopy beds. Some have 25' coffered ceilings, crystal chandeliers, tromp l'oeil decorated walls, and hand stenciling. Baths have limestone counters, marble shower, oversize bathtub, illuminated magnifying wall mirror, electric towel warmer and a fresh red rose. All rooms feature cable television, VCR, direct dial telephones, and refrigeration. An in-room fax machine is accessible at any time.

The Restaurant at National Hall features American regional and continental cuisine prepared with the freshest ingredients and beautifully presented.

The Inn is located in the heart of the National Hall Historic District on the Saugatuck River shoreline in Westport. Referred to by some as "Beverly Hills East," Westport offers visitors an abundance of stimulating cultural and recreational activities. Excellent shops, antique stores, restaurants, galleries and the Westport Playhouse provide charm to this creative community by the sea.

Address: 2 Post Road West, Westport, CT 06880
Phone: 203-221-1351
Toll-Free: 800-NAT-HALL
Fax: 203-221-0276
Room Rates: $$$$
Suite Rates: $$$$
Credit Cards: Visa, MC, AmEx, DC
No. of Rooms: 15 **Suites:** 7
Services and Amenities: Ample parking, Car hire, Laundry service, Turndown service, Card/game area with Snooker table, Individual climate control, Cable TV, VCR, Telephones, Radio, Robes, Complimentary morning coffee/tea & newspaper, Complimentary Crabtree & Evelyn toiletries
Restrictions: No pets allowed, No smoking
Concierge: 9:00 a.m.–9:00 p.m.
Room Service: 24 hours
Restaurant: The Restaurant at National Hall, Lunch, Dinner and Sunday Brunch
Bar: Service bar
Business Facilities: Built-in screen, Overhead & 35mm slide projector, VCR & monitor, Teleconferencing, Fax, Copier
Conference Rooms: 1 boardroom, capacity 16
Sports Facilities: Complimentary use of YMCA 2 blocks away
Location: Downtown Westport, 1 hour drive from New York's LaGuardia airport
Attractions: Within walking distance to Shops, Restaurants, Galleries and The Westport Playhouse, Numerous antique shops, Beach nearby

BOARDWALK PLAZA HOTEL

Not your typical beach resort, the family owned and operated Boardwalk Plaza Hotel in Rehoboth Beach, Delaware combines the privacy and all the amenities of a luxury hotel with the charm and personal service of a Victorian-style bed and breakfast. The postcard-pretty exterior—pink paint, white fretwork and picket balconies -gives way to an interior carefully planned to transport guests back to the grand Victorian era. Select from a variety of graciously appointed accommodations, from standard rooms to oceanfront deluxe rooms, all tastefully decorated with a blend of antiques and reproductions. All accommodations are designed to offer ambiance as well as comfort. Oceanfront deluxe rooms artfully team poster beds with whirlpool baths, while oceanfront suites feature separate bedroom, bath, and sitting areas with private oceanfront balconies.

For your dining pleasure, experience the service of a time gone by in the three-level, oceanfront Victoria's restaurant—where the only thing they overlook is the ocean. Grand Victorian decor and a gourmet menu of regional cuisine make any meal at Victoria's a special occasion. Dine on creations by chef Robert Webster, including blackened shrimp and scallops on a red pepper coulis, garlic-encrusted, roast rack of lamb with tri-color sauces, and broiled lump crab cakes—then finish with a home-made dessert. Complement your meal with a selection from the thoughtful list of imported and domestic wines.

At the Boardwalk Plaza, luxury is a priority, with complimentary parking, bellhop service, room service, and checkout day changing rooms. Relax and unwind in the heated indoor-outdoor spa pool, or stroll along the boardwalk and visit nearby shops where you'll find unique gifts and souvenirs.

The Boardwalk Plaza is truly a hotel for all seasons!

Address: 2 Olive Avenue at the Boardwalk, Rehoboth Beach, DE 19971
Phone: 302-227-7169
Toll-Free: 800-33-BEACH
Fax: 302-227-0561
E-mail: bph@boardwalkplaza.com
Room Rates: $
Suite Rates: $
Credit Cards: Visa, MC, AmEx, Disc., Diners
No. of Rooms: 84 **Suites:** 45
Services and Amenities: Garage/parking, 6 rooms with kitchens, 60 rooms with private balconies, Some whirlpool baths available, Cable TV, VCR available, Telephone, Radio, Heat/air-conditioning control, In-room coffee/refreshments, Complimentary toiletries/newspaper, Ocean views
Restrictions: No pets allowed, Children 6 & under free, May-Oct. 2-3 minimum night stay if Saturday inclusive
Room Service: 7:00 a.m.–10:00 p.m.
Restaurant: Victoria's Restaurant, 7:00 a.m.–10:00 p.m., Catered banquets for up to 100 persons by prior arrangement
Business Facilities: Copiers, Audio-Visual, Teleconferencing, Fax, Modems
Conference Rooms: 1 room, capacity 100, catering available
Sports Facilities: Tennis, Golf, Sailing, Water sports nearby (within 5-10 minutes), Indoor/outdoor spa pool, Exercise room on premises
Location: Near downtown, 3 blocks north of Rehoboth Avenue
Attractions: Beach and boardwalk, Amusements, Wonderful antique shops, 5 minutes from Factory Outlet center Rated four diamonds by AAA

The Bed and Breakfast Inn at La Jolla, La Jolla, California. PAGE 23

Westwood Marquis Hotel and Gardens, Los Angeles, California. PAGE 28

BRANDYWINE SUITES HOTEL

European style and charm are the keynotes of Wilmington's Brandywine Suites Hotel. The historic brick twin atrium hotel with fireside lobby was built in the 1880s and restored as a hotel in 1985. It is close to the Market Street Mall with its shops and restaurants and is within walking distance of the Quaker Hill Historic District, the Grand Opera House and the Playhouse. The nearby Brandywine Valley also beckons.

Each suite features traditional cherry furnishings and such convenient touches as in-room coffee brewers, microwaves, refrigerators, blow dryers and lighted make-up mirrors. Luxurious bathrooms offer a full array of toiletries and a private phone.

Guests enjoy a complimentary breakfast. Dinner is available at the Mediterranean Grille, with its upscale but casual ambiance. Guests recommend the jumbo baked crabcakes and for dessert, tiramisu.

The hotel provides business facilities, a full-scale conference room and access to a nearby fitness center. Service is intimate and "user friendly."

Address: 707 North King Street, Wilmington, DE 19801
Phone: 302-656-9300
Toll-Free: 800-756-0070
Fax: 302-656-2459
Suite Rates: $$$
Credit Cards: MC, Visa, AmEx, Discover
No. of Suites: 49
Services and Amenities: Valet service, Garage & parking, Car hire, Laundry service, House doctor, Baby-sitting service by request, TV lounge, Cable TV, Radio, 2 telephones, Complimentary toiletries & newspaper
Restrictions: No pets allowed, Children under 16 free with parents
Concierge: 24 hours
Room Service: Varying hours
Restaurant: Mediterranean Grille, 6:30 a.m.–8:30 a.m., 11:30 a.m.–2:00 p.m. Monday—Friday, 5:00 p.m.–10:00 p.m. Monday—Sunday, 8:00 a.m.–10:00 a.m. weekends, Dress code
Bar: 11:30 a.m.–2:00 p.m., 5:00 p.m.–10:00 p.m.
Business Facilities: Message center, Secretarial center, Copiers, Audio-Visual, Fax, Modems, Translators
Conference Rooms: 5 rooms, capacity 330
Sports Facilities: Moderate fitness equipment on property, Fitness center close by at a nominal fee
Location: Downtown
Attractions: Market Street Mall with shops and eateries behind hotel, Walking distance to Opera House and Play House

GEORGETOWN DUTCH INN

This all-suite European hotel is located on the street where Thomas Jefferson once lived in the heart of historic Georgetown. Since colonial times, when the fashionable Union Tavern opened nearby, Georgetown has offered fine accommodations in one of the world's most desirable neighborhoods, among superb restaurants, boutiques, night spots, tranquil tree-lined streets, landmark brick mansions and the famous C&O Canal. The business and tourist centers of Washington, D.C.—the Smithsonian, many national monuments, Capitol Hill, the Kennedy Center and more—are just minutes away.

One can imagine that Jefferson himself would have felt at home in the understated colonial elegance the Inn's one- and two-bedroom suites decorated in peach, burgundy, beige and green, each with separate living room and full kitchen. Amenities Jefferson would not have been familiar with include remote controlled cable TV, exercise facilities, telephones in the bathrooms, and air-conditioning. Guests are treated to a complimentary breakfast, complimentary parking, and a host of other conveniences such as secretarial service, valet and laundry service, and accommodations for guests with disabilities.

Business facilities include a conference room, message center, fax and modem, and copiers.

Address: 1075 Thomas Jefferson Street N.W.; Washington, DC 20007
Phone: 202-337-0900
Toll-Free: 800-388-2410
Fax: 202-333-6526
E-mail: gdidc@aol.com
Suite Rates: $$
Credit Cards: MC, Visa, AmEx, Discover
No. of Suites: 47
Services and Amenities: Valet, Garage/parking, Car hire, House doctor, Laundry, Baby-sitting service by request, Full kitchen, Iron & ironing board, Walk in closet, Hair dryer, Cable TV, Radio, 2 telephones, Some balconies, Complimentary toiletries/shoeshine/continental breakfast
Restrictions: No pets allowed, Children under 15 free with parents
Concierge: 24 hours
Room Service: Varying hours
Business Facilities: Message center, Secretarial center, Copiers, Audio-Visual, Fax, Modems, Translators
Conference Rooms: 1 room, capacity 60
Sports Facilities: Free privileges at Westend Fitness Center
Location: Historic Georgetown
Attractions: Many historic and tourist sites within walking distance, 12 blocks to the White House, Close to Kennedy Center and the Smithsonian Museum

THE HAY-ADAMS HOTEL

Whether you are attending a presidential inaugural celebration or having a power lunch, vacationing with your family or hosting a wedding—at The Hay-Adams Hotel in Washington, D.C., nothing is overlooked but the White House.

A welcome haven from Washington's hectic pace, The Hay-Adams Hotel is both classic and romantic. Its warm, inviting atmosphere combines contemporary lifestyle with traditional graciousness and evokes images of a timeless past amidst elegant English period furnishings, walnut paneling, gilt molding and ornate architectural details.

The Hay-Adams Hotel is the place to stay for comfort, personal service and attention to detail. The individually furnished guest rooms are tastefully decorated with rich fabrics, marble-clad baths and state-of-the-art amenities such as two-line telephone sets with dataports, speaker phones and voice mail.

Guests may experience the innovative Contemporary American Cuisine served in the hotel's renowned Lafayette restaurant. Social and business functions are often held in the light and airy Concorde room which faces historic St. John's Church and features hand-painted wallpaper depicting an 18th-century Parisian scene. Other possibilities are the John Hay room or the handsome Windsor room.

In 1884 John Hay, private secretary to President Lincoln, and Henry Adams, great-grandson of John Adams, built adjacent homes across from the White House on Lafayette Square. The inspiring view of the White House remains spectacularly unchanged today.

This class hotel, the only privately-held real estate on Lafayette Square, has been refurbished and its staff is dedicated to a tradition of hospitality and service excellence. The Hay-Adams Hotel is an island of civility in the sea of power that is Washington, D.C.

Address: 800 16th Street NW, Washington, D.C. 20006
Phone: 202-638-6600
Toll-Free: 800-424-5054
Fax: 202-638-2716
Room Rates: $$$$
Suite Rates: $$$$
Credit Cards: Most credit cards accepted
No. of Rooms: 117 **Suites:** 18
Services and Amenities: Weekend rates and packages available, Valet service, Garage and parking, Concierge, Laundry service, Complimentary shoeshine, Butler service, 2-line phones with dataports, Bath phone, Robes, Color TV, Complimentary newspaper, Radio
Restrictions: No pets allowed, Handicapped access to 3 rooms (limited access)
Concierge: 7:00 a.m.–midnight
Room Service: 24 hours
Restaurant: The Lafayette, breakfast, lunch and dinner, Afternoon tea and brunch on Sunday
Business Facilities: Secretarial service, Copiers, Fax, Arrangements made for other business services
Conference Rooms: 6 rooms, capacity 10–150
Attractions: White House, Capitol, Ten museums, Georgetown, Five universities

THE MORRISON-CLARK INN

The Morrison-Clark Historic Inn and Restaurant is Washington D.C.'s only historic inn listed with the National Trust for Historic Preservation. The Inn incorporates two Victorian townhomes built in 1864 and features a stunning Victorian/Chinois facade with a Chinese Chippendale porch. When guests enter the Inn through formal glass doors, into a marble floored foyer, a tuxedo-clad doorman immediately greets them. Adjoining the foyer, guests may rest in the turn-of-the-century parlor with wine colored Scalamandre upholstered Victorian furnishings.

Each of the guestrooms is individually and exquisitely decorated featuring impressive ten-foot ceilings or marble fireplaces, while others evoke a French-country flair with hand made quilts, floral patterns and wicker furniture. Delicate color schemes with hues of blue, rose, cream and peach are used throughout and all the guestrooms feature modern bathrooms with travertine marble vanities and fresh-cut flowers.

The Morrison-Clark Restaurant is listed among the area's top-20 restaurants. Its dining room is reminiscent of a Victorian drawing room with gilded mirrors, Italian marble fireplaces and lace curtains. Chef Lindeborg is nationally renowned and her menu features traditional American cuisine with Southern accents and regional specialties.

A delicious continental breakfast is served each morning in the richly detailed Club Room, reminiscent of an exclusive club with its custom-made bar, mahogany trim, marble fireplaces and handsome collection of nineteenth century art.

Guests may want to burn off their extra calories in the Inn's on-property fitness center or walk to the nearby attractions such as the Smithsonian Museums, White House, Fords Theater and Capitol Hill.

Address: Massachusetts Avenue & 11th Street, NW, Washington, D.C. 20001
Phone: 202-898-1200
Toll-Free: 800-332-7898
Fax: 202-289-8576
Room Rates: $$$
Suite Rates: $$$
Credit Cards: Most credit cards accepted
No. of Rooms: 54 **Suites:** 13
Services and Amenities: Valet parking, Laundry services, Nightly turndown service, TV, Radio, Individual heat & air-conditioning control, Hair dryers, Dataports, Complimentary newspaper & toiletries, Complimentary continental breakfast
Restrictions: Children welcome—under 16 years of age free with parents, No pets allowed
Concierge: 24 hours
Room Service: 7:00 a.m.–10:00 p.m.
Restaurant: Morrison-Clark Restaurant, 7:00 a.m.–9:30 p.m.
Bar: The Club Room, 11:00 a.m.–2:00 p.m., 5:00–11:00 p.m.
Business Facilities: Message center, Secretarial services, Copiers, Fax, Audio-Visual, Teleconferencing, Translators
Conference Rooms: 2 rooms, capacity 25
Sports Facilities: Fitness center on property
Location: Downtown Business District
Attractions: 3 blocks from the Convention Center & 4 blocks from the closest Metro Stop, White House, Smithsonian Museums, Fords Theater, Capitol Hill, Kennedy Center, Georgetown

GRAND BAY HOTEL COCONUT GROVE

If the ultimate in style and a "jet set" social scene appeal to you, you will love the Grand Bay. The first American hotel to be developed by the Italian firm CIGA, the Grand Bay Hotel is Miami *par excellence*.

Guest balconies at the Grand Bay Hotel view Biscayne Bay or Downtown Miami from the fashionable Coconut Grove area of Miami, Florida. Convenient for sailing on the bay and shopping the designer boutiques of Bal Harbour, the hotel also takes full advantage of Miami's year-round cultural offerings.

The royal treatment begins at check-in, accompanied by fresh Florida orange juice in the terra-cotta floored lobby and comfortable designer furniture in the rooms. Perhaps, best of all, every room and suite has floor-to-ceiling windows which open to a spacious bay-view or city-view balcony.

The comforts of home include fluffy bathrobes, minibars, TVs with VCRs, stereo systems with CD and tape players, safes, personal fax machines, and multilingual voice mail. Bathrooms provide hair dryers, custom toiletries, and two phone extensions. The personal luxuries are hard to beat.

Not to be missed, however, are the Grand Bay's public dining pleasures. The world famous BICE Restaurant is nestled on the mezzanine level overlooking the garden terraces. The BICE offers the finest Italian fare available in Miami. For a light lunch and cocktails, guests gather at the Poolside Bar & Grill. For Mozart, Brahms, and Chopin and an updated afternoon tea, guests may visit the Lobby Terrace, as inviting as an English club with its deep leather sofas and chairs. After hours, guests may relax with live music at The Bar, which rounds out another clublike atmosphere with a light menu, wine and cocktails.

Guests will truly enjoy the Grand Bay's sophisticated blend of service, discretion, luxury, style and class.

Address: 2669 South Bayshore Drive, Coconut Grove, FL 33133
Phone: 305-858-9600
Toll-Free: 800-327-2788
Fax: 305-858-1532
E-mail: grandbay@vcn.net
Room Rates: $$$
Suite Rates: $$$$
Credit Cards: Most credit cards accepted
No. of Rooms: 132 **Suites:** 46
Services and Amenities: Valet service & parking, Car hire, Sundry boutique, Beauty salon, Currency exchange, Laundry service, Baby-sitting service, Cable TV, Radio, Robes, Complimentary newspaper & toiletries
Restrictions: No pets allowed
Concierge: 24 hours
Room Service: 24 hours
Restaurant: BICE, 7:00 a.m.–3:00 p.m., 6:30 p.m.–11:00 p.m., Dress code
Bar: The Bar
Business Facilities: Full-scale business center
Conference Rooms: 7 rooms, capacity 20–400
Sports Facilities: Outdoor swimming pool, Exercise room with sauna, Massage, Weight training, Access to water sports
Location: Coconut Grove, Fifteen minutes from airport, Across from Biscayne Bay
Attractions: Shopping, Vizcaya, Key Biscayne, Downtown Miami, Seaquarium, Planet Ocean, Mayfair shops, Cocowalk

HERON HOUSE

In the heart of Historic Key West is the Heron House, meticulously designed by Key West's most gifted artists and craftsmen specifically for the discerning traveler. Combining the artistic sensitivity with open hearts, a genuine sense of caring pervades every aspect of this unique, private retreat. Lacking pretense, this style has been inspired by the informality of the Florida Keys' natural environment, revealing itself in a casually elegant style in which you will feel totally free, welcome and relaxed.

With generous private decks and balconies, guestrooms merge with luxurious tropical gardens. Interior and exterior spaces blend and flow together. The multi-level decks provide guests with space to lounge and view the gardens. There is ample use of natural materials. Many of the rooms feature "signature walls" of teak, oak or cedar. Granite baths and tile floors are cool and tropical. The stained glass transoms above French doors create a glow of natural sunlight and sparkling colors throughout the room. Interiors feature originally commissioned watercolors from local Keys artisans.

When it comes to Key West activity, Heron House is just one block from world famous Duval Street with its epicurean delights, lively entertainment, shopping, and art galleries. Guests may wander away to the beach which is only four blocks away.

Heron House has always meant attention to fine detail. Whether it is a Honeymoon Special or just a special time away, guests will find Heron House vintage champagne ready to put on ice, bubble bath for the jacuzzi, robes placed in every room, reef snorkeling and sunset champagne sails. Come and see for yourself.

Address: 512 Simonton Street, Key West, FL 33040
Phone: 305-294-9227
Toll-Free: 888-676-8648
Fax: 305-294-5692
E-mail: heronkyw@aol.com
Web site: http://www.fla-keys.com/heronhouse
Room Rates: $
Suite Rates: $$$
Credit Cards: Most credit cards accepted
No. of Rooms: 23 **Suites:** 13
Services and Amenities: Balconies, Cable TV, Telephones, Radio, Robes, Individual air-conditioning control, Wet bar in suites, Whirlpool bath in some rooms, Robes, Complimentary newspaper & toiletries, 2nd story sundeck, Orchid gardens
Restrictions: Limited handicapped access, Children over 16 years of age welcome, No pets allowed
Concierge: 8:00 a.m.–8:00 p.m.
Room Service: 9:00 a.m.–8:00 p.m.
Business Facilities: Message center, Copiers, Fax
Sports Facilities: Outdoor heated swimming pool, Sundeck, Orchid Gardens
Location: Old Town, Downtown
Attractions: Historic district, One block from most attractions

PILOT HOUSE

This grand two-story Victorian mansion, built circa 1900 by Julius Otto as his private home, stands proudly in the center of Key West's Old Town. Adorned with gingerbread trim and hand-milled spindles on its porches and verandas, the Pilot House earned the Florida Keys Preservation Board's prestigious "Excellence Award for Preservation" following its 1990 restoration. The guest rooms with their hardwood floors, massive moldings and twelve-foot ceilings are appointed with a blend of antiques and tropical furnishings. Innkeeper Ed Cox has carefully chosen wallpapers and fabrics to complement the original character of the Pilot House. Private Italian-tiled baths, kitchenettes, color cable TVs, phone, air conditioning and paddle fans are part of the package.

As befits the tropics, the focus here is on airy outdoor living. The adjoining poolside Cabana Suites, which feature in-room Jacuzzis, mini-bars and modern tropical decor, open onto the palm-shaded clothing-optional pool.

Intimate and convenient to the magic ambiance of Key West, the Pilot House is designed to be a home away from home for the experienced, discriminating traveler.

Address: 414 Simonton Street, Key West, FL 33040
Phone: 305-293-6600
Toll-Free: 800-648-3780
Fax: 305-294-9298
E-mail: keywestlodging@sprynet.com
Web site: http://www.pilothousekeywest.com
Room Rates: $$
Suite Rates: $$$$
Credit Cards: Most credit cards accepted
No. of Rooms: 12 **Suites:** 3
Services and Amenities: Kitchen/cooking facilities, 2 fireplaces, 8 balconies/decks, Cable TV, Telephones, Radios, Wet bar, 5 whirlpool baths, Clothing-optional pool and spa
Restrictions: 1 room with handicapped access, No children please, No pets allowed
Concierge: 9:00 a.m.–6:00 p.m.
Sports Facilities: Outdoor swimming pool, Whirlpool
Location: Old Town
Attractions: Shops, restaurants and boutiques of Old Town, Walking and biking tours

THE COLONY BEACH AND TENNIS RESORT

Sun worship is the central purpose of this casually elegant, tropical-feeling island resort, just minutes from Sarasota and yet a world apart. White powder beaches strewn with seashells stretch the 12-mile length of Longboat Key. Sunbathe, windsurf, enjoy an evening stroll along the sand for a spectacular sunset over the Gulf on the Colony's 800-foot private beach.

The resort buildings are nestled among beautiful flowering shrubs and trees from the entrance to the beach. All units are one-and two-bedroom apartment-style suites or two- and three-bedroom private beach houses. Full kitchen facilities include dishwashers, microwaves, and refrigerators with ice makers. Marbled master baths have mini-spa steam showers and whirlpools. One-bedroom lanais and oversized apartments in the main clubhouse building are reserved exclusively for adults.

The award winning Colony Restaurants overlook the Gulf of Mexico surf. The Dining Room's wine cellar, which has received national and international praise, offers a marvelous selection to the budding connoisseur and oenophile alike. Seafood is the house specialty. A typical deluxe dinner might be a medley of jumbo Gulf shrimp and Florida stone crab, a caesar salad and pan roasted American Red Snapper with lump crabmeat and sundried tomatoes. The Colony Bistro serves regional favorites in a casual setting, and the Colony Patio and Bar serves light lunches alfresco.

Recreation opportunities abound. There is complimentary play on 21 tennis courts (10 soft), free match-making service and certified pros offering clinics and private lessons for all ages and levels. Golf can be arranged at several championship courses nearby. There are complete complimentary health spas for men and women, as well as an aerobic and fitness center with a wide variety of daily classes and shape-up programs. Also complimentary is a year round daily program of fun-filled activities designed especially for children ages 3–6, 7–12, and a seasonal program for teens. The watersports center offers instruction in sailing and windsurfing.

Address: 1620 Gulf of Mexico Drive, Longboat Key, FL 34228
Phone: 941-383-6464
Toll-Free: 800-426-5669
Fax: 941-383-7549
E-mail: colonyfl@ix.netcom.com
Web site: http:// www.colonybeachresort.com
Suite Rates: $$$
Credit Cards: Visa, AmEx, MC
No. of Suites: 235
Services and Amenities: Tennis Pro shop, Le Tennique Boutique, Tastebuds gourmet market, Valet service, Free Parking, Laundry, Drycleaning, Cable TV, Radio, In-room Whirlpool, Microwave, Complimentary children's activity program
Restrictions: Limited handicapped access, No pets allowed
Concierge: 8:00 a.m.–11:00 p.m.
Restaurant: The Colony Dining Room, lunch, dinner, Sunday brunch, The Colony Bistro, breakfast, dinner, The Colony Patio and Bar, lunch and light fare
Bar: The Colony Lounge, noon-closing
Business Facilities: Full service business center, Audio-Visual, Equipment available
Conference Rooms: 7 rooms, capacity 10-200
Sports Facilities: Outdoor heated swimming pool, 21 tennis courts, Golf nearby, Fitness center, Full service spa, Watersports center
Location: Beachfront island resort on Gulf of Mexico
Attractions: Boutique shopping at St. Armands, Selby Botanical Gardens, Ringling Museum, Mote Marine Aquarium, Tampa's Busch Gardens (1 hour); Disney World, Epcot, and Sea World are just two hours away in Orlando

THE RESORT AT LONGBOAT KEY CLUB

Set amid a bird sanctuary on 410 acres of lush landscaping, The Resort at Longboat Key Club is one of the few Florida resorts featuring both beach and golf.

Located off the coast of Sarasota on the Gulf of Mexico, and home to the annual Florida Winefest and Auction in April, this tropical island resort is one of Florida's most sophisticated. All accommodations offer dramatic views of the Gulf of Mexico, lagoon and golf course fairways.

Club suites, one- and two-bedroom suites, and Deluxe two-bedroom suites have expansive living areas, fully equipped kitchens, washer/dryer, spacious dressing rooms and large private balconies. Guest rooms feature a single king or two twin beds, dressing area, icemaker/refrigerator and a private balcony. All the fabrics and furnishings are custom designed to emphasize the ambiance of tropical elegance.

The Resort provides a full array of opportunities for invigorating the body and recharging the spirit. Tennis, 45 holes of golf, a golf school and a breathtaking stretch of sparkling white sandy beach are just a step away. Four full-service Pro shops and a staff of resident professionals are available to complement your golf or tennis game. There is also a fully equipped fitness center featuring aerobic classes, weight and cardiovascular training and massage. Tennis and Fitness Centre usage are complimentary.

Guests choose from several dining options including traditional favorites in casual poolside surroundings at the Grille, The Dining Room and the elegant classic Italian cuisine and sophisticated ambiance of Orchid's Restaurant, overlooking the beach and the Gulf of Mexico. Live entertainment is featured at Orchid's Tuesday-Saturday.

Address: 301 Gulf of Mexico Drive, Longboat Key, FL 34228
Phone: 941-383-8821
Toll-Free: 800-237-8821
Fax: 941-383-0359
E-mail: reservations@longboatkeyclub.com
Web site: http://www.longboatkeyclub.com
Suite Rates: $$$
Credit Cards: Most credit cards accepted
No. of Suites: 232
Services and Amenities: Valet service, Garage & parking, Car hire, House doctor, Laundry, Baby-sitting, Pro shops, Library, Kitchen/cooking facilities, Balconies, Cable TV, Radio, Wet bar, Individual heat/AC control, Complimentary newspaper, toiletries, mini-bars, safes & coffee
Restrictions: No pets allowed, Kids free with parents, Handicapped access to all rooms (some with shower bars)
Concierge: 7:00 a.m.–11:30 p.m.
Room Service: 7:00 a.m.–midnight
Restaurant: Orchids, 7:00 a.m.–midnight, The Grille, 8:00 a.m.–10:00 p.m., The Dining Room, 5:30–10:00 p.m. (seasonal)
Bar: Orchid's Lounge and Barefoot's (poolside), 11:30 a.m.–midnight
Business Facilities: Message center, Secretarial services, Copiers, Audio-Visual, Translators, Conference facilities
Conference Rooms: 7 rms, cap. 150
Sports Facilities: Outdoor swimming pool, Whirlpool, Massage, Steam rooms, Aerobics & weight training, Golf, Sailing, Tennis, Deep-sea fishing, Bikes
Location: Beachfront, Nearest airport is SRQ or TPA
Attractions: St. Armands Circle, One mile to over 100 upscale boutiques, Restaurants, Galleries, The Ringling Museum Complex, Selby Botanical Gardens, Mote Marine Labs

DELANO

Delano is a world-class destination resort set directly on Miami Beach, in the heart of one of America's most exciting cities. First built in 1947, Delano has just completed a "fabulously surreal" renovation by the renowned French designer, Philippe Starck. Creating a nationwide wave of publicity since its reopening in 1995, the 16-story hotel offers an understated mix of quiet quality, value and tranquility—along with cutting-edge sensibility, excitement and style.

Delano's unique indoor/outdoor lobby is composed of a series of eight beautifully conceived areas that create the feel of an interwoven "village." With furnishings and objects spanning over a century and the continents of Europe, Asia, Africa and Australia, these areas include a wide variety of dining and beverage options, a uniquely designed lounging area and swimming pool with private cabanas, a mini-forest that provides cooling shade, and an outdoor children's play area.

Each of the custom-painted white and pearl-grey, pristine guest quarters are corner rooms, with furniture and lamps designed especially by Starck for Delano, showcasing high style, comfort, and intimacy without pretension. Every convenience is provided, including entertainment centers, private telephone numbers, data port connections, black-out shades, refrigerators and mini-bars. The bathrooms feature a blend of technology and art, with free-standing tubs, custom-made porcelain sinks, and multi-head showers. Poolside duplex guest bungalows, inspired by those in Beverly Hills, allow separate access from the street.

Delano has a private beach area providing extensive water sports recreation for guests. The David Barton Gym with private trainers and fitness classes on the beach is available to guests for a fee, as is Agua, the rooftop bath house and spa offering a full menu of spa beauty and relaxation services and a solarium with health bar.

A full-service business center, along with extensive meeting and banquet facilities make Delano a perfect setting for social and business events.

Address: 1685 Collins Avenue, Miami Beach, FL 33139
Phone: 305-672-2000
Toll-Free: 800-555-5001
Fax: 305-532-0099
Room Rates: $$$
Suite Rates: $$$$
Credit Cards: Most credit cards accepted
No. of Rooms: 210 **Suites:** 28
Services and Amenities: International news and gift shop, Private telephone numbers, Data-port connections, In-room refrigerator, Cable TV, Video on demand, Radio and CD player, Turndown service, Outdoor children's play area, Complimentary newspaper
Restrictions: Non-smoking rooms available, No pets allowed
Concierge: 24 hours
Room Service: 24 hours
Restaurant: Five distinct indoor and outdoor food and beverage areas on premises
Business Facilities: Business center, Audio-Visual equipment, Fax, Portable computers & telephones
Conference Rooms: Variety of Multi-service meeting spaces available
Sports Facilities: $15/day for state-of-the-art David Barton Gym with private trainers & fitness classes, $10/day plus spa fees for use of Bath House
Location: In the heart of Miami Beach Art Deco District
Attractions: Near all Miami Beach attractions, Shopping, Night Clubs, Restaurants

THE CHESTERFIELD HOTEL

"More like an exclusive club than a hotel" is the hotel's long-standing motto, and the red carnation worn by every staff member embodies the Chesterfield's attitude of responsiveness to every need and attention to every detail.

Built in Mediterranean Revival style in 1926 and completely refurbished last year, the Chesterfield embodies the elegance of an earlier time. Inside is an English country manor style lobby and library furnished with antique Persian rugs, English and French antique furniture and oversized sofas and chairs. There is also a landscaped courtyard and a cigar club on the premises.

Rooms feature antiques, traditional fabrics and hand-buffed walls and trim. Suites are provided with fresh flowers, refrigerators and 2 phones. All rooms have cable TV; plush robes, mineral water, hair dryers, and fine soaps and sachets await guests in the marble bathrooms. Guests are served sherry on arrival, and English tea with scones, preserves and clotted cream is served every afternoon. A round-the-clock concierge is available for every need.

The ambiance of the hotel's Leopard Lounge and Supper Club can best be described as "exotic playfulness." Handpainted mural ceilings and leopard printed walls and carpet envelope the guest from behind Asian palm fronds. Seating is in red leather booths or red lacquered chairs. Guests can watch the meal being prepared in the central "theater kitchen."

This intimate hotel is within strolling distance of the shores of the Atlantic or the famous shops of Worth Avenue. The financial center of West Palm Beach is a short cab ride away.

Address: 363 Cocoanut Row, Palm Beach, FL 33480
Phone: 561-659-5800
Toll-Free: 800-243-7871
Fax: 561-659-6707
E-mail: chesterpb/cpbo.htm
Room Rates: $
Suite Rates: $$$
Credit Cards: Most credit cards accepted
No. of Rooms: 55 **Suites:** 11
Services and Amenities: Valet service, Car hire, House doctor, Library, Telephones, Radio, Air-conditioning, Robes, Complimentary toiletries & newspaper, Complimentary sherry on arrival, Complimentary afternoon tea
Restrictions: No pets allowed, Children free in room with parents, 1 room handicapped-equipped
Concierge: 24 hours
Room Service: 24 hours
Restaurant: The Leopard Lounge Restaurant and Supper Club, 6:00–10:30 p.m., Dress code in season
Bar: Leopard Lounge, Lunch-2:00 a.m.
Business Facilities: Copiers, Audio-Visual, Teleconferencing, Fax, Translators, Modem hookups
Conference Rooms: 1 room, capacity 150
Sports Facilities: Outdoor swimming pool, Nearby golf, Tennis
Location: Palm Beach, Near the beach
Attractions: Beach, Historical landmarks, Museums, Theaters, Exclusive Worth Avenue shopping

GOVERNORS INN

Located in the center of the Adams Street Commons, Governors Inn is the crowning touch in a bid to restore a sense of history to the heart of the city. Imposing heart-of-pine overhead beams and warm pine paneling help to maintain the charm of the original 50 year old buildings. Antique furniture, quality reproductions, traditionally patterned wall coverings with chair rails and cove moldings complement the French Country style.

No two of the 40 guest rooms are identical. Each has its own spirit and is uniquely decorated. Antiques are used throughout and armoires act as closets and hide modern amenities. Some rooms feature sleeping lofts, corkscrew staircases, wood-burning marble fireplaces, clerestory windows, a bar, or jacuzzi. The staff provides turndown service, terrycloth robes, valet parking, continental breakfast, complimentary cocktails, newspapers and many personal care amenities.

Governors Inn is fortunate to have one of the capitol city's finer restaurants—"Andrew's Second Act"—within easy walking distance. In addition, guests wishing to dine in the comfort of their own room may order room service from "Andrew's."

Many guests are corporate executives and the hotel's professional staff can help arrange for conferences up to 50 people.

Address: 209 South Adams Street, Tallahassee, FL 32301
Phone: 850-681-6855
Toll-Free: 800-342-7717
Fax: 850-222-3105
Room Rates: $$
Suite Rates: $$$
Credit Cards: Visa, MC, AmEx, DC, CB
No. of Rooms: 40 **Suites:** 6
Services and Amenities: Valet service, Garage and parking, Card/game area, Cable TV, Telephone, Robes, Complimentary newspaper and toiletries
Restrictions: No pets allowed
Room Service: 6:00 p.m.–10:00 p.m.
Restaurant: Room service is available through "Andrew's Second Act" located across the street from Governors Inn
Business Facilities: Message center, Copiers, Fax
Conference Rooms: 2 rooms, capacity 12-45
Location: Adams Street Common, Nearest airport is Tallahassee Regional
Attractions: Central City, ½ block north of Capitol building

REGENCY SUITES HOTEL

This classic European Hotel in the center of Atlanta's Midtown brings guests quiet elegance, along with friendly service in a homelike setting. With ninety-six well designed and carefully furnished suites, it offers a welcome stay for the business or leisure visitor. All suites feature king, queen, or double/double beds and living rooms with queen-size convertible sofas. Kitchens are equipped with microwave ovens, refrigerators, coffee maker, small appliances, and table service for four people.

Regency Suites Hotel is located in the center of Atlanta's cultural and business district, just 2 blocks from I-75/85. Marta's Midtown Station, conveniently located a few steps away, offers a quick ride to Underground Atlanta, Downtown, the Georgia Dome, World Congress Convention Center, Woodruff Arts Center and Buckhead. Also located nearby is the Georgia Tech Campus and Piedmont Park.

Monday through Thursday evenings guests are invited to a complimentary meal with a different menu nightly. In addition, a complimentary breakfast is served daily in the Club Room. Here guests can watch a movie, borrow a book, read the complimentary daily newspaper or just relax with friends.

Guests will also find valet service, covered parking, and on-site laundry. Choice microwavable food is available in the mini-convenience store.

The Executive Board Room offers business guests a professional atmosphere in which to conduct meetings. Furnished with Chippendale-style conference table and chairs, this room can be scaled to accommodate executive meetings for up to 12 people. The accompanying audio-visual center is at your command. Larger meeting space is also available as is catering.

Address: 975 West Peachtree Street, Atlanta, GA 30309
Phone: 404-876-5003
Toll-Free: 800-642-3629
Fax: 404-817-7511
E-mail: sales@regencysuites.com
Web site: http://www.regencysuites.com
Suite Rates: $
Credit Cards: Most credit cards accepted
No. of Suites: 96
Services and Amenities: Valet service, Garage and parking, Car hire, Library, Cable TV, VCR, Exercise room, Non-smoking suites, Suite service, Complimentary toiletries and newspaper, Daily complimentary breakfast and Monday—Thursday complimentary dinner
Restrictions: No pets allowed, 4 suites handicapped-equipped
Business Facilities: Message center, Copiers, Audio-Visual, Overhead projector, VCR-½", Fax equipment, Notary
Conference Rooms: 2 rooms, capacity 50, 1 executive boardroom
Location: Midtown, Nearest airport is Hartsfield International
Attractions: Six Flags, Underground Atlanta, High Museum of Art, Fox Theatre, 4 blocks from Atlanta Symphony's home and Woodruff Art Center, Carter Center, Georgia Tech Campus, Martin Luther King, Jr. Center, Atlanta Botanical Gardens, Center for Puppetry Arts

FOLEY HOUSE INN

For travelers who value a sense of place and time, the 100-year-old Foley Inn on historic Chippewa Square has been lovingly and authentically refurbished to reflect Savannah in its Victorian hey-day. The parlor glows with the jewel-tones of deep burgundy, green and gold. Two carved fireplaces, crystal chandelier and fresh flowers remind guests that they are not in some faceless large hotel.

The amazingly quiet rooms in this downtown location are individually decorated with antique English dressers and armoires, lace-canopied 4-poster beds, complimented by sumptuous wallpaper and drapes in old Savannah's signature colors of peach, crimson and salmon. Many rooms have fireplaces, marble bathrooms with whirlpool baths, and balconies. Guests may enjoy a complimentary movie in their private VCR. The adjacent Carriage House offers simpler rooms at surprisingly modest prices.

Guests enjoy a continental breakfast in the parlor or open-air courtyard. The afternoon hors d'oeuvres hour features fresh fruit, cheese, crackers, and wine or lemonade. Owner Inge Svensson Moore enjoys providing European-style personal attention that makes guests feel truly special. "That's why I love this business." During the holiday season, she adds a touch of her native Denmark with a month-long traditional advent celebration.

All the delights of landmark Old Savannah, with its restaurants, theaters and historic riverfront walk, await guests who venture forth to tour the area on foot or by horsedrawn carriage or trolley.

Address: Chippewa Square, 14 West Hull Street, Savannah, GA 31401
Phone: 912-232-6622
Toll-Free: 800-647-3708
Fax: 912-231-1218
Web site: http://www.bbonline.com/ga/savannah/foley/index.html
Room Rates: $$
Credit Cards: Visa, MC, AmEx
No. of Rooms: 19
Services and Amenities: Cable TV, VCR, Telephones, Radio, Air-conditioning, Complimentary newspaper and toiletries, Complimentary breakfast, afternoon tea, cordials and hors d'oeuvres
Restrictions: No pets allowed, Children under 12 free, No handicapped-equipped rooms
Concierge: 7:00 a.m.–11:00 p.m.
Room Service: Breakfast hours
Business Facilities: Copiers, Fax, Modems
Sports Facilities: Privileges by special arrangement at First City Club & Downtown Athletic Club, Golf & tennis available at Southbridge Country Club
Location: Downtown, Chippewa Square, Historic landmark district
Attractions: Trolley tours, Jazz festivals, Shakespeare in the Park, River front festivals, Antique shops

THE GASTONIAN

You will step into the past when you enter the Gastonian's lovely drawing room, with its antique Persian rug, Waterford Crystal chandelier and authentic English antiques. The inn is actually comprised of two adjacent mansions built in 1868. A walkway, which gives an overview of the garden filled with fragrant myrtle and flowering dogwood, connects the two houses, and a two-story carriage house has been transformed into a private honeymoon suite.

Each of the rooms and suites has its own theme, and each is appointed with high ceilings, operating fireplaces, Charleston canopied beds and ample whirlpool or soak tubs. The Caracalla Suite, named for the pleasure-loving Roman emperor, has an eight-foot jacuzzi bathtub with solid brass hardware on a corian-stepped platform. Draped at its four corners with floor-to-ceiling sheer curtains, the luxurious bath sits in the center of a parquet floor, looking like the set piece for a Roman toga party!

In the morning you may choose from a sumptuous hot breakfast in the parlor or Silver Service continental breakfast in your room or courtyard with complimentary newspaper. Afternoons, enjoy complimentary tea and in the evening, turndown service including Savannah sweets and cordials. Upon arrival, wine, fresh fruit and flowers will welcome you. The inn's concierge service is available which will arrange everything from dinner reservations to horsedrawn carriage tours.

Address: 220 East Gaston Street, Savannah, GA 31401
Phone: 912-232-2869
Toll-Free: 800-322-6603
Fax: 912-232-0710
Web site: http://www.gastonian.com
Room Rates: $$$
Suite Rates: $$$$
Credit Cards: AmEx, Visa, MC, Discover
No. of Rooms: 14 **Suites:** 3
Services and Amenities: Offstreet parking, Gift shop, Kitchen (2 rooms), Operating fireplaces, Balconies, Sundeck, Cable TV, Individual heat & air-conditioning, Telephones, Robes, Whirlpool, Caswell Massey toiletries, Complimentary full breakfast & afternoon tea
Restrictions: 1 room handicapped-equipped, No children under 12, No pets, No smoking
Concierge: 24 hours
Room Service: 8:00 a.m.–10:00 p.m.
Restaurant: Recommended restaurant nearby: Elizabeth on 37th Street
Business Facilities: Copiers, Audio-Visual
Conference Rooms: 2 rooms, capacity 25
Sports Facilities: Whirlpool, Tennis & golf nearby by arrangement, Privileges at Southbridge & Sheraton
Location: Downtown, Savannah Historic District, Nearest airport is Savannah Int'l.
Attractions: Historic landmark district with many gourmet restaurants, Museums, Antique shops, Riverboat dinner & historic tours

THE CLOISTER

Five miles of private beach and 10,000 acres of surrounding forest and marsh make this sunny sub-tropical island playground a paradise for honeymooners, family vacationers and sports enthusiasts. The Spanish-architecture resort complex, built in 1928, offers accommodations in the main hotel, the River House, and an array of guesthouses and beach cottages. Lodging locations and sizes vary considerably, and rates adjust accordingly.

The entire property is a garden a-bloom the year around. Flowers grace the tables and the rooms. The food is superb—from the exquisite Beach Club buffet to breakfast served on your own private balcony overlooking the ocean. Full American plan dining is offered year round at your choice of four unique dining facilities including the Beach Club. The Cloister orchestra plays nightly for dancing in the Clubrooms.

The sporting life reigns supreme. America's finest golf is to be found here, with 54 championship holes on what were once the cotton fields of an antebellum seaside plantation. Guests can also enjoy clubhouse facilities at two excellent golf clubs, as well as 17 fast-dry clay tennis courts, two pools at Sea Island Beach Club, full-service spa, trap, skeet and sporting clays at the Sea Island Shooting School, bicycles, fishing, inland cruising boats, including the vintage yachts: Zapala and Lady Patricia sailboats, and horses for ring, trail or beach riding.

Children stay year round in room with parents without charge except for meals, based on age. During Summer Family Festival, meals are included for the under-19 sharing parents' room. No charge for golf green fees and tennis for young guests staying at The Cloister. The Junior Staff hosts the youth during holiday periods, Spring break and Summer.

Winter festivals at The Cloister include Bridge festivals, Food/Wine Classic, Personal Financial Planning Seminar and Cloister Garden Series. There are also exceptional conference facilities.

Address: Sea Island Drive, Sea Island, GA 31561
Phone: 912-638-3611
Toll-Free: 800-SEA-ISLAND
Fax: 912-638-5159
Room Rates: $$$
Suite Rates: $$$$
No. of Rooms: 262 **Suites:** 28
Services and Amenities: Full-service garage & parking, Car hire, Valet service, Laundry service, Baby-sitting service, Business Center, Gift shop, Florist, Beauty shop, Game area, Cable TV, Telephones
Restrictions: No pets allowed, Handicapped access
Concierge: 7:00 a.m.–9:00 p.m.
Room Service: 7:00 a.m.– Midnight
Restaurant: The Cloister Dining Room, Sea Island Beach Club, Sea Island Golf Club, St. Simons Island Club
Bar: Several, open daily except Sunday
Business Facilities: Business Center, Fax, Computer service, Secretarial service, Copiers, Audio-Visual
Conference Rooms: 12 rooms, capacity 350
Sports Facilities: 54 holes of golf, Golf Learning Center, 17 tennis courts, 1 automated practice court, 2 pools, Horseback riding, Sailing, Croquet
Location: On 5-mile beach off the southern coast of Georgia
Attractions: Full-service spa, 5 miles of private beach, Winter Festivals

THE LODGE ON LITTLE ST. SIMONS ISLAND

Virtually untouched for centuries, Little St. Simons Island is a privately-owned 10,000-acre barrier island along the Georgia coast. The owners of Little St. Simons Island have welcomed family and friends since the early 1900s. Accessible only by boat and allowing just 30 overnight guests, the Lodge provides comfort in a natural setting highlighted by a seven mile stretch of pristine beach.

The classic Hunting Lodge, built in 1917, is the very heart of Island life. Reminiscent of a Hemingway novel, its great room is the gathering spot for each evening's social hour. An informal bar is available, and healthy regional cuisine utilizing the bounty of the area is served family style in the Hunting Lodge dining room. This is the perfect setting to enjoy delicious regional specialties such as oyster roasts, blue crab boil, crispy fried flounder and homemade ice cream and sorbets.

Among the five lodges and cottages, the elegant Helen House is a favorite. This historic house was constructed in 1928 of tabby, a building material made of all indigenous materials which was used extensively in coastal Georgia during colonial times. Shaded by a small grove of live oaks bedecked with Spanish moss and situated along the creek, the Helen House offers three gracious bedrooms, two baths, a large living room with grand fireplace, and a screened porch which overlooks a quiet courtyard and the expansive marsh beyond. The home provides ideal accommodations for families and groups of friends as well as individual travelers.

The Island is a haven for wildlife. The unique diversity of habitat provides an exciting opportunity for birdwatching, as well as viewing European fallow deer, alligators, dolphins and the many other creatures that share the Island and its waters. It may take a while to explore all seven miles of beaches as well as the inland waterways and woods. It would be tempting to become part of the wildlife, except for the very civilized care and service of the staff on Little St. Simons Island.

Address: P.O. Box 21078, St. Simons Island, GA 31522
Phone: 912-638-7472
Toll-Free: 888-SEE-LSSI
Fax: 912-634-1811
E-mail: lssi@mindspring.com
Web site: http://www.pactel.com.au/lssi
Room Rates: $$$$
Suite Rates: $$$$
Credit Cards: Visa, MC
No. of Rooms: 15 **Suites:** 1
Services and Amenities: Gift shop, Library, Card or game area, Midweek packages, Full island rental available, Personal checks accepted, Washer/dryer available, Ceiling fans, Individual heat and air-conditioning control, Complimentary toiletries, All meals included in room rates
Restrictions: No pets allowed, 2-night minimum stay, Children over eight welcome
Restaurant: Family style for breakfast, lunch and dinner
Bar: In the Hunting Lodge
Conference Rooms: 5 rooms, capacity 30
Sports Facilities: Expertly guided saltwater fly fishing excursions, Bird watching, Horseback riding, Hiking, Bicycling, Boating, Outdoor pool
Location: Private 10,000-acre barrier island in Georgia's Golden Isles
Attractions: Accessible only by boat, Seven miles of pristine beach, Three surrounding islands offer golf, tennis, shopping and historical tours

ASTON WAIKIKI BEACHSIDE HOTEL

Hawaii's Royalty once occupied estates throughout Waikiki where visiting guests would be hosted and entertained with lavish luaus and social teas. It was a time when royal children were schooled abroad in the rich traditions and cultures of European monarchies.

Built on the former estate of Prince Kuhio, the Aston Waikiki Beach Hotel recreates subtle opulence exhibited in those Hawaiian estates. A privileged collection of antiques and artwork includes an intricately carved coromandel Malaysian wood screen, Louis XV chests, a 17th century French sculpture, a 100 year old Emperor's chair and an 18th century Chinese altar table.

The extravagance is continued in the guestrooms with hand painted Oriental screens and Chinoiserie bath vanities gilded with accents of real gold. An open air courtyard is lined with palms and a soothing Italian fountain, and it is here that afternoon tea and the island's only high tea is served on the weekends. Tales of our monarchs are shared by the tea time staff.

The royal tradition of entertaining visitors with gracious Hawaiian hospitality is continued at the Aston Waikiki Beachside Hotel—an elegant boutique hotel overlooking Waikiki Beach.

Address: 2452 Kalakaua Avenue, Honolulu, HI 96815
Phone: 808-931-2100
Toll-Free: 800-922-7866
Fax: 808-931-2129
Web site: http://www.aston-hotels.com
Room Rates: $$$
Suite Rates: $$$$
Credit Cards: Visa, MC, AmEx, Diners
No. of Rooms: 79 **Suites:** 2
Services and Amenities: Laundry service, Cable TV, Telephone, Video player, Radio, Air-conditioning, Mini-refrigerator, Complimentary newspaper, toiletries and continental breakfast
Restrictions: No pets allowed, Children must be accompanied by an adult, Handicapped-equipped rooms available
Concierge: 24 hours
Restaurant: A Special Tea Affair, Saturday & Sunday, 3:00 p.m.–6:00 p.m.
Business Facilities: Message center, Copiers, Audio-Visual, Fax, Translators
Sports Facilities: Nearby aerobics, Weight training, Sailing, Surfing, Canoeing, Tennis, Archery, Jogging paths
Location: Waikiki
Attractions: Waikiki Beach, Dinner cruises, Sightseeing tours; Walking distance to Hermes, Gucci, Chanel, Louis Vuitton, Cartier, Dior

THE NEW OTANI KAIMANA BEACH HOTEL

On the quiet end of Waikiki Beach at the foot of Diamond Head in Kapiolani Park is The New Otani Kaimana Beach Hotel. In a setting that is simply incomparable, the Kaimana, as it is affectionately known, literally sits on secluded Sans Souci, a golden strand of beach shared by only a few exclusive residences and two private clubs. In fact, it was Robert Louis Stevenson who once wrote, "If anyone desires lovely scenery, pure air, clear sea water and heavenly sunsets, I recommend him cordially to the San Souci."

Soft pastels and private balconies with stunning views of Waikiki, Diamond Head and the park make the guest rooms uncommonly inviting. The spacious ninth floor suites, done in dramatic color schemes, are exceptionally pleasing in this boutique hotel.

The hotel's restaurants typify the harmony achieved between the relaxes attitudes of a tropical paradise and the centuries-old Japanese innkeeping tradition based on perfect hospitality for every guest. The open-air, beachfront Hau Tree Lanai specializes in creative and flavorful entrees using fresh island ingredients. Dinner, served by candlelight and torchlight, might be papaya salad, local fish prepared steamed, broiled or sautéed, Oahu gourmet ice cream and fresh-ground Kona blend coffee.

The Miyako, is among the finest Japanese restaurants anywhere outside of Tokyo. It offers Western-style seating as well as tatami rooms for traditional dining, and its prices are surprisingly reasonable.

With Kapiolani Park at its front doorstep, the Kaimana is at the heart of sports and culture. Its parkside location gives guests ideal access to jogging, cycling, tennis and golf, as well as a front row seat to floral parades, concerts and hula shows. The Kaimana is also headquarters for the Diamond Head Climbers Hui, for adventurers who have hiked to the top of Hawaii's most famous landmark. For ocean lovers, equipment is available for snorkeling and kayaking.

Address: 2863 Kalakaua Avenue, Honolulu, HI 96815
Phone: 808-923-1555
Toll-Free: 800-356-8264
Fax: 808-922-9404
E-mail: kaimana@pixi.com
Web site: http://www.kaimana.com
Room Rates: $$
Suite Rates: $$$
Credit Cards: Most credit cards accepted
No. of Rooms: 124 **Suites:** 30
Services and Amenities: Valet service, Parking, Beauty shop, International currency exchange, Baby-sitting service, Laundry service, Cable TV, Video cassette player, Radio, Phone in bath, Complimentary toiletries, Access to New Otani Frequent Visitor Club
Restrictions: No pets allowed, Some handicapped access
Concierge: 8:00 a.m.–4:00 p.m.
Room Service: 7:00 a.m.–9:00 p.m.
Restaurant: Hau Tree Lanai, 7:00 a.m.–9:00 p.m., Miyako Japanese Restaurant, 6:00 p.m. nightly
Bar: Sunset Lanai, 11:00 a.m.–11:30 p.m., weekdays, 11:30 a.m.–11:30 p.m. weekends
Business Facilities: Message center, Secretarial service, Copiers, Audio-Visual, Fax, Personal computer
Conference Rooms: 3 rooms
Sports Facilities: Fitness Center, Park adjacent to hotel, Public tennis courts, Bicycling, Riding, Kayaking, Snorkeling
Location: Waikiki on Pacific Ocean, Gold Coast/Diamond Head area, 5 miles to downtown
Attractions: Hike Diamond Head and receive Diamond Head Climbers Hui certificate, 10 minutes walk from Waikiki, On Sans Souci Beach

IHILANI RESORT & SPA

The feeling of serenity is very special at Ihilani which translates as "heavenly splendor." Guests feel as if they are on a private, outer island, yet Honolulu and the night life of Waikiki are within a half hour's drive. Once a place where ancient Hawaiian royalty played, the Ihilani is situated in an unspoiled area with two miles of pristine, white-sand beaches, tropical vegetation and the sparkling Pacific Ocean teeming with active marine life.

Perched on one of four magnificent lagoon sites, Ihilani Resort & Spa features 387 rooms in its sleek fifteen-story structure, illuminated by a magnificent glass-domed atrium complete with tropical fish, soft foliage and orchids. 42 beautiful suites, including a stunning Presidential Suite, offer prime appointments and the ultimate in amenities.

Guest rooms feature soft white tones, plush carpeting, individually controlled air-conditioning, large screen TV and floor-to-ceiling sliding glass doors which open onto a private lanai, edged with bougainvillea and dressed with cushioned teak garden furniture. The luxurious marble bathroom, stocked with complimentary spa products, includes a deep-soak tub with European hand-held sprayer wand. 85% of all guest rooms showcase ocean or lagoon vistas.

Azul, Ihilani's signature restaurant, draws from a Mediterranean theme for both food and decor. A wood-burning brick oven and grill greets visitors in the mahogany wood-trimmed dining room ornamented with hand-painted ceramics.

A showcase of the Ihilani is its full-service spa. Among the truly unique treatments is Thalasso therapy, an underwater massage in saltwater. Other services available include Swedish massage, Shiatsu or Lomi Lomi massage, herbal wraps of relaxing chamomile or sassafras, and hydro treatments. To complete the resort spa experience, there is an outdoor swimming pool, complete fitness center and tennis club.

Address: 92-1001 Olani Street, Kapolei, HI 96707
Phone: 808-679-0079
Toll-Free: 800-626-4446
Fax: 808-679-0080
E-mail: ihilani@oceanic.net
Web site: http://www.ihilani.com
Room Rates: $$$$
Suite Rates: $$$$
Credit Cards: Most credit cards accepted
No. of Rooms: 387 **Suites:** 36
Services and Amenities: Valet service, Garage & Parking, Beauty shop, Gift shop, House nurse, International currency exchange, Laundry service, Baby-sitting service, Cable TV, Wet bar, Complimentary newspaper & toiletries
Restrictions: No pets allowed, 14 rooms equipped for handicapped access, Children welcome
Concierge: 7:00 a.m.–11:00 p.m.
Room Service: 24 hours
Restaurant: Azul Restaurant, 6:30 p.m.–10:00 p.m., Dress code
Bar: Hokulea, 5:00 p.m.–Midnight
Business Facilities: Full scale conference facilities, E-mail, Copier, Audio-Visual, Modem, Fax
Conference Rooms: 9 rooms, capacity 420
Sports Facilities: Spa, Outdoor swimming pool, Whirlpool, Sauna, Massage, Weight training, Golf, Tennis-6 Kramer Sports surfaces, Children's program
Location: Adjacent to Paradise Cove Luau
Attractions: Guests feel as if they are on a private island, Honolulu night life and Waikiki are within half hour drive, Complimentary shopping shuttle to Waikiki, Waikele and Ala Moana Shopping Centers, Thalasso therepy available

LAHAINA INN

Voted one of the ten most romantic country inns by American Historic Inns, the Lahaina Inn is steeped in turn-of-the-century charm. Built originally as a general merchandise store by the Maui Trading Company, Ltd., the Inn retains the frontier storefront facade, while the 12 guest rooms represent perhaps the most lavish combination of restored authentic frontier opulence and modern comfort in Hawaii.

Each room is designed in a different style of period wallpaper and coordinated hangings, with the rich warmth of Oriental rugs, romantic beds and furnishings of carved wood or brass, handquilted bed covers, antique armoires and stained glass lamps. Many of the furnishings come from owner Rick Ralston's own antique collection.

Guests may listen to taped classical music in air-conditioned comfort while relaxing in yukatas—Japanese cotton robes. Breakfast is savored on private balconies overlooking historic Old Lahaina Town.

Old Lahaina offers many fine restaurants. The best of them is David Paul's Lahaina Grill, located right in the Lahaina Inn. Voted best Maui restaurant for each of the past three years by Honolulu Magazine, the Lahaina Grill is known for David's innovations in North American and Pacific Rim cuisine. Try the tequila shrimp with firecracker rice, after an appetizer of eggplant Napoleon or lobster gazpacho Martini. Finish with Macadamia Nut Caramel Flan. Nightly selections also include fresh-caught Hawaiian fish.

Guests can walk to the beach for snorkeling, sailing, ocean cruises, and whale-watching, visit the Lahaina Whaling Museum, tour the square-rigged Brig Carthaginian, or go antique and art hunting. Tennis and golf are also nearby. Another option is that private balcony with its wicker rocker for just enjoying the lazy tropical ambiance of Old Hawaii.

Address: 127 Lahainaluna Road, Lahaina, Maui, HI 96761-1502
Phone: 808-661-0577
Toll-Free: 800-669-3444
Fax: 808-667-9480
Room Rates: $
Suite Rates: $$
Credit Cards: Visa, MC, AmEx, Discover
No. of Rooms: 9 **Suites:** 3
Services and Amenities: Parking, Balconies/decks, Complimentary newspaper, Telephones, Robes, Complimentary toiletries
Restrictions: No pets allowed, Children 15 and over welcome
Concierge: 10:00 a.m.–4:00 p.m.
Restaurant: David Paul's Lahaina Grill, 6:00 p.m.–1:00 a.m.
Bar: 6:00 p.m.–1:00 a.m.
Business Facilities: Copiers, Fax
Sports Facilities: Sailing, Snorkeling, Scuba, Waterskiing, Parasailing, Hiking, Biking, Golf and Tennis nearby
Location: Old Lahaina Town
Attractions: Beaches, Water sports, Whale watching, Harbor and sunset cruises, Antique and art shopping, Pacific Rim cuisine

THE LODGE AT KOELE

The Lodge at Koele has the ambiance of a worldly plantation-owner's residence. It is designed in the manner of a grand estate or country lodge, with heavy timbers, beamed ceilings and natural stone fireplaces. A large porch with lounging chairs provides a relaxing spot from which to view spectacular Hawaiian sunsets.

The Great Hall, the heart of the Lodge, is appointed with comfortable, large-scale furnishings and unique art objects, paintings, sculptures and rare artifacts of the Pacific. Striking octagonal corner rooms offer the perfect place for the most care worn traveler to retreat.

The guestrooms continue the "plantation" theme with carved fourposter beds, quilted pillows, colorful paintings by local artists, and carpets custom-made in radiant Hawaiian colors. The bathrooms feature Verde Issorie marble counter tops and floors in blue and white tiles.

For casual dining, the Terrace Dining Room overlooks the Lodge's Great Hall and outdoor gardens. The formal Dining Room is a fine dining area which features sophisticated cuisine, blending the best of Lanai's freshest ingredients with classic contemporary American and Pacific Rim techniques. A favorite dish here is the Lanai venison loin with Molokai sweet potato puree. The Tea Room is a cozy area for drinks, hors d'oeuvres and music.

The Lanai Pine Sporting Clays is the only resort sporting clays course in Hawaii. The rustic 14-station course is situated within a 200 -acre pine-wooded valley overlooking Molokai. The course is designed to appeal to both skilled and new shooters alike. Guests may choose to participate in the different sporting games, or just stroll along paved walkways and enjoy the unmatched scenery.

Address: P.O. Box 310, Lana'i City, HI 96763
Phone: 808-565-7300
Toll-Free: 800-321-4666
Fax: 808-565-4561
E-mail: reservations@lanai-resorts.com
Web site: http://www.lanai-resorts.com
Room Rates: $$$$
Suite Rates: $$$$
Credit Cards: Most credit cards accepted
No. of Rooms: 102 **Suites:** 14
Services and Amenities: Valet, Parking, Car hire, Beauty & Gift shops, Laundry, Currency exchange, Baby-sitting, Children's program, Card/game area, Library, Some suites with fireplace/wet bar, Balconies, Cable TV/VCR, Radio, Robes, Complimentary toiletries, minibars & shoeshine
Restrictions: No pets allowed, Children under 15 free with parents, 12 rooms handicapped-equipped
Concierge: 6:30 a.m.–10:30 p.m.
Room Service: 6:00 a.m.–9:30 p.m.
Restaurant: Terrace Dining Room, 7:00 a.m.–9:30 p.m., Formal Dining Room (dress code evenings), 6:00 p.m.–9:30 p.m.
Bar: Tea Room, 11:00 a.m.–11:00 p.m., Koele Club House, Afternoon Tea
Business Facilities: Secretarial service, Copiers, Audio-Visual, Full-scale facility at Lana'i Conference Center
Conference Rooms: 4 rooms, capacity 25
Sports Facilities: Fitness center, Outdoor swimming pool, Jacuzzi, Croquet, 18-hole golf course, Sailing, Tennis, Horseback riding, The Spa at Manele
Location: 1 mile to Lana'i City
Attractions: Four-wheel drive excursions, Mountain biking, Hunting, Hiking, Sporting clays, Scuba & snorkeling, Tackle fishing, Ocean rafting, Executive putting course

THE MANELE BAY HOTEL

The Manele Bay Hotel sits high above Hulopo'e Bay, Lanai's finest white sand beach, overlooking the nearby island of Kaho'olawe. The brilliant red lava cliffs and rock formations provide a dramatic contrast to the blue-green waters of the sea below. Multi-level gardens are in five different themes—Hawaiian, Japanese, Chinese, Bromeliad and Kama'aina—with waterfalls, ponds and streams, exotic plants and flowers.

The lobby features stunning views and original works of Lanai's native artists. Guests may browse through books, photography and view artifacts on display.

Guestrooms are spacious and offer views of the ocean, sculptured gardens and waterfalls. Interior decor reflects Mediterranean and Asian influences—custom-designed tile and wall-coverings incorporate five different color schemes—English yellow, Caribbean blue, Mandarin red and other hues. The bathroom features his and hers marble sinks, wall mirror, marble countertop, separate shower stall and separate toilet room. A lighted make-up mirror, hair dryer and other accessories are available for guest use.

The dramatic setting of the Manele Bay Hotel affords many opportunities for guests to enjoy a variety of dining experiences with unparalleled views. Utilizing Hawaii's unique fresh products and reflecting a diverse blend of cultures, the Hulopo'e Court serves contemporary Hawaii regional cuisine. Dine informally under a bougainvillea covered trellis at the Pool Grille, which offers an array of sandwiches and lighter fare keeping today's healthier lifestyle in mind. Ihilani (heavenly splendor) is an intimate dining room featuring French Mediterranean gourmet cuisine. Here, guests will be greeted by staff and seated at tables with crystal and silver. A favorite dish is the Sauteed Fresh Shrimp, Hearts of Palm and Prosciutto Salad with Mango. For dessert, don't miss the Strawberry Sunburst.

For those with an adventuresome spirit, Lanai is an explorer's mecca. There are many excellent hiking trails through lush forests, over rugged grasslands and beside pristine shorelines.

Address: P.O. Box 310, Lana'i City, HI 96763
Phone: 808-565-7700
Toll-Free: 800-321-4666
Fax: 808-565-2483
E-mail: reservations@lanai-resorts.com
Web site: http://www.lanai-resorts.com
Room Rates: $$$$
Suite Rates: $$$$
Credit Cards: Most credit cards accepted
No. of Rooms: 250 **Suites:** 26
Services and Amenities: Valet service, Parking, Car hire, Beauty shop, Laundry, Gift shop, TV lounge, Baby-sitting service, Card/game area, Children's program, Library, Balconies, Cable TV, VCR, Radio, Air-conditioning, Robes, Complimentary toiletries, shoeshine, paper & coffee
Restrictions: No pets allowed, Children under 15 free with parents, 4 rooms handicapped-equipped
Concierge: 6:00 a.m.–10:30 p.m.
Room Service: 6:00 a.m.–9:30 p.m.
Restaurant: Hulopo'e Court, 7:00 a.m.–9:30 p.m., Pool Grille, 11:00 a.m.–5:00 p.m., Ihilani, 6:00–9:30 p.m. (dress code), Challenge at Manele Clubhouse, 11:00 a.m.–5:00 p.m.
Bar: Pool Grille & Challenge Bars 11:00 a.m.–5:00 p.m., Hale Ahe Ahe 5:00–11:00 p.m.
Business Facilities: Message center, Secretarial service, Copiers, Audio-Visual
Conference Rooms: 6 rooms plus Lanai Conference Center, capacity 299
Sports Facilities: Outdoor swimming pool, Croquet, Jacuzzi, Sauna, Massage, Aerobics, Weight training, Golf, Sailing, Horseback riding, Tennis, Spa
Location: Hulopo'e Bay, 20 minutes-Manele Bay airport, 30 minutes-Honolulu Airport
Attractions: Four-wheel drive excursions, Hiking, Nearby ocean activities: beachcombing, scuba, snorkeling, rafting and fishing

OLD NORTHERN INN

With its steep shingled roof, plank floors, cedar paneling and wrap-around verandahs, the Old Northern Inn represents a nostalgic return to the rustic country lodges of the 1890s. Once a home away from home for miners on vacation, the original log building has been completely and authentically restored by owners Phil and Lorraine Battaglia. It is set on the shores of Priest Lake, a scenic 90-minute drive from Spokane and just over an hour's drive from beautiful Lake Coeur d'Alene and Lake Pend Oreille.

Amenities include a small marina, swimming and sunning beach, volleyball court and fishing, as well as a large deck overlooking the lake with comfortable lounge chairs and a huge outdoor fireplace. Not far away are hiking trails, canoe and sailboat rentals, lakeside resorts with gourmet restaurants, and museums. Guided fishing excursions may also be arranged.

Each room features antique country furnishings, a goosedown comforter and forest-green Ralph Lauren bathrobes. Room rates include a home-cooked breakfast for two served in the Cedar Dining Room with fresh specialties including Priest Lake Huckleberries. Wine, cheese and fruit are served every afternoon.

The comfortable living room is filled with old books and antique furniture, some with hand-painted folk designs. The mahogany mantel over the huge stone fireplace is inscribed "Warm your hands and warm your hearts." The Old Northern Inn is perfect for those who seek the slow rhythm of a simpler time.

Address: P.O.Box 177, Lakeshore Road, Priest Lake, Coolin, ID 83821
Phone: 208-443-2426
Fax: 208-443-2426
Room Rates: $
Suite Rates: $$
Credit Cards: Visa, MC
No. of Rooms: 6 **Suites:** 2
Services and Amenities: Garage and parking, Card/game area, Telephones, Robes, Complimentary toiletries and newspaper, Complimentary breakfast, afternoon wine and cheese
Restrictions: No pets allowed, 1 room handicapped-equipped, No children under 12 please
Concierge: 8:00 a.m.–7:00 p.m.
Restaurant: Cedar Dining Room, 8:00–10:00 a.m. (breakfast)
Business Facilities: Message center, Secretarial center and Fax available
Sports Facilities: Golf, Sailing, Swimming, Boating, Water skiing, Hiking, Fishing, Volleyball, Private marina
Location: South Shore, Priest Lake
Attractions: Large 26 mile lake with timbered islands in the Selkirk mountains, Bordering on Canada, Entree Gallery, Museum at Luby Bay

HOTEL ALLEGRO CHICAGO

Located in the heart of Chicago's downtown Loop area, the Hotel Allegro Chicago brings with it a sense of excitement and entertainment celebrating the city's rich musical, artistic and theatrical style. Following a dramatic renovation of the former Bismarck Hotel, the once elegant grande dame of Chicago hotels has been transformed into a stylish, energetic environment. The hotel's decor features a mix of the classic and the contemporary, thanks to the vision of award-winning designer Cheryl Rowley, who has preserved elements of the Bismarck's original 1920 design, while incorporating deluxe, modern furniture looks and textures.

The guest rooms at the Hotel Allegro Chicago are unique in every aspect. There are nine varieties of guest rooms and suite types to choose from, each awash in brilliant color. A typical guest room may include walls wrapped in a lively pink grapefruit wall-covering with beds draped in a luxurious melon and magenta colored bedspread. Sea foam green throw pillows sprinkled with gold stars and an over-scaled, black wood trim headboard with wide, cream and bittersweet chocolate stripes complete the bed. Each rooms boasts an oval, cherry wood desk that rolls on casters for maximum usability. A plethora of amenities are provided in guest rooms including a two-line speaker telephone with data ports, fax machine, custom designed armoire, an honor bar, remote color television, CD "boombox" stereo with cassette player, hair dryer, and a variety of toiletries.

The Hotel Allegro Chicago's outstanding restaurant, 312 Chicago, features the Italian-inspired cuisine of Chef Dean Zanella for breakfast, lunch and dinner. A delightful, savory dining experience can be expected with a wide variety of fresh, skillfully blended ingredients. Start with a bibb, raddicchio and endive salad with fresh mozzarella and vine ripened tomatoes complimented by a light balsamic vinaigrette dressing. Move onto the next course with chilean sea bass in a lemon white wine broth and three pepper confetti. End with a mouth watering dessert such as a piece of truffled chocolate mousse cake topped with white chocolate sauce.

Offering a rare combination of high style, sophistication and exemplary personal service, the Hotel Allegro Chicago will do doubt meet the needs of the most discerning leisure or business traveller.

Address: 171 West Randolph Street at LaSalle, Chicago, IL 60601
Phone: 312-236-0123
Toll-Free: 800-643-1500
Fax: 312-236-3177
Room Rates: $$
Suite Rates: $$$
Credit Cards: Most credit cards accepted
No. of Rooms: 483 **Suites:** 31
Services and Amenities: Valet service, Same-day laundry service, Early morning coffee service & evening wine hour, Safety deposit boxes available, Gift shop, Hair salon, Shoe shine, Color TVs with remote & on-demand movies, Two-line speaker telephones, Modem ports, In-room fax
Restrictions: Non-smoking rooms available
Concierge: Full services
Room Service: 6:30 a.m.–10:30 p.m.
Restaurant: 312 Chicago, 220-seat free-standing restaurant with access to hotel lobby serving breakfast, lunch and dinner
Business Facilities: Printer, Fax, Overnight delivery
Conference Rooms: 12 rooms, capacity 400, 13,500 sq. ft.
Sports Facilities: On-site fitness center, Access to nearby health club with indoor swimming pool
Location: Heart of Chicago's downtown Loop area, Directly across from City Hall
Attractions: Minutes from shopping the "Magnificent Mile" including Water Tower Place & Bloomingdale's, State Street, Grant Park, Art Institute of Chicago, New Symphony Center, Navy Pier, McCormick Place, United Center, City Hall, State of Illinois Building,

LENOX SUITES

The inviting lobby of Chicago's Lenox Suites is the prelude to the hotel's intimate European style. Traditional details such as polished cherry woods, marble flooring and rich tapestry fabrics gracing the upholstered walls provide a familiar comfort. Guests are welcomed by fresh flowers and an original bronze sculpture by J. Seward Johnson, Jr., which adds a touch of whimsy.

Suites are done in soothing tones of hunter green, burgundy, gold and blue, with handsome traditional furnishings. Each suite includes a wet bar with fresh coffee and tea, a complimentary in-suite continental breakfast, a complimentary weekday newspaper, a mini-snack and beverage bar, two telephones, cable TV and private bath with a full line of toiletries. Corner suites are exceptionally large and provide panoramic views of world-renowned Michigan Avenue and Lake Michigan.

Freshly decorated meeting facilities accommodate up to 35 in a theater-style arrangement, up to 30 for conferences and banquets, and receptions up to 60 persons.

For dining, visit the nationally acclaimed Houston's Restaurant serving lunch, dinner and cocktails in a warm and friendly atmosphere that is casually elegant with oak paneling and comfortable banquets.

Other on-site amenities at "Chicago's European-Style Hotel" include a fitness center, valet and self parking, a gift and sundry shop, laundry and valet services, and Business Center and services. Chicago's most celebrated shops, restaurants, nightlife, galleries and museums are just a short walk away.

Address: 616 North Rush Street, Chicago, IL 60611
Phone: 312-337-1000
Toll-Free: 800-44-LENOX
Fax: 312-573-3586
E-mail: lenoxsuite@aol.com
Web site: http://www.hotelbook.com
Suite Rates: $$
Credit Cards: Most credit cards accepted
No. of Suites: 324
Services and Amenities: Valet service, Garage parking, Chauffeured town car transportation, Concierge service, Laundry service, Gift shop, Cable TV, Modem-ready telephones, Radio, Wet bar, Toiletries, Complimentary weekday newspaper, Complimentary continental breakfast
Restrictions: No pets allowed, One child under 17 free if sharing parent's room, 15 handicapped-equipped rooms
Concierge: 7 days a week
Room Service: 6:00 a.m.–11:00 p.m.
Restaurant: Houston's, Monday-Thursday 11:00 a.m.–11:00 p.m., Friday-Saturday 11:00 a.m.–midnight, Sunday 11:30 a.m.–10:00 p.m.
Bar: Houston's, same hours
Business Facilities: Message center, Secretarial center, Copiers, Audio-Visual, Fax, Modems
Conference Rooms: 2 rooms
Sports Facilities: Complimentary fitness center
Location: Downtown Chicago, the "Magnificent Mile" area
Attractions: Michigan Avenue, Shopping, Restaurants, Theatre, Nightlife, Lake Michigan beaches, Cultural center, Water Tower Place, Navy Pier/North Pier, Art Institute of Chicago, Opera House, Orchestra Hall, John G. Shedd Aquarium, Adler Planetarium, Numerous museums

THE CHECKERBERRY INN

A solid retreat in the unspoiled rolling countryside of Northern Indiana, the Georgian-style Checkerberry Inn sits on 100 acres surrounded by Amish farms. This elegant country inn is ideal for quiet relaxation and re-charging. Sit on the wicker-lined front porch and watch the rush hour traffic of horse-drawn buggies clip-clop by. Walk the extensive grounds and lose yourself in the 20 acres of wild woods. Many also come to the area to visit Notre Dame or to shop for Amish quilts and antiques.

The Inn itself sparkles with freshness and flowers. The style is crisp and elegant country, reflecting a clean and comfortable midwestern ambiance. Guest rooms are individually decorated and named after flowers, each with a spectacular green and tranquil view. Suites are spacious and airy with cathedral ceilings and original art.

Dinner is served in The Checkerberry Restaurant with its French doors, large fireplace with French tile, fresh flowers, hand embroidered tablecloths and brass chargers. The menu is not extensive, but is exquisite and varies with the season. Don't miss the grilled duck breast, but check for the evening's specials. Your plate will be full of the best and freshest produce from the surrounding farmlands. Desserts vary nightly, but don't worry, chocolate should be on the menu.

Guests can spend their days lounging around the library and common rooms, shopping and touring, or catching a college football game. There is an outdoor swimming pool, professional croquet court, tennis court, and routes for cycling and jogging. Whatever choice you make The Checkerberry Inn and its caring staff will pamper you and send you off refreshed.

Address: 62644 Country Road 37, Goshen, IN 46526
Phone: 219-642-4445
Fax: 219-642-4445
Room Rates: $$
Suite Rates: $$$
Credit Cards: AmEx, Visa, MC
No. of Rooms: 11 **Suites:** 2
Services and Amenities: Breakfast included, Lunch available, No minimum stay, Parking, TV lounge, Card/game area, Library, Baby-sitting service, Television, Telephone, Radio, Central heat and air-conditioning, Complimentary toiletries
Restrictions: No pets, No smoking, Children limited, No out-of-state checks, 1 room equipped for handicapped
Room Service: 8:00 a.m.–8:00 p.m.
Restaurant: The Checkerberry Restaurant, 6:00 p.m.–10:00 p.m., Casual elegant attire
Business Facilities: Message center, Copiers
Conference Rooms: 3 rooms, capacity 30
Sports Facilities: Outdoor swimming pool, Croquet, Tennis court (asphalt), 10 golf courses nearby, Biking, Walking
Location: Pastoral countryside, 30 miles from South Bend Michiana Regional Airport
Attractions: Notre Dame, Amish communities, Working farms, Good walking

DAUPHINE ORLEANS HOTEL - FRENCH QUARTER

Beautifully situated in the historic Storyville section of downtown New Orleans is the quaint French Quarter Dauphine Orleans Hotel. This 109-room landmark is a tribute to the successful blend of restored townhouses and faithfully recaptured design of Vieux Carré. Carefully maintained, the Hotel is resplendent with palm-draped courtyards, wrought iron balconies and shaded patios.

Extended courtesies begin on arrival, with an invitation to cocktails and hors d'oeuvres in May Baily's Place, whose name recalls the boisterous era of the city's "sporting house" past. Charmingly-appointed rooms and suites are amply complemented with amenities such as mini-bars stocked with wines, liquors, soft drinks and snacks. EverGreen Rooms are also available which are allergen and smoke free. Your morning paper arrives in time to accompany you to a complimentary bountiful continental breakfast in the cheerful Coffee Lounge. Enjoy, too, the cable TV with HBO, nightly turn-down service, outdoor swimming pool and extensive library.

The Audubon Room, named for John James Audubon, who completed his acclaimed "Birds of America" while a resident here, is an accommodating and artistic setting for conferences and meetings.

Famous restaurants are within a short stroll of Dauphine Orleans, and a jaunt away are the sights, sounds and colorful attractions of legendary New Orleans.

The Dauphine Orleans Hotel—French Quarter will pamper you with its unsurpassed hospitality.

Address: 415 Rue Dauphine, New Orleans, LA 70112
Phone: 504-586-1800
Toll-Free: 800-521-7111
Fax: 504-586-9630
E-mail: dohfq@aol.com
Web site: http://www.dauphineorleans.com
Room Rates: $$
Suite Rates: $$$
Credit Cards: AmEx, DC, CB, Visa, MC, DS
No. of Rooms: 109 **Suites:** 9
Services and Amenities: Valet service, Garage, Downtown transportation, Welcome cocktail, Complimentary continental breakfast & newspaper, Afternoon tea, Baby-sitting service, Library, Cable TV, Radio, Mini-bar, Climate control, Patios, Suites with whirlpool, Robes, In-room safe
Restrictions: Non-smoking rooms available, Children under 17 stay free
Concierge: 6:00 a.m.–11:00 p.m.
Room Service: Breakfast, Cocktails
Bar: May Baily's Place, weekdays: 3:30 p.m.–midnight, weekends: noon—midnight
Business Facilities: Copiers and Fax service
Conference Rooms: 3 rooms
Sports Facilities: Outdoor swimming pool, Whirlpool, Fitness facility, Rivercenter Racquetball Club privileges extended to guests
Location: French Quarter, 2 miles from highway, 15 miles from airport
Attractions: Lively French Quarter attractions, Boutiques, Antique shops, Restaurants, Riverboats, Music, Plantation & Swamp Tours

BALANCE ROCK INN

This beautifully restored oceanfront mansion has spectacular views which can be seen from most of the 14 guestrooms. Built in 1903 in the Colonial Revival style, the Balance Rock is located on 3 acres of oceanfront land.

The foyer uses rose and grey colors along with oriental rugs, polished hardwood floors and ornate painted woodwork. The sunny living room has a fireplace, grand piano, overstuffed furniture and oil paintings throughout.

A typical guestroom is large and sunny with a queen-size canopy bed, writing desk, sitting area with fireplace, reproduction antique furniture, print wallpaper and wall-to-wall carpeting. Fresh flowers and plants add to the cozy atmosphere.

Breakfast is served in the lovely dining area with plush navy blue carpeting, floral wallpaper, and cushioned Queen Anne chairs. Wedgewood china and Oneida silver are used for the service. The Balance Rock is famous for its crepes! Afternoon tea is also available from 3-5 p.m.

There are many ocean activities if you so choose… whale watching, cruises, sailing, kayaking, island explorations and of course beaches for lounging and swimming.

The Balance Rock is the only restored oceanfront mansion with modern amenities in the area.

Address: 21 Albert Meadow, Bar Harbor, ME 04609
Phone: 207-288-2610
Toll-Free: 800-753-0494
Fax: 207-288-5534
Room Rates: $$
Suite Rates: $$$
Credit Cards: MC, Visa, AmEx, Discover
No. of Rooms: 19 **Suites:** 2
Services and Amenities: Laundry, Baby-sitting, Fireplaces (8 rooms), Balconies (11 rooms), Cable TV/VCR, Audio cassette player, Wet bar, Individual heat/air-conditioning controls, Gilcrest & Somes toiletries, Whirlpool, Complimentary newspaper, breakfast & afternoon tea 3-5 p.m.
Restrictions: No infants, Children under 4 free, One room for pets
Concierge: 8:00 a.m.–11:00 p.m.
Room Service: 8:00 a.m.–10:00 a.m.
Restaurant: Breakfast only, 8:00 a.m.–10:00 a.m.
Business Facilities: Message center, Copiers
Conference Rooms: 1 room, capacity 20
Sports Facilities: Exercise room
Location: Oceanfront/Historic Shorepath
Attractions: Acadia National Park & Carriage Paths, Whale watching cruises, Beaches, Birdwatching

BAR HARBOR HOTEL – BLUENOSE INN

Set atop a granite-terrace hillside with spectacular views of sparkling Frenchman Bay and close proximity to Acadia National Park, the Bar Harbor Hotel—Bluenose Inn is one of the most beautiful spots on the Atlantic.

Attention to detail and gracious service are why the Bar Harbor Hotel—Bluenose Inn is the only Oceanview Resort in Maine to earn the prestigious AAA Four Diamond and Mobil Guide Four Stars Awards of Excellence with AAA Four Diamond dining at the Rose Garden Restaurant.

In the beautifully appointed Queen-Anne style rooms, amenities include air-conditioning, cable TV with HBO movies, telephones and mini-refrigerator. Guests in the spacious Mizzentop suites, beautifully detailed in mauve, burgundy and green Waverly fabrics, may relax in fluffy robes to view breathtaking sunrises over Frenchman Bay. A king bed, love seat, easy chairs and crystal chandeliers provide comfort and grace. Walls are adorned with distinctive artwork. Many rooms and suites also have romantic fireplaces.

Creative cuisine, candle light, classic white china and Waverly "Roses" fabrics amid potted plants provide the perfect setting for Four Diamond dining at the Rose Garden. Try the Maine crab cakes and a decadent dessert of flourless chocolate cake while perusing the expertly prepared Wine List. Enjoy a selection of ports and single malt whiskies here or in the Great Room with its plush and inviting furnishings, magnificent fireplace and handcrafted cherry-wood bar—offering entertainment most evenings.

Sports facilities include a spa, fitness center, and outdoor heated pool with ocean views and undoubtedly New England's most beautiful indoor pool.

The Bar Harbor Hotel—Bluenose Inn is a leisurely stroll from Bar Harbor with its many activities and historic sites, and is only 600 yards to the dock where the famed Bluenose Ferry makes its daily trip to and from Nova Scotia. Bicycling, kayaking, harbor cruises and whale watching are among the favorite ways to enjoy Bar Harbor and Acadia National Park.

Address: 90 Eden Street, Bar Harbor, ME 04609
Phone: 207-288-3348
Toll-Free: 800-445-4077
Fax: 207-288-2183
E-mail: bhotel@acadia.net
Web site: http://www.acadia.net/bluenose
Room Rates: $$
Suite Rates: $$
Credit Cards: Visa, MC
No. of Rooms: 97 **Suites:** 31
Services and Amenities: Garage & parking, Gift shop, Balconies/decks, Laundry service, Cable TV, Telephones, Radio, Air-conditioning, Robes, Complimentary toiletries and newspaper
Restrictions: No pets allowed, 52 rooms handicapped-equipped
Room Service: 7:00 a.m.–9:30 p.m.
Restaurant: The Rose Garden, 7:00–11:00 a.m., 6:00–9:30 p.m., Dressy/Casual
Bar: The Great Room, 5:00 p.m.–closing
Business Facilities: Copiers, Fax
Conference Rooms: 1 room, capacity 65
Sports Facilities: Indoor & outdoor pools, Whirlpool, Fitness Center, Nearby massage, Sailing, Riding, Tennis, Hiking, Biking—Acadia National Park
Location: Eden Street
Attractions: Acadia National Park, Village pier, Shops and restaurants, Bluenose ferry to Nova Scotia

INN BY THE SEA

Located within Crescent Beach State Park, one of Maine's finest sand beaches, is the Inn by the Sea. The award-winning architecture of the Inn is reminiscent of the Cottage Shingled design of the 1890s. Surrounded by lush green lawns and ever-blooming perennials, the main house offers 25 one-bedroom suites and the adjacent cottages offer 18 two-bedroom suites—each with full kitchen, living/dining areas and patio or porch overlooking the Atlantic Ocean.

Guest rooms in the main house are furnished with Chippendale cherry and floral chintz fabrics, while the cottages are furnished with natural wicker and simple white pine pieces; all are accented with original art. A unique collection of hand colored engravings by John J. Audubon are on display throughout the dining room and lobby area.

Indulge your senses and enjoy a gourmet dining experience in the romantic and intimate atmosphere of the Audubon Room. The menu offers new American regional cuisine with contemporary French overtones. There is always a variety of menu selections, offering only the freshest and finest of Maine's local gardens, fields and orchards. Native hand-picked seafood specialties provide the perfect compliment to the most impressive wine selections. Some house favorites include Grilled Salmon with an Orange Basil Vinaigrette, Wild Mushroom Risotto, Sauteed Oysters with Porcini Mushrooms, and for dessert, Chocolate Marquis with Cappuccino Hazelnut Cream. Breakfast and dinner are served daily. During the summer, lunch and poolside service are available. The outdoor terrace is also open during the warmer months for evening cocktails and hors d'oeuvres.

A private boardwalk, leading through a beautiful natural estuary to the white sandy shore of Crescent Beach, is one of the highlights of the Inn. Amenities such as bicycles, tennis, outdoor pool, croquet field and shuffleboard are also offered. Sailing and excursion tours are available at the nearby Portland waterfront, as is an eclectic array of shops and restaurants in the Old Port district.

Address: 40 Bowery Beach Road, Route 77, Cape Elizabeth, ME 04107
Phone: 207-799-3134
Toll-Free: 800-888-4287
Fax: 207-799-4779
E-mail: innmain@aol.com
Web site: http://www.innbythesea.com
Suite Rates: $$
Credit Cards: Visa, MC, AmEx, DS
No. of Suites: 43
Services and Amenities: Valet service, Parking, Baby-sitting service, Library, Balconies, Cabel TV, Radio, 3 telephones per suite, Individual heat controls, Robes, Complimentary toiletries
Restrictions: No smoking
Room Service: 7:00 a.m.–9:00 p.m.
Restaurant: The Audubon Room, 7:00 a.m.–9:00 p.m.
Business Facilities: Full-scale conference facilities
Conference Rooms: 2 rooms, capacity 60
Sports Facilities: Outdoor swimming pool, Croquet, Volleyball, Shuffleboard, Bicycles, Walking/jogging trails, Golf and sailing nearby
Location: Quiet, Non-commercial location, Seaside setting, Nearest airport: Portland
Attractions: Walk the "Old Port" with specialty shops, Cobblestone streets and Brownstone buildings, 30 minutes to LL Bean, Portland Headlight just 7 minutes away

HARRASEEKET INN

The Harraseeket Inn is situated in the center of Freeport Village just two blocks from L.L. Bean. Upon entering the Harraseeket, the elegant mahogany panelling and cozy fireplaces exude the welcoming feel of an English country house.

In the guest rooms, the Colonial Revival theme is apparent from decorate touches of upholstered reproduction Colonial and Federal furniture and draperies. Many of the guest rooms and suites have working fireplaces.

The Harraseeket Inn's kitchen relies for its inspiration on locally-raised ingredients—the justly famous seafood of the Gulf of Maine, produce from area gardens, and game from farms just down the coast. The Inn encompasses two restaurants: The Main Dining Room, known as one of New England's best restaurants, serving exciting interpretations of New England regional cuisine; the Broad Arrow Tavern offering traditional Downeast cooking in an open kitchen with wood fired oven and grill with all the antique charm of an upcountry Maine hunting lodge. Al *fresco* dining on the terrace of the Inn's formal gardens makes for a perfect summertime repast. In keeping with the Inn's commitment to fresh, local, organically-raised foods, the menus change with the seasons. The Inn's award-winning wine list is one of the best in the Northeast.

Complimentary tea is served daily in the Drawing Room. Full breakfast buffet is also included in the room rates. Cocktails are served in the Tavern.

The Harraseeket Inn is perfectly located for day-trips to the rocky coastline, including Freeport's Wolfe Neck State Park and Mast Landing Audubon Society Center. Golf and skiing are within easy reach, and Portland, with its recreational, business, and cultural attractions, as well as its exciting night-life, is only a half-hour away.

The Inn's conference and banquet facilities and attention to the details of old-fashioned Maine hospitality are making it a destination of choice for business meetings, receptions, and unique weddings.

Address: 162 Main Street, Freeport, ME 04032
Phone: 207-865-9377
Toll-Free: 800-342-6423
Fax: 207-865-1684
E-mail: harraseeke@aol.com
Web site: http://www.stayfreeport.com
Room Rates: $$
Suite Rates: $$$
Credit Cards: Most credit cards accepted
No. of Rooms: 54 **Suites:** 4
Services and Amenities: Parking, Library, Game area, Gift shop, 40 non-smoking rooms, 15 in-room fireplaces, Cable TV, Radio, Robes, Whirlpool bath, Complimentary toiletries, Sewing kit, Complimentary breakfast and afternoon tea, Children welcome
Restrictions: No pets allowed
Concierge: Seasonal
Room Service: 7:00 a.m.–10:30 p.m.
Restaurant: Maine Dining Room, 7:00 a.m.–9:30 p.m., Broad Arrow Tavern, 11:30 a.m.–Midnight
Bar: Broad Arrow Tavern, 11:30 a.m.–Midnight
Business Facilities: Full conference facilities, Message center, Copiers, Audio-Visual, Fax
Conference Rooms: 4 rooms, capacity 250
Sports Facilities: Croquet, Fitness center, Indoor pool
Location: Center of Freeport Village, Nearest airport is Portland International
Attractions: L.L. Bean, 100-plus Outlets and Specialty shops, Wolfe Neck State Park, Close to: Portland, Bath Maritime Museum, Entire rockbound coast of Maine, Beaches

The Willows Historic Palm Springs Inn, Palm Springs, California. PAGE 37

VailGlo Lodge, Vail, Colorado. PAGE 73

The Wit's End Guest Ranch & Resort, *Durango, Colorado.* PAGE 72

THE COLONY HOTEL

Built in 1914, The Colony Hotel is a historic grand resort hotel serving the discerning guest from May through October. With majestic ocean front views and Edwardian architecture, this landmark establishment guides working and pleasure boats up into the mouth of the Kennebunk River. The Colony is Maine's first environmentally responsible hotel, certified and designated as a "US Backyard Wildlife Habitat".

The 125 smoke-free guestrooms are divided into four buildings with either garden or ocean views. The typical guestroom is "like your grandmother's summer house" with Waverly floral wallpapers, hardwood floor, antique needlepoint rugs, antique furniture, and mostly king sized beds. Each bath contains antique sinks, low flow toilets and massage showers. There is no television in the Main Hotel but there is a television room on the first floor for viewing. In other buildings there are color cable TV's in the rooms. There is no need for air-conditioning as the architecture has been designed to capture the sea breezes through the windows.

The Colony Hotel Dining Room is open to the public and features award-winning New England fare including lobster, the freshest seafood, local produce and sumptuous homemade desserts. Homemade breakfasts are served daily and the Ocean Terrace Lounge serves lunch poolside in July and August. The Marine Room Lounge offers drinks, entertainment and dancing almost every night. Complimentary refreshments are a Colony Hotel tradition serving afternoon tea with homebaked sweets. On Monday nights, there is a Manager's Cocktail Park for hotel guests.

The hotel offers naturalist programs on coastal Marine ecology as well as social programs including the history of lobstering, Marine art and architecture, dance lessons, movies and bingo. There are also outdoor activities such as putting, shuffleboard, horseshoes, croquet, bicycle rentals and volleyball. Guest may linger in the heated saltwater swimming pool, overlooking the ocean, or play in the surf of a private sandy beach. Guests are also extended privileges to the Cape Arundel Country Club for golf, and the River Club for tennis.

Address: 140 Ocean Avenue, P.O. Box 511, Kennebunkport, ME 04046
Phone: 207-967-3331
Toll-Free: 800-552-2363
Fax: 207-967-5551
E-mail: info-me@thecolonyhotel.com
Web site: http://www.thecolonyhotel.com/maine/
Room Rates: $
Credit Cards: Visa, AmEx, MC
No. of Rooms: 125
Services and Amenities: Parking, Gift shop, TV lounge, Card/Game Area, Library, Cable TV in some rooms, Telephone, Iron & Ironing board, Hair dryer, Individual heat control, Complimentary toiletries
Restrictions: Extra charge for children as well as pets, Smoke-free guestrooms
Room Service: Dining Room Hours
Restaurant: Colony Hotel Dining Room, 8:00 a.m.–8:30 p.m.
Bar: Marine Room Lounge
Business Facilities: Message center, E-mail, Copiers, Audio-Visual, Fax
Conference Rooms: 8 rooms, capacity 250
Sports Facilities: Heated outdoor saltwater pool, Croquet, 18-hole Putting Green, Volleyball, Biking, Horseshoes, Additional Sports Facilities Nearby
Location: Cape Arundel, Oceanside
Attractions: Within walking distance to Kennebunkport, art galleries, and boutiques; One mile to President George Bush's summer estate

KENNEBUNKPORT INN

The heart of the Kennebunkport Inn is a gracious late Victorian mansion built for a sea captain in the 1890's. The ideal blend of sophisticated small hotel and country inn, it has an intimate, personalized approach to service, yet is large enough to be entirely professional. Additional guest accommodations are located in the adjacent 1930's River House.

Each guest room is individually decorated with period antiques, reproductions, and selected wallpapers and fabrics. Many include poster beds and comfortable sitting areas, and some rooms have views of the salt-water river and waterfront.

The two gracious dining rooms are elegantly appointed with two working fireplaces, original paintings by local artists, chandeliers, deep carpeting and tables dressed in white linen. Under the direction of chef William Griffin, signature dishes including a real bouillabaisse, a grilled boneless duck breast with cranberry chutney, and desserts such as seasonal berry trifle are served elegantly by candlelight. In addition, the summer terrace called Martha's Vineyard provides an inviting warm-weather dining alternative. It overlooks Dock Square, with umbrella-topped tables, potted plants, and pleasant salt breezes. Guests enjoy nightly piano music in the Turn of the Century Pub, featuring an extensive wine list.

Perfectly located in the center of the charming village at Dock Square, the Inn is within walking distance to wonderful shops and galleries. The waterfront and the Historic District, a neighborhood of white-clapboard sea captains' homes, tree-shaded gardens and white picket fences are also just steps away.

The Kennebunkport Inn is a sophisticated small hotel with the authentic atmosphere of an elegant sea captain's mansion.

Address: One Dock Square, P.O. Box 111, Kennebunkport, ME 04046
Phone: 207-967-2621
Toll-Free: 800-967-2621
Fax: 207-967-3705
Room Rates: $
Suite Rates: $$
Credit Cards: Visa, MC, AmEx
No. of Rooms: 34 **Suites:** 1
Services and Amenities: Parking, Cable TV, Telephones, Private bath, Complimentary toiletries, Views of village and river, Kitchen and fireplace available
Restrictions: No pets allowed, Children welcome
Restaurant: Kennebunkport Inn Dining Room and seasonal Martha's Vineyard terrace dining, 8:00–10:00 a.m., noon-2:30 p.m., 6:00–9:00 p.m.
Bar: Turn of the Century Pub, 5:00 p.m.–Midnight
Business Facilities: Fax, Copier
Sports Facilities: Nearby five 9-and 18-hole golf courses, Tennis, Outdoor swimming pool
Location: Center of Kennebunkport, 1½ hours—Boston, 25 miles—Portland Jetport
Attractions: Walking distance to shops, Historic District and harbor, Day sailing, Sightseeing, Deep-sea fishing excursions, Boat charters, 1 mile to beach

THE WHITE BARN INN

One of the interesting features of East Coast vacation spots from New York northward is the number of historic farmhouses that have been restored and converted to lodgings. An example of this is the White Barn Inn, which is situated between woodlands and the rugged shoreline of Maine.

The hardwood floors of the original structure built in 1840 are still in place throughout the Inn today, complementing the 19th century antiques in the lobby. Period furnishings and armoires, accented by color-coordinated fabrics and wall coverings have been used throughout the guest accommodations. Suites feature king-size four-poster beds, wood-burning fireplaces, over-size marble bathrooms with whirlpool baths, fresh flowers, and a complimentary basket of fresh fruit. Among the amenities are twice daily maid service and thick robes.

The restaurant is in a carefully-restored three-story barn, with large picture windows. Tables are set with Villeroy and Boch China, crystal stemware and fresh flowers. Guests dine by candlelight and are entertained by a pianist as they enjoy their choices from a menu that lives up to the elegant surroundings and wine selections from a vastly expanded wine cellar. Dinner might begin with Foie Gras. The entree of choice is—what else—a steamed Maine Lobster on fresh fettucine, with carrots and ginger in a cognac and coral butter sauce. For dessert there is a rich chocolate mousse in a thin pastry crust with toasted hazelnuts and Frangelico whipped cream. A wine list is featured, as well as a variety of liquors, ports and cognacs.

Complimentary afternoon tea with fresh patisseries is served daily to hotel guests. Outdoor activities available nearby include riding one of the Inn's bicycles along a stunning stretch of coastline, sailing, deep sea fishing, ocean swimming, whale watching, monastery tours, or a five-minute walk to the heart of Kennebunkport with its antique shops, theater and galleries.

The White Barn Inn was named one of the most romantic hideaways for 1996 by *The Discerning Traveler*, and the restaurant has held the prestigious AAA Five Diamond rating consecutively for five years.

Address: 37 Beach Street, P.O. Box 560C, Kennebunkport, ME 04046
Phone: 207-967-2321
Fax: 207-967-1100
E-mail: innkeeper@whitebarninn.com
Room Rates: $$$
Suite Rates: $$$$
Credit Cards: Visa, MC, AmEx
No. of Rooms: 17 **Suites:** 7
Services and Amenities: Parking, Laundry service, TV lounge, Fireplaces, Cable TV, Suites have whirlpool baths, Twice daily maid service, Robes, Complimentary toiletries and newspaper, Complimentary breakfast
Concierge: 8:00 a.m.–9:00 p.m.
Room Service: Breakfast only
Restaurant: White Barn Inn, 6:00–9:00 p.m., Jackets required
Bar: Piano Bar, 6:30 p.m.–midnight
Business Facilities: Message center, Secretarial service, Copiers, Audio-Visual
Conference Rooms: 2 rooms, capacity 40
Sports Facilities: Outdoor heated pool, Poolside spa treatments, Two 18-hole golf courses, Sailing, Riding, Deep-sea fishing, Whale watching, Tennis
Location: Lower Village, ½ hour from Portland Airport, 1½ hours from Logan
Attractions: Boutiques, Galleries, Antique shops, Trolley tours, Local theater, Woodland, Ocean

THE LENOX

Built in the turn of the century as a gathering place for proper Bostonians, The Lenox stands proudly in its original Back Bay location, providing eloquent testimony to its distinguished heritage. Recent, award-winning renovations combine the gracious elegance of the past with the modern conveniences of today in this 212-room landmark hotel.

Spacious guest rooms and suites are designed with comfort in mind, featuring such luxurious necessities as plush terry bathrobes and walk-in closets. Modern amenities, such as a fax machine, dual-line speaker phone with modem port, and personal voice mail are also included. Simpler needs may be filled by a crackling fire in one of the hotel's select rooms with a fireplace, or the complimentary newspaper waiting at the door each morning.

New to The Lenox is Anago, the nationally acclaimed restaurant of Chef Bob Calderone. Guests of the hotel can now enjoy Calderone's exceptional, Mediterranean-inspired cuisine either in Anago's dramatic dining room or in the privacy of their guest room through the hotel's In-Room Dining service.

Guests searching for a taste of Boston's patriotic past will find it at the Samuel Adams Brew House. This popular local gathering place serves twelve distinct styles of freshly-tapped Samuel Adams beer and pub-style food.

The Lenox can accommodate a wide variety of social and business events. The elegant Dome Room, with its gilded central dome and superb acoustics, has been the proud setting of many a grand function in the course of Boston's social history. The Board Room, with its oak paneling, antique furniture, and ornamental fireplace, brings a note of dignified refinement to small meetings and private luncheons.

Ideally located in the heart of Boston, The Lenox provides its guests with the perfect blend of old world charm and modern extravagance.

Address: 710 Boylston Street, Boston, MA 02116
Phone: 617-536-5300
Toll-Free: 800-225-7676
Fax: 617-236-0351
Web site: http://www.lenoxhotel.com
Room Rates: $$$$
Credit Cards: Most credit cards accepted
No. of Rooms: 212
Services and Amenities: Valet service, Garage & valet parking, Car hire, International currency exchange, House doctor, Laundry service, Baby-sitting service, Cable TV, Telephone in bathroom, Radio, Robes, Hair dryers, Iron & ironing board, Complimentary toiletries and newspaper
Restrictions: No pets allowed, 4 rooms with handicapped access
Concierge: 24 hours
Room Service: 6:30 a.m.–Midnight
Restaurant: Anago, lunch (Monday-Friday), dinner (daily), Sunday brunch, Reservations recommended
Bar: Samuel Adams Brew House, 11:30 a.m.–1:30 a.m. daily, Smoking in bar
Business Facilities: Message center, Audio-Visual, Fax, Modem ports, Full-scale conference facilities
Conference Rooms: 6 rooms
Sports Facilities: Exercise room with cardiovascular machines and weights
Location: Downtown Back Bay at Copley Square
Attractions: Walking distance to Newbury Street, Shopping at Prudential Center and Copley Place, Trolley and Duck Tours, Hynes Convention Center, Boston Common and Public Gardens, Faneuil Hall Marketplace

THE RITZ-CARLTON

For 70 years, gracious service and time-honored elegance have combined to make The Ritz-Carlton a Boston tradition. From its magnificent Grand Ballroom, to its exclusive Back Bay location, to its highly professional 400-person staff, this hotel sets the standard by which excellence is measured.

Attention to detail shows in the gold service, hand polished brass, white-gloved elevator operators, and fresh flowers everywhere. On weekdays, the hotel provides complimentary chauffeured limousine service to guests with appointments in the financial district and other areas of the city.

The guest rooms are furnished in classic French provincial style accented with imported fabrics and distinctive works of art. Fluffy robes hang in baths of Vermont marble with porcelain fixtures and oversized tubs. The Presidential Suite on the seventh floor has full-height windows overlooking historic Beacon Hill.

A delightful meal in The Dining Room, with its expansive view of Boston's Public Garden, might begin with caviar, followed by poached salmon with lobster sauce, then a pear sorbet; as an entrée, a rack of lamb with vegetables; and for a sweet conclusion, a sky-high chocolate soufflé. The wine cellar contains 10,000 bottles—you will undoubtedly find one you like.

Tea is served daily in the Lounge, and after-dinner cigars and cognac are a nightly ritual. The clublike Bar, with its glowing fireplace, popular pianist and rich warm panelling, is a Boston favorite.

Address: 15 Arlington Street, Boston, MA 02117
Phone: 617-536-5700
Toll-Free: 800-241-3333
Fax: 617-536-0055
Room Rates: $$$$
Suite Rates: $$$$
Credit Cards: Most credit cards accepted
No. of Rooms: 275 **Suites:** 34
Services and Amenities: Valet service, Garage and parking, Barber shop, Currency exchange, Baby-sitting service, "Jr." Presidential Suite for children, Laundry service, Gift shop, TV, Clock-radio, Hair dryers, Robes, Complimentary newspaper and shoeshine
Restrictions: Pets on leash by prior arrangements, 8 rooms handicapped-equipped
Concierge: 24 hours
Room Service: 24 hours
Restaurant: Dining Room, 5:30 p.m.–11:00 p.m., Dress code, Sunday brunch, The Cafe, Less formal, Breakfast-Dinner, Weekend Brunch, The Roof, Seasonal dining/dancing, Thur.-Sat., Informal Sunday Jazz Brunch
Bar: The Bar, Monday—Saturday, 11:30 a.m.–1:00 a.m., Sunday, noon—midnight
Business Facilities: Business center, Secretarial service, Copiers, Telex
Conference Rooms: 13 rooms, capacity 500
Sports Facilities: Fitness center, Sauna, Massage, Weight training, Candela of Boston
Location: Downtown Back Bay, Arlington stop on public transport
Attractions: Boston Public Garden, Theatre, Newbury Street

CHATHAM BARS INN

Chatham Bars Inn is a historic Cape Cod landmark and one of the last of America's grand oceanfront resorts. The 172 room resort preserves the traditional gracious service and ambiance of lavish leisure that makes it a year round destination famous for its elegance, cuisine and the natural beauty of its surroundings. Built in 1914 by a wealthy Boston family, Chatham Bars Inn is celebrating its eighty-fourth anniversary with an extensive restoration program that will, over the course of the next two years, return the resort to its original splendor.

The Main Inn, with beautifully appointed rooms, is perched gracefully atop a rise overlooking Pleasant Bay, the Outer sand bars and the open Atlantic. Outstanding ocean vistas are also enjoyed from the Inn's famous veranda and from the acclaimed Main Dining Room. Twenty-six charming Cape Cod style cottages dot the 23 acre property, some situated on the quarter mile of private, sandy beach.

Three award-winning restaurants offer dining experiences not to be missed. The Main Dining Room features signature New England cuisine accompanied by panoramic ocean views and classic elegance. The North Beach Tavern & Grille delights families and friends with its traditional favorites and cozy atmosphere. The Beach House Grill, on the water's edge, has Cape Cod's best summertime seats for luncheons, clambakes and festive beach parties.

Relax in the luxury of a quarter mile of private sandy beach; heated outdoor pool, complimentary children's program, beachside clambakes and barbecues, fitness room, tennis courts and adjacent golf. Request a gourmet picnic lunch and take a short ride on the hotel launch to explore the miles of beach on the uninhabited Outer sand bar. The charming village of Chatham is just steps away and boasts many historic sites, unique shops and galleries.

Address: 297 Shore Road, Chatham, Cape Cod, MA 02633
Phone: 508-945-0096
Toll-Free: 800-527-4884
Fax: 508-945-5491
E-mail: resrvcbi@chathambarsinn.com
Web site: http://www.chathambarsinn.com
Room Rates: $$$
Suite Rates: $$$$
Credit Cards: Most credit cards accepted
No. of Rooms: 172 **Suites:** 20
Services and Amenities: Valet service, Parking, Car hire, Barber & beauty shops nearby, International currency exchange nearby, Library, Baby-sitting service, Laundry service, TV, Radio, Beachside clambakes & barbecues, Complimentary toiletries & children's program
Restrictions: No pets allowed, Non-smoking except in designated areas
Concierge: 7:00 a.m. -9:00 p.m.
Room Service: 7:00 a.m. -1:00 a.m.
Restaurant: Main Dining Room, 7:30–11:00 a.m., 12:30–2:00p.m., 6:30–8:30 p.m., Dress Code; The North Beach Tavern & Grille, luncheon & dinner daily; Beach House Grill, open seasonally for lunch & dinner
Bar: Tavern Bar, Noon—1:00a.m.
Business Facilities: Message center, Secretarial service, Fax, Copiers, Audio-Visual
Conference Rooms: 5 rooms, capacity 300
Sports Facilities: Heated outdoor pool, 4 tennis courts, Fitness room, 9-hole golf course, 18-hole championship golf nearby, Numerous outdoor sports
Location: Beachfront, Steps to Chatham Village
Attractions: Short walk to Chatham's antique shops, art galleries, fine shops; Deep sea fishing & whale watching charters, Historic sites & museums nearby, National Seashore Park

HAWTHORNE INN

Located in the Historic Zone of Concord, the Hawthorne Inn, erected c. 1870, is on the same road the founders trod, the famed "Battle Road" of 1775.

The rooms are appointed with antique furnishings, beautifully designed hand-made quilts, and wood floors graced with oriental and rag rugs all highlighted by wonderful colors that rest the soul and warm the heart. Throughout the Inn are displayed original art works, both ancient and modern, antique Japanese Ukiyoye prints and sculpture by the Innkeeper. The Common Room provides a numerous selection of books and up-to-date magazines along with a warm fire on chilly evenings. In the guest rooms will be found poetry books, magazines, am-fm clock radios and perhaps bowls of fresh fruit and flowers.

Each morning at a common table guests are served a continental breakfast featuring wholesome home-baked breads, heaps of fresh fruit, seasonal berries and grapes from the garden, juice, a selection of teas or the house special blend of freshly ground coffee, and soon, if the bees keep working, honey for your enjoyment.

The Hawthorne Inn is situated on land that once belonged to Ralph Waldo Emerson, the Alcotts and Nathaniel Hawthorne. Hawthorne purchased the land and repaired a path leading to his home with trees planted on either side. Two of these trees yet stand and can be viewed on the west side of the Inn. In the yard is a small pond with carp and the errant frog, vegetable gardens, fruit trees, grape vines, berry bushes and flowers. Far from normal walking paths work the bees.

The town is alive with history, with beauty and with peacefulness. The Hawthorne Inn has captured a small part of what is Concord.

Address: 462 Lexington Road, Concord, MA 01742
Phone: 978-369-5610
Fax: 978-287-4949
E-mail: hawthorneinn@concordmass.com
Web site: http://www.concordmass.com
Room Rates: $$$
Credit Cards: AmEx, MC, Visa, Discover
No. of Rooms: 7
Services and Amenities: Off-street parking, Baby-sitting service by reservation, Card/game area, Library, 1 room with fireplace, Air-conditioning, TV and VCR by request, View of home of Nathaniel Hawthorne, Complimentary fine toiletries, beverage and snack
Restrictions: No pets allowed, Minimum stay on holidays
Concierge: 9:00 a.m.–9:00 p.m.
Restaurant: Breakfast served to over-night guests at a common table set with Wedgewood and Dedham pottery, Walking distance to local diner and restaurants
Business Facilities: Fax
Sports Facilities: Nearby rivers for canoeing, Parkland for walking, running, picnicking, meditating or just plain enjoying
Location: American Mile Historic Village, 20 miles to Logan Airport-Boston
Attractions: Walk to authors' homes: Hawthorne, Alcott (Little Women), Ralph Waldo Emerson and Henry D. Thoreau cabin site at Walden Pond, Near to site of First Battle of Revolution at Old North Bridge, "Shot Heard Round the World," DeCordova Museum, Concord Museum

DEERFIELD INN

Built in 1884, the Deerfield Inn is the quintessential New England hostelry, situated in historic Deerfield on what has been called "the loveliest street in New England." Deerfield was settled around 1670 and was recognized for its unspoiled antiquity as early as 1819. There are now 14 museum houses to explore, along with the cultural history, art and craftsmanship of the Pioneer Valley. Many art galleries, museums, bookstores and antique shops are close by.

The Deerfield Inn has been carefully modernized to maintain its New England atmosphere—and not disturb the Inn's two celebrated ghosts, Cora and Hershel. Guestrooms feature antiques and period reproductions, designer fabrics and wallcoverings, and tile bathrooms. Each guest enjoys individual climate control, telephone and television.

All guests partake of a full country breakfast and afternoon tea and "nibbles."

The Deerfield Inn Dining Room, with its Queen Anne chairs, mahogany tables and white napery, is a step into New England history. Period sideboards, brass chandeliers and portrait-lined walls provide a sense of the past. A not-to-be-missed entree is the sashimi-quality tuna cooked rare with leeks, wrapped in a scallopini of veal and sauteed and served with a light marsala tomato sauce. For dessert, a favorite is the Deerfield Inn Indian pudding. Guests may choose from an abundant selection of wines and local ales.

Address: 81 Old Main Street, Deerfield, MA 01342
Phone: 413-774-5587
Toll-Free: 800-926-3865
Fax: 413-773-8712
E-mail: frontdesk@deerfieldinn.com
Web site: http://www.deerfieldinn.com
Room Rates: $$
Credit Cards: AmEx, MC, Visa, DC
No. of Rooms: 23
Services and Amenities: Parking, Gift Shop, Baby-sitting service, Card/Game area, TV, Telephones, Radio, Hair dryers, Irons & ironing boards, Individual heat & air-conditioning control, Robes, Complimentary toiletries & newspaper, Complimentary full breakfast & afternoon tea
Restrictions: 2 rooms handicapped-equipped, No pets allowed
Restaurant: Deerfield Inn Dining Room, 6:00–9:00 p.m., Dress code; Terrace Cafe, open year-round for light lunches
Bar: Yes
Business Facilities: TTY phone, Assistive listening devices, Copiers, Audio-Visual, Fax
Conference Rooms: 1 room, capacity 20
Sports Facilities: Nearby 18-hole golf course, Whitewater rafting, Hiking, Fishing, Tennis, Skating, Skiing, Cross-country skiing
Location: Deerfield
Attractions: National historic landmark village with museums, farms, country walks, antiques and beautiful scenery of the Pioneer Valley

THE WAUWINET

The Wauwinet originally opened in the mid-19th century as a restaurant serving shore dinners to patrons arriving by boat. It evolved into a hotel and soon became a Nantucket landmark. Featuring 30 guest rooms, an award-winning restaurant, a 254-foot dock, and a wide range of recreational options, the Wauwinet also offers thoughtful and innovative services and amenities.

The gracious, sunny guest rooms are located over three floors of the inn, and in five private guest cottages. Each is individually decorated with country antiques, fine paintings and other art. Some offer water views and all have private baths.

A complimentary full breakfast is served to guests daily, either in-room or at Topper's restaurant. Cheeses, port and sherry are served in the library each afternoon. Guests also have complimentary use of all recreational equipment and facilities.

Topper's restaurant, with dining in two indoor rooms and alfresco on the umbrella-shaded Bayview Terrace, is the recipient of Wine Spectator's Grand Award. Chef Chris Freeman creates American Regional cuisine focusing on fresh local ingredients that celebrate the distinct natural flavors of the season. A dinner might include an appetizer of Lobster and Scallop "Navarin" with Morel Mushrooms and English Peas followed by an entree of Grilled Stripped Bass on a Jonah Crab Broth with Fennel, Leek and Shoestring Potatoes. The award-winning wine list features more than 800 American and French vintages.

Drinks and light fare for lunch are also served in the bar or on the Bayview Terrace, and customized, gourmet picnic baskets are available.

The Wauwinet Lady, a custom 26-passenger open launch, sails to town twice a day (a 50-minute ride). Guests also enjoy complimentary sailing aboard the Topper, Too, a 21-foot Mako Runabout, to Coatue, a secluded beach. Complimentary bay cruises are scheduled in the summer.

Address: 120 Wauwinet Road, P.O. Box 2580, Nantucket, MA 02584
Phone: 508-228-0145
Toll-Free: 800-426-8718
Fax: 508-228-6712
Web site: http://www.wauwinet.com
Room Rates: $$$
Suite Rates: $$$$
Credit Cards: Visa, MC, AmEx, DC
No. of Rooms: 25 **Suites:** 5
Services and Amenities: Parking, Library, Video Library, Television, VCR, Telephone, Radio, CD Player, Some kitchens and balconies available, Complimentary newspaper
Restrictions: No pets, 2 rooms wheelchair accessible, Children welcome in family cottages, Non-smoking areas
Concierge: 7:00 a.m.–11:00 p.m.
Room Service: 8:00 a.m.–9:00 p.m.
Restaurant: Topper's, 8:00 a.m.–11:00 p.m., Dress code after 6:00 p.m.
Bar: Topper's Bar, Noon to 11:00 p.m.
Business Facilities: Message center, Copiers, Audio-Visual, Fax
Conference Rooms: 1 room, capacity 25
Sports Facilities: Clay tennis courts, Bicycles, Atlantic Ocean and Nantucket Bay swimming and boating
Location: In Wauminet, 8 miles northeast of downtown, 8 miles to airport
Attractions: 26 miles of secluded nature preserve beaches, Atlantic Ocean sunrises, Nantucket Bay sunsets, Historic Nantucket Town, Taste of Nantucket: 5 special natural history and dining experiences midweek during Spring and Fall

RALPH WALDO EMERSON INN

Fully restored and renamed for the celebrated American poet who vacationed here in the 1850s and "made his acquaintance with the sea," the Emerson combines modern comfort with the unspoiled atmosphere of an earlier, more gracious era. Here the fast pace of modern life yields to tranquil days filled with sun and sea, leisurely strolls along quiet tree-shaded streets, and visits to art galleries and shops. There are party boats for fishing, sightseeing or whale watching. Nearby are golf, tennis and an excellent summer theater. Or guests can simply stroll the spacious grounds or loaf in a comfortable chair on the wide, old-fashioned veranda overlooking the sea.

Emerson would still feel at home in the Greek Revival style inn's guestrooms with their spool beds, old-fashioned dressers and commodes, and flowered wallpapers. Modern guests also enjoy telephones and private baths. Soft tones of plum and rose dominate the decor of the intimate dining room and spacious living room.

Business and group meetings, special events and other social gatherings are welcome at the Emerson Inn, where the proud tradition of Cape Ann hospitality dates from a time when the American country inn was at its peak.

Address: 1 Cathedral Avenue, P.O. Box 2369, Rockport, MA 01966
Phone: 508-546-6321
Fax: 508-546-7043
E-mail: emerson@cove.com
Room Rates: $
Suite Rates: $$
Credit Cards: Visa, MC, Novus
No. of Rooms: 36 **Suites:** 2
Services and Amenities: Parking, TV lounge, Card/game area, Laundry serivce, Baby-sitting service, Telephones, Air-conditioning, Complimentary toiletries, Complimentary afternoon lemonade and cookies
Restrictions: No pets allowed, 2 rooms handicapped-equipped
Concierge: 7:00 a.m.–3:00 p.m.
Room Service: 8:00 a.m.–11:00 p.m.
Restaurant: Poets Corner, 8:00–10:00 a.m., 6:00–9:00 p.m., Dress code
Business Facilities: Message center, Copiers, Audio-Visual, Fax
Conference Rooms: 3 rooms, capacity 10, 30, 45
Sports Facilities: Outdoor swimming pool, Croquet, Whirlpool, Sauna, Massage available, Nearby golf, tennis and sailing
Location: Pigeon Cove, By the ocean
Attractions: Whale watching, Famous Bearskin Neck area, Historic Salem, Newbury Port, Portsmouth

SEACREST MANOR

Amid surroundings of two beautiful acres of lawns and gardens, Seacrest Manor sits only 300 yards from the shore, on a hill overlooking the woods and the sea. It offers an escape for that special relaxation without overly programmed activities. Room phones are purposely avoided here as are all forms of business facilities. A house phone is available, however, for emergencies or local contacts.

The guest rooms are Victorian in style with floral wallpaper, deep plush carpets, fine paintings and prints and traditional furniture with some antiques. Some rooms have picture-window views of the ocean. Bathrooms are tiled and wallpapered and provide plush oversize towels in complementing colors.

The Manor dining room overlooks the garden and features tables set with rose

and burgundy linens, Wedgewood "Flying Cloud" china, and a fireplace. A typical breakfast includes a fresh fruit cup and spiced Irish oatmeal with chopped dates. Tea with teabreads and sweets is available in the living room at 4 p.m. daily. The staff will gladly help with advice and reservations for dinner at local restaurants and menus are available. A filled apple tray and candy dish tide guests over till dinner time. The complimentary breakfast includes a variety of pancakes, French toast, or corn fritters, plus eggs and bacon.

"...Sophistication and refined elegance are the bywords of this home, which could easily be along the Southern Coast of England..." —*The Discerning Traveler.* "One of the Outstanding reasons to visit New England" —*Yankee Magazine's Travel Guide to New England.*

Address: 99 Marmion Way, Rockport, MA 01966
Phone: 978-546-2211
Web site: http://www.rockportusa.com/seacrestmanor/
Room Rates: $$
Suite Rates: $$
Credit Cards: Personal and travelers checks
No. of Rooms: 8 **Suites:** 1
Services and Amenities: Complimentary full breakfast, shoeshine and toiletries, Parking, Card/game area, Library, Large ocean view deck, Two acres manicured grounds & prize-winning gardens, Nightly turndown, Rain hats & umbrellas, Cable TV, Hair dryers, Fresh flowers throughout
Restrictions: No pets, No smoking, Not recommended for children, Minimum stay 2 days on-season, 3 days on holidays
Concierge: 6:00 a.m.–9:00 p.m.
Room Service: Setups as requested
Restaurant: Inn Dining Room, 7:30–9:30 a.m., Guests only
Sports Facilities: Rockport Country Club (9 holes)
Location: South End—Residential, Shore, 35 miles to Logan Airport, Boston
Attractions: Art galleries, Antique shops, Restaurants, Whale Watching, Schooner trips, Fishing, Lobstering trips, Island boat trips, Trolley tours, John Kieran Nature Reserve, Shore walks, Guided nature walks, Halibut Point State Park, Rockport Chamber of Music

THE SALEM INN

The Salem Inn comprises three restored and renovated homes, the West House(c.1834), the Curwen House(c.1854) and the Peabody House(c.1874), all on the National Registry of Historic Places. Located just 18 miles from Boston, the Inn's convenient location in the heart of the downtown McIntire Historic District is within easy walking distance to the National Park Maritime Historical Site, the Peabody Essex Museum, fine restaurants and the waterfront.

Each of the thirty-nine individually decorated rooms and suites reflects the fine craftsmanship of the Federal period. Amidst the old world charm emanated by canopy beds, antique furnishings and period details are the many modern day conveniences of a full-service inn. Some rooms have whirlpool baths and wood-burning fireplaces.

A complimentary light breakfast is served to guests each morning in the Courtyard Cafe, which offers outdoor seating in our rose garden brick patio during warm weather. Afternoon Sherry is also served in the hospitality room, with its warm fireplace and fireside Queen Ann chairs.

The Salem Inn, with its convenient hospitality services and complete line of audio-visual equipment, provides an intimate environment ideal for social functions, receptions and business meetings.

Address: 7 Summer Street, Salem, MA 01970
Phone: 978-741-0680
Toll-Free: 800-446-2995
Fax: 978-744-8924
E-mail: saleminn@earthlink.net
Web site: http://www.salemweb.com/biz/saleminn
Room Rates: $$
Suite Rates: $$
Credit Cards: Most credit cards accepted
No. of Rooms: 39 **Suites:** 11
Services and Amenities: Parking, Color and Cable TV, Telephones, Radios, Some rooms with kitchens or fireplace
Restrictions: Pets accepted by prior arrangement, Children welcome
Concierge: 8:00 a.m.–8:00 p.m.
Business Facilities: Message center, Audio-Visual, Fax, Modems
Conference Rooms: 1 room, capacity 25, Adjacent hospitality room for beverages
Sports Facilities: Nearby sailing, Some rooms have whirlpool bath
Location: Downtown Salem, Historic district, 18 miles to Boston's Logan Airport
Attractions: Walking access to Salem's shops, restaurants, museums, waterfront, and National Park Historic Site, 35-minute train ride to downtown Boston

DAN'L WEBSTER INN

The Dan'l Webster Inn is located on the site of a tavern built before the American Revolution, and named for its most famous 19th century guest.

Wood panelling, oriental carpeting, and colonial reproduction furniture dominate the Inn's lobby. A grandfather clock ticks quietly and the warm glow of a fire invites guests to relax and enjoy. A cozy Gathering Room offers an intimate place for reading, game playing or just good conversation.

Double rooms decorated with colonial charm feature comfortable beds, highboy dressers, desks and easy chairs. All the rooms of the Inn have private baths with numerous amenities. Elegant two-room suites are available in the two restored, antique homes that are part of the Inn. The Fessenden House and The Quince Tree feature canopy beds, whirlpool baths and several working fireplaces. The Dan'l Webster Suite, set atop the main inn, features a king-size master bedroom with balcony overlooking the Great Marsh, and a marble bathroom with jacuzzi for two with skylight.

The Inn, known for its innovative American cuisine also features a changing Chef's Menu which highlight local and seasonal specialties. Four dining rooms including the glassed Conservatory that overlooks the ever-changing gardens, offer award-winning cuisine and wine list. The new Tavern at the Inn features casual dining serving items such as wood grilled pizza, burgers, and vegetable burritos in a more relaxed atmosphere.

The same award-winning quality is evident at banquet functions. Numerous dance bands are available for hire, and the size and placement of the dance floor may be adapted to each room. For unique entertainment, inquire about arranging a cabaret show.

In addition to the Inn's outdoor swimming pool, guests have access to a local private health club and local golf courses.

The Dan'l Webster Inn requires a two-night minimum stay on weekends and some holidays, but guests will find at least two days worth of historical sights and recreational opportunities around Sandwich and nearby Plymouth.

Address: 149 Main Street, Sandwich, MA 02563
Phone: 508-888-3622
Toll-Free: 800-444-3566
Fax: 508-888-5156
E-mail: dwi@capecod.net
Web site: http://www.danlwebsterinn.com
Room Rates: $
Suite Rates: $$$
Credit Cards: AmEx, Visa, MC, DC
No. of Rooms: 38 **Suites:** 9
Services and Amenities: Parking, Gift shop, Gathering room for guests, TV lounge, Equipment for physically impaired, Nightly turndown service, Cable TV, Individual climate control, Hair dryer, Toiletries
Restrictions: No pets, 2-night minimum stay on weekends and some holidays, Children under 12 free with parents
Concierge: Daily
Room Service: 8:00 a.m.–8:00 p.m.
Restaurant: 8:00 a.m.–9:00 p.m.
Bar: Tavern, 11:30 to midnight
Business Facilities: Audio-Visual equipment, Copiers, Teleconferencing, Message center
Conference Rooms: 6 rooms, capacity 10-150
Sports Facilities: Outdoor swimming pool—Golf and tennis nearby
Location: Sandwich Village
Attractions: Historic attractions, Museums, Factory outlet malls, Antique shops, Cape Cod Canal, Ocean nearby

THE INN AT STOCKBRIDGE

Set far back from the road on twelve secluded acres, just one mile from downtown Stockbridge, is the white-pillared Inn at Stockbridge. This turn of the century Georgian-style mansion was built in 1906 and has been lovingly restored to a bed and breakfast inn. Filled with antiques, the Inn remains elegant and comfortable. Once guests enter the lobby, they are transformed to a different time where grand formal furnishings, warm fireplaces and a baby grand piano invited guests to stay and linger. Whether chatting over complimentary wine and cheese or splashing in the pool, the atmosphere of being among friends predominates.

Guestrooms feature king, queen or double beds with original headboards, spacious antique armoires and unique period wallcoverings. Suites offer additional features such as fireplaces and whirlpool tubs. Each suite has a unique theme ranging from Indian, Scottish, African to French.

Each morning guests may indulge in an elegant gourmet breakfast by candlelight, featuring fresh seasonal fruit, home-baked goods and sumptuous entrees.

There are two conference rooms to meet guests' business needs. Copier and fax services are provided. For the active traveler, golf and horseback riding are nearby. Tanglewood and the Shakespeare Company are also nearby for summer entertainment.

The Inn at Stockbridge offers the perfect combination of elegance, comfort and personal attention for the discerning traveler.

Address: Route #7 North, P.O. Box 618, Stockbridge, MA 01262
Phone: 413-298-3337
Toll-Free: 888-466-7865
Fax: 413-298-3406
E-mail: innkeeper@stockbridgeinn.com
Web site: http://www.stockbridgeinn.com
Room Rates: $$
Suite Rates: $$
Credit Cards: Most credit cards accepted
No. of Rooms: 12 **Suites:** 4
Services and Amenities: TV lounge, Card/game area, Library, Some rooms with fireplace and/or deck, Telephones, Radios, Individual air-conditioning control, Whirlpool bath in some rooms, Large fluffy towels, Complimentary toiletries and breakfast
Restrictions: Handicapped access, Children over 12 years of age welcome, No pets allowed
Concierge: 24 hours
Business Facilities: Copiers, Fax
Conference Rooms: 2 rooms
Sports Facilities: Outdoor swimming pool, Whirlpool, 5 miles from skiing, Golf and Horseback riding nearby
Location: Along route #7, Mass. Turnpike
Attractions: Tanglewood, Norman Rockwell Museum, Berkshire Theatre, Jacobs Pillow, Antique and outlet shopping, Shakespeare and Company, 12 acres wonder gardens

THE RED LION INN

"The new hotel is a graceful structure in the colonial style, simple yet elegant and appointed after the luxurious fashion of a gentleman's country house." So reported *The Berkshire Courier* in an April 1987 article about The Red Lion's reconstruction following a devastating fire that burned the original structure to the ground. The Red Lion Inn, built in 1773 as a stop between Boston and Albany, was a meeting spot for dissident colonists, and later host to at least five presidents of the United States.

The inn is a white Victorian clapboard structure with a magnificent porch full of white wicker, perfect for watching the comings and goings of this lovely Berkshire Hills town, which its late resident Norman Rockwell loved to sketch. To step inside is to enter a world of memorabilia, much of it saved from the original inn. Public areas display antiques, beautiful flowers, colonial pewter, Canton china, and photographs of Old Stockbridge.

The guest rooms are comfortably furnished with period pieces, cozy comforters, and each has a unique color scheme, delicate wallpapers, and Oriental rugs. Delicious contemporary New England cuisine is served in the elegant main dining room, and more casual Widow Bingham's Tavern. Within walking distance of the Inn are the Norman Rockwell Museum, antique shops, boutiques, and Mission House, a museum of early colonial life.

Whether you visit this picturesque village as spring unfolds, in summer to enjoy the Tanglewood Music Center, in colorful fall when foliage beckons, or to ski at a nearby mountain in winter, you'll enjoy one of New England's best-loved hostelries.

Address: 30 Main Street, Stockbridge, MA 01262
Phone: 413-298-5545
Fax: 413-298-5130
E-mail: innkeeper@redlioninn.com
Web site: http://www.redlioninn.com
Room Rates: $
Suite Rates: $$$
Credit Cards: Most credit cards accepted
No. of Rooms: 111 **Suites:** 22
Services and Amenities: Parking, Baby-sitting service, Gift shop, Library, Special packages, Cable TV, Vintage clawfoot bathrubs, Eyelet shower curtains, Shaving mirrors, Complimentary robes and Country Inn toiletries
Restrictions: No pets allowed, Handicapped accessible (inquire)
Room Service: Restaurant hours
Restaurant: The Main Dining Room, breakfast 7:30 a.m.–10:00 a.m., lunch noon-2:00 p.m., and dinner 5:30–9:00 p.m., Dress code
Bar: Lion's Den Pub, 4:00 p.m.–1:00 a.m., Lunch, Weekends, In season
Business Facilities: yes
Conference Rooms: 5 rooms, capacity 2-100
Sports Facilities: Outdoor swimming pool, Massage, Tennis, Golf, Riding, Sailing and skiing nearby
Location: Center of village, 40 miles to Albany Airport
Attractions: Close to Tanglewood concerts, Jacob's Pillow (oldest dance festival in US), Berkshire Theatre Festival, Berkshire Garden Center, Mission Wildlife Santuaries, Lenox, Williamstown, Norman Rockwell Museum, Chesterwood and Naumkeg

PUBLICK HOUSE HISTORIC INN

Just minutes from main routes between New York and Boston, The Publick House Historic Inn and Country Motor Lodge invites you to take a detour into living history.

Founded by Colonel Ebenezer Crafts in 1771, the Public House Historic Inn still retains the pre-Revolutionary fireplaces and hand-hewn beams of the original establishment. A visit here and to nearby Old Sturbridge Village is a must for those interested in authentic recreations of Yankee colonial history.

Guests have a choice of accommodations. The Publick House Historic Inn and the Colonel Ebenezer Crafts Inn feature rooms and suites authentically designed in 18th-century antique and reproduction furnishings, wallpaper and accessories. Innkeepers have worked hard to provide guests with a combination of genuine colonial ambiance and attention to every need. Lodgers at Crafts Inn peruse the morning paper over a breakfast of fresh muffins, sticky buns, juice and coffee, and also enjoy complimentary afternoon tea. For convenient modern accommodations, cable TV, and individual decks at modest prices, the Country Motor Lodge is another option.

Of the three dining establishments on the premises, the Publick House Inn, a 4-star restaurant, is an experience not soon to be forgotten. Guests savor such traditional fare as baked lobster pie and Indian pudding at wooden tables before an open hearth and open-beam ceiling. Fresh flowers and candlelight lend intimacy and charm.

For those in need of a meeting site, The Public House maintains full conference facilities and two large conference rooms.

Address: P.O. Box 187, Sturbridge, MA 01566
Phone: 508-347-3313
Toll-Free: 800-PUBLICK
Fax: 508-347-5073
E-mail: bdion@gnn.com
Web site: http:// www.publickhouse.com
Room Rates: $
Credit Cards: AmEx, Visa, MC, CB
No. of Rooms: 125
Services and Amenities: Parking, Laundry service, Gift shop, Cable TV in Motor Lodge, Telephones, Air-conditioning, Complimentary toiletries, At Crafts Inn: Complimentary toiletries, Robes, Afternoon tea, Breakfast
Restrictions: Pets, $5 extra (must be attended), Children 17 & under free in room, 2 rooms handicapped-equipped
Restaurant: Publick House Historic Inn Restaurant, 7:00–11:00 p.m.
Bar: Ebenezer's Tavern, 11:30 a.m.–12:00 a.m., 4:00 p.m.–12:00 a.m. on weekends
Business Facilities: Copiers, Fax, Full-scale conference facilities
Conference Rooms: 2 rooms, capacity 225
Sports Facilities: Outdoor pool, Handball, Croquet, Tennis, Children's play area, Nearby golf, Skiing, Racquet ball, Hiking, Cross-country skiing
Location: The Common
Attractions: Old Sturbridge Village, Antiques, Boutiques, Higgons Armory, Worcestor Common Outlet

STAFFORD'S PERRY HOTEL

Stafford's Perry Hotel, glistening under its new exterior restoration, will celebrate its centennial in 1999. A beacon in the city's historic Gaslight District, the pale yellow Hotel sits atop a gentle bluff overlooking sparkling Little Traverse Bay. The lobby is boldly decorated with persimmon walls, original white pressed tin ceilings, antique furniture, and a teal and salmon patterned carpet reminiscent of the opulent Gay '90s.

Well known for its warm hospitality, the Hotel boasts gracious guestrooms individually decorated and furnished with period reproductions. Some accommodations feature balconies with sunset views of the bay. Although nineteenth century in flavor, the comforts of the twentieth century prevail with private baths, air-conditioning, cable television, and telephones.

An experienced and competent staff caters to every detail of the many meetings and small conferences held in the fully-equipped boardroom suite and other banquet facilities. A corporate hospitality suite with kitchenette serves as a sales suite where vendors can set up product displays and trunk shows.

Guests choose from a variety of dining options for breakfast, lunch and dinner. The H.O. Rose Dining Room features a menu of international cuisine with a panoramic view of the water. Weather permitting, the Depot Porch, with its wicker chairs and hanging plants, is one of the town's most popular dining spots. The Salon, adjacent to the H.O. Rose Dining Room, offers refreshments in a quiet atmosphere for those who stop by after a play, concert, or film. The Noggin Room Pub on the lower level of the hotel is known locally for its "Hall of Foam," a list of nearly 50 specialty beers, imports, and micro-brews to pair with the light dinner fare offered. The Rose Garden Veranda offers outdoor dining overlooking perennial gardens and the bay.

Stafford's Perry Hotel, surrounded by shady parks and the shops of the Gaslight District, is a short walk from the yacht docks, history museum, arts center and county buildings. A short drive puts hotel guests on the best ski hills and golf courses in the midwest. Boaters from around the world call Little Traverse Bay, Petoskey, and the Perry Hotel, a charming haven.

Address: Bay at Lewis Street, Petoskey, MI 49770
Phone: 616-347-4000
Toll-Free: 800-737-1899
Fax: 616-347-0636
E-mail: stafford@freeway.net
Web site: http://www.staffords.com
Room Rates: $
Suite Rates: $$$
Credit Cards: Visa, MC, AmEx
No. of Rooms: 79 **Suites:** 1
Services and Amenities: On site parking, Car rental, Valet laundry service, Gift shop, Hot tub, Cable TV, Individual climate control, Complimentary newspaper and toiletries
Restrictions: No pets allowed, 4 rooms with barrier-free accommodations, Non-smoking room available
Room Service: 7:00 a.m.–10:00 p.m.
Restaurant: H.O. Rose Dining Room, 7:00 a.m.–10:00 p.m., Noggin Room, 11:00 a.m.–11:00 p.m., The Rose Garden Veranda, 11:00 a.m.–sunset
Bar: Salon, 11:00 a.m.–11:00 p.m., Noggin Room, 11:00 a.m.–11:00 p.m.
Business Facilities: Message center, Audio-Visual
Conference Rooms: 4 rooms, capacity 16, 16, 16, 70
Location: Heart of Gaslight Shopping District in Petoskey on Little Traverse Bay
Attractions: Excellent shopping, Sight-seeing, Boating, Golf, Tennis, Petoskey State Park with hiking, cross country ski trails and sand beaches

MILLSAPS BUIE HOUSE

When the Millsaps Buie House came to life in 1888, two mules pulled the city's streetcar along its intended route. Now, the Inn offers its guests cable television and a telephone with computer dataport. It is unique in that it has been in the same family for five generations.

Built in Queen Anne style, the four, two-story fluted columns with their Ionian capitals that were added later suggest a stately home. Once you step inside, you are left with no doubt that this was a stately home, now converted to a boutique hotel for your enjoyment. Ceilings are 14 feet high; hardwood floors are carpeted with oriental rugs. Lace curtains and draperies cover the windows. There is a grand piano in the drawing room and all of the rooms are furnished with antiques and period reproductions.

Guest rooms are unusually spacious. Some have four-poster beds with canopy, French dressing tables or English tables and chairs. It is all warmth and intimacy in an opulent setting. Many of the furnishings are original to the house. The library, foyer and parlor provide guests with privacy for reading or an opportunity for cocktails.

The Millsaps Buie House is located on the crest of one of Jackson's highest hills and commands a view of the downtown area. It is within a short distance of the Governor's Mansion, the Old Capitol Museum and The Oaks. Tours are available of the Old Capitol Museum, the Mississippi Museum of Art, and during the season, semi-professional theater, opera and ballet are available.

Address: 628 North State Street, Jackson, MS 39202
Phone: 601-352-0221
Toll-Free: 800-784-0221
Fax: 601-352-0221
Room Rates: $
Credit Cards: Most credit cards accepted
No. of Rooms: 11 **Suites:** 1
Services and Amenities: Secured Parking, Library, Cable TV, Telephone in bath, Radio, Individual heat & air-conditioning control, Complimentary toiletries & sewing kit, Complimentary breakfast
Restrictions: No pets allowed, Children under 12 discouraged
Concierge: Innkeeper on duty
Business Facilities: Fax, Copier
Conference Rooms: 1 room, capacity 10
Sports Facilities: Privileges to Mississippi Baptist Fitness Center (fee)
Location: 5 blocks from downtown
Attractions: Short distance from historical buildings, Governor's Mansion, Old Capitol Museum, The Oaks

THE CORNHUSKER

The Cornhusker is a Nebraska Tradition. Located in the heart of downtown Lincoln, the Hotel is a true reflection of the midwestern ideals and values which surround it. Within walking distance of the historic Haymarket district, the Lied Center for Performing Arts and other entertainment, guests find themselves in the heart of the activity. Adjacent to the Hotel is The Burnham Yates Conference Center which is comprised of over 4,400 square feet, accommodating more than 2,500 people.

The Cornhusker offers ten floors of guest rooms, decorated with the richest fabrics and colors including pieces from the owner's personal collection of antiques and oriental rugs. An entire level is dedicated to the Executive traveler boasting plush robes, turndown service and complimentary refreshments in the Executive Lounge for floor guests. Also, eight suites, a Governor's Suite and an Extended Stay Suite, provide an alternative for whatever need guests may have.

The Hotel also offers two distinctive choices in dining. The Renaissance, the City's only AAA Four Diamond Restaurant, is located on the second floor of the Hotel. Offering a formal atmosphere and gourmet dining, The Renaissance's menu allows one to chose from a seven course dining experience to a special prix fixe menu geared to fit into any busy schedule. Choose from a wide array of sumptuous desserts, including tableside preparation and an award winning wine list. Offering a more casual atmosphere, Terrace Grille is located on the lobby level and is open all day for breakfast, lunch and dinner. Featuring walls adorned with hand-painted trompe l'oeil murals of garden scenes from countries around the world, the atmosphere is one designed to change with the hours as the day passes from dawn to dusk. Room Service is also available through this restaurant 24 hours a day.

The Cornhusker offers a welcome surprise in its combination of warm hospitality and elegance to business and vacation travelers alike.

Address: 333 South 13th Street, Lincoln, NE 68508
Phone: 402-474-7474
Toll-Free: 800-793-7474
Fax: 402-474-1847
E-mail: reservations@thecornhusker.com
Web site: http://www.thecornhusker.com
Room Rates: $$
Suite Rates: $$$$
Credit Cards: Most credit cards accepted
No. of Rooms: 290 **Suites:** 9
Services and Amenities: Valet service, Garage and parking, Gift shop, TV lounge, Laundry service, Cable TV, Radio, Wet bar, Individual heat and air-conditioning control, Robes, Complimentary newspaper and toiletries
Restrictions: Dogs under 25 lbs. allowed with deposit, 8 rooms handicapped-equipped, Children under 18 free
Room Service: 24 hours
Restaurant: The Renaissance, lunch and dinner served, coat & tie preferred; Terrace Grille, breakfast, lunch and dinner
Bar: The Five Reasons, 4:00 p.m.–1:00 a.m., Monday thru Saturday
Business Facilities: Full-scale conference facilities, Audio-Visual, Teleconferencing, Telex, Full printing capabilities
Conference Rooms: 40,000 sq.ft., capacity 15-1500
Sports Facilities: Indoor swimming pool, Complete health facility
Location: Downtown
Attractions: Historic Haymarket District, University of Nebraska, Sheldon Memorial Art Gallery, Morrill Hall Museum, State Historical Society Museum and Archives, Nebraska State Capitol

CRESTWOOD PAVILION

Crestwood Pavilion is often called a fantasy experience. The 200-acre hilltop estate looks out from Scofield Mountain, in Southwestern New Hampshire, over 100 miles from Connecticut through Massachusetts Pioneer Valley and the Green Mountains of Vermont. The Pavilion is a completely outfitted and well appointed 2-bedroom accommodation which stands in a garden on manicured grounds. Other rooms are located in the Main House. The Rectory features a private suite on the first level that is fully handicapped accessible. There is an open concept space with a kitchen, livingroom and full bath. The upstairs features a balcony overlooking Vermont's Green Mountains. Inside the upper suite there are two bedrooms and two baths, both with views of the mountains and a sitting room.

The American Georgian style buildings and grounds are geared to provide the perfect location for an event, wedding, business gathering, or whatever you can imagine. Several special features await your use, including the Grand Salon which shines as a ballroom, a commodious Club Room complete with bar and fireplace, a sun porch, a greenhouse conservatory and galleries. Formal French and English gardens add a sense of definition to the expansive lawns. A Japanese Tea House appears to float above the Chapel gardens located between the Rectory of the Historic Crestwood Chapel.

The beautifully maintained Victorian Chapel and its recently refurbished 1895 sanctuary are available for weddings along with appropriate presentations. Your culinary wish is an easily obtainable command for the multi-lingual and cultural staff of Crestwood. Grand cuisine from artichokes to zabaglione is featured. While there is no specific meal, as no two guests are the same, a breakfast may be Belgian waffles with whipped cream or decadently rich chocolate croissants or New Hampshire's own Stoneyfield non-fat yogurt and seasonal berries picked on the grounds of the estate. You may choose a picnic to be packed for and excursion on one of many local lakes, rivers or a climb on nearby Mt. Monadnock.

With the exceptional privacy and personalized care offered at the Crestwood Pavilion it is easy to embellish in life's little pleasures.

Address: 400 Scofield Mountain Road, Ashuelot, NH 03441
Phone: 603-239-6393
Fax: 603-239-7342
E-mail: meg910@sover.net
Web site: http://www.sover.net/~meg910
Suite Rates: $$$$
Credit Cards: AmEx, Visa, MC, Discover
No. of Suites: 3
Services and Amenities: Special packages, Baby-sitting, Laundry, Library, Kitchen facilities, Fireplaces, Satellite TV, VCR, Cassette players/CD, Radio, Telephones, Whirlpool bath, Individual climate control, Robes, Massage (on call), Complimentary newspaper, Breakfast included
Restrictions: 1 suite handicapped-equipped, Specific pets welcome, Seasonal minimum stays, Children welcome
Room Service: 24 hours
Restaurant: Chef at your request
Bar: The Club
Business Facilities: Message center, Copiers, Teleconferencing
Conference Rooms: 2 rooms, capacity 50
Sports Facilities: Croquet, Hiking, Whirlpool, Horse-drawn carriages and Sleighs, Nearby: Golf, Sailing, Skiing one hour away, Hinsdale Race Track
Location: Private mountain-top estate, 1½ hours to HFD-CT, BOS-MA, MHT-NH Airports
Attractions: Easy access to Boston MA, Hartford CT, Manchester VT, Tanglewood, Rural Vermont and New Hampshire, Antique shops

THE BRETTON ARMS COUNTRY INN

This gracious country inn sits on the expansive grounds of the fabulous Mount Washington Resort area. Built as a private home in 1896, the inn first opened its doors to guests in 1907, then was meticulously restored in 1986, when it was given its National Historic Landmark designation. Within easy walking distance to the grand Mount Washington Hotel, The Bretton Arms Country Inn combines elegant service with the warm atmosphere of traditional country hospitality. During the summer months when The Mount Washington Hotel is open, it offers all its amenities to guests of The Bretton Arms Country Inn, including golf and tennis.

The inn's spacious guestrooms are decorated in Victorian style, with drapes and bedding done in floral prints. Large windows look out onto the Rosebrook Mountain Range or flower gardens. Each bathroom has a tiled floor, modern cast tub with shower, pedestal sink and brass fixtures.

The intimate Bretton Arms Dining Room provides candlelit dinners in front of a welcoming fireplace. In addition to delicious gourmet cuisine, you may also enjoy wintertime entertainment, such as light jazz or folk music. The cozy Club Bar and fireplaced parlor are comfortable spots to relax after a day on the slopes.

Summer is the perfect time to meander around the grounds and delight in the Perennial Gardens or indulge in a peaceful respite seated on the veranda. Winter offers additional delights. Skiers need not go any further than the front door of the inn to put on their skis; there are 100 km of cross-country trails right there. Non-skiers can take a romantic ride on a horse-drawn sleigh, then just sit back and enjoy the glorious view.

Address: Route 302, Bretton Woods, NH 03575
Phone: 603-278-1000
Toll-Free: 800-258-0330
Fax: 603-278-8838
Room Rates: $
Suite Rates: $$
Credit Cards: Visa, MC, AmEx, DS
No. of Rooms: 34 **Suites:** 3
Services and Amenities: Live entertainment, Wine tastings, Shuttle service, Baby-sitting service, Children's programs, Gift shop, Library, Card/game area, TV, Radio, Complimentary toiletries, Discounted ski tickets, Ski & stay packages available
Restrictions: No pets allowed, 2 rooms equipped for handicapped, Children welcome
Restaurant: The Bretton Arms Dining Room, breakfast and dinner served
Bar: The Bretton Arms Club Bar, 4:30–10:00 p.m.
Business Facilities: Message center, Copier, Audio-Visual, Teleconferencing
Sports Facilities: Golf, Tennis, Horseback riding, Biking, Carriage rides, Hiking, Fishing, Downhill & cross-country skiing, Indoor heated pool
Location: Rural White Mountain National Forest, Centrally located
Attractions: Major attractions & outlet shopping within minutes, 5 major ski areas within a 30 mile radius, Bretton Woods Ski Area across the street, Access to amenities of Mount Washington Hotel at established guest rates, Access to Bretton Woods Sports Center (fee)

THE MOUNT WASHINGTON HOTEL & RESORT

Opened in 1902, The Mount Washington Hotel & Resort continues as one of the last of the great Grand Hotels in the beautiful White Mountains, 18,000 acres of National Forest at the base of the Presidential Range. A white-columned 900 foot long veranda, decorated with geraniums and white wicker furniture, wraps around most of the huge building, offering a peaceful place from which to contemplate the beauty of the surrounding countryside.

The main lobby area is elegantly decorated in creams, rich reds, blues and rose, with coordinating couches and easy chairs providing many cozy niches to sit in and read or people-watch. Sparkling chandeliers, wall-length windows and a large fireplace enhance the room's splendor.

Guestrooms are done in light pastels and floral wallpaper accents, with coordinating bedding and drapes, couch and/or easy chairs in deep tones, brass fixtures and floor lamps. Two large windows provide magnificent mountain views. Most bathrooms contain antique claw-foot tubs with showers, large antique marble sinks and brass fixtures.

The Grand Main Dining Room is designed in a unique octagonal fashion, with crystal chandeliers and stained-glass accents. Large wall-length windows allow for sweeping views. The menu changes daily and dinner is accompanied by the resort orchestra, which plays everything from contemporary jazz to traditional orchestral arrangements.

The hotel provides an ample array of amenities, among which is a supervised resort activities program for children, geared for ages 5–12. The King of the Mountain Kids Kamp is staffed by a crew experienced in structured children's programs. For grownups, there are five major ski areas, just half an hour away, in addition to full resort amenities.

Address: Route 302, Bretton Woods, NH 03575
Phone: 603-278-1000
Toll-Free: 800-258-0330
Fax: 603-278-8838
Room Rates: $$$
Suite Rates: $$$$
Credit Cards: Visa, MC, AmEx, Discover
No. of Rooms: 200 **Suites:** 56
Services and Amenities: Valet, Barber shop, Beauty shop, Gift shop, TV lounge, Card/game area, Library, Laundry service, Baby-sitting service, Full activities programs for kids & adults, Radio, Individual heat & air-conditioning, Complimentary toiletries, 2 meals included
Restrictions: 5 rooms equipped for handicapped, No pets allowed, Hotel open from mid-May to mid-October
Concierge: 24 hours
Room Service: 24 hours (limited)
Restaurant: The Grand Main Dining Room, 7:00–9:30 a.m., 6:00–9:00 p.m., Dress code at dinner
Bar: The Princess Lounge, Stickney's, The Cave, 11:30 a.m.–12:30 a.m.
Business Facilities: Message center, Copiers, Audio-Visual, Teleconferencing
Conference Rooms: 16 rooms, capacity 5–1000
Sports Facilities: Indoor/outdoor pools, Handball/squash, Croquet, Whirlpool, Sauna, Massage, Weight training, Tennis, Skiing, Golf—27 PGA holes
Location: Rural—White Mountain National Forest
Attractions: Centrally located with over 12 major attractions within minutes, Extensive outlet shopping within 30 miles, 5 major ski areas within 30 minutes

THE HANOVER INN AT DARTMOUTH COLLEGE

The Hanover Inn is conveniently located on the Dartmouth College green, where guests enjoy access to all of the school's athletic facilities as well as its art exhibits, plays, concerts and films. The architecture is Georgian brick, and the environs are those of a small New England Village. The inviting lobby features a fireplace and sitting area offering a view of the College Green.

Colonial styling in shades of beige accented with rose and green is featured throughout the inn, and each guest room is individually decorated. The lounge and six guest rooms were recently renovated. Baths have telephones, robes, and ample deluxe personal care amenities.

The award-winning Daniel Webster Room serves classic American fare in an atmosphere of Edwardian elegance. Recently opened Zins Restaurant and Wine Bar, with its upbeat contemporary ambiance, serves American cuisine and offers an extensive wine by the glass list. Afternoon high tea is served Tuesday and Thursday in the lobby, which is appointed like a fine living room. Included is a wide assortment of pastries made on the premises.

The surrounding Upper Connecticut River Valley, one of America's most scenic areas, provides ample opportunities for picnicking, hiking, swimming, fishing and skiing.

Intended as lodgings for visiting parents and alumni, Hanover Inn is open to the public and offers a unique taste of the Ivy League environment. Business meetings may be arranged at the Dartmouth College Conference Center, with support facilities at Kiewit Computation Center, where the concept of computer time-sharing originated.

Address: East Wheelock & Main Street, P.O. Box 151, Hanover, NH 03755
Phone: 603-643-4300
Toll-Free: 800-443-7024
Fax: 603-646-3744
E-mail: hanover.inn@dartmouth.edu
Room Rates: $$$
Suite Rates: $$$$
Credit Cards: Visa, MC, AmEx, Diners
No. of Rooms: 92 **Suites:** 22
Services and Amenities: Valet service, Garage and parking, Baby-sitting service, Laundry service, Exercise room, Three floors are non-smoking, Cable TV, Radio, Telephone, Robes, Computer hookup in rooms, PC's available to guests, Complimentary toiletries
Restrictions: Small pets, Handicapped access
Room Service: 8:00 a.m.–10:00 p.m.
Restaurant: Daniel Webster Room, Zins, breakfast, lunch and dinner, Dress code, 4 Diamonds
Bar: Zins, 11:00 a.m.–midnight
Business Facilities: Copiers, Audio-Visual
Conference Rooms: 8 rooms, capacity 300
Sports Facilities: Access to sports club, Guest privileges to Hanover Country Club
Location: Dartmouth College Campus
Attractions: Museums, Shopping, Quechee Gorge, Dartmouth College

THE BERNARDS INN

The Bernards Inn encompasses the service, style, intimacy and elegance of a small European luxury hotel while preserving the rural charm of a historic American country inn. Situated in the quaint country town of Bernardsville in New Jersey's picturesque Somerset Hills, the Mission-style building was constructed in 1907, just steps away from a delightful turn-of-the-century train station. Today, the lovingly restored Inn is host to discerning travelers. Culinary connoisseurs are attracted by the world class cuisine of Chef Edward Stone.

Upon entering The Bernards Inn, guests are enveloped in an aura of refined luxury. A massive floral arrangement soars from a burnished mahogany table toward the impossibly high ceiling of the lobby area. Richly hued in deep burgundy and emerald green, this room exudes warmth, both from a blazing fireplace and from inviting seating areas. Large paintings are graceful notes here and throughout the Inn, lending an air of residential-style elegance.

Each of the spacious deluxe guestrooms and suites is custom designed and furnished in the simple, classical tradition of great Edwardian manor houses, with superb architectural detailing, 19th century armoires, lavish English chintz window treatments and white matlasse coverlets. Behind the painstakingly reproduced period decor are all the amenities of a modern luxury hotel, including a fully stocked mini-bar and a color television. Baths are replete with plush terry robes and oversized towels.

Two magnificent dining rooms and a warm, clubby bar with jazz pianist are apt settings for the outstanding American cuisine of Chef Edward Stone. Dedicated to offering guests exceptional food and gracious service, Chef Stone derives inspiration from fresh, seasonal ingredients. Signature dishes include an enticing juxtaposition of grilled venison shop and roast loin of venison with cranberry-apple relish, and the seared Arctic char with lobster and crab risotto and chive sauce.

Address: 27 Mine Brook Road, Bernardsville, NJ 07924
Phone: 908-766-0002
Toll-Free: 888-766-0002
Fax: 908-766-4604
E-mail: info@bernardsinn.com
Web site: http://www.bernardsinn.com
Room Rates: $$$
Suite Rates: $$$
Credit Cards: Most credit cards accepted
No. of Rooms: 20 **Suites:** 3
Services and Amenities: Parking, Limousine & car rental, Laundry/dry cleaning, Maid service, Nightly turndown with ice service & chocolates, Iron/ironing board, Hair dryer, Cable TV, Telephone, Clock radio, Mini-bar, Robes, Complimentary paper, toiletries & continental breakfast
Concierge: 9:00 a.m.–5:00 p.m.
Restaurant: The Bernards Inn Great Room, The Garden Room and The Bar, 11:30 a.m.–10:00 p.m., Closed Sunday, Dress code, Continental breakfast for guests, 6:30—10:30 a.m. daily
Bar: Same as dining room hours
Business Facilities: Message center, Copiers, Fax, Audio-Visual projection screens, Microphones, Podium, Teleconferencing
Conference Rooms: 6 rooms, capacity 225
Location: In the Somerset Hills, Nearest airport is Newark, Next to New Jersey Transit
Attractions: Antique shopping, Heart of "horse country," Historic sightseeing, Hot air balloon festival (August), Home of US Equestrian Team and US Golf Association and Museum, Walk to movies and shopping

THE QUEEN'S HOTEL

The Queen's Hotel is a small, intimate, historic hotel in the center of Cape May's Historic District, one block from the ocean. Rooms all feature Victorian revival wallpapers, custom European duvets and bed skirts, custom designed headboards and Axminster carpets. Within minutes' walk guests can enjoy some of the State's best restaurants and shops. Numerous tours of the historic district and the town's well-known inns start within two blocks. From several rooms, guests will marvel at the ocean view framed by some of the town's spectacular Victorian architecture down Ocean Street.

The Queen's hotel is owned and operated by the Wells family, who over the past 15 years have established a national reputation for quality hospitality, comfort and service at The Queen Victoria bed and breakfast inn across the street from the Hotel. The Queen's Hotel offers guests the same quality of lodging and restoration that made The Queen Victoria so famous, while providing a different type of hospitality and additional features. The emphasis is on privacy and modern conveniences for guests' comfort, all in a historical setting.

In keeping with Cape May's reputation as a mecca for birding and natural studies, The Queen's Hotel has taken a leadership position in water and energy conservation as well as waste management. Guests, for example, have the choice to have their linens changed daily or reuse them throughout their stay. The savings in water and other resources will fund a donation towards local environmental programs.

The Hotel's professional staff, trained at The Queen Victoria Inn, will make sure that each room is immaculate while making themselves available to help guests find a special restaurant or nearby shop. In the morning, guests can start their day off with a cup of freshly-brewed coffee in their room, then venture out at their leisure to a nearby restaurant for breakfast or brunch.

Address: 601 Columbia Avenue, Cape May, NJ 08204
Phone: 609-884-1613
E-mail: reservation@queenshotel.com
Web site: http://www.queenshotel.com
Room Rates: $
Suite Rates: $$
Credit Cards: Visa, MC
No. of Rooms: 9 **Suites:** 2
Services and Amenities: Parking available, 5 rooms have decks, Pantry w/ice & soda machine, Individual climate control, In-room coffee makers/refrigerators, Phones, Cable TV, Marble sink tops, Heated towel bars, Hair dryers, Whirlpool in 3 rooms, Iron/ironing board, Toiletries
Restrictions: No pets allowed, Smoking permitted on porches and outdoors only
Concierge: 8:00 a.m.–9:00 p.m.
Restaurant: Walking distance to a variety of restaurants
Conference Rooms: 220 square feet
Sports Facilities: 1 block to beach
Location: Downtown Cape May historic district, 40 miles from Atlantic City Airport
Attractions: 2 blocks to Washington Street Pedestrian Mall, Antiques, Boutiques, Specialty shops, 1 block from the ocean

THE CHATEAU

Located in Spring Lake, one of New Jersey's most unspoiled seaside resorts, The Chateau is a jewel of a Victorian summer hotel. Built in 1888, it was most recently refurbished in 1995. One enters the lobby through oak and bevelled-glass doors. Marble floors, a Victorian desk, fresh flowers, ceiling fans, and stained glass windows usher you into the era of yesteryear.

The Chateau's guest accommodations are decorated in white wicker furniture and Waverly fabrics. All rooms and suites feature individual heat and air-conditioning, color cable TVs and VCRs, Casablanca paddle fans, in-room safes, refrigerators, two telephones and private bathrooms. Luxury suites and parlors feature marble baths with double soaking tubs for two, wet bars, sofa sitting areas, marble woodburning fireplaces and private balconies overlooking Spring Lake Park.

The Chateau is located at the foot of Spring Lake, for which the town was named. It also overlooks two parks with ancient shade trees and footbridges, and Constitution Gazebo. A trolley departs every half hour from its front door for a scenic tour of this quaint Victorian town.

The staff can advise you on dining, shopping, and other activities. The Chateau provides complimentary beach, pool, and tennis passes. Bicycles can be rented from the hotel. The Atlantic Club, a private full-service fitness center, is available to Chateau guests at a nominal fee.

A newly opened Conference Room has 800 square feet of space. Also, a new breakfast room serves a Continental Breakfast—optional at $4.75 per person.

Open year round, the Chateau offers a lovely respite one hour from New York, Philadelphia, or Atlantic City.

Address: 500 Warren Avenue, Spring Lake, NJ 07762
Phone: 908-974-2000
Toll-Free: 800-873-2392
Fax: 908-974-0007
Room Rates: $
Suite Rates: $
Credit Cards: Visa, MC, AmEx, DC, DS
No. of Rooms: 38 **Suites:** 5
Services and Amenities: Non-smoking rooms available, Baby-sitting service, Laundry service, Game area, Cable TV, VCR, Radio, Refrigerator, In-room safe, 2 telephones per room, Complimentary toiletries
Restrictions: No pets allowed, 5 rooms handicapped-equipped
Room Service: 8:00–11:00 a.m.
Business Facilities: Message center, Copiers, Audio-Visual
Conference Rooms: 1 room, capacity 40
Sports Facilities: The Atlantic Club available to Chateau guests (fee)
Location: Historic district of Spring Lake, 1 hour from New York
Attractions: The beachfront community of Spring Lake, Six Flags Great Adventure, Allaire State Park, Garden State Arts Center, Monmouth Park Race Track and Freehold Raceway

THE LODGE AT CLOUDCROFT

Widely recognized as New Mexico's finest country inn, The Lodge at Cloudcroft has also gained international acclaim with its celebrity guests. In its 99-year history, such diverse luminaries as Pancho Villa, Judy Garland, and Clark Gable have appreciated the hospitality of this imposing Bavarian-style mountain resort which blends unobtrusively in its lush primeval setting. Two newly acquired properties house a special conference facility called The Lodge Retreat, while the historic Pavilion, Cloudcroft's oldest dwelling, is a bed and breakfast conversion.

Nestled among the fresh aspen, fir, and maple trees, this forested retreat reflects, as owners planned, "great sensitivity to the beauty of the landscape."

A commitment to provide relaxed, congenial surroundings continues in the mezzanine-encircled lobby, replete with inviting leather couches, warming fireplace and fine antiques. The 47 suites and guest room accommodations reflect Victorian charm—high ceilings, lazy fans, cheery hues, and down comforters. Rebecca's offers a choice of two dining rooms—one boasting leaded-glass windows and cheerful, plant-filled decor—the other a cozy mahogany-walled fireside retreat. Culinary delights are prepared by an award winning chef. For convenience, the golf shop has a snack area.

Tee off at one of the world's highest and oldest (1895) mountain golf courses, or seasonally, take advantage of cross country skiing, inner tubing and snowmobiling. Fishing, jogging, and nearby horseback riding remain favorite activities. Natural wonders abound at The Lodge—the glorious mountain scenery, pine-scented air, and spectacular sunsets.

Address: #1 Corona Place, P.O. Box 497, Cloudcroft, NM 88317
Phone: 505-682-2566
Toll-Free: 800-395-6343
Fax: 505-682-2715
E-mail: thelodge-nm@zianet.com
Room Rates: $
Suite Rates: $$
Credit Cards: Most credit cards accepted
No. of Rooms: 47 **Suites:** 7
Services and Amenities: Babysitting service, Gift shop, Golf shop, Cable TV with HBO, Radio, Some rooms with whirlpools, Fireplaces, Balconies, Children under 12 years free of charge, Entry designed for handicapped
Restrictions: No pets allowed
Concierge: Summer season
Restaurant: Rebecca's Fine Dining, 7:00 a.m.–10:00 p.m. daily, Dress Code
Bar: Evening hours during summer, Weekends in winter, Lobby service
Business Facilities: Message center, Secretarial service, Copiers, Audio-Visual
Conference Rooms: 5 rooms, largest seats 150
Sports Facilities: Golf, Cross-country skiing, Snowmobiling, Fishing, Jogging, Pool, Whirlpool & Sauna, Tennis & Horseback riding nearby, On-site massage
Location: 9200 ft. above & 18 mi. from Alamogordo and White Sands National Monument
Attractions: Sweeping 150-mile mountain views from one of the world's highest and oldest (1895) mountain golf courses, Southernmost ski area in the U.S., Carlsbad Caverns, White Sands National Monument, Great sightseeing

ELDORADO HOTEL

The Eldorado, opened in 1986, is a small luxury hotel in the heart of Santa Fe's historic district.

Built in Pueblo Revival-style, its interior design has a southwestern theme. The dramatic lobby features tiled floors, high ceilings, and many works of original local art.

Carpeted guest rooms are decorated in tones of mauve, turquoise, and bone. Hand-carved furniture designed by Peter Gould, original tile work, light walls with prints by Pueblo Indians, and patterns bordering the ceiling all lend local flavor. There are 18 suites. The Presidential Suite features five luxurious rooms with ample space for small board meetings and receptions. Its VIP accommodations include two fireplaces, a wet bar, Jacuzzi, and tiled terrace with panoramic views of Santa Fe and the Sangre de Cristo Mountains.

The Eldorado has two restaurants, each with its own lounge. The Old House offers gourmet dining five nights per week. A more casual ambience is found at the Eldorado Court, which is open daily.

The hotel has full conference facilities, including a courtyard capable of accommodating banquets for 500 or receptions for 700. Two blocks away is the Sweeney Convention Center with generous exhibit space and room to seat 1500 theater-style.

Only two blocks from Santa Fe's Plaza, the Eldorado is convenient to all the historic, commercial, and cultural sites of "The City Different" where Indian, Spanish, and Anglo cultures blend. The hotel's bilingual staff will do everything possible to help guests fully enjoy their Santa Fe experience.

The Eldorado has just completed a renovation of all guest rooms and has recently become the managing agent of the Zona Rosa which is comprised of eight beautifully appointed suites and the Las Palmas, which consists of twenty-one uniquely Santa Fe casitas and studios.

Address: 309 West San Francisco Street, Santa Fe, NM 87501
Phone: 505-988-4455
Toll-Free: 800-252-7466
Fax: 505-995-4555
E-mail: rez@eldoradohotel.com
Room Rates: $$
Suite Rates: $$$$
Credit Cards: Most credit cards accepted
No. of Rooms: 218 **Suites:** 18
Services and Amenities: Valet and concierge service, Valet parking in underground garage, Laundry service, Baby-sitting available, Gift shop, Cable TV, Robes, Nightly turndown, Fully stocked honor bar, Complimentary toiletries
Restrictions: Pets allowed, 20 non-smoking rooms, 3 rooms handicapped-equipped
Concierge: 8:00 a.m.–6:00 p.m.
Room Service: 6:30 a.m.–11:00 p.m.
Restaurant: The Old House Restaurant, Tuesday-Sunday 5:30 p.m.–10:00 p.m.; The Eldorado Court, daily 5:30 p.m.–10:00 p.m.
Bar: The Old House Tavern, 5:30–10:00 p.m., Eldorado Court Lounge, 11:00 a.m-midnight
Business Facilities: Message center, Secretarial service available, Copiers, Audio-Visual, Fax
Conference Rooms: 10 rooms, capacity 15–600
Sports Facilities: Heated rooftop swimming pool and jacuzzi, Whirlpool, Sauna, Massage
Location: Historic district of Santa Fe
Attractions: The Plaza, Outdoor markets and festivals, Shopping, Art, Theater, Opera, Museums, Historic churches, Sports: Rafting, Hot air ballooning, Skiing, Golfing, Tennis and Soaking in nearby hot springs

HACIENDA DEL CEREZO

Secluded and intimate, Hacienda del Cerezo is a "hideaway" guest ranch, bordering the desert solitude of 150,000 acres of federal and Native American land, yet only 20 minutes from the world-renowned art and cultural center of Santa Fe. The ten guest suites provide modern luxury within an architecturally stunning framework of hand-carved beams and massive doors, polished Saltillo tile floors and kiva fireplaces burning with the aroma of native pinon.

Each suite has its own private enclosed patio, fireplace and sitting area, king bed, and radiant heating. Oversize baths have huge Jacuzzi tubs, stone counters with double sinks, separate showers, water closets and bidets, and their own heating zone for maximum comfort. Magical details abound, with each suite's separate southwestern motif, such as "Sol" (sun), or "Pottery," carved into ceiling beams, hand-painted on tile, and etched on glass shower doors. Arranged around a walled courtyard planted with native shrubs and fruit trees, all suites have views of the Sangre de Cristo Mountains or the Jemez Mountains.

Strains of classical guitar reverberate from the Great Room's 100-year-old ceiling beams as guests enjoy a candle-lit dinner that might include: seared Ahi tuna Hoisin with Wasabi guacamole and a Cilantro infused oil; or a roasted rack of Australian lamb with noisette of Muscovy duck breast; prepared under the direction of a master chef.

Guests may enjoy horseback riding from the Inn's own stable, tennis court, and a vanishing edge pool with outdoor spa.

Address: 100 Camino del Cerezo, Santa Fe, NM 87501
Phone: 505-982-8000
Toll-Free: 888-982-8001
Fax: 505-983-7162
E-mail: hacienda@rt66.com
Suite Rates: $$$$
Credit Cards: AmEx, Visa, MC
No. of Suites: 10
Services and Amenities: Parking, Limited laundry service, Library, Fireplaces, Balconies, Satellite TV, VCR, Telephone, Whirlpool bath, Robes, Complimentary shampoo, conditioner and lotion, All meals provided
Restrictions: No pets allowed, Only 2 guests per room, No rollaways, 1 room with handicapped access
Room Service: Per arrangement
Restaurant: Hacienda, breakfast, lunch and dinner hours
Business Facilities: Fax, Modems
Conference Rooms: 1 room, capacity 25
Sports Facilities: Outdoor swimming pool, Whirlpool, Massage, Tennis (hard surface), Horseback riding along ancient Indian trails, Hiking
Location: In the desert, Northwest of Santa Fe
Attractions: 20 minutes from Santa Fe art markets, opera and fiestas, Nearby rafting and world class fly fishing, Native American pueblo tours

HOTEL ST. FRANCIS

Santa Fe is situated on a 7,000-foot-high plateau with clear air, the heritage of Pueblo Indians and Spanish Conquistadors followed by American traders, and 20th-century names such as Georgia O'Keeffe and Max Weber. To this, add inspiring architecture, an incredible outdoor opera theatre, and what some consider the best Indian-art shopping in the Southwest. The Hotel St. Francis, which first opened in 1924 as the De Vargas Hotel, presented an enormous challenge to renovators a few years ago. The program required extensive research to update the building, and the architects had to meet the standards of the National Register of Historic Places.

Today's hotel, renamed, is a short block from the Plaza, the center of the town for centuries. Guests will find 1920s art deco-inspired decor and an open, airy concept, with large street-view windows, palms, and plenty of access to the verandas. The original light fixtures were refurbished for public areas, and artifacts from the earlier hotel are displayed throughout. All guest rooms feature period furniture of cherry and mahogany, and brass and iron beds topped with colorful quilts. Bathrooms are marble with brass and porcelain fixtures and pedestal sinks.

The new restaurant, The Club, offers good food with an Italian flair at affordable prices. A standout among the dishes is Pasta Alla Santa Fe, a fresh red chile fettucine sauteed with chicken, Parmesan cheese, green chile, and cream.

Santa Fe is a pleasure to walk around. In the immediate area are the Palace of the Governors, Sena Plaza, St. Francis Cathedral (housing the oldest madonna in the United States), the Museum of Fine Arts, and shops selling kachinas, pottery, rugs, and irresistible turquoise and silver jewelry.

Address: 210 Don Gaspar, Santa Fe, NM 87501
Phone: 505-983-5700
Toll-Free: 800-666-5700
Fax: 505-989-7690
Room Rates: $
Suite Rates: $$$
Credit Cards: Visa, MC, AmEx, DC, CB
No. of Rooms: 81 **Suites:** 2
Services and Amenities: Parking, Afternoon tea, Individual safes, Refrigerators, Television, Complimentary toiletries
Restrictions: No pets allowed, Handicapped access to 1 room
Concierge: 9:00 a.m.–6:00 p.m.
Room Service: 7:00 a.m.–12:00 a.m.
Restaurant: The Club, 7:00 a.m.–12:00 midnight
Bar: Artist's Pub, 11:00 a.m.–12:00 midnight or 1:00 a.m.
Business Facilities: Banquet facilities
Conference Rooms: 1 room, capacity 65, All meeting plans customized
Sports Facilities: None on premises; In the area: White water rafting, Hiking, Rock climbing, Ballooning, Tennis, Golf, Santa Fe Ski Basin (14 miles)
Location: Historic downtown
Attractions: Five major museums, Horseracing May through Labor Day, Nearby pueblos, Opera and Chamber Music Festival July and August, State Capital, Canyon Road galleries, Skiing, Santa Fe Ski Basin

INN ON THE ALAMEDA

Warm personal service and an inviting atmosphere make this small hotel a must for your next visit to Santa Fe. Nestled between Canyon Road and the historic Plaza in old Santa Fe, the Inn on the Alameda offers comfort and peace within its adobe walls. The Inn blends an intimate atmosphere with an impeccable combination of convenience and privacy.

The city of Santa Fe is a mecca for artists. Across from the Inn, Canyon Road is brimming with galleries showcasing artists and their creations. The historic Plaza, shopping, dining and many other activities are just a stroll away. A short drive will take you to the Santa Fe Ski Basin, white water rafting, fishing, golfing or exploring.

Each of the Inn's uniquely designed Southwestern rooms have an individual personality and style. The essence of Santa Fe is best captured in one of the 19 deluxe rooms and 10 suites offering private balconies and romantic kiva fireplaces with handmade Spanish tile accents.

A delicious complimentary gourmet breakfast buffet with homemade muffins, bagels, pastries, cinnamon rolls, fresh fruit juices, teas and locally roasted coffee, is offered each morning in the Inn's delightful country kitchen or in the privacy of your own room.

The corporate guest will enjoy the variety of meeting styles that can be created with the Inn's conference facilities. Natural light, kiva fireplaces create a warm and intimate setting for almost any gathering. Audio-Visual equipment and gourmet catering are available for all meeting rooms and facilities.

Address: 303 East Alameda, Santa Fe, NM 87501
Phone: 505-984-2121
Toll-Free: 800-289-2122
Fax: 505-986-8325
E-mail: info@inn-alameda.com
Web site: http://www.inn-alameda.com
Room Rates: $$
Suite Rates: $$$
Credit Cards: Visa, MC AmEx, Diners Club
No. of Rooms: 69 **Suites:** 10
Services and Amenities: Free parking, Laundry service, Dry cleaning service, Baby-sitting service, Beauty shop, Library, Fitness center, 2 outdoor jacuzzis, Massage, Cable TV with HBO, Complimentary breakfast
Restrictions: Pets allowed, Handicapped access to 3 rooms, Children under 18 stay free
Concierge: Yes
Room Service: 7:00 a.m.–11:00 a.m.
Bar: 4:00 p.m.–11:00 p.m.
Business Facilities: Conference center, Intimate meeting rooms, Audio-Visual equipment, Gourmet catering service
Conference Rooms: Conference Center, capacity 62
Sports Facilities: White water rafting, Bicycling, Hiking, Skiing, Tennis, Golf, Fishing, Exploring countryside and cultures
Location: Downtown Santa Fe, Nearest airport is Albuquerque International
Attractions: Restaurants, Concerts, Theatre, Opera, Nightclubs, Craft fairs, Indian Market, Art galleries, Museums, Shops and Historic Plaza nearby

LA FONDA

Located in the heart of Santa Fe on the historic plaza, this elegant Spanish colonial Adobe hotel is surrounded by historic churches, museums, shops and galleries. This landmark hotel is famous for its timeless charm and its commitment to excellent service. La Fonda has been on this site since 1610 and has been providing the best in Southwestern hospitality for generations. Numerous celebrities from Kit Carson to Errol Flynn to John F. Kennedy have enjoyed La Fonda.

Each of the 153 rooms and 21 suites are unique including mountain views, balconies, fireplaces, colorful hand-decorated wooden furniture, air-conditioning, cable TV, room service and covered parking. Rooms are accented by local Pueblo Indian artists. After a day of skiing, shopping or sightseeing, guests can enjoy a hot tub soak or plunge into the hotel's year round outdoor swimming pool.

La Fonda is famous for their Margaritas whether at the La Fiesta Lounge, the patio bar with music and nightly dancing, or The Bell Tower Bar on the fifth floor offering magnificent sunset views of the mountains. Enjoy New Mexican and American favorites from award-winning chef, Maurice Zeck, at La Plazuela, an enclosed skylit courtyard. Such favorites include Chile Rellenos de La Fonda.

La Fonda is a favorite spot for gatherings of all kinds. There is a ballroom for up to 600 guests as well as several different sized meeting rooms. In addition, there is a new roof-top banquet room to meet all your business and special event needs.

Address: 100 East San Francisco Street, Santa Fe, NM 87501
Phone: 505-982-5511
Toll-Free: 800-523-5002
Fax: 505-988-2952
Web site: http://www.travelbase.com/destinations/Santa-Fe/La-Fonda/
Room Rates: $$
Suite Rates: $$$$
Credit Cards: Most credit cards accepted
No. of Rooms: 153 **Suites:** 21
Services and Amenities: Garage & parking, Gift shop, Lounge, Laundry service, Baby-sitting service, Fireplaces, Balconies, Cable TV, Radio, Individual heat & air-conditioning control, Hair dryers, Irons & ironing boards, Complimentary toiletries
Restrictions: 1 room with handicapped access, No pets allowed, Children under 12 no extra charge in room
Concierge: 9:00 a.m.–6:00 p.m.
Room Service: 7:00 a.m.–10:00 p.m.
Restaurant: La Plazuela, 7:00 a.m.–10:00 p.m.
Bar: La Fiesta Lounge, 11:00 a.m.–Midnight
Business Facilities: Copiers, Fax, Modems (guest telephones)
Conference Rooms: 7 rooms, capacity 6–600
Sports Facilities: Outdoor swimming pool, Whirlpool, Massage, Skiing nearby
Location: Downtown Historic Plaza
Attractions: Only hotel on the historic Plaza, Galleries, Shopping, Historic churches, Museums, Restaurants

Delano, Miami Beach, Florida. PAGE 88

Heron House, Key West, Florida. PAGE 84

Old Northern Inn, Coolin, Idaho. PAGE 102

Seacrest Manor, Rockport, Massachusetts. PAGE 121

RIVEREDGE RESORT HOTEL

Located in the heart of the beautiful 1000 Islands, the Riveredge Resort Hotel is as spectacular as its surroundings. Rising four floors above the majestic St. Lawrence River and overlooking magnificent Boldt Castle, the resort offers an elegant, yet comfortable atmosphere complemented by superior service and hospitality.

With 129 deluxe accommodations, most with a river view, the Riveredge has earned the coveted AAA Four Diamond rating. The French Provincial furnishings and soft color schemes lend an air of elegance and comfort to the well-equipped rooms. The wide array of services and the activities at hand create a haven for business meetings and for unforgettable intimate weddings.

Windows on the Bay, the Hotel's main dining room, offers casual dining on the main floor overlooking the main shipping channel of the St. Lawrence Seaway. The Jacques Cartier Room's chef James Collar boasts the AAA Four Diamond rating for fine dining. Located on the fourth floor concierge level, its floor- to-ceiling windows on three sides provide spectacular panoramic views of the St. Lawrence River and Boldt Castle. The decor is French Provincial with table service consisting of Schonwald China, Bohemian Crystal, and Oneida Silver. One of the most celebrated entree selections is the Cajun Lobster Tails, and for dessert, the tableside Bananas Foster. The RiverWatch Lounge offers the best in beverage service in a relaxed atmosphere with live entertainment.

Guests may relax on a balcony and enjoy the sights and sounds of the beautiful St. Lawrence River. For those in pursuit of activity, options abound. In the spring, summer and fall the river is alive with pleasure boats and ocean-going freighters from all over the world. Within walking distance is the village of Alexandria Bay with its shops, boutiques, nightclub and restaurants, and where sightseeing vessels depart regularly from the docks for guided cruises through the islands. A stop at Boldt Castle, a 122-room replica of a Rhineland castle, is a must.

The Riveredge Hotel Resort is easily accessible from both Highway 401 in the province of Ontario and Route 81 in New York State.

Address: 17 Holland Street, Alexandria Bay, NY 13607
Phone: 315-482-9917
Toll-Free: 800-ENJOY-US
Fax: 315-482-5010
Room Rates: $
Suite Rates: $$
Credit Cards: Most credit cards accepted
No. of Rooms: 129 **Suites:** 41
Services and Amenities: Fun Time Packages, Parking, Valet, Beauty shop, Gift shop, TV lounge, Card and game area, Laundry service, Baby-sitting service, Cable TV, Wet bar, Radio, Two telephones, Complimentary toiletries
Restrictions: No pets allowed, 6 rooms equipped for handicap
Concierge: 8:00 a.m.–8:00 p.m.
Room Service: 6:30 a.m.–10:00 p.m.
Restaurant: RiverWatch Lounge, 11:00 a.m.– 1:00 a.m.
Bar: 11:00 a.m.–1:00 a.m.
Business Facilities: Message and Secretarial center, Copiers, Audio-Visual, Fax
Conference Rooms: 8 rooms, capacity 10-250
Sports Facilities: Indoor pool & Jacuzzi, Fitness room, 2,000 feet of dock space with power, Water & cable TV hook-ups, Near 18-hole golf course
Location: Walk to Alexandria Bay, Hancock airport 99 miles
Attractions: A short drive to the Antique Boat Museum, The Frederic Remington Art Museum, and Old Fort Henry in Kingston, Ontario; The St. Lawrence River, In the heart of beautifull 1,000 Islands, Unparalleled natural beauty

DE BRUCE COUNTRY INN ON THE WILLOWEMOC

Located within the Catskill Forest Park, the De Bruce Country Inn offers a secluded and elegant setting for enjoying wooded trails, wildlife and game, trout-fishing streams, and lake and mountain views from the Inn's own private preserve. Guests experience unpretentious but heartfelt hospitality, the offerings of a gifted chef, and all the amenities of a lovingly and authentically restored turn-of-the-century country hostelry.

You enter this 1914 Federal-style building through a parlor lined with bookshelves and contemporary art, with yellow pine floors, a fieldstone fireplace and comfortable antique couches and chairs. Rooms—all with private baths and telephones—feature brass beds with posturepedic mattresses and homemade bedspread, Indian or Oriental rugs, Victorian hurricane lamps and ceiling fans, and color-coordinated custom drapes and wallpaper. Original art and decorative craft items provide a unique touch.

After a day of fly-fishing, fall foliage viewing or just lounging on the front porch, you may enjoy an Apple Toddy at the Dry Fly Lounge, followed by fresh Willowemoc trout at Ianine's Restaurant. The formal dining room with its long-leaf yellow pine floors, coffered ceiling, silk drapes, and white Picasso china features a collection of small artifacts and antique tools. The summer dining terrace allows full enjoyment of the fresh air and views of the valley and mountains.

There is a fly-fishing museum nearby and the many activities of the state park. Local antique shops and discount malls offer interesting resources for bargain and gift hunters.

Address: De Bruce Road #286A, De Bruce, NY 12758
Phone: 914-439-3900
Web site: http://www.debrucecountryinn.com
Room Rates: $$$
Suite Rates: $$$
Credit Cards: American Express
No. of Rooms: 15 **Suites:** 2
Services and Amenities: Parking, Gift shop, TV lounge, Library, Two meals included, Complimentary toiletries
Restrictions: Children & pets at owner's discretion, No handicapped-equipped rooms
Restaurant: Ianine's, 8:00–10:00 a.m., 7:00–10:00 p.m.
Bar: The Dry Fly Lounge, 5:00–10:00 p.m.
Business Facilities: Fax, Copiers
Conference Rooms: 1 room, capacity 15
Sports Facilities: Whirlpool bath, Sauna, Swimming pool, Some weight training equipment, Nearby golf, Skiing, Boating, Riding, Tennis, Fishing
Location: Catskill Forest Preserve
Attractions: Antiques, Herb gardens, Covered bridges, Fly-fishing Museum, Music festivals, River rafting, On nearby Delaware River, Discount malls, State park with boating, swimming and trails

CHESTNUT INN AT OQUAGA LAKE

Built in 1928, the Chestnut Inn at Oquaga Lake is a classic example of American-style architecture and craftsmanship. The Inn is almost totally constructed of the now extinct North American chestnut. The lobby, dominated by a natural stone fireplace, is furnished in antiques, with fabrics in warming hues of pink and green.

Guests enjoy the relaxed atmosphere and many amenities of a lakeside resort, with excellent service and elegant furnishings. Guest rooms feature private baths, decorative floral touches, and soothing lakeside or woodland views. A short stroll on flower-lined walkways brings guests to the banks of Oquaga Lake and the boat dock.

A cruise aboard Pickles, a replica of the Inn's original launch that once graced the waters, provides an entertaining experience. Canoes and paddleboats are available upon request, and the Activities Director is on hand to arrange an activity for everyone. Guests can fish, waterski, or hike the beautiful shores of the lake. Golf and tennis are just minutes from the Inn.

The ultimate in dining is offered by Chef Chris McGee both in the relaxed elegance of the main Chestnut Inn Dining Room with its lamp-lit tables, and in the Lakeside Sun Room with views of the lake from its windows on all sides. Weather permitting, more casual dining is available on the Waterfront Terrace. The Waterside Tavern provides daily beverage service.

The Chestnut Inn prides itself in providing a fully-equipped conference facility that accommodates up to 100 people, complete with catering capabilities. The relaxed atmosphere and multitude of activities at hand create the perfect meeting place.

Address: 498 Oquaga Lake Road, Deposit, NY 13754
Phone: 607-467-2500
Toll-Free: 800-467-7676
Fax: 607-467-5911
Room Rates: $
Suite Rates: $
Credit Cards: Visa, MC, Diners, Discover
No. of Rooms: 30 **Suites:** 6
Services and Amenities: Valet service, TV lounge, Library, Some rooms have televison, Complimentary toiletries
Restrictions: No pets allowed, No charge for children under 12 with parent
Restaurant: Chestnut Inn Dining Room, 7:00 a.m.–9:00 p.m.
Bar: Waterside Tavern, 11:00 a.m.–11:00 p.m.
Business Facilities: Business workspace with Copiers, Audio-visiual, Teleconferencing, Fax
Conference Rooms: 1 room, capacity 100
Sports Facilities: Canoes, Paddleboats, Water skiing, Fishing, Hiking, Swimming, Mountain biking, Nearby 9 holes of golf and tennis
Location: Off Route 17, 40 miles to Link Field at Binghamton, NY
Attractions: Binghamton Mets baseball team, Carousel Museum, Antique shops, Movie theatre, Shopping Mall

J. HARPER POOR COTTAGE

On the site of the former 1650 Baker Tavern stands the magnificently refurbished J. Harper Poor Cottage of East Hampton. This stately English manor house incorporates a distinctly American saltbox theme with oak hand-hewn beams and expansive fireplaces. Luxurious sitting rooms and library invite guests to linger, relax and take in the incredible interior details: carved wood ornaments, scrolled brackets and plaster relief ceilings. It is no surprise that this stately inn has been featured in Travel & Leisure and Town & Country Magazines.

The Cottage is within walking distance to some of the finest beaches on the Atlantic coast, unique shops, churches, galleries, restaurants, Herrick Park and the Village Green. Off-street parking, beach-parking passes and beach towels are available for guests' convenience.

Spacious, sun-bright rooms are all discerningly decorated. Each room includes a queen or king bed, lavish bath with spa or clawfoot tubs, individually controlled air-conditioning and heat, an in-room security safe, TV and VCR. All rooms overlook the village green or the gardens.

A 200-year old wisteria vine presides over a formal garden, with outdoor tables and chairs for breakfast, reading, lounging and drinks. Each morning guests begin their day with a sumptuous complimentary breakfast cooked to order. Guests may dine outdoors during the summer and by a wood burning fireplace in the winter. The private dining room, with its original 18th century ceiling beams, fireplace and paneling, is available for catered dinners. A fully stocked bar with select choices of wines, by the glass or by the bottle, is available for guests and event purposes. Enjoy your wine with daily hors d'oeuvres.

Town & Country Magazine said the Cottage "...offers the kind of plush overnight accommodations that you'd expect to find in an area famous for its residential real estate; the five-room inn is poor in name only."

Address: 181 Main Street, East Hampton, NY 11937
Phone: 516-324-4081
Fax: 516-329-5931
E-mail: info@jharperpoor.com
Web site: http://www.jharperpoor.com
Room Rates: $$$
Credit Cards: AmEx, Visa, MC, DC
No. of Rooms: 5
Services and Amenities: Laundry service, Card/game area, Library, Fireplaces, Cable TV, VCR, Telephones, Individual heat and air-conditioning control, Robes, Whirlpool bath, Complimentary toiletries, Breakfast included in room rate
Restrictions: No pets allowed
Room Service: 8:00 a.m.–10:00 p.m.
Bar: Noon–11:00 p.m.
Business Facilities: Fax
Sports Facilities: Massage
Location: Village Main Street
Attractions: Boutique shopping and beach within easy walking distance, Surrounded by historic buildings

INN AT GREAT NECK

Located in the heart of Great Neck Village on picturesque Long Island, minutes from Manhattan surrounded by 300 shops, restaurants and entertainment spots, the Inn at Great Neck offers 85 luxurious guest rooms and suites. Valet, concierge, twice daily maid service, 24 hour room service and a health facility are just the beginning of what the Inn at Great Neck has to offer.

Every guest room features two-line speaker telephones with facsimile and personal computer capabilities, mini-bars, stereo CD players, video cassette players, multi-phase lighting, separate reading and work areas, spacious vanities and marble bathrooms with oversized bathtubs or Jacuzzis. Art Deco in style, guest rooms are furnished and appointed in a style reminiscent of the golden era of the 1920's. The Inn's state of the art telephone system was specifically designed to serve the demanding needs of the business traveler. The system is without peer in its ease of use, privacy and the flexibility it affords guests.

The restaurant at the Inn offers innovative American cuisine with seafood, meats and game from the bountiful Long Island area. Two banquet rooms, a ballroom and a boardroom provide the setting for unequalled catering and reception events, corporate meetings, weddings and social gatherings.

Minutes from Manhattan and moments from Long Island's famed North Shore, The Inn at Great Neck offers the perfect location for the business or leisure traveler visiting New York City and points East on Long Island. The Inn provides the perfect atmosphere for a relaxing escape.

Address: 30 Cutter Mill Road, Great Neck, NY 11021
Phone: 516-773-2000
Toll-Free: 800-777-4151
Fax: 516-773-2020
Room Rates: $$$
Suite Rates: $$$$
Credit Cards: AmEx, DC, Visa, MC
No. of Rooms: 85 **Suites:** 6
Services and Amenities: Valet, Twice daily maid service, Spacious vanities, Multi-phase lighting, Marble bathrooms with oversized bathtubs/Jacuzzis, Mini-bars, Cable TV, Video cassette player, Video tapes & compact discs available, 2-line telephones, Fax & computer data ports
Concierge: Front desk
Room Service: 6:00 a.m.–11:00 p.m.
Restaurant: Restaurant at Inn, 7:00 a.m.–11:00 p.m.
Bar: Restaurant Bar, 12:00 noon–1:00 a.m.
Business Facilities: Catering & conference facilities
Conference Rooms: 4 rooms, capacity 350
Sports Facilities: Exercise room
Location: 6 miles from JFK, Minutes from Manhattan
Attractions: Great Neck Village, Over 300 shops, restaurants & entertainment spots, Downtown Manhattan, Shea Stadium, Belmont Race Track, National Tennis Center

MIRROR LAKE INN

The Mirror Lake Inn is "your home away from home," located on eight acres in the quiet residential area of Lake Placid. The Inn was a famous resort even before the Winter Olympics came to town in 1932. The 1980 Winter Olympics increased the area's wintertime recreational opportunities, which now include skating rinks, cross-country skiing, downhill skiing nine miles from the Inn (at Whiteface Mountain), bobsledding, toboggan, dogsledding, and snowmobiling.

Situated on the shores of Mirror Lake, the Inn offers a private beach and summertime recreation as well. Its full service spa/salon and swimming facilities are open year round.

The Inn's ambiance is one of casual Adirondack elegance. Its lobby and public areas feature mahogany, stone fireplaces, chandeliers, and antiques. Complimentary afternoon tea is served in the living room.

Guest rooms are well appointed in classic traditional style. Most have mountain or lake views with private terraces. Suites feature king-size beds and double Jacuzzi tubs with showers.

Breakfast and dinner are served in the Averil Conwell Dining Room, a romantic spot overlooking Mirror Lake and the High Peaks, named for the artist who executed its oil paintings of Lake Placid at the turn of the century. The dining room's Adirondack flapjacks with hot maple syrup are a famous breakfast item, and the Adirondack mixed grill is popular in the evening.

The Cottage Café, known as the skiers' meeting place, serves lunch and supper and stays open until the wee hours.

The Mirror Lake Inn offers full conference facilities. For a vacation or conference in a modern resort that values tradition and service, this is the place. The Inn is Lake Placid's only four diamond resort.

Address: 5 Mirror Lake Drive, Lake Placid, NY 12946
Phone: 518-523-2544
Fax: 518-523-2871
E-mail: info@mirrorlakeinn.com
Web site: http://www.mirrorlakeinn.com
Room Rates: $$
Credit Cards: Visa, MC, AmEx, DC
No. of Rooms: 128 **Suites:** 17
Services and Amenities: Parking, International currency exchange, Full service spa and salon, Library, Activities desk, Baby-sitting service, Game area, Gift shop, Cable TV, Radio, Complimentary toiletries
Restrictions: No pets allowed, 2 rooms handicapped-equipped
Restaurant: Averil Conwell Dining Room, 7:30–10:00 a.m. Monday-Friday, 7:30–11:00 a.m. Saturday-Sunday, The Cottage Cafe, 11:30 a.m.–1:00 a.m. daily
Bar: The Terrace Suite Lounge, 4:00 p.m.–11:00 p.m.
Business Facilities: Message center, Secretarial service, Translators, Copiers, Audio-Visual, Fax
Conference Rooms: 3 rooms, capacity 300
Sports Facilities: Indoor & outdoor swimming pools, Tennis court, Sailing, Windsurfing, Fishing, Hiking, Cross-country skiing, Whirlpool, Sauna, Massage
Location: Mirror Lake Drive, Olympic Village, Lake Placid
Attractions: International sports events, Outdoor recreational activities, Boutiques

BEEKMAN TOWER SUITE HOTEL

Located in a charming Eastside neighborhood near exclusive Sutton Place and the United Nations, The Beekman is ideally situated in a quiet neighborhood only a stones throw away from the corporate headquarters of Midtown. Personal service and attention, combined with the neighborhood setting, creates a welcome "home in New York" feeling.

Built in 1928, The Beekman has long been a distinctive sight on the New York skyline. This landmark building, whose elaborate tower is an outstanding example of the art deco style, successfully combines elegance and art. The hotel offers 173 handsomely furnished studios, as well as one and two-bedroom suites, all with complete kitchens. Suites are decorated in soft shades of moss, rose and gold. French prints adorn the walls creating an elegant sophistication. A typical deluxe one-bedroom suite features an oversized living room, dining room with queen-size pull-out sofa, 25" TV/VCR, spacious bedroom with king-size bed, one and a half baths, and fully equipped kitchen. These spacious suites give guests all the room they need to spread out their work, hold a meeting, entertain friends or even bring along the family.

The hotel's on-site Zephyr Grill restaurant features contemporary American cuisine prepared with a New York flair. The unique modern art deco setting evokes the romance of the Zephyr trains in the 1930's. Giant glass murals, featuring etchings of the trains, are complemented by mahogany wood paneling and "Bauhaus" banquettes in tones of blue and salmon.

A delicious assortment of food will tempt even the most discerning palate at the Grill. Known for their extensive seafood appetizers, home-style chicken pot pie, and Mississippi mud pie, guests are guaranteed to have a delicious experience.

For those travelers who love art deco settings and are concerned with personal service and attention to detail, The Beekman Tower will fulfill all your needs.

Address: 3 Mitchell Place, New York, NY 10017
Phone: 212-355-7300
Toll-Free: 800-637-8483
Fax: 212-753-9366
E-mail: info@mesuite.com
Web site: http://www.mesuite.com
Suite Rates: $$$$
Credit Cards: Most credit cards accepted
No. of Suites: 173
Services and Amenities: Valet & parking service, Laundry service, Kitchen facilities, Cable TV/VCR, 2-line telephones, Radio, Individual heat & air-conditioning, Complimentary toiletries
Restrictions: 2 rooms with handicapped access, No pets, Children under 12 years free, No charge for baby crib
Concierge: 11:00 a.m.–7:00 p.m.
Room Service: 7:00 a.m.–1:00 a.m.
Restaurant: Zephyr Grill, 7a.m.–10p.m.(Mon.-Sat.), Open Sunday
Bar: 5p.m.–2a.m. (Mon.-Sun.)
Business Facilities: Voicemail, Copiers, Audio-Visual, Fax, Dataports
Conference Rooms: 3 rooms, capacity 160
Sports Facilities: Fitness center with saunas
Location: Midtown East, Turtle Bay
Attractions: Restaurants & shops nearby, Sutton Place, United Nations, Adjacent gardens

HOTEL PLAZA ATHENEE

New York City's Plaza Athenee captures the spirit of its renowned sister hotel in Paris. This former penthouse apartment hotel, on a quiet residential street on the upper East Side, has been redesigned by architect John Carl Warnecke. The result is a unique small luxury establishment offering the type of personal service for which only a few European hotels, including the Plaza Athenee's French namesake, are justly famous.

Interiors were done by Valerian Rybar and Daigre Design Corporation. Each room is richly appointed and beautifully decorated using Swiss Zumsteg fabrics. Such features as upholstered headboards, Irish Navan carpets and Directoire night tables set the tone. Most rooms also have wet bars, stoves and refrigerators, and safe deposit boxes. Baths are clad in Portuguese marble; Porthault bathrobes, hair dryers, scales, telephones and lovely Crabtree & Evelyn toiletries are provided.

Among the exquisite suites, the most notable are two duplex suites on the top stories. Each has a living room and a dining room downstairs and bedrooms upstairs. A solarium adjoining the bedroom commands a stunning roofscape view of Manhattan. Le Regence restaurant has 12-foot-high vaulted ceilings handwoven carpets and imported English chandeliers. Its delightful specialties are the creations of the French chef: Marcel Agnez.

Address: 31 East 64th Street, New York, NY 10021
Phone: 212-734-9100
Toll-Free: 800-447-8800
Fax: 212-606-4682
Room Rates: $$$$
Suite Rates: $$$$
Credit Cards: Most credit cards accepted
No. of Rooms: 153 **Suites:** 37
Services and Amenities: Valet service, Car hire, Laundry service, Complimentary shoeshine and newspaper, House doctor, Baby-sitting service, Cable TV, Radio, Porthault bath robes, Crabtree & Evelyn toiletries, Hair dryers, Scales, 2-line phones
Restrictions: Small pets allowed, Handicapped access to 1 room
Concierge: 24 hours
Room Service: 24 hours
Restaurant: Le Regence, 7:00 a.m.–10:30 p.m., Dress Code
Bar: Lounge
Business Facilities: Message center, Secretarial service, Translators, Copiers, Audio-Visual, Telex
Sports Facilities: Health Lounge complimentary
Attractions: Famous boutiques, Museums and gallery district, Near business district

THE KIMBERLY HOTEL

Offering European style elegance service, this 186-room hotel is conveniently located in the heart of midtown Manhattan's fashionable East side, steps away from Park Avenue, New York's world renowned Madison and Fifth Avenue shops and the Waldorf-Astoria.

The Kimberly guests enjoy the luxury of oversized one and two bedroom suites which feature a separate living room with dining area, marble bathrooms, a fully-equipped kitchen, and private balcony.

Complimentary membership at the New York Health & Racquet Club provides guests of the hotel with the most extensive network of sports facilities available in Manhattan, inclusive of swimming pools, tennis, squash, racquetball, indoor golf, strength training and cardiovascular equipment. The club's most recent addition offers spa facilities for which guests receive attractive discounts and complimentary transfers. Complimentary sunset cruises during the Spring and Summer months allows hotel guests to luxuriate on a 75-foot yacht during evening sunset cruises.

Tam-Tam Bar is the hotel's new restaurant known for eclectic American bistro cuisine. It provides a classic and elegant setting for breakfast, lunch and dinner. Tatou, a favorite New York Supper Club, was one of the celebrated venues where President Clinton and his saxophone took center stage during his campaign swing of Manhattan.

The Penthouse Suite, extending the entire length of the hotel's 31st floor, is surrounded by a wrap-around veranda that offers panoramic views of Manhattan's Upper East Side. An opulent back-drop for festive receptions, intimate weddings and executive board meetings.

Address: 145 East 50th Street, New York, NY 10022
Phone: 212-755-0400
Toll-Free: 800-683-0400
Fax: 212-486-6915
Room Rates: $$$$
Suite Rates: $$$$
Credit Cards: Most credit cards accepted
No. of Rooms: 26 **Suites:** 160
Services and Amenities: Same-day valet, Turndown service (upon request), Complimentary health club membership, Bath robes, Honor bars, Daily newspaper, Seasonal sunset cruises on 75' yacht
Concierge: 8:00.a.m.–11:00 p.m.
Room Service: 6:00 a.m.–11:00 p.m.
Restaurant: Tam-Tam Bar, 7:00 a.m.–11:00 p.m., Tatou Supper Club, noon-11:00 p.m., Dancing 11:00 p.m.–4:00 a.m.
Business Facilities: In-room two-line telephones with dataport, In-room fax
Conference Rooms: 1 executive meeting room, cap. 25; receptions, cap. 75
Sports Facilities: Complimentary off-site tennis, Squash, Racquetball, Indoor golf, Swimming pools, Strength training & cardiovascular, Spa services
Location: Midtown Manhattan's fashionable East Side, 30 minutes-LaGuardia, 1 hr. JFK
Attractions: Park Avenue, Madison Avenue, Fifth Avenue shops, Rockefeller Center, UN Headquarters, Radio City Music Hall, Museum of Modern Art, New York Public Library and St. Patrick's Cathedral

THE LOWELL

The Lowell hotel, in its historic landmark building, combines the atmosphere of a European retreat with the warmth and familiarity of home. Its prestigious Upper East Side address is just steps from Madison Avenue boutiques, restaurants and cafes. With its heritage of luxurious service since 1928, The Lowell has perfected a standard of excellence which remains the hotel's hallmark among the world's most discriminating travellers.

Individually-appointed deluxe guest rooms and suites reflect The Lowell's immaculate attention to detail. From Scandinavian down comforters to Chinese porcelains, the decor of the rooms embodies an old-world charm. Each has a marble bath with aromatic Bulgar toiletries. All accommodations are outfitted with mini-bars including gourmet snacks, fully-equipped kitchens, home entertainment centers, and multi-line telephones with voicemail and faxes. Suites additionally feature wood-burning fireplaces.

The Post House award-winning restaurant is reminiscent of a distinguished Gentleman's dinner club, with its spacious dining room and long, polished bar flanked by glass wine cases. A collection of American artifacts, treasured paintings, and handsome leather armchairs decorate this venerable New York establishment. Befitting one of the finest steak and seafood restaurants in America, a library of rare Cabernet, Bordeaux and Burgundy wines as well as an extensive list of California wines are available for connoisseurs to relish.

Address: 28 East 63rd Street, New York, NY 10021
Phone: 212-838-1400
Toll-Free: 800-221-4444
Fax: 212-319-4230
E-mail: lowellhtl@aol.com
Room Rates: $$$$
Suite Rates: $$$$
Credit Cards: Most credit cards accepted
No. of Rooms: 21 **Suites:** 44
Services and Amenities: Valet service, Express laundry & drycleaning, Cable TV/VCRs, Two line telephone with voicemail, Telephone with ports for PC's and fax machines, Phone in bath, Hair dryers, Robes, Soaps, Shampoo, Conditioner, Hand lotion, Complimentary shoeshine & newspaper
Restrictions: No handicapped access
Concierge: 24 hours
Room Service: 6:00 a.m.–1:00 a.m.
Restaurant: The Post House, noon to midnight, weekends 5:30 p.m. to midnight, The Pembroke Room, breakfast, afternoon tea, weekend brunch, special holiday dinners, social affairs
Bar: The Post House, noon to midnight
Conference Rooms: 2 rooms, capacity 12 & 75, Also specialty suites available
Sports Facilities: Fully-equipped fitness center on second floor
Location: Upper East Side, 30 minutes from LaGuardia, 1 hour from JFK Airport
Attractions: Madison Avenue shopping, Museums, Central Park, Broadway Theatres

THE MARK

This venerable hotel has been part of Manhattan's prestigious Upper East Side scene since 1936. Located in an elegant residential district within a stroll of the Metropolitan and other renowned museums, chic shops, and galleries, the 16-story landmark has a new name, The Mark, and has been extensively refurbished and updated by Rafael Hotels Ltd., and E. William Judson of Judson Ream.

The canopied glass and granite entrance leads to a three-tiered lobby lounge. On floors 4 to 16, spacious rooms and suites are offered in 11 different-styled units—all with two-line phones, cable TV, gleaming pantries with stove, sink and refrigerator, and custom-designed furnishings of graceful neo-classical Italian design. Black and white tiled baths have separate glass shower stalls, tub and vanity, marble counters, heated towel racks, heat lamps, and Kohler soak tubs. Bath amenities include 18 oz. terry robes and top-quality toiletries. The top three floors showcase the hotel suites, resplendent with separate living, dining, and bedroom areas, many with libraries, wet bars, and canopied terraces.

Offered here too are Fax machines and multiple phone lines. The Mark devotes its second floor to splendid meeting and banquet facilities—all surrounding a large airy greenhouse. Available to the corporate guest are six conference rooms, where fully-equipped business and catering facilities ensure success for meetings, conferences, and social gatherings.

Milan-based St. Ambroeus, with its internationally known Tuscan culinary artistry, has established a namesake restaurant at The Mark. Its widely heralded succulent veal dishes are unsurpassed, as are inventive and savory pastas. Homemade confections are gelati and dessert treats, offered all day. Guests may also dine in the Italian marble-clad three-tiered Mark's restaurant, where meals, tea, and cocktails are served continously. It's also a charming, tranquil place to relax.

The Mark's newly restored vigor, beauty, and service are evident throughout.

Address: 25 East 77th Street at Madison Avenue, New York, NY 10021
Phone: 212-744-4300
Toll-Free: 800-223-1588
Fax: 212-744-2749
Room Rates: $$$$
Suite Rates: $$$$
Credit Cards: AmEx, Visa, MC, DC, CB, JCB
No. of Rooms: 182 **Suites:** 60
Services and Amenities: Valet service, Garage & parking nearby, Car hire, International currency exchange, House doctor nearby, Baby-sitting service, Cable TV, VCRs, Heat lamps, Robes, Hair dryers, Phone in bath, Complimentary toiletries, shoeshine and newspaper
Restrictions: Small dogs and seeing-eye dogs only, 8 rooms equipped for handicapped
Concierge: 7:00 a.m.–10:00 p.m.
Room Service: 24 hours
Restaurant: Mark's Restaurant, 7:00 a.m.–10:00 p.m.
Business Facilities: Full-scale conference facilities, Copiers, Audio-Visual, Telex
Conference Rooms: 6 rooms, capacity 25-200
Sports Facilities: Guests are extended priviledges to Apple Health Club
Location: Upper East Side, 15 miles from LaGuardia airport, 20 miles from JFK airport
Attractions: Walk to Metropolitan, Whitney, Frick and Guggenheim museums, Elite Madison Avenue shops, galleries and restaurants, Near Central Park and theatre district

THE MICHELANGELO

As you enter the Italian marble lobby of the Michelangelo you will wonder whether you are in New York or Rome. The classic decor, light woods, peach marble and chandeliers are reminiscent of a magnificent Italian residence. Fresh flowers and potpourri are among the elegant touches everywhere.

The guest rooms range in decor from Art Deco to Country French. The marble bathrooms feature over-sized tubs and European amenities.

Just off the lobby is the world-renowned Limoncello restaurant. This Northern Italian style restaurant is very popular with local theater-goers. Risotto Primavera is one of the favorite entrees while the cakes and pies (which are prepared on the premises) are superb.

Located in the heart of Manhattan's business, theater, shopping and cultural districts, the Michelangelo is an oasis of calm in the heart of the most exciting city in the world. It offers personalized service in an elegant yet relaxed atmosphere with Italian style.

Address: 152 West 51st Street, New York, NY 10019
Phone: 212-765-1900
Toll-Free: 800-237-0990
Fax: 212-541-6604
Room Rates: $$$$
Suite Rates: $$$$
Credit Cards: Most credit cards accepted
No. of Rooms: 178 **Suites:** 52
Services and Amenities: Valet service, Garage & parking, Laundry, International currency exchange, Complimentary shoeshine, toiletries & newspaper, House doctor & baby-sitting on call, Cable TV/VCR, Radio, Individual heat & air-conditioning control, Robes, TV & phone in bathroom
Restrictions: No pets allowed, 2 rooms with handicapped access, Children under 16 free
Concierge: 24 hours
Room Service: 24 hours
Restaurant: Limoncello; 7:00 a.m.–10:30 a.m., 11:30 a.m.–3:00 p.m., 5:00 p.m.–1:00 a.m., Dress code: Jackets for men
Bar: Lobby Lounge, 11:00 a.m.–1:00 a.m.
Business Facilities: Fax, Printer, Message center, Secretarial serv., Copiers, Audio-Visual, Teleconferencing, Translator
Conference Rooms: 3 rooms, Full scale conference facilities
Sports Facilities: Nearby outdoor swimming pool, whirlpool, and massage
Location: Midtown near Rockefeller Center, Nearest airports: JFK, La Guardia
Attractions: Fifth Avenue shopping, Theatre district, Restaurants, and all the excitement of New York City

THE NEW YORK PENINSULA

The New York Peninsula, which opened in 1905 as the Gotham Hotel, has been fully restored to its original beaux arts elegance and designated for landmark preservation. Entering the lobby is like stepping into the grandeur of the Belle Epoque. Rich marble abounds and a multifaceted crystal chandelier highlights renaissance details of the original Gotham ceiling.

Spacious guest rooms are decorated in Art Nouveau style, most with king-size beds, writing desks, and seating areas. Oversized marble bathrooms feature luxurious six-foot tubs.

Two restaurants provide a variety of dining delights. The Adrienne, with its soft mauve tones and art nouveau decor, features elegant French cuisine. Le Bistro's lunch and dinner menu offers more provincial stews and grilled items.

In the Gotham Lounge, English high tea can be enjoyed in the afternoon. Later in the evening, the lounge has piano entertainment.

The crowning feature of this hotel is the Peninsula Spa, a rooftop tri-level glass-enclosed health club offering the most extensive facilities of any hotel in New York. It includes an indoor swimming pool and whirlpool, massage, aerobics, weights, fully equipped exercise rooms, and steam and saunas in the dressing rooms. The Pen-Top Bar and Terrace are also part of the spa.

For those seeking European elegance, proximity to Manhattan's cultural, entertainment and shopping opportunities, and all the facilities to renew oneself after a long day, The New York Peninsula is the place.

Address: 700 Fifth Avenue, New York, NY 10019
Phone: 212-247-2200
Toll-Free: 800-262-9467
Fax: 212-903-3949
Room Rates: $$$
Suite Rates: $$$$
Credit Cards: Most credit cards accepted
No. of Rooms: 250 **Suites:** 30
Services and Amenities: Valet service, Garage and valet parking, 2 non-smoking floors, Laundry service, Baby-sitting service, Cable TV, Radio, Refrigerators, Phone in bath, Robes, Complimentary toiletries, NY Times and shoeshine
Restrictions: No pets allowed, No handicapped access, Children welcome
Concierge: 24 hours
Room Service: 24 hours
Restaurant: Adrienne, 7:00 a.m.–10:30 p.m., Dress Code
Bar: The Gotham Lounge, 11:00 a.m.–1:00 a.m.
Business Facilities: Message center, Copiers, Audio-Visual, Teleconferencing, Telex
Conference Rooms: 6 rooms, Full-scale conference facilities
Sports Facilities: Full health spa, Whirlpool, Sauna, Massage, Aerobics, Weight training
Location: Fifth Avenue & 55th Street, Downtown/theater district
Attractions: In the heart of Manhattan's cultural, entertainment, and shopping district

THE RIHGA ROYAL HOTEL

The Rihga Royal Hotel is the only luxury all-suite hotel in New York City. Its ambiance lends a feeling of an intimate private club with a maximum of 12 suites on the lower floors and six suites on the higher floors. The lobby, international in style, is inspired by Park Avenue residential lobbies.

Each elegant suite offers a living room in the shape of an elongated octagon, with bay windows at one end and an entry foyer with a bar unit at the other. A pair of mirrored French doors opens onto the bedroom, expanding the striking views from the bay windows. There is a large marble bathroom with glass enclosed shower and a separate tub. Multiple telephone lines and communication options provide the latest in technology. Suites with additional business amenities and the added luxury of a dining room, kitchen, whirlpool bath and sauna, and views of Central Park and the Hudson Valley are also available. In addition to the extensive services offered to all Rihga Royal guests, a chauffeur-driven Town Car is available for private transport to Wall Street.

For those who demand even more, the top floor Pinnacle Suites add special guest services including chauffeur-driven Town Car to and from La Guardia, Kennedy or Newark airports, in-suite check- in and check-out, private in-suite communications system with computer capability and, in a leather case, personalized business cards printed with the private suite phone numbers.

The Halcyon Restaurant serves breakfast, lunch, pre-theater dinner, dinner, late-night supper, and a Sunday Marketplace Brunch located on the 54th floor with panoramic views of the city. One of Executive Chef John A. Halligan's favored dinner entrees is the Lightly Smoked and Roasted Rack of Lamb.

Two hospitality suites with striking views of Manhattan are designed to accommodate a wide range of events. The eleven distinctively designed meeting and banquet rooms offer panoramic Manhattan skyline and river views and 1930's style glamour, providing the perfect setting for business or social functions of 10 to 500 people. Full-service catering and event planning services are available.

Address: 151 W. 54th Street, New York, NY 10019
Phone: 212-307-5000
Toll-Free: 800-223-1888
Fax: 212-765-6530
Suite Rates: $$$$
Credit Cards: Most credit cards accepted
No. of Suites: 500
Services and Amenities: Weekend packages from $225, Valet parking, Car Hire, Same day valety/dry cleaning, International currency exchange, Baby-sitting, Complimentary shoe shine & newspapers, Robes, Hair dryer, Mini-bar, In-suite safe, VCP, Two TVs, Two phones
Restrictions: No pets allowed, No charge for children under 15 with parent
Concierge: 7:00 a.m.–11:00 p.m.
Room Service: 24 hours
Restaurant: Halcyon 6:30 a.m.–1:00 a.m.
Bar: 6:30 a.m.–1:00 a.m.
Business Facilities: Private chauffered car to Wall Street, Computer, Fax
Conference Rooms: 10 rooms, capacity 200 for receptions
Sports Facilities: Cardiovascular machines, Sauna, Massage, Weight training, Sauna
Location: Steps from Broadway, Fifth Avenue shops, Midtown
Attractions: Central Park, City's finest Museums, Carnegie Hall; This hotel excels in service, also it is the only luxury all-suite hotel in New York City

STANHOPE HOTEL

The Stanhope, on Fifth Avenue overlooking Central Park, has been a tradition for the world's most discerning clientele since 1926. Enter the landmark 16-story neo-Italian building to find yourself in an opulent 18th century French style lobby with antiques, marble floors and handcarved wall moldings gilded with 24-carat gold leaf.

The hotel's total commitment to excellence is evident in the extraordinary two-to-one staff-to-guest ratio. The Assistant Manager, not a bellman, escorts guests to their rooms or suites.

Guest accommodations, completely redecorated in the course of a $26 million renovation in 1986, feature Louis XV style furniture custom designed for the Stanhope by Claude Moulin, including cozy sitting areas with couch, table and chairs. Remote control TVs are concealed inside armoires stocked with antique books and oriental accessories. Two-line telephones, clock-radios with tape machines, and satin hangers are among the special touches revealing extraordinary attention to guests' comfort.

The Stanhope is located across from the Metropolitan Museum of Art and a moment's walk from Madison Avenue's shops and art galleries. Complimentary limousine service will take guests to midtown Manhattan and Wall Street on weekday mornings, and evening transportation is provided to Lincoln Center, Carnegie Hall and the theatre district.

Address: 995 Fifth Avenue, New York, NY 10028
Phone: 212-288-5800
Toll-Free: 800-828-1123
Fax: 212-517-0088
Web site: http://www.thestanhope.com
Room Rates: $$$$
Suite Rates: $$$$
Credit Cards: Most credit cards accepted
No. of Rooms: 106 **Suites:** 63
Services and Amenities: Valet service, Laundry service, International currency exchange, Cable TV with in-room movies, CD Player, In-room fax, 2-line telephones, Wet bar, Robes, Complimentary toiletries, shoeshine & newspaper, Children under 12 free with parents
Concierge: 8:00 a.m.–11:00 p.m.
Room Service: 24 hours
Restaurant: Cafe M, 7:00 a.m.–11:00 p.m., Outdoor terrace
Bar: Gerard's, 3:00 p.m.–Midnight
Business Facilities: Message center, Secretarial service, Translators, Copiers, Audio-Visual, Telex, Fax
Conference Rooms: 5 rooms, capacity 100
Sports Facilities: Fitness center in hotel with state-of-the-art equipment, Sauna
Location: Upper East Side, Nearest airport is LaGuardia
Attractions: Across the Central Park, Metropolitan Museum of Art, Museum Mile, Art galleries, European boutiques

THE SURREY HOTEL

If it's the upper East Side you want, and you'd like to find something reasonable in price, look no further! The Surrey, with studios and one-and two-bedroom suites, offers terrific value and comfort in an appealing neighborhood of stately brownstones, Madison Avenue's dramatic boutiques, and the Metropolitan Museum of Art (without a doubt one of the best art museums this side of the Louvre). You'll be right on the corner of Madison and 76th Street, a block from Central Park, and within walking distance of the Metropolitan. Step into a large lobby, where antique reproductions stand out against highly polished marble floors and walls. Crystal chandeliers, fresh flowers, and an outgoing concierge complete the picture of a special environment.

The fully furnished suites feature executive-size desks, two-line telephones with voice mail, and well-equipped kitchens or kitchenettes. Our favorite suite has an oriental rug on the gleaming hardwood foyer floor, a large living room with mahogany bookcases, beveled mirrors, fireplace, terrace, and a striking marble bathroom.

Daniel Boulud's restaurant "Daniel" at the Surrey Hotel is an artful addition to the Upper East Side's museum mile. The Mediterranean decor features arched passageways, attractive earth tones and a terra-cotta tiled floor leading into an intimate bar area. Chef Boulud's menu highlights regional American produce prepared in a distinctive contemporary French style, one that made him famous at Le Cirque and has earned him the coveted 4 stars from the New York Times. The ambiance is sophisticated yet warm, the service attentive, and the food in harmony with the seasons. The a la carte menu is complemented with creative tasting menus and an extensive wine list. During summer months patrons may enjoy cocktails on the charming sidewalk terrace. Daniel also provides room service for the hotel guests.

Address: 20 East 76th Street, New York, NY 10021
Phone: 212-288-3700
Toll-Free: 800-637-8483
Fax: 212-628-1549
E-mail: info@mesuite.com
Web site: http://www.mesuite.com
Suite Rates: $$$$
Credit Cards: AmEx, MC, Visa, DC, CB, JCB
No. of Suites: 131
Services and Amenities: Valet parking, Fully equipped kitchens or kitchenettes, Grocery shopping service, Cable TV and VCR, Individual heat and air-conditioning control, Laundry, Radio, Hair dryer, Iron and ironing board, Bath robes
Concierge: 11:00 a.m.–7:00 p.m.
Room Service: 7:30 a.m.–11:00 p.m.
Restaurant: Daniel, Dinner: Monday through Saturday, Breakfast, Lunch: Tuesday through Saturday
Bar: Noon-3:00 p.m., 5:30–11:00 p.m.
Business Facilities: Voice mail, Copiers, Fax, Dataport for in-room fax & computer hookups, 2-line phones, Secretary
Conference Rooms: 1 room, capacity 20
Sports Facilities: Fitness center in hotel, Horseback riding, Jogging paths nearby
Location: Upper East Side Manhattan, Near Central Park, Airports—JFK & LaGuardia
Attractions: Metropolitan Museum of Art, Guggenheim Museum, Whitney Museum, Yorkville and Gracie Mansion, Shopping at Menage a Trois, Bloomingdale's, Armani, Sonia Rykiel, Ungaro, Gucci, Kenzo

ADELPHI HOTEL

It was called the Queen of the Spas. And no wonder. The legendary Adelphi Hotel was built in the high Victorian style that prevailed just before the turn of the century, with 12-foot ceilings and window treatments to match. Today it remains replete with classic Victorian furnishings, and reflects all of the opulence of that era. Although the hotel has added a beautifully landscaped outdoor swimming pool and has undergone a major renovation and updating to full baths, air-conditioning, and other modern conveniences, it presents the original facade of ornamental brickwork and three-story Victorian columns with elaborate fretwork at the top, and retains the aura of the era.

Guest rooms are unusually large, and each is uniquely decorated with a variety of wall coverings and color schemes. Suites are furnished in Adirondack style with original Stickley mission oak furniture, period arts and crafts wall coverings and photographs.

There are several dining rooms, one featuring a wrap-around wall mural, and another with an enclosed patio area overlooking the courtyard. The dinner menu lists a number of grilled items, and for dessert offers pastries for which the hotel is famous. The Cafe Adelphi, with its outdoor Courtyard, offers special blended drinks, exotic coffees and unique wines. As in the past, it is a popular gathering place after the theater or the track for cocktails, supper, or coffee and desert.

Saratoga Springs is a charming town in which to stroll, and guests of the hotel find interesting antique shops and restaurants. Also of interest is the Saratoga Performing Arts Center, the Saratoga Raceway, and several large and small museums.

Address: 365 Broadway, Saratoga Springs, NY 12866
Phone: 518-587-4688
Fax: 518-587-0851
Room Rates: $
Suite Rates: $$
Credit Cards: Visa, MC, AmEx
No. of Rooms: 38 **Suites:** 16
Services and Amenities: Cable TV, Air-conditioning, Telephone, Complimentary toiletries, Complimentary breakfast
Restrictions: No pets allowed, Children welcome
Restaurant: Cafe Adelphi, July and August, 6:00 p.m.–midnight
Bar: Cafe Adelphi, 5:00 p.m.–midnight
Sports Facilities: Outdoor swimming pool
Location: Broadway, Nearest airport is Albany
Attractions: Near Saratoga Performing Arts Center, Saratoga Raceway, Museums, Antique Shops, Restaurants

COPPERHOOD INN & SPA

Nestled in the lush Catskill mountains, just a two and a half hour drive from New York City, this subtly elegant European style Inn and Spa provides the ideal environment for rejuvenating both body and spirit, for rediscovering the peace there is to be found here.

Guests enjoy a wide range of spa services and sport facilities but are never burdened by strenuous exercise regimes; meals are flavorful and nutritious, beautiful and light, but happily... starvation is not part of Copperhood's philosophy.

All of the accommodations are equipped with modern conveniences such as telephone, television, hair dryer and, in deluxe rooms, plush terry robes. Each room is exquisitely decorated in an original manner, offering guests a unique experience each time they return to the Catskills. The Copperhood's standard accommodations are reminiscent of a charming bed and breakfast. All of the suites and duplexes' access balconies from which guests enjoy the captivating view of steady Garfield mountain towering over the ever-shifting Esopus Creek. The deluxe rooms and suites are furnished in Italian Louis XVI reproduction furniture, Bergere armchairs and oriental rugs. Deluxe baths include Italian mosaic tile with Jacuzzi tubs, bidets, separate shower stalls, hair dryers and complimentary toiletries.

A feeling of comfort, warmth and home prevails throughout the inn, while varieties of pampering services await to add to one's sense of well being. A guest's daily routine may include a game of tennis, canoe trip down the Esopus, fly fishing for the prize winning trout, cross country skiing on Copperhood's private island trails or...do nothing at all. Just relax in warmth of the Jacuzzi tub or take a dip in the cool blue water of the competition sized indoor pool; soak up some sun while watching river course over rocky bottom, murmuring gently as it passes banks of wildflowers.

The Copperhood Inn & Spa features a variety of rooms suitable for meetings of differing scale and character. From intimate to grand, all of them provide a private, quiet, distraction free environment where needs can be met in a professional and timely manner.

Address: 70 – 38 Route 28, Shandaken, NY 12480
Phone: 914-688-2460
Fax: 914-688-7484
E-mail: info@copperhood.com
Web site: http://www.copperhood.com
Room Rates: $$$
Suite Rates: $$$$
Credit Cards: Visa, MC, AmEx
No. of Rooms: 13 **Suites:** 7
Services and Amenities: Laundry service, Baby-sitting service, Card/game area, Library, Balconies, Cable TV, VCR, Telephones, Radio, Some rooms with audio cassette player, Individual air-conditioning, Robes, Whirlpool bath, Complimentary toiletries
Restrictions: No pets allowed in rooms, Outdoor kennel available
Room Service: 9:00 a.m.–10:00 p.m.
Restaurant: Private dining room for breakfast and dinner
Bar: Open evenings
Business Facilities: Message center, Secretarial center, E-mail, Copiers, Audio-Visual, Fax, Modems
Conference Rooms: 3 rooms, capacity 80
Sports Facilities: 60 ft. indoor pool, Sauna, Whirlpool, Massage, Herbal & mud wraps, Aerobics, Croquet, Tennis, Esopus Creek Fishing, Skiing
Location: Catskills Forest Preserve
Attractions: Woodstock, Bellayre and Maverick Concerts, Antiques, Arts and Crafts shopping

THE VILLAGE LATCH INN

This famous Country House Hotel, situated on a lovely 5-acre estate, was the grand annex to Southampton's oldest hostelry, the Irving Hotel. It is perfectly located within walking distance to Southampton village's most fashionable shopping streets and beautiful ocean beaches.

The main house is "old Southampton, turn-of-the-century, Gatsby-style." Fascinating collectibles from around the world have been strikingly arranged throughout the mansions interwoven with the rich elegance of the Inn's eclectic decor.

Guestrooms, distributed between the main building and several former estate buildings, are all distinctive, decorated with a collection of antiques from different periods and style. The tone is sophisticated and elegant. Along with modern comforts, phones, air-conditioning and televisions, accommodations are also equipped with thick rugs, stripped oak furniture, tweed-covered chaises, lazy ceiling fans, private baths and easy chairs. One of the fireplace suites has English pine furniture, an antique sleigh bed, Laura Ashley print curtains and wallpaper and dusty rose wall-to-wall carpeting. Despite its lavishness, the Inn is cozy—the sort of place where guests can help themselves to coffee or a cold drink any time of day, even if the sign says "Kitchen Closed."

There is a continental breakfast, and a full breakfast on weekends, which might include bagels, cream cheese, ham, cheese, yogurt, fruit and homemade breads and cakes. Breakfast is served in the dining room with its lush green Italian chairs.

Guests can also rent a private villa for exclusive use when arranging events such as family reunions, wedding groups, corporate outings and photo-shoots. The villas include a magnificent living room, country kitchen and from 5–15 bedrooms, depending upon groups needs, all with modern conveniences too. Additional rooms are available in the main buildings. Charming meeting and party rooms in a Victorian greenhouse, "the potting shed" or the estate grounds.

Between the main and other buildings, stretches a large lawn for croquet, a pool with a private hedge providing privacy, and a tennis court. A former conservatory now contains a hot tub. Bicycles are available for rent. Arrangements can easily be made for horseback riding, golfing, fishing, antiquing and more.

Address: 101 Hill Street, Southampton, NY 11968
Phone: 516-283-2160
Toll-Free: 800-54-LATCH
Fax: 516-283-3236
Room Rates: $
Suite Rates: $$$$
Credit Cards: Visa, MC, AmEx, Discover
No. of Rooms: 67 **Suites:** 8
Services and Amenities: Free parking, Baby-sitting service, 7 rooms with fireplaces, 15 with balconies, Cable TV, Individual heat and air-conditioning control, Complimentary toiletries
Restrictions: Some pets by prior arrangements, Some rooms available for children, Minimum stay on peak weekends
Business Facilities: Message center, Fax, Copiers
Conference Rooms: 1 room, capacity 10-100
Sports Facilities: Outdoor swimming pool, Hot tub, Tennis court, Bicycle rentals, Special Health Club priviledges at the American Fitness Factory
Attractions: Art galleries, Boutiques, Wineries, Theatre, Boating, Cultural events, Miles of world famous unspoiled beaches

HAYWOOD PARK HOTEL

For many years it was the Ivey's Department Store—the Tiffany of department stores. After extensive remodeling it opened in 1985 as the Haywood Park Hotel. Consisting of 33 suites, this small world-class hotel offers the ambiance of a luxurious executive home-away-from-home.

In keeping with the Art Deco style of the building, the lobby is done in soothing pastels, with golden oak woodwork accented by gleaming brass.

The beautiful, spacious suites are remarkably larger than an average hotel room. Fully appointed with a wet bar, work desk, TV with remote control, and king or queen size beds, they feature bedroom sitting areas and large walk-in closets. Baths are done in Spanish marble and have double vanities, lighted make-up mirrors, hair dryer, TV and telephone. The Master Suites also feature Jacuzzi tubs. Guests are pampered with evening turndown service including a chocolate truffle, and with continental breakfast served in-room.

The restaurant, 23 Page, is done in Aubergine tones with special paint treatment and an open kitchen. Among the scrumptious dinner menu selections, favorites are the popular wild mushroom crepe hors d'oeuvres and an entree of grilled lamb chops.

The hotel has business and conference facilities available. Its two conference rooms have a capacity of 150 and can accommodate any equipment or decorating needs.

A state-of-the-art fitness center is available for guest use at no additional charge, and massage therapy is available by appointment. Guests may relax in the sauna after a workout.

Located in the heart of the Blue Ridge mountains in downtown Asheville, North Carolina, the Haywood Park Hotel is a four-diamond gem.

Address: One Battery Park Avenue, Asheville, NC 28801
Phone: 704-252-2522
Toll-Free: 800-228-2522
Fax: 704-253-0481
Web site: http://www.haywoodpark.com
Room Rates: $$
Credit Cards: Visa, MC, AmEx, Diners, Disc.
No. of Rooms: 33
Services and Amenities: Valet service, Garage & parking, Dry cleaning service, Baby-sitting service, Gift shop, Cable TV, Telephone, Radio, Wet bar, TV & phone in bath, Complimentary toiletries & newspaper, Complimentary in-room continental breakfast
Restrictions: No pets allowed, 3 rooms handicapped-equipped
Concierge: Yes
Room Service: 11:00 a.m.–10:00 p.m
Restaurant: 23 Page Restaurant
Bar: New French Bar, 11:00 a.m.–10:00 p.m.
Business Facilities: Message center, Secretarial center, Copiers, Audio-Visual, Teleconferencing, Haywood Business Center
Conference Rooms: 2 rooms, capacity 150
Sports Facilities: Fitness Center privileges, Sauna, Massage, Weight training, Access to golf & tennis, 30 mi. to skiing, Nearby white water rafting
Location: Downtown, Nearest airport is Asheville
Attractions: Specialty shops adjacent, Guided historical walking tours, Biltmore Estate and Gardens (2 miles)

RICHMOND HILL INN

Built in 1889 as the private residence of U.S. Congressman and ambassador Richard Pearson, Richmond Hill was a center of North Carolina social, literary and political activity for many years. Each of the twelve lovingly restored guest rooms is named after a family member or prominent literary figure of the Asheville area, and furnished with Queen Anne Style antiques and four-poster and canopy beds. Many rooms have fireplaces.

Guests may also stay in one of 5 Victorian-style "croquet cottages" surrounding their own croquet court, or the Garden Pavilion, overlooking the Parterre Garden with its geometrically designed flower beds, mountain brook and serene waterfall.

In the Oak Hall, guests can bask in front of a roaring fire that reflects warmly the walls entirely paneled in polished oak. Or they can peruse the extensive collection of books on Western North Carolina, as well as a selection of Richard Pearson's own first editions, in the Library. The grand octagonal ballroom is an ideal site for meetings, receptions and banquets.

It would be a mistake to miss dinner at Gabrielle's, nationally acclaimed continental cuisine, in the mansion's cherry-paneled dining room. Recent seasonal house specials included Gabrielle's signature mountain apple-and-vidalia onion soup gratinee with aged Gruyere, and grilled spicy pink shrimp with peach glaze, fresh peach slaw, and potato-leek pancake.

Surrounded by the beautiful Blue Ridge Mountains, Richmond Hill House is also just minutes from downtown Asheville with its symphony, theater, art and antique shopping. Golf, skiing, the Biltmore Estate and the Blue Ridge Parkway are also just a short drive away.

Address: 87 Richmond Hill Drive, Asheville, NC 28806
Phone: 828-252-7313
Toll-Free: 800-545-9238
Fax: 828-252-8726
Web site: http://
www.richmondhillinn.com
Room Rates: $$
Suite Rates: $$$$
Credit Cards: AmEx, MC, Visa
No. of Rooms: 36 **Suites:** 3
Services and Amenities: Valet service, Parking, Laundry, Gift shop, Library, Fireplaces in many rooms, Cable TV, Telephones, Radio, Wet bar in some rooms, Robes, Whirlpool in some rooms, Complimentary toiletries & newspaper, Complimentary breakfast & afternoon tea
Restrictions: No pets allowed, Handicapped access to two rooms
Concierge: 24 hours
Restaurant: Gabrielle's and The Arbor Grille, Reservations required
Business Facilities: Copiers, Audio-Visual, Fax
Conference Rooms: 3 rooms, capacity 50
Sports Facilities: Croquet, Weight training, Exercise room, Golf and horseback riding by appointment
Location: Near downtown
Attractions: Garden tours, Blue Ridge Parkway, Antique/art shopping, Symphony, Theater, Biltmore Estate, 1 hour to skiing

THE MOREHEAD INN

Just minutes from Uptown Charlotte in one of the city's most picturesque neighborhoods, the Morehead Inn is an elegant Southern estate endowed with quiet elegance and fine antiques. Built in 1917 and renovated in 1995, the Inn is registered as a Charlotte Historic Landmark, and served as a showcase house for the local chapter of the American Society of Interior Designers before becoming a country inn in 1984. The Inn's combination of historic charm and Southern hospitality with all the modern necessities has earned it numerous awards for renovation, cuisine and service.

The lobby features original early American and English antiques and 24-carat gold-painted crown molding. An aviary with rare finches adorns the library. The spacious public rooms, magnificent staircase and secluded outdoor courtyard provide a gracious setting for every gathering, from business luncheons and executive meetings to parties and weddings—complete with in-house wedding consultant. The full-service catering staff can help plan a menu for any event.

All rooms and suites in the main building and carriage house are appointed with antiques and period pieces. All have telephones and cable TV. The unique Solarium suite is bright and open with white rattan and wicker furniture and ultrasuede sofa in the den, a king bed, hand-painted tile floor and sunken whirlpool tub.

Located in the historic, tree-shaded Dilworth district, The Morehead Inn is surrounded by Charlotte's finest restaurants, many within walking distance. The Inn is less than a mile from the Panther Stadium and Performing Arts Center.

Address: 1122 East Morehead Street, Charlotte, NC 28204
Phone: 704-376-3357
Toll-Free: 888-667-4323
Fax: 704-335-1110
Web site: http://charlotte.zip2.com/morehead
Room Rates: $$
Suite Rates: $$
Credit Cards: AmEx, MC, Visa, DC
No. of Rooms: 13 **Suites:** 7
Services and Amenities: Car hire, Laundry service, Baby-sitting service, Gift shop, Card and game area, Cable TV, Telephones, Radio, VCR and audiocassette available, Air-conditioning, Robes, Complimentary toiletries and breakfast
Restrictions: No pets allowed, No handicapped facilities
Restaurant: Morehead Inn Catering by appointment for private parties
Business Facilities: Message center, Copiers, Audio-Visual, Teleconferencing, Fax, Modems
Conference Rooms: 4 rooms, capacity 200
Sports Facilities: Indoor/outdoor pools, Handball/Squash, Whirlpool bath, Sauna, Massage, Aerobics, Weight training, Complimentary membership in YMCA
Location: Historic Dilworth
Attractions: Fine restaurants within walking distance, Panther Stadium and Performing Arts Center

THE PARK HOTEL

The Park Hotel, the luxurious centerpiece of Charlotte's celebrated South Park neighborhood, is small and privately owned. Nestled among the area's prestigious shops, homes, and businesses, it is convenient to the airport and downtown, the Coliseum complex, and the merchandise and apparel markets. Within walking distance are over 100 shops, theaters, and restaurants. In this incomparable location, guests of The Park Hotel discover hospitality at its most gracious.

Warmth and comfort are evident in the 194 oversized guestrooms and 7 suites, renovated in 1994. Each is as beautifully appointed as a fine residence, with 18th-century furnishings, marble vanities, original art, and modem-compatible two-line telephones. The one- and two-bedroom suites offer a variety of additional luxuries, such as dining rooms, separate parlors, wet bars, and sound systems.

Guests receive the kind of care and attention one would expect in the best small European hotels. The 24-hour room service, valet laundry and shoeshine, nightly turndown and the Nautilus-equipped health club set The Park Hotel apart.

Morrocrofts Restaurant and Bar resembles a fine private club. Warmly lighted and paneled in rich mahogany, its open fireplace sets the mood to meet friends and enjoy the American continental cuisine. Featuring only the finest meats and freshest seafood, Morrocrofts is a favorite with hotel guests and area neighbors alike!

Quiet elegance plus comfortable surroundings create the perfect combination for successful meetings at the Park Hotel. The finer touches abound. A detailed-oriented staff, fresh flowers, and candy in crystal bowls on each boardroom table add that something special.

The Park Hotel, with its gracious hospitality, uncompromising service, and finely detailed amenities, has earned the esteemed status of membership in Preferred Hotels Worldwide and is North Carolina's only Mobil 4-Star, AAA 4-diamond hotel.

Address: 2200 Rexford Road, Charlotte, NC 28211
Phone: 704-364-8220
Toll-Free: 800-334-0331
Fax: 704-365-4712
Room Rates: $$$
Suite Rates: $$$$
Credit Cards: MC, AmEx, Visa, CB, DC
No. of Rooms: 194 **Suites:** 7
Services and Amenities: Valet parking, Airport limousine service available, Gift shop, Nightly turndown service, Cable TV with movie channels, Complimentary newspaper, toiletries and valet shoeshine, Non-smoking rooms available, 2 modem-compatible two-line telephones in rooms
Restrictions: No pets allowed, Handicapped access to 10 rooms
Concierge: Available
Room Service: 24 hours
Restaurant: Morrocrofts, Weekdays 6:30 a.m.–10:30 p.m., Weedends 7:00 a.m.–11:00 p.m., Dress Code
Bar: Morrocrofts Bar, Mon.-Sat. 11:00 a.m.–1:00 a.m., Sun. 1:00 p.m.–1:00 a.m.
Business Facilities: Message center, Translators, Copiers, Audio-Visual, Fax, Teleconferencing, Conference facilities
Conference Rooms: 6,000 sq. ft. exhibit and meeting space
Sports Facilities: Heated outdoor swimming pool, Full health spa
Location: South Park (South Charlotte) area, Nearest airport is Charlotte Douglas
Attractions: Within walking distance of specialty shops, also South Park Mall

SANDERLING INN RESORT

In the lobby of the Sanderling Inn Resort is an intricately carved group of sanderlings, the small coastal birds indigenous to the area, crafted by world-renowned wildlife artist Grainger McCoy. It is complemented by a complete set of Audubon prints and an extensive collection of Boehm bird porcelains. Such details mark the Sanderling Inn's faithfulness to the very special character of North Carolina's Outer Banks at the turn-of-the-century.

The Sanderling is a 12-acre sound-to-sea Beach Resort, adjacent to the hiking trails of the Pine Island Audubon Sanctuary. From the lobby's soft wood tones, soaring staircase and museum quality artworks celebrating the coastal setting, to the Pallachick wicker furnishings of the guest rooms and suites, casual coastal elegance is the theme. Individual balconies or decks, coffeemakers, bathrobes and beach towels encourage guests to savor the quiet seashore atmosphere in comfort and privacy.

The Sanderling Restaurant is a restored turn-of-the-century life-saving station, featuring custom china and unique antiques of a nautical theme. Guests may choose between shrimp, crab and corn chowders, and among hearty entrees such as crab cakes made with jumbo lump crabmeat. For dessert, try the unique chocolate pecan pie with Bourbon ice cream.

Recreational facilities at the Sanderling Inn include indoor and outdoor pools, whirlpool, tennis courts and fitness center. For business needs, there are full-scale conference facilities.

Address: 1461 Duck Road, Duck, NC 27949
Phone: 252-261-4111
Toll-Free: 800-701-4111
Fax: 252-261-1352
E-mail: sanderlinginn@outerbanks.com
Web site: http://www.outerbanks.com/sanderling.html
Room Rates: $$
Suite Rates: $$$$
Credit Cards: Most credit cards accepted
No. of Rooms: 77 **Suites:** 13
Services and Amenities: Parking, Laundry, Gift shop, Individual heat & air-conditioning, All rooms with balconies or decks, Cable TV/VCR, Radios, Coffee makers, Refrigerator, Bathrobes, Beach towels, Complimentary newspapers, amenities, afternoon tea & continental breakfast
Restrictions: 4 rooms with handicapped access, Additional fee per child, Not pets allowed
Concierge: 9:00 a.m.–5:00 p.m.
Room Service: 8:00 a.m.–9:00 p.m.
Restaurant: Sanderling Restaurant, 8:00 a.m.–9:00 p.m.
Bar: Swan Bar, 12 p.m.–10 p.m.
Business Facilities: Copiers, AV, Fax, Message service
Conference Rooms: 4 rooms, capacity 100
Sports Facilities: Indoor & outdoor swimming pools, Tennis courts, Fully-equipped health club, Golf & Pine Island Racquet Club nearby
Location: Northern Outer Banks, 1.5 hours from Norfolk Airport
Attractions: Twelve acre beach resort, Adjacent to Pine Island Audubon Sanctuary, Eco-center offering numerous outdoor pursuits, Boutique shopping in Duck, Racquet Club & Golf nearby

WASHINGTON DUKE INN & GOLF CLUB

Located on the campus of Duke University, the Washington Duke Inn and Golf Club opened in 1988, introducing to Durham a new adventure in elegance.

The hotel, built in modern Gothic architecture to blend with the university, overlooks the Robert Trent Jones championship 18-hole golf course. This "classic" course was recently renovated by Ress Jones. Today you would be overwhelmed by the beauty and improved playability of the course. The other three sides of the hotel property are embraced by the Duke Forest.

Antiques and Duke family memorabilia grace the lobby and halls. Floor-to-ceiling windows overlook the flowered terrace and golf course. Slate floors, brass elevator doors, mahogany, and rich blues welcome the traveler.

In the recently decorated guest rooms, dark wood is featured in headboards, mirror frames, desks, chairs, and armoires. Each room has a multiple access phone for fax or personal computer, and comfortable chairs with ottomans and accompanying reading light. Draperies open to views of the beautifully landscaped entrance or the manicured golf course.

The Fairview Restaurant, overlooking the golf course, is a popular Durham dining spot. Its menu offers a medley of international specialties. For alfresco dining try the Terrace-on-the-Green.

One can relax with friends at the Bull Durham Bar, where piano entertainment is featured four nights per week. Guest privileges are extended to the 24-hour Metrosport facility for those who prefer to unwind in a health club.

Reminiscent of a personal library, the Duke University Room is perfect for small conferences. Groups of up to 600 can be accommodated in the Ambassador Ballroom.

Comfort and convenience are found at the Washington Duke Inn, which is a AAA Four Diamond Award and Mobil Four star award recipient, along with personal service and that famous Southern hospitality.

Address: 3001 Cameron Boulevard, Durham, NC 27706
Phone: 919-490-0999
Toll-Free: 800-443-3853
Fax: 919-688-0105
E-mail: JLTasker@duke.EDU
Web site: http://www.WASHINGTONDUKEINN.com
Room Rates: $$$
Suite Rates: $$$$
Credit Cards: Most credit cards accepted
No. of Rooms: 171 **Suites:** 7
Services and Amenities: Valet parking, Library, Baby-sitting service, Laundry service, Gift Shop, Cable TV, Radio, Voice mail, Mini bars, In room safes, Complimentary toiletries and newspaper, 43 non-smoking rooms
Restrictions: No pets allowed, 8 rooms handicapped-equipped
Room Service: 7:00 a.m.–10:30 p.m.
Restaurant: The Fairview Restaurant, 7:00 a.m.–10:00 p.m.
Bar: Bull Durham Bar, 10:30 a.m.–1:00 a.m.
Business Facilities: Secretarial service, Copiers, Audio-Visual, Fax
Conference Rooms: 8 rooms, capacity 600
Sports Facilities: Robert Trent Jones 18-hole championship golf course and pro shop, Outdoor swimming pool, 6 clay tennis courts, Duke Forest jogging
Location: Duke University Campus at Golf Course, 18 miles from Raleigh Durham Airport
Attractions: Duke University, Sarah P. Duke Gardens, Museums, Shopping

FIRST COLONY INN

The Outer Banks' only historic B&B inn offers comfortably elegant accommodation and real Southern hospitality at the beach. The Lawrences saved this handsome shingle-style building wrapped by unique continuous double verandas by moving it three and a half miles to a setting of five landscaped acres, doing a complete historic rehabilitation, and placing it in the National Register of Historic Places.

Rooms are individually appointed with English antiques, traditional furnishings and king, queen, or twin beds. Some are tall four posters, and some are canopied with hand-tied lace. Children are accommodated in daybeds or trundle beds. All rooms have television, telephone, and individual climate control with remote. Most have wet bars with microwaves or kitchenettes with dishwashers. Private tiled baths feature heavy towels on heated towel bars and English toiletries, and some have Jacuzzi tubs. Sitting rooms or comfortable seating areas, books, plants, and old local photographs and antique prints lend a homelike touch.

Guests begin the day at First Colony in a sunny breakfast room with a bountiful buffet including such specialties as ham and cheese braid hot from the oven, then stroll to the ocean for beachcombing, fishing, swimming, or a long walk by the surf. Some may choose to windsurf, hangglide, sail, take an aero tour or a deep sea fishing trip, or go on a dolphin watching expedition. The secluded pool and a rocking chair on the veranda wait to be enjoyed along with a good book from the library.

Guests can also spend the afternoon at the NC Aquarium or the *Elizabeth* II (a replica sixteenth century ship), or stroll through the Elizabethan Gardens, returning in time for tea. After dining at a fine restaurant, guests enjoy the sunset over Roanoke Sound from the veranda where a little wine and cheese is served. Chess, bridge, and a jigsaw puzzle are available in the library. *The Lost Colony*, the country's oldest outdoor drama, is one of the nearby attractions.

First Colony is located conveniently near Fort Raleigh (The Lost Colony), the Wright Brothers Memorial, and Jockey's Ridge which is the tallest dune on the East Coast.

Address: 6720 South Virginia Dare Trail, Nags Head, NC 27959
Phone: 252-441-2343
Toll-Free: 800-368-9390
Fax: 252-441-9234
E-mail: first.colony.inn@worldnet.att.net
Room Rates: $
Suite Rates: $$$
Credit Cards: Visa, MC, AmEx, Discover
No. of Rooms: 20 **Suites:** 6
Services and Amenities: Smoke-free building, Valet service weekdays, Parking on site, Gift shop, Baby-sitting service, Card/game area, Library, Some kitchens, Balconies, Cable TV, VCR, Wet bar, Complimentary toiletries & newspaper, Complimentary breakfast, afternoon tea & snacks
Restrictions: No pets allowed, First floor and 1 room handicapped-equipped
Room Service: 8:00 a.m.–9:30 a.m.
Restaurant: Penguin Isle (across street) 5:00 p.m.–10:00 p.m.
Bar: Room service wine/beer setups, Licensed for parties
Business Facilities: Copiers, Audio-Visual rental, Secretarial services by arrangement, Dataports, Fax
Conference Rooms: 2 rooms, capacity 30
Sports Facilities: Outdoor swimming pool, Croquet, Massage by arrangement, Golf, Sailing & Tennis nearby, Fishing, All beach activities
Location: Beach resort/ Outer Banks, Nearest airport is Norfolk, VA
Attractions: Wright Brothers Memorial, The Elizabeth II, Aquarium, Ocean beach, Jockey's Ridge (tallest sand dune on East Coast), Birdwatching, Dolphin watching, Fort Raleigh, Rated four diamonds by AAA

THE COUNTRY INN AT WALDEN

Set on thirty-two rolling acres, the Country Inn at Walden appeals to both business and recreational guests with world-class charm and amenities. The Inn beckons guests with a stone fireplace in the lobby and beautifully appointed furnishings. Through the glass-enclosed foyer, views of horses grazing and extensive landscaping welcome the senses.

The Inn has 25 suites, each with their own distinct design: cedar-paneled ceilings, sky lights, large fireplaces, oversized cushioned headboards and decorative tile accent on stairs and countertops. Whirlpool baths with separate showers, PC-compatible writing desks, spacious living spaces and balconies all compliment the luxurious accommodations. Soothing green, blue and neutrals add to the home-like quality. Each suite is equipped with state-of-the-art control panels on the telephone to operate the TV, temperature, lighting and 25 different types of stereo music. A sumptuous breakfast is included in the room rate.

The Barn Restaurant offers country club dining at its best with piano entertainment Saturday nights. The 175 year old elegantly restored barn includes a wine cave and private dining room overlooking English gardens. Chef Thomas Dech prepares light, typically low-fat cuisine such as roasted New Zealand lamb rack with caramelized shallots and herb mashed potatoes or fresh Maine lobster over handmade linguini. The Blue Ribbon Cafe offers more casual dining surrounded by walls of glass soaring 25 feet overlooking vistas and gardens. A wide variety of foods are offered ranging from cinnamon croissants to salads, pizzas and heartier fare. The Walden Clubhouse provides a third dining experience where guests can enjoy breakfast, lunch and dinner six days a week. In mild weather, the new outdoor patio is a special place to enjoy.

A glass-enclosed hallway leads to the Inn's meeting rooms, conference room and an executive board room, all of which have high-tech equipment to meet every business guest's needs.

The Country Inn at Walden is a country inn in the true sense of the word. Guest can expect personal service and attention to detail throughout their stay.

Address: 1119 Aurora Hudson Road, Aurora, OH 44202
Phone: 330-562-5508
Toll-Free: 888-808-5003
Fax: 330-562-8001
E-mail: dlcdl@aol.com
Suite Rates: $$$
Credit Cards: Visa, AmEx, MC, DC
No. of Suites: 25
Services and Amenities: Valet, Garage & parking, Car hire, Laundry, Library, Card/game area, Kitchen facilities in 4 suites, Fireplaces, Balconies, Cable TV, VCR, Radio, Wet bar, 2nd powder room in many suites, Plush cotton bath robes, Complimentary shoeshine & toiletries
Restrictions: 1 room with handicapped access, Pets allowed in some rooms
Concierge: 8:00 a.m.–11:00 p.m.
Room Service: 24 hours, customized
Restaurant: The Barn Restaurant, open 5 days a week, Dress Code; The Blue Ribbon Cafe, open 7 days a week, Casual attire; The Clubhouse, open 6 days a week; All meals served between the three establishments
Bar: Jodhpur's Lounge, 6 p.m.–close
Business Facilities: Message center, Secretarial center, E-mail, Copiers, Audio-Visual, Teleconferencing, Fax, Modems
Conference Rooms: 5 rooms, capacity 10-100, Small Theatre
Sports Facilities: Outdoor pool, Whirlpool in rooms, Massage, Fitness Center, 4 tennis courts, Indoor riding arena, Championship 18-hole Golf Course
Location: Western Reserve, 2 minutes off turnpike I-80
Attractions: Extensive outlet shopping, Sea World of Ohio, Geauga Lake Amusement Park, Fine antiquing, Tinkers Creek State Park, Cleveland Rock-n-Roll Hall of Fame, Science Museum, Severence Hall (Cleveland Orchestra), Skiing nearby

THE CAMPBELL HOUSE - A CITY INN

The Campbell House is a Queen Anne shingle style Victorian nestled in an acre of beautifully landscaped grounds adjacent to hiking trails in the East Skinner Butte Downtown Historic District of Eugene. Originally built in 1892 by gold miner and timber owner John Cogswell for his daughter Idaho, this City Inn was completely renovated in 1993.

Elegant, light guest rooms, beautifully appointed, and sporting Waverly fabrics and wallpapers, create an English country ambiance. The most popular suite offers hardwood floors, high dormer ceilings, four-poster bed, gas fireplace and a jetted tub for two.

After you've settled in, your hosts recommend lunch or dinner at Willie's on 7th Street. The entree menu just begins with Apricot-Rosemary Pork, Fresh Chinook Salmon, and Szechuan Chicken. The walk to Willie's can take you by restaurants, boutiques, antique shops, the river walk, and the Hult Center for the Performing Arts.

The Campbell House is also ideal for a business meeting or retreat, with 3-becomes-1 conference rooms, most office amenities, and catering available.

Whether you come to Eugene for a sports vacation, business, to visit someone at the University of Oregon, or just kick back and relax, the genteel and quiet marble floored lobby, well-stocked library and lovely gardens help chase away the business of the day. There are also special events sprinkled across the year, including Murder Mystery Nights in October!

Address: 252 Pearl Street, Eugene, OR 97401
Phone: 541-343-1119
Toll-Free: 800-264-2519
Fax: 541-343-2258
E-mail: campbellhouse@campbellhouse.com
Web site: http://www.campbellhouse.com
Room Rates: $
Suite Rates: $$$
Credit Cards: Visa, MC, AmEx, Discover
No. of Rooms: 18 **Suites:** 8
Services and Amenities: Breakfast included, Parking, Laundry, Gift shop, Card/game area, Library, Complimentary newspaper, toiletries & refreshments, Cable TV, Telephones, Video cassette players, Individual heat control, Air-conditioning, Robes, Corporate rates, Event packages
Restrictions: No pets allowed, Minimum stay some weekends, 1 room handicapped-equipped
Concierge: 8:30 a.m.–midnight
Room Service: Noon-10:00 p.m.
Business Facilities: Copier, Audio-Visual, Teleconferencing, Data port for computer and fax, Full catering menu available
Conference Rooms: 3 rooms, capacity 20 each room
Sports Facilities: Guest passes to Downtown Athletic Club, 2 golf courses, Skiing, Riverside bicycle paths, Whitewater rafting, Fishing
Location: Eugene's downtown historic district, 15 miles to Mahlon Sweet Airport
Attractions: Walking distance to fabulous restaurants, boutiques, antique shops, Hult Center for Performing Arts, 2 blocks to the River

COLUMBIA GORGE HOTEL

The Columbia Gorge Hotel was built in 1921 on a cliff above the mighty Columbia River at the foot of majestic Mount Hood, and quickly became a favorite retreat for the jazz-age rich and famous. Now listed in the National Registry of Historic Places, the hotel continues to delight visitors with its spectacular natural setting and superlative service.

The spacious guest rooms are individually decorated, many with brass, canopy, or antique beds. Evening turn-down service comes with a rose as well as a chocolate.

The world-famous Farm Breakfast, a multi-course extravaganza, is definitely worth waking up for. The Columbia River Court dining room serves fine Northwestern cuisine, such as fresh Columbia River salmon, dry-aged Eastern prime beef, and Hood River apple torte.

The multitude of outdoor activity possibilities includes river rafting, water sports, skiing on Mt. Hood, fishing, hiking, and more. The waterfall that plunges from the hotel's "backyard" to the river 206 feet below has been the scene of romantic interludes for generations of visitors.

The Columbia Gorge Hotel is a favorite conference locale for small high-level meetings. Every effort is made throughout the hotel to provide thoughtful service. The staff is dedicated to making each guest's visit—whether business or pleasure—a memorable one.

While in the area, be sure to visit the Maryhill Museum, with its world-renowned collection of Rodin sculptures.

Address: 4000 Westcliff Drive, Hood River, OR 97031
Phone: 541-386-5566
Toll-Free: 800-345-1921
Fax: 541-387-5414
Room Rates: $$$
Suite Rates: $$$$
Credit Cards: Most credit cards accepted
No. of Rooms: 42 **Suites:** 4
Services and Amenities: Gift shop, Parking, Laundry, Baby-sitting service, Complimentary newspaper, Cable TV, Phone, World-famous farm breakfast included with your room
Restrictions: Handicapped access to two rooms, Pets and children welcome
Restaurant: Columbia River Court 8:00 a.m.–11:00 p.m.
Bar: 11:00 a.m.–midnight
Business Facilities: Copiers, Audio-Visual, Fax
Conference Rooms: 2 rooms, capacity 40-150
Sports Facilities: 18-hole golf course 1 mile, Nearby tennis courts, Half mile to whitewater rafting, Summer skiing, Salmon fishing, Hiking, Windsurf
Location: From Portland I-84 to Exit 62
Attractions: Blossom Festival each April, 250,000 Christmas lights in yard Thanksgiving thru Valentines Day, View of Mt. Hood

FIFTH AVENUE SUITES HOTEL

Set in an historic 1912 building, the 10-story Fifth Avenue Suites Hotel in downtown Portland is the very picture of comfort and sophistication, opening its arms to business travelers as well as vacationing families.

The hotel lobby, with its soaring ceilings and floor-to-ceiling windows, is light and airy. The decor is accented by mahogany, leather and brass, and is anchored by an inviting corner fireplace. Guests may gather in this inviting area for an early evening glass of wine or simply admire the artwork.

Of the hotel's 221 rooms, 135 are suites, 4 grand suites, and 82 deluxe guest rooms. Suites are divided by curtained sliding French doors rather than the standard solid doors, so they always feel airy and light. Plush overstuffed upholstered chairs, ottomans and a small sofa evoke the feeling of home. Comfortable beds are made cozier by padded brocade, fabric trimmed headboards and lush, thick bedspreads.

The bustling Red Star Tavern & Roast House, located on the ground floor, features regional produce and specialty comfort foods cooked in brick wood-burning ovens, rotisseries and grills. This food foundry is open for all meals daily.

Fifth Avenue Suites Hotel offers a wealth of facilities and accommodations for every type of traveler. Business travelers will enjoy the on-site fitness center and Aveda Environmental Lifestyle Spa. Guests will also enjoy access to meeting and conference sites within the hotel equipped with all the amenities, plus easy access to Portland's central business district.

The home-like ambiance is underscored by the luxury and exemplary service of a boutique hotel that excels in mastering the finest detail.

Address: 506 SW Washington Street, Portland, OR 97204
Phone: 503-222-0001
Toll-Free: 800-711-2971
Fax: 503-222-0004
Web site: http://www.5thavenuesuites.com
Room Rates: $$
Suite Rates: $$$
Credit Cards: Most credit cards accepted
No. of Rooms: 96 **Suites:** 135
Services and Amenities: Valet service, Garage and parking, Telephones with two line data port, Fax, Cable TV, VCR in Grand Suites, Movies, Radio, Audio cassette player, Wet bar in Grand Suites, Robes, Complimentary toiletries, shoeshine and newspaper
Restrictions: Pets Allowed, 13 rooms equipped for handicapped, Children under 18 stay free with parents
Concierge: 24 hours
Room Service: 24 hours
Restaurant: Red Star Tavern and Roast House, 6:30 a.m.–11:00 p.m., Casual/Bistro attire
Bar: Red Star Tavern and Roast House Bar 11:30 a.m.–midnight
Business Facilities: Computers, Message center, E-mail, Audio-Visual, Modems, Copiers, Fax, Complete business facility
Conference Rooms: 6 rooms, capacity 10–150
Sports Facilities: Complete executive fitness center, Massage, Weight training, Universal gym, Access to Princeton Athletic Club
Location: Downtown, City center
Attractions: Pioneer Place, Yamhill Market Place, Concert Hall, Performing Arts Center, Shopping, Cultural districts

HOTEL VINTAGE PLAZA

Built in 1894 and listed on the historical registry is the charming European-style Hotel Vintage Plaza which enjoys urban luxury and elegance in the heart of downtown Portland. The dramatic atrium lobby and comfortable piano lounge, classically decorated in rich jewel tones, features a marble fireplace and vineyard fresco. The winery theme is celebrated throughout the hotel including a wine cellar located in the lobby with an extensive vintage collection and unique wine tasting area. Complimentary local vintage wines are served each evening by the lobby fireplace, accompanied by live piano music.

All 107 guest rooms are named for and dedicated to Oregon wineries and vineyards. Each is stylishly appointed in rich color schemes of hunter green, deep plum, cerise taupe and gold compliment the custom neo-classic cherry furniture. There are 9 deluxe two-story town house suites offering large two-person jacuzzi soak tubs. There are also 9 unique "starlight" rooms on the top floor boasting solarium style windows which capture the spectacular views of the surrounding areas.

The Pazzo Ristorante located in the Hotel provides guests with a truly memorable dining experience. Pazzo offers savory regional Italian cuisine served in an upscale, yet casual setting. Chef David Machado prepares such specialties as smoked salmon ravioli in asparagus-lemon cream and grilled pork chops with garlic-ricotta stuffed potatoes. To compliment the menu, Pazzo carries one of the largest collections of Italian wines in the Pacific Northwest.

If business takes you to The Hotel Vintage Plaza, there are 8 conference rooms, an elegantly appointed executive boardroom, fully equipped business center and executive gym. The hotel staff prides itself on their attentiveness to detail and guest's needs.

Address: 422 Southwest Broadway, Portland, OR 97205
Phone: 503-228-1212
Toll-Free: 800-243-0555
Fax: 503-228-3598
Web site: http://www.holog.com/vintage
Room Rates: $$$
Suite Rates: $$$$
Credit Cards: Most credit cards accepted
No. of Rooms: 107 **Suites:** 19
Services and Amenities: Valet, Gift shop, International currency exchange, Laundry, Baby-sitting referrals, Balconies/decks, Cable TV, Telephones, Radio, Fully stocked honor bars, Hair dryer, Iron/board, Alarm clock, Complimentary wine tasting each evening by lobby fireplace
Restrictions: Pets allowed–$50 deposit, 7 rooms equipped for handicapped, Children under 18 free with parents
Concierge: 10:00 a.m.–7:00 p.m.
Room Service: 24 hours
Restaurant: Pazzo Ristorante, 7:00 a.m.–10:00 p.m., Casual/Formal
Bar: Pazzo Bar, Private wine cellar
Business Facilities: Voice mail, Copiers, Audio-Visual, Fax, Modems
Conference Rooms: 7 rooms
Sports Facilities: Whirlpool, Weight training, Treadmill, Stairmaster, Lifecyle, Rowing machine
Location: Downtown
Attractions: Two blocks to Pioneer Courthouse Square, Shopping at Pioneer Place, Nordstrom, Saks Fifth Avenue, and the Galleria, Two block walk to the Light Rail Transit System and close to Performing Arts Center

THE HEATHMAN HOTEL

This National Historic Landmark in downtown Portland is next door to the Center for the Performing Arts and just a few steps from the Portland Art Museum and downtown business and shopping districts. The Heathman was completely renovated in 1984 under the supervision of San Francisco's master interior designer, Andrew Delfino. Original works by leading American artists are displayed throughout the hotel. The lobby, featuring rare eucalyptus panelling, a grand piano, and a fireplace, is the setting for afternoon tea, a burgeoning Portland custom.

Each spacious guest room is decorated with teak wood and art deco furnishings. Carrara white and Verona red marble, Roman travertine, and Burmese teak have been artfully blended to create an unabashedly luxurious decor. A complimentary 225-plus film library is available to all guests. Baths are fitted with marble and provided with robes, hair dryers and abundant complimentary toiletries.

The Heathman has become a Portland dining favorite, thanks in part to its proximity to cultural events, and to their award winning chef, Philippe Bowlot. The restaurant prides itself on serving the finest and freshest northwest regional seafood, vegetables, and meat. Menus change seasonally; in the spring, dinner began with northwest game pâté with red rémoulade, then the Heathman salad of Romaine butter lettuce, garlic croutons bacon, and mint tossed together in a delectable dressing. The entrée was rack of Oregon lamb, and dessert a chocolate raspberry torte served along with the Heathman's house blend coffee.

The elegant Marble Bar, named for its exquisite marble furnishings, is a popular après-theatre meeting place, serving bistro-style small plates until 2:00 a.m.

The care and thought that have gone into refurbishing this hotel, combined with courteous professional service, will surely please.

Address: 1001 SW Broadway at Salmon Street, Portland, OR 97205
Phone: 503-241-4100
Toll-Free: 800-551-0011
Fax: 503-790-7110
Room Rates: $$$
Suite Rates: $$$$
Credit Cards: Most credit cards accepted
No. of Rooms: 103 **Suites:** 47
Services and Amenities: Valet service, Garage and parking, Car hire, Laundry service, Baby-sitting service, Currency exchange, Library (featuring volumes signed by guest authors), Video library, TV, Radio, Robes, Complimentary newspaper and toiletries
Restrictions: No pets except seeing-eye dogs, Handicapped access to 8 rooms
Concierge: 24 hours
Room Service: 24 hours
Restaurant: Heathman Restaurant & Bar, 6:00 a.m.–11:00 p.m.
Bar: Marble Bar & Lobby Lounge, 11:00 a.m.–2:00 a.m.
Business Facilities: Check with concierge
Conference Rooms: 7 rooms, capacity 104 (seated), 150 (standing)
Sports Facilities: In-room exercise equipment available, Access to athletic club and on-site fitness suite
Location: Downtown, 10 miles from Portland International
Attractions: Shopping, Business district, Performing Arts Center, Portland Art Museum

Bar Harbor Hotel - Blue Nose Inn, Bar Harbor, Maine. PAGE 108

Chatham Bars Inn, Chatham, Massachusetts. PAGE 116

THE RIVERPLACE HOTEL

European in style and service, Portland's stately new RiverPlace Hotel maintains a uniquely Northwestern character in its wood and brick exterior. The location, on the Willamette River at Governor Tom McCall Park in the prestigious RiverPlace neighborhood, is convenient to the downtown financial district, shopping and theatres.

The spacious rooms are well appointed with traditional furnishings that reflect the aura of warmth and comfort felt throughout the hotel. Each bath is lushly accoutered with plush towels and a basket of personal care amenities. Guests enjoy choice of morning newspaper, overnight shoeshine, twice-daily maid service with evening turndown and complimentary continental breakfast.

The Esplanade Restaurant has a spectacular view of the riverfront. Fine cuisine has made it a Portland favorite—be sure to try the special seafood and pasta dishes. The Sunday Brunch is a Portland favorite, served to you at your table. During the summer months, enjoy casual outdoor riverside dining at the Patio Restaurant. The Bar at RiverPlace offers a river view and jazz entertainment seven nights a week.

Guests enjoy the hotel spa and whirlpool. Additional exercise facilities are available in the RiverPlace Athletic Club, to which guests are extended privileges.

Address: 1510 Southwest Harbor Way, Portland, OR 97201
Phone: 503-228-3233
Toll-Free: 800-227-1333
Fax: 503-295-6161
E-mail: riverplace@ossnw.com
Web site: http://www.riverplacehotel.com
Room Rates: $$$
Suite Rates: $$$$
Credit Cards: Most credit cards accepted
No. of Rooms: 84 **Suites:** 45
Services and Amenities: Valet service, Garage & parking, Car hire, Laundry service, Baby-sitting service, Cable TV, Radio, Robes, Whirlpool bath, Shampoo, Lotion, Bath gel, Complimentary newspaper & shoeshine
Restrictions: Pets by pre-arrangement
Concierge: 24 hours
Room Service: 24 hours
Restaurant: Esplanade Restaurant, 6:30 a.m.–10:00 p.m., Outdoor Patio Restaurant open during the summer
Bar: The Bar, 11:00 a.m.–1:00 a.m.
Business Facilities: Message center and other business services available on request
Conference Rooms: 3 rooms, capacity 300
Sports Facilities: Water skiing, Sailing, Whirlpool, Sauna, Access to full service health club
Location: Overlooking Willamette River, Financial district
Attractions: Major city park, Esplanade walkway of shops & boutiques, Pike Marketplace

EVERMAY ON-THE-DELAWARE

Nestled on 25 acres of pastures, woodland and gardens between the Delaware River and Canal, EverMay On-The-Delaware exudes a quiet elegance that makes it the perfect place for a romantic getaway. The hotel was built in the 1700's, was remodeled and underwent a considerable expansion in 1871, and is now listed on the National Register of Historic Places. The double Victorian parlor across from the main dining room features a gas fireplace, antique grandfather clock, baby grand piano, period-style tapestries and a carved armoire. Here guests enjoy Afternoon Tea from 4 to 5 p.m., which includes individual trays of tea, cookies, sweet breads, and tea sandwiches.

All of the guest rooms are furnished in Eastlake or Renaissance Victorian-style. Most have oriental rugs, carved headboards and marble-topped dressers. Rooms at the front of the inn offer views of the river, while those at the back overlook the fields. Some very special touches you will find in your room include baskets of fruit bedside and fluted glasses of bedtime sherry.

The formal Victorian dining room is set with Bavarian china. An elegant dinner is served, with one seating on Friday, Saturday, Sunday and holidays. Dinner is prix fixe and begins with champagne and hors d'oeuvres followed by six courses with a choice of entrees. The menu changes each evening. Dinner here is an evening's entertainment and deserves to be eaten in a leisurely fashion so that every bite is savored. A complimentary breakfast, served in the conservatory, includes juice, fresh fruit compote, granola, cheese and a basket filled with croissants and rolls.

EveryMay on-the-Delaware prides itself in providing substance, style and country comfort, with a lack of pretense and the utmost charm.

Address: River Road, P.O. Box 60, Erwinna, PA 18920
Phone: 610-294-9100
Fax: 610-294-8249
E-mail: moffly@evermay.com
Web site: http://www.evermay.com
Room Rates: $$
Suite Rates: $$$$
Credit Cards: Visa, MC
No. of Rooms: 16 **Suites:** 1
Services and Amenities:
Complimentary breakfast & afternoon tea, Sherry, Fresh fruit, Garage & parking, Card/game area, Library/parlor, Individual heat & air-conditioning control, Complimentary toiletries, Two rooms equipped for handicapped access
Restrictions: Minimum 2 nights on weekends, May not be appropriate for children under 12, No pets allowed
Room Service: 8:30 a.m.–10:00 p.m.
Restaurant: Evermay on-the-Delaware, One seating 7:30 Friday, Saturday, Sunday and holidays, Jacket & tie required for the formal dining room
Business Facilities: Copiers, Audio-Visual, Fax, Computer jacks
Conference Rooms: 2 rooms, capacity 20 in each
Sports Facilities: Nearby outdoor swimming pool, Massage, Aerobics, Weight training, Horseback riding, Tennis
Location: Historic Bucks County, Nearest airports are Newark & Philadelphia
Attractions: New Hope—antiquing, Historic Doylestown, Delaware Canal—walking, Cross-country skiing, Canoeing, Rafting on the Delaware River

THE MOUNTAIN VIEW INN

The Mountain View Inn, built in Early American style, prides itself on the tradition of innkeeping established in colonial America. Guests are welcomed in a lobby featuring dark wood panelling, a stone fireplace, and an outstanding collection of Pennsylvania country antique furniture and plates.

Each room has a different character; some have the spacious formality of an elegant 18th-century boudoir, others the cozy charm of an Early American country home. Bathrooms are individually decorated to complement the rooms. All bathrooms have phones; the honeymoon suites have sunken tubs for two.

The Inn's 1776 House serves three meals daily. Its brick walls, two large fireplaces, and antiques create a colonial ambience. One can dine by candlelight while listening to soft music from a Steinway and enjoying a view of the Laurel Highlands. The menu includes such delicacies as oysters Mountain View, scallops of veal Williamsburg, fresh sautéed green beans and peppers, and Early American desserts such as oatmeal cake or apple rum bread pudding. On Sundays meals are served family-style. The 1776 Tavern serves beverages and lighter fare.

The Mountain View Inn has executive suites, conference facilities, and can accommodate receptions for up to 500 persons. Its gracious grounds include lawns facing the mountain, a lily pond, an herb garden, perennial gardens, an outdoor pavilion, a croquet court and a swimming pool.

In winter, the Inn offers musical weekend packages, such as an overnight stay for two with dinner and dancing to the big band sound. Located 30 miles east of Pittsburgh in the foothills of the Alleghenies, the Mountain View Inn offers warm hospitality and a convenient location to many tourist attractions in western Pennsylvania.

Address: 1001 Village Drive, Greensburg, PA 15601
Phone: 412-834-5300
Toll-Free: 800-537-8709
Fax: 412-834-5304
Room Rates: $
Suite Rates: $$$
Credit Cards: Visa, MC, AmEx, DC, Discover
No. of Rooms: 56 **Suites:** 6
Services and Amenities: Laundry service, Victoria's Garden Gift shop, Cable TV, Radio, Complimentary toiletries, shoe mit and sewing kit
Restrictions: No pets allowed, 2 rooms handicapped-equipped, Children under 16 stay free with parents
Room Service: 7:00 a.m.–11:00 p.m.
Restaurant: 1776 House, 7:00 a.m.–9:00 p.m., Dress code
Bar: 1776 Tavern, 11:30 a.m.–1:30 a.m.
Business Facilities: Message center, Secretarial service, Copiers, Audio-Visual
Conference Rooms: 7 rooms, capacity up to 500
Location: Suburbs of Greensburg, 30 miles east of Pittsburgh
Attractions: Bushy Run and Fort Ligonier battlefields, Frank Lloyd Wright's "Fallingwater," Idlewild Park and Storybrook Forest, Georgia Place outlet mall, Skiing downhill and cross-country nearby, Antique stores abound

CLIFF PARK INN & GOLF COURSE

In 1820 George Buchanan built the family farmstead in a grassy meadow. In 1900 Annie Buchanan, wife of George Buchanan's grandson, turned the old farm house into Cliff Park House, a small summer hotel. The inn's old fireplaces and other details trace the family history. Ancestral portraits, bronze sculptures, a Civil War era family Bible, and original Victorian furnishings reflect the life and times of the family.

In 1913 a family friend and outstanding golf course architect converted the surrounding fields into a 9-hole course, all located in front of the Inn so the non-playing guests could sit on the porch and watch. Keeping pace with the game and the times, the course has been rearranged, modified and enlarged. The fairways with their long par fives are challenging to the low-handicapper, yet the openness of the course invites the less accomplished golfer. Spectators still enjoy watching from the inn's long veranda, which is shaded by stately maples and comfortably furnished with high-backed rockers.

At the Cliff Park Inn, golf and good food are among life's essentials. There are two dining rooms, the Colonial Room is cozy with its fireplace and antiques. The Buchanan Room sports the family tartan. The food is hearty, savory and fresh, like Stuffed Mushrooms, Potato Crusted Halibut, and Bumbleberry Pie.

The rooms and suites are comfortable and well-appointed. The decor is light and airy, with each room different. The overall effect is of a charming English countryside inn. The Buchanans, with generations of innkeeping experience, are pleased to extend a warm welcome and invite you to their family and their lovely Victorian retreat.

Address: 155 Cliff Park Road, Milford, PA 18337
Phone: 717-296-6491
Toll-Free: 800-225-6535
Fax: 717-296-3982
E-mail: cpi@warwick.net
Web site: http://www.cliffparkinn.com
Room Rates: $
Suite Rates: $$$
Credit Cards: Most credit cards accepted
No. of Rooms: 18 **Suites:** 2
Services and Amenities: Golf packages, Breakfast included, Children welcome, International currency exchange, Personal checks accepted, Parking, Card/game area, Library, Television Lounge, Individual climate control, Cable TV, VCR's, Telephones, Balconies
Restrictions: No pets allowed, 6 rooms equipped for handicapped, Seasonal minimum 2-night weekend stay
Concierge: 9:00 a.m.–5:00 p.m.
Restaurant: The Restaurant at Cliff Park Inn, 8:00–10:00 a.m., noon-3:00 p.m., 6:00–9:00 p.m.
Bar: The Bar, Noon 'til closing
Business Facilities: Clubhouse meeting room with both formal and informal meeting areas, Message center, 5 IBM PCs
Conference Rooms: 3 rooms, capacity 60
Sports Facilities: 9-hole golf course, Full service Golf Pro Shop on premises, 7 miles of cross-country ski trails in winter, Ski shop on premises
Location: 600-acre estate with long-established golf course amid dramatic setting
Attractions: One and a half miles to Milford, a quaint Victorian town with many antique shops; 2 miles to the Delaware River: Swimming, Fishing, Whitewater rafting and Canoeing

THOMAS BOND HOUSE

Thomas Bond was a doctor best known, along with Benjamin Franklin and Dr. Benjamin Rush, for helping to found the first public hospital in the United States. His house, built in 1769, is an important example of the classic revival Georgian style architecture. Today it stands as a carefully restored townhouse with an ambiance of quiet luxury, and is listed on the National Register of Historic Places.

The guest rooms and suites have private baths, and are exquisitely furnished with period furniture and authentic accessories. In keeping with the custom of the Federal Period, the most luxurious accommodations are those closest to the first floor. The charming parlor serves as a gathering place where guests relax and enjoy a game of chess or bridge at the game table while sipping a complimentary glass of Sherry or Brandy, or start their evening with complimentary wine and cheese. Freshly baked cookies are also on hand. During the week guests are served a continental breakfast featuring freshly-squeezed orange juice and freshly-baked muffins, and, on weekends, a sumptuous full breakfast is served.

In the heart of Philadelphia's Old City with easy access to downtown, The Bond House is walking distance to many historic sites, including Independence Hall. It is on the doorstep of fine restaurants, theaters, museums, world-class shopping and the internationally acclaimed Academy of Music and Philadelphia Orchestra.

Thomas Bond House has been selected as one of the 25 best Historic Inns and has been rated by AAA and Mobil.

Address: 129 South Second Street, Philadelphia, PA 19106
Phone: 215-923-8523
Toll-Free: 800-845-2663
Fax: 215-923-8504
Room Rates: $
Suite Rates: $$$
Credit Cards: Visa, MC, AmEX
No. of Rooms: 12 **Suites:** 2
Services and Amenities: Parking, Car hire, Game room, Library, Cable TV, Telephone, Radio, In-room heat & air-conditioning control, Hair dryer, Desk, Some rooms with fireplaces/whirlpool tub, Complimentary coffee/soft beverages & wine/cheese in evening, also toiletries in rooms
Restrictions: Children welcome under supervision, No pets allowed
Concierge: Innkeeper
Restaurant: Complimentary continental breakfast on weekdays, Full breakfast on weekends, Also nearby restaurants for dining
Bar: Walk to City Tavern, noon—10:00 p.m.
Business Facilities: Copiers, Fax
Conference Rooms: 1 room, capactiy 25
Sports Facilities: Sheraton Health Club privileges at a modest fee
Location: Old City Area
Attractions: University of Pennsylvania, Barnes Art Collection, All sites in Philadelphia, Independence Park

THE 1661 INN & HOTEL MANISSES

The 1661 Inn and Hotel Manisses are situated on eleven acres of lawn on Block Island, a thirteen-mile ferry ride from the coast of Rhode Island.

The 1661 Inn and 1661 Guest House, named for the year that Block Island was settled, offers visitors 18 individually decorated guest rooms. Most have private baths, some have Jacuzzis, ocean views, sundecks, and refrigerators and/or kitchenettes. Each room is named after one of the original settlers. Both the inn and the Guest House overlook the ocean and guests can watch the sun rising over the Atlantic.

The Hotel Manisses, built in 1870, has been completely restored and is lovelier now than it was in the nineteenth century. It now has 17 rooms individually decorated with antique furnishings. All rooms have telephones and private baths, and some have Jacuzzis. Each room is named after a famous ship wrecked before 1870. The award-winning Hotel Manisses Dining Room is known for chef Andre Wlodowski's outstanding seasonal seafood dishes. After dinner drinks and flaming coffees are served at the Top Shelf Bar in the parlor.

The animal farm on the premises features llamas, goats, black swans, Indian runner ducks, geese, emus, and more. The gardens east of the animal farm provide many of the herbs and vegetables served to guests and the flowers found in the guest rooms, parlors and dining rooms. Historic Old Harbor, with many shops and sights, is within short walking distance, as are the renowned white sandy beaches. Hundreds of acres of nearby Conservancy Land are perfect for biking and hiking.

Address: 1 Spring Street, Block Island, RI 02807
Phone: 401-466-2421
Toll-Free: 800-626-4773
Fax: 401-466-3162
E-mail: biresorts@aol.com
Room Rates: $
Credit Cards: MC, Visa, AmEx
No. of Rooms: 38
Services and Amenities: Parking, Gift Shop, TV lounge, Game area, Library, Cable TV, Radio, Honor bar, Snacks. Soaps, Shampoo, Conditioners. Some: Kitchens, Fireplaces, Porches, & Ceiling Fans.
Restrictions: Hotel Manisses: no children under 10 welcome; 1661 Inn: children welcome; No pets allowed
Concierge: On demand
Room Service: 8:00 a.m.–10:00 p.m.
Restaurant: Hotel Manisses Dining Room and Bar
Business Facilities: Copiers, Fax, Courtesy van to airport
Conference Rooms: Conference space 75–300 people
Sports Facilities: Whirlpool, Sailing, Tennis nearby, Beaches on Island, Hiking
Location: Near Ocean, Zoo, Gardens, Town and Harbor
Attractions: 11 acres of lawn, Farmland gardens, Walking distance to all island attractions, Whale and Seal watching, Bird walks

CLIFFSIDE INN

Located on a quiet, tree-lined street, the Cliffside Inn is one block from Newport's renowned "Cliff Walk," known for lover's strolls and warm nights. Guests can stroll down the promenade, walk five minutes to the beach, or wander along the famed Gilded Age mansions. The inn itself is an elegant blend of Victorian splendor, period antiques, luxurious fabrics and modern fixtures.

Since its purchase in 1989, Winthrop Baker has renovated the inn to what is now a beautiful inn including four-poster beds, carved armoires, plump wing chairs, private baths, working fireplaces, brass-appointed whirlpools, and more. Elegance and grace abound throughout this lovely Victorian creating a relaxed, tranquil setting for guests to lavish in.

Each guestroom and suite has its own unique character creating a fanciful mood. The two-level Garden Suite with narrow iron spiral staircase, queen-size bed, fireplace and reading nook sets the scene for a romantic getaway. Sunlight filters through the hallway from the private enclosed patio adding light and space to this already grand suite. The Tower Suite, with private outside entrance, features a 25-foot turret tower with a cupola. If that weren't enough, guests may choose to lounge in the double whirlpool or read on a window seat basking in the warmth from the fireplace.

The inn's long history of inhabitants has left its mark on this establishment. The renowned painter and recluse, Beatrice Turner, once occupied this home at the turn of the century. More than 1,000 self-portraits were found on the estate, and many remain today for guest's viewing pleasure.

Whether it's a romantic getaway weekend or midweek business stay, the Cliffside Inn offers guests an array of luxuries and comforts that makes ones stay a memorable one.

Address: 2 Seaview Avenue, Newport, RI 02840
Phone: 401-847-1811
Toll-Free: 800-845-1811
Fax: 401-848-5850
E-mail: cliff@wsii.com
Web site: http://www.cliffsideinn.com
Room Rates: $$$
Suite Rates: $$$$
Credit Cards: Most credit cards accepted
No. of Rooms: 15 **Suites:** 7
Services and Amenities: Garage & parking, Laundry service, Gift shop, Library, Fireplaces, Individual heat and air-conditioning, Cable TV/VCR, Telephones, Radio, Robes, Complimentary toiletries and newspaper
Restrictions: Children over 14 welcome, No pets allowed
Concierge: 9 a.m.–9:00 p.m.
Location: Seaside, 20 miles to airport
Attractions: Bellevue Avenue mansions, Antique shops along the harborfront, Tennis Hall of Fame, Newport Art Museum, Historic Cliff Walks, Beach access

BATTERY CARRIAGE HOUSE INN

The Battery Carriage House Inn is "No. 20 on the Battery," built in 1843, and the childhood summer home of the owner's grandmother. Beyond the wrought iron gates of No. 20 lies beautiful White Point Gardens in Charleston's Historic Residential District at the quiet end of the Battery overlooking Charleston Harbor.

Eight guest rooms are located in the old carriage house in the garden of the antebellum mansion, and another three rooms are on the ground floor in what was once the kitchen area of the mansion. Each room has a private entrance and each is individually decorated. The atmosphere is European, garden-centered, history-laden, romantic and intimate. Of course, all conveniences are provided, including private steam bath shower units in some rooms, whirlpool tubs in others, computer hook-ups for business travelers, and a private phone line with answering machine in each room.

The most unusual room is a small suite which was the old cistern of the house! This extremely private lodging has its own sitting area under the porch.

Guests begin their day with the deluxe continental breakfast served with the morning newspaper, either in-room or under the Lady Bankshire rose arbor. For dinner, it's just a 10- to 15-minute walk up High Battery to Charleston's celebrated selection of fine restaurants.

This is definitely the right spot for a gracious, relaxing, European-style getaway south of the Mason-Dixon line.

Address: 20 South Battery, Charleston, SC 29401
Phone: 803-727-3100
Toll-Free: 800-775-5575
Fax: 803-727-3130
Room Rates: $
Suite Rates: $$$
Credit Cards: Visa, MC, AmEx, DS
No. of Rooms: 11 **Suites:** 1
Services and Amenities: Breakfast included, Checks accepted, Card/game room, Cable TV, Telephone, Radio, Whirlpools, Robes, Complimentary newspaper
Restrictions: No pets allowed, No smoking, 2 night minimum stay on weekends
Concierge: 9:00 a.m.–10:00 p.m.
Sports Facilities: Golf nearby
Location: Quiet historic waterfront residential district, 10 miles to airport
Attractions: Historic Charleston, Fort Sumter, Plantations and House museums

JOHN RUTLEDGE HOUSE

John Rutledge was one of 55 men who signed the Constitution of the United States. His home, which he built in 1763 as a wedding gift to his wife, is one of only 15 belonging to those signatories that have survived and the only one that is now a boutique hotel accommodating lodging guests.

The Inn is a complex of three buildings—the main house and two carriage houses—that enclose a courtyard garden of plants indigenous to coastal Southern Carolina. There are tables in the courtyard for guests who wish to have breakfast out of doors.

All rooms have parquet floors, Italian marble fireplaces and 14-foot ceilings with equally tall classic window treatments, and crystal chandeliers. The second floor ballroom is a public area where the Colonial experience is recreated for the edification of guests. Wine and sherry are offered.

Guest rooms are decorated with accurate period reproduction furniture and some antiques, individual climate control, remote control color TV and refrigerators. Suites feature fireplaces in the bedrooms, parlors and have double jacuzzis and a separate shower.

There is no full service restaurant at the Inn, but afternoon tea and refreshments in season are served.

The Inn specializes in small, upscale meetings and offers the full range of meeting and catering services. Guests are extended privileges to Wild Dunes and Kiawah, two golf resorts nearby.

The Inn is located in the heart of Charleston's historical district, directly across from the famous antebellum mansions. Fine restaurants, theaters, shopping, Charleston Place and the Market are within a few minutes' walking distance.

Address: 116 Broad Street, Charleston, SC 29401
Phone: 843-723-7999
Toll-Free: 800-476-9741
Fax: 843-720-2615
E-mail: jrh@charminginns.com
Web site: http://www.charminginns.com
Room Rates: $$$
Suite Rates: $$$$
Credit Cards: Most credit cards accepted
No. of Rooms: 19 **Suites:** 3
Services and Amenities: Parking, Laundry, Baby-sitting service, Library, Some rooms with fireplaces and/or whirlpool baths, Individual climate controls, Telephone, Radio, Wet bar, Cable TV, Stocked refrigerator, Robes, Complimentary paper, toiletries, wine, sherry, tea & snacks
Restrictions: No pets allowed, 2 rooms handicapped-equipped
Concierge: 24 hours
Room Service: 7:00 a.m.–10:00 a.m.
Business Facilities: Message center, Secretarial center, Copiers, Audio-Visual, Complete business service center
Conference Rooms: 1 room, capacity 20
Sports Facilities: Golf resorts nearby
Location: Historic District, downtown Charleston, 12 miles to Charleston Airport
Attractions: Convenient to tours, Shopping, Dining, Battery and Market Areas

KING'S COURTYARD INN

Here you inhabit a slice of Charleston's history. The 3-story building of the Inn was built in 1853 in Greek Revival Style with unusual Egyptian detail. The adjoining building dates to the 1830's and still has the original heartpine floors and plaster ceilings.

The Inn has served a variety of functions over the years, now offering a selection of rooms around two inner courtyards and a rear garden. Extreme care has been taken to ensure the necessary architectural and historic accuracy for which Charleston is famous, maintaining the residential atmosphere of lower King Street. Rooms are furnished in 18th-century reproduction furniture, with large windows, high ceilings, and oriental rugs over hardwood floors. In one suite the original 1830's living room maintains the ornate plaster ceiling moldings and the original fireplace.

From the moment you arrive you realize comfort and service are of primary importance to the staff of the King's Courtyard. The gracious surroundings are a pleasant respite for an afternoon cocktail in the courtyard.

The Inn is within easy walking distance of Charleston's historic homes, gardens, churches, and the City Market area. Explore one interesting shop after another, barter for the unusual in the open market, or enjoy a delicious meal at one of the many delightful restaurants. King Street is a center for the antique trade, and the Inn is literally surrounded by shops filled with fine collectibles.

Business travelers can take advantage of the services at the Inn. There is an elegantly restored room with original tin ceiling available for small meetings or receptions. This is an elegant, time-stopping treat in old Charleston.

Address: 198 King Street, Charleston, SC 29401
Phone: 843-723-7000
Toll-Free: 800-845-6119
Fax: 843-720-2608
E-mail: kci@charminginns.com
Web site: http://www.charminginns.com
Room Rates: $$
Suite Rates: $$$
Credit Cards: Most credit cards accepted
No. of Rooms: 41 **Suites:** 4
Services and Amenities: Special packages, Valet, Parking, Currency exchange, Baby-sitting service, Card/game room, Outdoor jacuzzi, Fireplaces, Balconies, Cable TV, Telephones, Radio, Individual climate control, Complimentary toiletries, Complimentary wine/sherry and breakfast
Restrictions: No pets allowed, 2 rooms handicapped-equipped, Children welcome
Concierge: 7:00 a.m.–11:00 p.m.
Room Service: 7:00 a.m.–11:00 a.m.
Bar: Courtyard Bar, 3:00 p.m.–11:00 p.m.
Business Facilities: Secretarial center, Copiers, Audio-Visual, Translators available
Conference Rooms: 2 rooms, capacity 20 and 75
Sports Facilities: Sailing nearby, Golf 5 to 25 miles away, Public tennis courts nearby, 3 blocks to the fully-equipped "Y"
Location: Center of Historic District surrounded by antique shops, 12 mi. to airport
Attractions: Walking distance to historic houses, High Battery, Waterfront park, Antique shop district, City Market, Over 40 restaurants

THE LODGE ALLEY INN

Nestled in the heart of the historic district and close to Charleston Harbor, The Lodge Alley Inn opened in 1983 and offers the finest of Southern hospitality. The design that was incorporated into these historical buildings allows many of the rooms to retain their original 18th century pine floors and brick walls.

Inn rooms and suites are both spacious and luxurious, taking you back to a time of endless beauty. Each room is individually decorated with period reproductions reflecting Charleston's European heritage. Room details vary with many offering high ceilings, detailed crown molding, fireplaces and oriental carpeting.

Guests may relax in the landscaped courtyard with fountain, featuring seasonal jazz entertainment. Meals are served daily in The French Quarter Restaurant with a glassed-in atrium overlooking the courtyard. Dinner specialties of Shrimp & Grits, Charleston Crab Cakes or Chateaubriand can be savored. Evening sherry is served in the parlor and the Tea Party Lounge features entertainment Thursday -Saturday nights.

The Lodge Alley Inn is conveniently located within easy strolling distance of many of the city's most desirable attractions. The Waterfront Park, the 18th Century city market area, historic churches, antebellum homes, carriage rides, restaurants, antique shops, and galleries are all located nearby.

Address: 195 East Bay Street, Charleston, SC 29401
Phone: 803-722-1611
Toll-Free: 800-845-1004
Fax: 803-722-1611 ext.7777
Room Rates: $$
Suite Rates: $$$
Credit Cards: AmEx, Visa, MC
No. of Rooms: 95 **Suites:** 60
Services and Amenities: Valet service, Complimentary parking, Turndown service with chocolates, Daily newspaper, Complimentary morning coffee in the lounge, Laundry service, Baby-sitting service, Cable TV, Children stay free with parents
Restrictions: No pets allowed
Concierge: Front desk
Room Service: 7:00–10:30 a.m.
Restaurant: The Frech Quarter, 7:00–10:30 a.m., 11:30–2:30 p.m., 6:00–10:00 p.m., Dress Code, Closed Sunday evening
Bar: Charleston Tea Party Lounge, Noon-Midnight, Closed Sunday
Business Facilities: Copiers, Full conference facilities
Conference Rooms: 6 rooms, capacity 70
Location: Historic district, French Quarter, Downtown, Nearest aiport is Charleston
Attractions: Within walking distance of fine restaurants, shopping, entertainment and stately Antebellum homes

MIDDLETON INN AT MIDDLETON PLACE

Adjacent to America's oldest landscaped gardens and secluded among tall pines and live oaks, the Middleton Inn provides magnificent views and exceptional comfort. The Inn's 20th-century architecture is an exciting counterpoint to the 18th- and 19th-century architecture of Middleton Place. This facility was given the American Institute of Architects' highest award.

Each of the 50 rooms has an expanse of ceiling-to-floor windows with views of the Ashley River. The rooms have handcrafted furniture, wood-burning fireplaces, large European-style bathrooms with ceramic tile counters, Carrara marble floors and sanded glass block walls.

The Cafe at the Inn serves continental breakfast, and beverages are available in the lobby. A short walk along the river path from the Inn, the Middleton Place Restaurant specializes in fine southern plantation cooking.

Middleton Place, on the banks of the Ashley River, is a carefully preserved 18th-century plantation. Today, the National Historic Landmark encompasses America's oldest landscaped Gardens, the Middleton Place House, and the Plantation Stableyards. The Gardens reflect the elegant symmetry of 17th-century European design and are magnificent throughout the year. The House museum interprets the lives of the Middleton Family, including Arthur Middleton, a Signer of the Declaration of Independence, through paints, silver, furniture and other decorate arts owned by the Middletons. The Plantation Stableyards recreate the activities of a self-sustaining Low Country plantation, bringing to life the era of rice cultivation.

Guests of Middleton enjoy unlimited access to the Gardens and Plantation Stableyards of Middleton Place and may tour the House for a small fee. The Inn offers swimming, tennis, volleyball, croquet, kayaking, and miles of scenic trails for jogging and nature walks. Golf is nearby, and tours of neighboring plantations are easily arranged. Historic Charleston is only 14 miles away, while a 45-minute drive takes you to Kiawah Island and other area beaches.

In any season, the Middleton experience is peaceful—one of quiet beauty and unfailing hospitality.

Address: 4290 Ashley River Road, Charleston, SC 29414
Phone: 803-556-0500
Toll-Free: 800-543-4774
Fax: 803-556-0500
E-mail: MiddletonInn.com
Room Rates: $
Suite Rates: $$
Credit Cards: Visa, MC, AmEx
No. of Rooms: 50 **Suites:** 7
Services and Amenities:
Complimentary continental breakfast and newspaper, Game area, Baby-sitting service, Each room offers a refrigerator, telephone, television and individual heat/air-conditioning controls
Restrictions: No pets allowed
Concierge: 9:00 a.m.–5:00 p.m.
Restaurant: Dining Room, 7:30 a.m.–8:00 p.m.
Bar: Yes, open lobby hours
Business Facilities: Full executive services, Copier, Fax
Conference Rooms: 3 rooms, capacity 275
Sports Facilities: Outdoor pool, Croquet, Tennis, Horseback riding, Scenic trails for jogging & nature walks, Middleton Outdoor Program, Nearby golf
Location: 14 miles from Charleston
Attractions: Middleton Place National Historic Landmark, Drayton Hall, Historic Charleston's House, Art museums and cultural events, Kiawah Island, Other nearby beaches

PLANTERS INN

Charleston's historic district, the 18th-Century city market area, abounds with antique shops, restaurants, flower vendors and boutiques. The district's bed-and-breakfast inns have traditionally played an important role in visitors' enjoyment of this venerable Old South seaport. The Planters Inn has set a whole new standard in cozy, elegant charm with courteous professional service. Designed in the manner of Charleston's fine antebellum homes, the lobby features detailed crown molding and fireplace mantle, antique furnishings and fine art. The 41 guest rooms and suites feature high ceilings, large closets, and beautiful oversized bathrooms done in travertine marble and equipped with telephone, TV, and toiletries. Guests are pampered with nightly turndown service and a silver service continental breakfast delivered to the room.

Planters Inn is home to the Peninsula Grill. Opened February 12, the grill has both an award-winning chef—Robert Carter and a general manager—Andrew Fallen backing its concept. The menu reflects the comfort of the 40s and 50s when a thick grilled steak, live Maine lobster and a glass of fabulous champagne were readily available.

This fine hotel has stood as a landmark overlooking Charleston's famous City Market for over 150 years. Complimentary refreshments in the lobby are a reminder of the Southern hospitality enjoyed throughout the Inn.

Address: 112 North Market Street, Charleston, SC 29401
Phone: 803-722-2345
Toll-Free: 800-845-7082
Fax: 803-577-2125
E-mail: plantersinn@charleston.net
Web site: http://www.plantersinn.com
Room Rates: $$
Suite Rates: $$$
Credit Cards: Visa, MC, AmEx, DC, DS
No. of Rooms: 56 **Suites:** 6
Services and Amenities: Silver service breakfast, Valet parking, Laundry, Gift shop, Baby-sitting service, Remote control cable TV, Radio, Phone, Individual climate control, Complimentary newspaper and evening refreshments, European turndown service
Restrictions: No pets allowed, Children stay free with adult
Concierge: 24 hours
Restaurant: Peninsula Grill, 5:00 p.m.–10:00 p.m.
Bar: Peninsula Grill, 4:00 p.m.–midnight
Business Facilities: Message center, Secretarial service, Copiers, Audio-Visual, Translators
Conference Rooms: 2 rooms, capacity 120
Sports Facilities: Massage, Nearby golf, Sailing and Riding, Access to nearby health club
Location: Historic district, 7 miles to Charleston airport
Attractions: Surrounded by Charleston's finest dining, Shopping, and Entertainment, Annual Spoleto Music Festival (May 24 to June 29)

VENDUE INN

The Vendue Inn has long been the definitive European-style inn in Charleston. Special service and attention to detail with a Southern flair are the Vendue's hallmark.

All 46 air-conditioned rooms and suites are individually decorated in 18th-century English or French period furnishings and color schemes. Bathrooms, with marble floors and counters, include robes, whirlpool baths, telephones, TV, and French-milled soaps and toiletries.

The lobby is done in wine, mauve and navy with English antiques and reproductions and Oriental rugs. The airy Garden Room features chamber music several nights a week. There is a small library and a rooftop deck and bar with views of the harbor and city of Charleston.

Guests are pampered with fresh-cut flowers, a full buffet breakfast or continental to the room served on a silver tray, afternoon wine and cheese tasting with live jazz or classical music, and liqueur and a chocolate mint at bedtime. For dinner, The Library Restaurant offers the finest Southern cuisine in a setting of soft gold painted walls and linen tablecloths. Meals can also be enjoyed on the rooftop terrace and bar. The shrimp *etouffe* and Southern Comfort pie are especially recommended.

For meetings and other gatherings, the Vendue provides full-scale conference facilities with wet bar and easy access to bathrooms. And for those who need to keep in touch, there are fax machines and computer hookups.

Getting out and about is easy at the Vendue, which is located it the historic French district and within walking distance of the harbor and its Waterfront Park.

Address: 19 Vendue Range, Charleston, SC 29401
Phone: 803-577-7970
Toll-Free: 800-845-7900
Fax: 803-577-2913
Web site: http://www.chas.net/com/vendueinn
Room Rates: $$
Suite Rates: $$$
Credit Cards: MC, Visa, AmEx, Disc., Diners
No. of Rooms: 46 **Suites:** 24
Services and Amenities: Valet service, Garage & parking, Laundry, Library, Kitchen & cooking facilities, Cable TV, Telephones, VCR, Radio, Air-conditioning, Robes, Whirlpools, Some rooms with fireplaces, Complimentary newspaper, toiletries, afternoon wine & cheese, breakfast
Restrictions: No pets allowed, 1 room handicapped-equipped
Concierge: 24 hours
Room Service: 8:00 a.m.–9:00 p.m.
Restaurant: The Library, 7:30 a.m.–10:00 p.m.
Bar: The Rooftop, 11:30 a.m.–10:00 p.m.
Business Facilities: Copiers, Audio-Visual, Fax, Complete business service center, Full-scale conference facilities
Conference Rooms: 2 rooms, capacity 25 & 50
Sports Facilities: Aerobics, Weight training, Nearby golf and tennis
Location: French District
Attractions: Historic areas, Boutiques, Saks Fifth Avenue, Waterfront Park and Charleston Harbor

WENTWORTH MANSION

Set proudly in the heart of historic Charleston, the Wentworth Mansion is one of the world's finest and most unique inns. Built in 1886 and designed not as a lodging house, but as an opulent private residence, the Wentworth Mansion is a place of hand-carved marble fireplaces, intricate woodwork, Tiffany stained glass windows and never-ending detail. The Mansion offers wine tastings, private tours of the city and exquisite buffet breakfasts served on the sunporch. For some, the highlight of their stay is the breathtaking view of Charleston, accessible via the spiral staircase that leads to the Mansion's towering cupola. Afternoon tea and evening cordials add to the experience. Guests may stroll through immaculate surroundings, unchanged since the days of the original owner, and sleep soundly in accommodations over a century old.

Each of the twenty-one guestrooms and suites have been historically restored and furnished with antiques. All of the most up-to-date conveniences and comforts have been discreetly added. All rooms have king beds and oversized whirlpools, most with a separate, spacious shower and working gas fireplace. Several rooms have day beds or sofa beds for additional guests.

The restaurant is located in a carriage house adjacent to the Mansion. The decor is deep rich woods, crisp white linens, polished glass and silver, large windows and in the winter, a romantic fireplace. Adjoining the restaurant is the Harleston Lounge. Enjoy top shelf spirits or sample wine from the Sommelier's Tasting Menu which features exceptional wines by the glass. In addition to cocktails, the Lounge offers a Vintner's Menu of select groupings of appetizers and specialties.

The world-class Wentworth Mansion promises guests an experience that will remain forever one of their fondest memories and bring them back year after year.

Address: 149 Wentworth Street, Charleston, SC 29401
Phone: 843-853-1886
Toll-Free: 888-INN-1886
Fax: 843-722-8634
E-mail: mgr@wentworthmansion.com
Web site: http://www.wentworthmansion.com
Room Rates: $$$$
Suite Rates: $$$$
Credit Cards: Visa, MC, AmEx, Disc., Diners
No. of Rooms: 21 **Suites:** 7
Services and Amenities: On-site parking, Library, Complimentary breakfast buffet, Afternoon tea, Wine tastings, Evening cordials, Turndown service, Private tours, Cable TV, Individual heat & air-conditioning control, Whirlpool bath, Complimentary newspaper
Restrictions: No pets allowed, Children welcome
Concierge: 24 hours
Restaurant: 5:00 p.m.–11:00 p.m., Last seating at 9:00 p.m.
Bar: The Harleston Lounge, 5:00 p.m.–11:00 p.m.
Business Facilities: Message center
Location: Historic downtown
Attractions: Historic Charleston, Fort Sumter, Plantations, High Battery , Waterfront park, City Market, Shopping, Antiquing and Dining

LITCHFIELD PLANTATION

Along the banks of the Waccamaw River in coastal South Carolina stands the Litchfield Plantation. Known for its beauty and magnificent natural setting at the end of a quarter-mile avenue of 250 year old live oaks, the stately Plantation House, circa 1750, overlooks former rice fields. The Plantation House is an 8,250-sq. ft. brick and stucco residential mansion surrounded by courtyards, landscaped patio, covered walkways, and natural pond.

In addition to the numerous suites available in the Plantation House, guests may also choose to stay in a private cottage. The cottages complement the Plantation by providing elegantly furnished country inn style accommodations with modern touches. The Tuckers Woods Cottages, for example, are situated around a quiet pond in a tranquil wooded setting. These spacious homes include two and three bedrooms, private bathrooms, modern kitchen and dining room, telephones, cable television, as well as a washer and dryer. The master bedrooms may feature a private veranda overlooking a lake, canopy bed, or whirlpool tub.

The handsome Carriage House Club, emulating a fine country home, provides the perfect setting for a romantic dinner for two, an intimate dinner party, or an elegant reception for 300 or more. The prestigious on-site dining facility gives guests the flexibility to enjoy a quiet night out while feeling pampered by an attentive staff. Guests can indulge in such culinary delights as House Grouper, Russian Blinis with Caviar, and Bourbon Pecan Pie. Other specialties include Chicken Mango, Grilled Salmon with Creamy Dill Cucumber Sauce, Honey Glazed Scallops, and Lemon Chess Pie.

The Plantation's extensive conference and recreational facilities compliment a guest's stay. Guests may choose from numerous conference rooms, an outdoor pool and cabana, tennis and golf, an on-site marina, fishing, boating, and horseback riding. The in-house concierge is always available to assist guests in their planning needs. Nearby attractions include historic Charleston and Georgetown, Brookgreen Gardens (the world's largest outdoor sculpture garden), Myrtle Beach, and live entertainment.

Address: P.O. Box 290, Pawleys Island, SC 29585
Phone: 803-237-5300
Toll-Free: 800-869-1410
Fax: 803-237-8558
E-mail: vacation@litchfieldplantation.com
Web site: http://www.litchfieldplantation.com
Room Rates: $$
Suite Rates: $$$
Credit Cards: Most credit cards accepted
No. of Rooms: 30 **Suites:** 8
Services and Amenities: Garage & parking, Baby-sitting service, Library, Kitchen facilities, Fireplaces, Balconies, Cable TV/VCR, Radio, Wet bar, Individual heat & air-conditioning, Whirlpool bath, Complimentary toiletries
Restrictions: 1 room with handicapped access, No pets allowed, Children welcome in guest cottages
Concierge: 8:30 a.m.–8:00 p.m.
Restaurant: Carriage House Club, 6:30 p.m.–9:00 p.m.
Bar: 6:30 p.m.–9:00 p.m.
Business Facilities: Message center, Secretarial center, E-mail, Copiers, Fax
Conference Rooms: 6 rooms, capacity 50
Sports Facilities: Outdoor swimming pool, Jacuzzi, Horseback riding, Tennis courts, Fishing, Boating, Golf nearby
Location: 2 miles to downtown, 22 miles south of airport
Attractions: 600 acre estate with small lakes & streams on property, 375 acres of ancient ricefields & canals, Brookgreen Gardens, Charleston, Georgetown and Myrtle Beach nearby

CHRISTOPHER PLACE, AN INTIMATE RESORT

Christopher Place is a colonial style mansion, newly constructed on 200 wooded acres at the edge of the Great Smoky Mountain National Park. This luxurious inn in the Smokies was created for romantic retreats. Reflections of crystal chandeliers on marbled floors welcome visitors. Massive fireplaces, hand-carved furniture, and resort amenities invite guests to stay.

The soothing calm of a mountain view, the hypnotic dance of a crackling wood fire and the seductive warmth of a whirlpool bath are all reasons why guests find it difficult to leave Christopher Place. Each room and suite is unique. The Tournament of Roses suite is secluded in the guest house with queen wicker bed and private entrance. All offer a private bath, soft terry robes, coffee maker, hair dryer, compact disc and cassette players.

Intimate meals for two are served exclusively to guests to complete the romantic retreat getaway. A full breakfast is served to order, accompanied by gourmet coffees, teas and fresh fruit. Allow the staff to pack a picnic for poolside or on the nature trails. Dinner by candlelight at a private table ends the evening, with service unobtrusive, yet unsurpassed. In select suites, in-room dining can be arranged.

The tranquility of the Smoky Mountains surrounds guests at Christopher Place, quietly boasting breathtaking views and serene silence. Away from one's hurried routines, there is relaxation, rediscovery and rekindling to be found at this intimate resort.

Address: 1500 Pinnacles Way, Newport, TN 37821
Phone: 423-623-6555
Toll-Free: 800-595-9441
Fax: 423-613-4771
E-mail: TheBestInn@aol.com
Web site: http://www.christopherplace.com
Room Rates: $$$
Suite Rates: $$$$
Credit Cards: Visa, MC, AmEx, Discover
No. of Rooms: 8 **Suites:** 3
Services and Amenities: Garage and parking, Gift shop, TV lounge, Card/game room, Library, Laundry service, Refreshments and light snacks, Television, CD players, Radio, Robes, Complimentary toiletries, Some rooms with whirlpool bath, Airport transfers with 24 hour notice
Restrictions: No pets allowed, Children 12 and over welcome
Concierge: 7:00 a.m.–10:00 p.m.
Room Service: 7:00 a.m.–10:00 p.m.
Restaurant: Max's, 6:00–10:00 p.m.
Business Facilities: Message center, E-mail, Copiers, Audio-Visual, Fax
Conference Rooms: 1 room, capacity 20
Sports Facilities: Outdoor pool, Croquet, Sauna, Weight training, One hard tennis court, Hiking/walking trails, Guided llama treks, Newport Golf Club
Location: Great Smoky Mountains
Attractions: Great Smoky Mountain National Park, Whitewater rafting, Fishing, Outlet shopping, Golf courses, Forbidden Caverns

HOTEL ST. GERMAIN

The antique-filled Hotel St. Germain, originally a residence built in 1906, is a step back in time to the old-world luxury of 19th century France.

No two suites are alike, but each is private and luxurious with fireplace, canopied bed dressed in fine linen and featherbeds, and soaking tub or jacuzzi. All bathrooms are decorated with clean, crisp black and white tile, have generous space, an extra telephone, ample vanity area and imported porcelain sinks. The two suites on the third floor are the most elaborate. One has a lofty gabled ceiling with a view overlooking the New Orleans-style walled courtyard; the sitting room is done in a red toile de Jouy, while the sleeping area is dominated by a draped Napoleonic sleigh bed. The premier guest room contains a 150-year-old Mallard suite, a pier glass cheval mirror and a carved wooden windscreen with glass insets.

The dining room is the romantic soul of the house. Elegantly laid tables draped to the floor overlook the garden and courtyard. Service is handled by white-gloved butlers, who set each place with 75-year-old Limoges, Waterford and Schotts-Zweisel crystal. The menu, which changes monthly, boasts a range of dishes from a familiar filet of Angus beef with orange bernaise sauce to an exotic hazelnut-dusted natural poussin with wild mushrooms. Reservations and menu selections must be made in advance.

Address: 2516 Maple Avenue, Dallas, TX 75201
Phone: 214-871-2516
Toll-Free: 800-683-2516
Fax: 214-871-0740
Web site: http://www.hotelstgermain.com
Suite Rates: $$$$
Credit Cards: Most credit cards accepted
No. of Suites: 7
Services and Amenities: Valet, Beauty/Barber shop across street, Laundry service, Lounges, Shoeshine, Fireplaces, Balconies-2 suites, Cable TV/VCR, Radio, CD/Cassette players, Wet bar, Robes, Whirlpools-3 suites, Complimentary toiletries & newspaper, European breakfast included
Restrictions: No pets allowed, No room with handicapped access
Concierge: 24 hours
Room Service: 24 hours
Restaurant: Hotel St. Germain Restaurant, Dinner Tuesday through Saturday
Bar: Hotel St. Germain, hours flexible for guests
Business Facilities: Message center, Secretarial services through concierge, Staff speak several languages
Conference Rooms: 3 rooms, capacity 150
Sports Facilities: Massage by appointment through concierge, Nearby full health facility for small fee
Location: Oak Lawn, Near downtown, Nearest airports: Love Field & Dallas Fort Worth
Attractions: Boutique shopping across the street, 30 restaurants, 25 art galleries, 20 antique shops

THE ARISTOCRAT HOTEL

Located in the Harwood Historical District (downtown), The Aristocrat Hotel of Dallas is a full-service historic landmark. The hotel was originally built in 1925 by Conrad Hilton and was the first hotel to carry his name. A $16 million dollar renovation in 1985 reduced the number of rooms from 320 to 172. Now a mostly-suite hotel, it is ideal for the business traveler as it is connected to an extensive skywalk system linking it to many corporate offices and a self-service garage.

Inside the lobby the decor is reminiscent of Europe's intimate hotels with rich wood paneling, crown molding, etched glass and brass period furniture. In addition to the lobby, hotel guests are invited to spend leisure time in the Clubroom—a private retreat for your morning coffee service and a tranquil relaxing spot for day or evening. Magazines, books, newspapers, plus a big screen TV are available here for guests' use.

The 74 one-bedroom suites all have refrigerator/dry bars (stocked), cherrywood writing table and side chairs, armchairs and loveseat with coffee table and console TV in the Parlor. All bathrooms have a two-line telephone and most have separate marble vanity areas. Extra pillows, fresh flowers and queen-size beds add to the comfort of the guest suites.

The Bar & Grill offers a full breakfast, luncheon and dinner with entrees grilled over mesquite wood. The bar features a wide choice of premium varietal wines by the glass, Texas-size frozen margueritas and superb espresso and capuccino. Fresh catch of the day, mesquite grilled with sauce is the most celebrated entree. The Bar & Grill is also a good spot to enjoy late-evening suppers and snacks.

Address: 1933 Main Street, Dallas, TX 75201
Phone: 214-741-7700
Toll-Free: 800-231-4235
Fax: 214-939-3639
E-mail: aristocrat@internetmci.com
Room Rates: $$
Suite Rates: $$$
Credit Cards: Most credit cards accepted
No. of Rooms: 172 **Suites:** 74
Services and Amenities: Valet service, Garage & parking, Car hire, Complimentary transportation upon availability, Cable TV, Complimentary newspaper
Restrictions: Small, trained dog or cat OK with deposit, Children up to 18 free with parent, 3 handicapped rooms
Concierge: 7:00 a.m.–9:00 p.m.
Room Service: 6:30 a.m.–10:30 p.m.
Restaurant: The Aristocrat Bar & Grill, 6:30 a.m.–10:30 p.m.
Business Facilities: Message center, Secretarial services, Copiers, Audio-Visual
Conference Rooms: 5 rooms
Sports Facilities: Privileges at Exchange Club and Texas Club
Location: Downtown Dallas, Nearest airports are Love Field and Dallas/Fort Worth
Attractions: Walking distance to Westend entertainment and shopping area, Close to Fair Park & Deep Ellum entertainment & dining districts

MANSION ON TURTLE CREEK

The internationally renowned Mansion on Turtle Creek was the first of the wonderful Rosewood Hotels & Resorts. The historic Mediterranean-style mansion, secluded within 4.6 acres of landscaped grounds, is only 5 minutes from Dallas' central business district.

The entrance foyer—a 32-foot-high rotunda with arched windows—sets the tone for the opulent interiors designed by James Northcutt/Hirsch Bedner and Associates.

All guest rooms are large, luxuriously comfortable and well-appointed. The furnishings are traditional and the art is original. French doors open onto individual balconies or private patios. Though all 14 suites vie for superiority, the 1200-square-foot Terrace Suite is truly incomparable.

The restaurant and bar occupy the original Sheppard King Mansion. In the main restaurant, a fireplace at each end and museum quality art on the walls create a grand ambiance. Our recent dinner there began with Louisiana crab cakes in a sauce of oysters and smoked peppers; then beefsteak tomatoes with Dallas mozzarella and avocado in a basil vinaigrette; roast Iowa lamb with artichoke tarragon sauce and wild mushrooms; and for dessert, white chocolate mousse in a tulip shell with raspberry sauce.

The Promenade restaurant serves breakfast and lunch. In the bar, the environment is like that of a most exclusive club; dark wood floor, low-beamed ceiling, forest green fabric walls and 18th-century hunting paintings and lithographs.

Management and staff join in a sincere effort to provide the most enjoyable possible atmosphere for the guests. The hotel offers extensive facilities for business and pleasure while creating a special, memorable warmth.

Address: 2821 Turtle Creek Boulevard, Dallas, TX 75219
Phone: 214-559-2100
Toll-Free: 800-527-5432
Fax: 214-528-4187
Room Rates: $$$$
Suite Rates: $$$$
Credit Cards: Most credit cards accepted
No. of Rooms: 142 **Suites:** 14
Services and Amenities: Valet, Car hire, Complimentary limousine service within 5 mile radius, Garage & parking, Beauty salon, Currency exchange, Baby-sitting, Laundry, House doctor, Cable TV, Radio, Bath phone, Robes, All-natural toiletries, Complimentary shoeshine & newspaper
Restrictions: Small pets (deposit required), Handicapped access to 1 room
Concierge: 24 hours
Room Service: 24 hours
Restaurant: The Mansion on Turtle Creek Restaurant, Dress Code except Sat.-Sun. before 5:00 p.m.
Bar: The Mansion Bar, 11:30 a.m.–1:00 a.m.
Business Facilities: Fax machines, Business & message center, Secretarial service, Copiers
Conference Rooms: 7 rooms, capacity 15–200
Sports Facilities: Heated swimming pool, Fitness studio
Location: 18 miles from Dallas/Ft. Worth Airport
Attractions: Near Highland Park Shopping Center, Art galleries, Boutiques, Central business district

STOCKYARDS HOTEL

Smack-dab in the middle of Fort Worth's Stockyards Historic District, this 1907 hotel has been dramatically restored by architect Ward Bogard. As an immense oak door opens onto the grand lobby, you are greeted by architecture and decor that can only be described as "Cattle Baron Baroque," with large leather Chesterfield sofas and carved wooden chairs bearing the hotel's longhorn steer emblem and upholstered with longhorn hide. The 52 rooms share four different decorative motifs: Indian, Mountain Man, Victorian and Western. Rams' head lamps and 200-year-old wormwood shutters that open to lace curtains remind you that you are deep in the heart of Texas.

The Booger Red restaurant specializes in (surprise!) Texas cuisine, featuring the house specialty, a 20-ounce Porterhouse steak, aged to perfection and cooked to order. If you still have room, don't miss the praline cheesecake. Saddle-topped barstools set the tone in the Booger Red Saloon, where Happy Hour is a Fort Worth tradition.

This hotel offers its guests a glimpse back into the cattle drive days on the Chisholm Trail. And, although many of the hotels in this guide have famous names in their guest registers, this is the only one we know of that can claim, "Bonnie and Clyde slept here": a gun carried by the bank-robbing duo is displayed on the lobby wall.

The hotel has three meeting rooms, the largest of which will accommodate up to 150 persons.

Address: 109 East Exchange Street, Fort Worth, TX 76106
Phone: 817-625-6427
Toll-Free: 800-423-8471
Fax: 817-624-2571
Room Rates: $
Suite Rates: $$
Credit Cards: Most credit cards accepted
No. of Rooms: 52 **Suites:** 4
Services and Amenities: Valet service, Parking, Laundry service, Baby-sitting service, Television, Radio, Telephone, Rose soap, Shampoo, Conditioner
Restrictions: No pets allowed, Handicapped access to one room
Room Service: 7:00 a.m.–10:00 p.m.
Restaurant: H3 Ranch, 7:00 a.m.–10:00 p.m.
Bar: Booger Red
Business Facilities: Secretarial service available upon request Monday-Friday
Conference Rooms: 2 rooms, capacity 15-150
Location: In center of historic stockyards district
Attractions: Walking distance to Billy Bob's Texas, Cattle sales, Western-related shopping

THE LUXURY COLLECTION HOTEL, HOUSTON

The Luxury Collection Hotel, Houston has been honored as one of the finest hotels in America. Nestled in the lovely residential setting of Post Oak Park, The Luxury Collection Hotel is near the prestigious Galleria and River Oaks area. Dramatic floral arrangements abound throughout the elegantly comfortable ambiance, while rich mahogany and glistening marble capture the essence of timeless elegance at every turn.

The guest rooms and suites are large and comfortably furnished in a traditional decor. Floor to ceiling windows offer sweeping views of the Houston skyline, Post Oak Park and the Galleria. The baths gleam with polished marble and travertine, and are accompanied by designer toiletries and terry cloth robes. Each of the uniquely different suites are reminiscent of a fine residence. Oversized living and bedroom areas are decorated with the finest quality furnishings and linens. Each suite shares a feeling of genuine opulence.

Featuring Classic Continental cuisine, the intimate and elegant Dining Room, with its hand stencilled walls and antique French tapestries, and glass enclosed Conservatory, offer a pastorale view of Post Oak Park. The Grill offers regional cuisine specializing in wild game, aged beef and grilled seafood. Considered Houston's most "in" spot, the cozy and club-like Bar offers an atmosphere of sophistication and world class luxury.

A commitment to excellence clearly defines The Luxury Collection Hotel, Houston.

Address: 1919 Briar Oaks Lane, Houston, TX 77027
Phone: 713-840-7600
Toll-Free: 800-241-3333
Fax: 713-840-8036
Room Rates: $$$$
Suite Rates: $$$$
Credit Cards: Visa, MC, AmEx, DC, CB
No. of Rooms: 221 **Suites:** 27
Services and Amenities: Valet service, Garage & parking, Car hire, Gift shop, Laundry service, Baby-sitting service, Cable TV, Phone in bath, Radio, Robes, Whirlpool, Complimentary shoeshine, newspaper and Gucci toiletries
Restrictions: No pets allowed, Handicapped access to 2 rooms
Concierge: 24 hours
Room Service: 24 hours
Restaurant: Garden Room/Conservatory, 6:30–11:00 a.m., 11:30 a.m.–2:00 p.m., 6:00–11:00 p.m., Dress code
Bar: Bar & Grill, 11:00 a.m.–2:00 a.m.
Business Facilities: Complete business center, Message center, Secretarial service, Translator, Teleconferencing
Conference Rooms: 6 rooms, capacity 300
Sports Facilities: Jogging track across street, Heated lap swimming pool
Location: Nearest airport: Hobby (Hou), Intercontinental (IAH)
Attractions: Galleria shopping within 2 miles, Theatre district within 5 miles, Limousine transportation available

STEIN ERIKSEN LODGE

Nestled amidst aspens and pines high in the Rocky Mountains mid-mountain at Deer Valley Resort, this four-star, four-diamond European-style lodge exudes rustic Norwegian elegance. Ski directly to Deer Valley's meticulously groomed slopes right from the doorstep. A skier's paradise, the Lodge is truly world class, and no wonder—it is the pride and joy of 1952 Olympic Gold Medalist Stein Eriksen. Old World charm pervades the Lodge from the lobby with its beamed cathedral ceiling, giant stone fireplace and grand piano, to each cozy guest room. Spectacular mountain scenery is seen from every window and balcony.

Guest rooms are extremely comfortable in the best Scandinavian tradition, featuring furnishings crafted from heavy brushed pine imported from Spain and European-imported fabrics. The baths have separate dressing and bathing areas, over-sized towels, whirlpool tub, gold-plated fixtures, telephone, plush terrycloth robes, complimentary toiletries and more. Suites are equipped with full kitchen, dining area, fireplace and master bedroom with fireplace.

After an exhilarating day on the slopes, enjoy the Lodge's spa facilities, which include an outdoor heated swimming pool, sauna, hot tub, fitness room and massage therapy.

When the snow melts, guests can golf at any of three nearby championship golf courses. The surrounding mountains are ideal for hiking or mountain biking; horseback riding, water sports, tennis, fishing, and hot air ballooning adventures can be arranged through the concierge.

Recipient of the *Wine Spectator* Award of Excellence consistently since 1991, the Lodge features an extensive wine list to complement the excellent fare prepared by award-winning chefs. Selected as Utah's Most Romantic Restaurant and Best Sunday Brunch, the Glitretind serves contemporary style cuisine with a European flair. The Birkebeiner Grill Room, open in winter season only, features American styled cuisine in a relaxed Bistro atmosphere.

Address: P.O. Box 3177, Park City, UT 84060
Phone: 435-649-3700
Toll-Free: 800-453-1302
Fax: 435-649-5825
E-mail: info@steinlodge.com
Web site: http://www.steinlodge.com
Room Rates: $$$
Suite Rates: $$$$
Credit Cards: Most credit cards accepted
No. of Rooms: 81 **Suites:** 49
Services and Amenities: Underground heated garage, Car rental, Valet service, Shuttle, Gift shop, Ski lockers, Baby-sitting service, Laundry service, Robes, Cable TV, Radio, Phone, Whirlpool bath, Complimentary newspaper
Restrictions: No pets, Handicapped access to most rooms, Children under 12 free with parents
Concierge: yes
Room Service: yes
Restaurant: Glitretind Restaurant, Birkebeiner Grill Room (winter only)
Bar: Troll Hallen Lounge
Business Facilities: Audio-Visual, Teleconferencing, Copiers, Secretarial service arranged on request
Conference Rooms: 5 rooms, capacity 140
Sports Facilities: Skiing, Golf, Tennis, Fishing, Health spa, Massage, Outdoor heated pool, Horseback riding
Location: Mid-mountain at Deer Valley Resort, 40 minutes from Salt Lake City Airport
Attractions: Skiing, Bear Hollow Sports Park, Hot air ballooning, Tennis, 3 championship golf courses, Mountain biking, Water sports, Art galleries, Scenic ride on steam locomotive, Alpine slide, Summer Arts Festival

GREEN VALLEY SPA & TENNIS RESORT

Located on the outskirts of St. George, the Green Valley Spa & Tennis Resort is an oasis waiting to be discovered by the discerning traveller who wants to relax mind, body, and soul. The Spa is situated on twenty-seven lush acres with extensive foliage and recreational facilities. All guest rooms are spacious suites decorated in southwestern or contemporary style. Suites include bedroom in warm color schemes, living room, full kitchen, and entertainment center with cable TV and VCP. Comfortable robes are provided in all bathrooms.

The Spa's extensive Relaxation Center and sports facilities are available to guests to escape from the anxieties and concerns of everyday life. The Spa is located on the bottom of an ancient inland sea which is presently transformed into a basin forming a great salty lake, world famous for its rich mineral assets. Each day the Center is replenished with fresh flowers, aromatics, music, and subtly flavored and scented water to tantalize the senses. For an additional price, guests may choose from a large array of services including: water treatments, massages, alternative therapies, facials, body works, consultant sessions, salon services, meditation training, and various other treatment programs. Those interested in outdoor activities may partake in guided hikes, rock climbing, tennis, aerobics classes, and yoga. Other activities nearby include mountain biking, five beautiful public golf courses, and horseback riding in Snow Canyon.

The Spa Dining Room is open exclusively to guests and offers a varied menu of delicious, healthy food. Fresh scrambled eggs, apple spice muffins and fruit are a typical breakfast to start the day off on the right foot. Every meal is served on a separate china service while tables are elegantly adorned with flowers and desert plants.

Address: 1871 West Canyon View Drive, St. George, UT 84770
Phone: 435-628-8060
Toll-Free: 800-237-1068
Fax: 435-673-4084
E-mail: mdavie@infowest.com
Web site: http://www.greenvalleyspa.com
Suite Rates: $$$
Credit Cards: Visa, AmEx, Discover
No. of Suites: 65
Services and Amenities: Barber/beauty shop, Garage & parking, Laundry, Gift shop, Baby-sitting service, Card/Game area, Kitchen facilities, Fireplaces, Balconies, Cable TV, VCR, Radio, Telephones, Individual heat & air-conditioning control, Complimentary newspaper & toiletries
Restrictions: 15 rooms equipped for handicapped, No pets, Children welcome
Concierge: 6:00 a.m.–9:00 p.m.
Restaurant: Spa Dining Room, 7:00 a.m.–7:00 p.m.
Business Facilities: Message center, Copiers, Fax
Conference Rooms: 1 room, capacity 50
Sports Facilities: Indoor/outdoor swimming pool, Handball/squash, Extensive Spa facilities, Massage, Aerobics, Weight training, 50 miles to skiing
Location: Five miles from airport and downtown area
Attractions: Forty-five miles to Zion National Park, 100 miles from Las Vegas, Nevada; Close to five major Golf Courses

THE CHARLES ORVIS INN AT THE EQUINOX

This elegant 19th century residence on historic Main Street has been completely restored. Located in Manchester Village, it was once home to Charles Orvis, the fly fishing entrepreneur and founder of the Orvis Company, and has been operating as an inn since 1883. Victorian in design with Tudor style windows, the Inn has nine one- and two-bedroom luxurious suites. Nestled in the village, it is surrounded by the Green Mountains and Battenkill River. The Inn offers special package rates including golf, skiing, spa, honeymoon, and anniversary stays.

Offering the highest level of service, this exclusive country retreat is ideal for both business and leisure travelers. The lobby sets an elegant tone with its coffered ceilings, oak floorings, and richly textured fabrics. The Tying and Billiard Rooms are beautifully appointed in the timeless club ambiance. The stately Board Room, with recessed audio/visual equipment, accommodates fifteen people. An experienced staff oversees the banquet facilities.

Complimentary breakfast is presented to guests daily, and afternoon tea is also served. Fine dining is available at the distinguished Colonnade Room at The Equinox, the Charles Orvis Inn's sister hotel next door.

The Equinox also shares with the Charles Orvis Inn its newly redesigned 18-hole Rees Jones golf course facilities, a fitness spa featuring an indoor pool, steam room, sauna, cardio-vascular equipment, Nautilus, pro shop, mountain bikes and 3 tennis courts. Adjacent to the fitness spa is a large outdoor pool.

The newest feature of The Equinox is the opening of The Land Rover Driving School, the first permanent manufacturer-supported 4x4 driving school of the US and the British School of Falconry.

Address: Main Street, P.O. Box 46, Manchester, VT 05254
Phone: 802-362-4700
Toll-Free: 800-362-4747
Fax: 802-362-4861
E-mail: postmaster@equinoxresort.com
Web site: http://www.equinoxresort.com
Room Rates: $$$$
Suite Rates: $$$$
Credit Cards: Most credit cards accepted
No. of Rooms: 14 **Suites:** 9
Services and Amenities: Parking, Airport transfers, Valet laundry service, TV lounge, International currency exchange, Card/game area, Library, Complimentary shoeshine and newspaper, Cable TV and VCR, 2 in-room telephones, Wet bar, Individual air-conditioning, Robes, Jacuzzi tub
Restrictions: No pets allowed
Concierge: 8:00 a.m.–9:00 p.m.
Room Service: 7:00 a.m.–10:00 p.m.
Restaurant: Colonnade Room at The Equinox, 6:00 p.m.–10:00 p.m.
Bar: Marsh Tavern, noon—closing
Business Facilities: Message center, Copier, Audio-Visual, Teleconferencing, Fax
Conference Rooms: 1 room, capacity 15
Sports Facilities: Indoor/outdoor pools, Croquet, Sauna, Massage, Aerobics, Weight training, Tennis, Golf nearby, Cross-country skiing, Canoes
Location: 1 mile from town center, 61 miles to Albany County Airport in NY
Attractions: Dorset Playhouse, Southern Vermont Art Center, Norman Rockwell Museum, Hildene (Robert Todd Lincoln's home), 120 outlet stores, 10 miles to ski lift, Snowmobile tours, Ice skating, Snowshoeing, Volleyball, Horseback riding

THE EQUINOX

Nestled in the heart of the spectacular Green Mountains of Vermont, The Equinox is located in the center of Manchester Village. Originally opened in 1769, and with 7 different past names, it is a noted national landmark with 224 years of intriguing history, 6 different architectural styles, and 17 separate buildings.

Having recently undergone a $14 million renovation, The Equinox offers old world hospitality in a style and setting that can be described as "Country Grand." New England style guest rooms are air-conditioned with private bath, color TV with cable and remote control. Presidential suites, which are named after presidents who visited The Equinox, are furnished with king-size poster beds and antiques.

The Colonnade, with its magnificently restored vaulted ceiling and expansive bay window, features contemporary American and European cuisine in the classic tradition. The Marsh Tavern welcomes guests with fine spirits and regional cuisine in a casual ambiance. The Dormy Grill on the deck of the Gleneagles Golf Clubhouse serves daily lunch and a fabulous weekend Lobsterfest dinner during summer and fall. The Artist's Palate Cafe at the Southern Vermont Art Center serves lunch mid-May through mid-October.

Facilities include a new redesigned 18-hole Rees Jones golf course, fitness spa with an outdoor pool, steam room, sauna, cardiovascular equipment, Nautilus, pro shop, mountain bikes and 3 tennis courts. Adjacent to the fitness spa is a large outdoor pool. The Land Rover Driving School at The Equinox is the first permanent, manufacturer supported 4x4 driving school in the U.S.

The new British School of Falconry at the Equinox is the first falconry school of its kind in America. Each program is hands-on lessons teaching the student to handle and fly native birds of prey. There are introductory lessons, hawk walks, hawking days, and half or full-day Country Pursuits programs which include falconry, fly fishing and clay pigeon shooting.

The resort also features miles of hiking, biking and cross country skiing trails and private fishing on a 12-acre pond. Local shopping includes over 130 designer outlets and a myriad of antique stores.

Address: P.O.Box 46, Route 7A, Manchester Village, VT 05254
Phone: 802-362-4700
Toll-Free: 800-362-4747
Fax: 802-362-4861
E-mail: postmaster@equinoxresort.com
Web site: http://www.equinoxresort.com
Room Rates: $$$$
Suite Rates: $$$$
Credit Cards: Most credit cards accepted
No. of Rooms: 144 **Suites:** 20
Services and Amenities: Gift shop, Valet service, Parking, Baby-sitting service, Telephone, Television, Complimentary shoeshine
Restrictions: No pets allowed
Concierge: 24 hours
Room Service: 7:00 a.m.–10:00 p.m.
Restaurant: The Colonnade, Sunday Brunch 11:30 a.m.–2:30 p.m., Fri. & Sat. Winter, 6:00–9:00 p.m., Wed.-Sun. Summer, 6:00–9:30 p.m., Marsh Tavern, 7:00 a.m.–9:30 p.m.
Bar: Marsh Tavern, noon-12:30 a.m.
Business Facilities: Message center, Secretarial service, Copier, Audio-Visual, Telex
Conference Rooms: 6 rooms, capacity 5-300
Sports Facilities: 3, Har-tru, 2 clay tennis courts, Golf course, Ice skating, Snow shoeing, Riding, Fly fishing, Canoeing, Paddle tennis, Spa
Location: Country, 1 mile from Manchester Center, 30 miles from Rutland Airport
Attractions: Equinox Ski Touring Center with rentals, Orvis fishing and shooting schools, Hildene, Lincoln Family Estate, Southern Vermont Art Center, Museums, Stratton & Bromley Mountains for downhill skiing & snow shoeing, Dorset Theatre

THE MIDDLEBURY INN

The prototype New England County Inn has long been the benchmark of fine innkeeping in the United States, and The Middlebury Inn continues that fine tradition. Middlebury is a Shire Town (county seat) in the middle of dairy country, and the site of Middlebury College. It is a historic, picturesque New England town which even has a bandstand on the village green.

Middlebury Inn overlooks the village green within the Green Mountains of Robert Frost country. A community landmark since 1827, the Inn is an imposing 3-story Georgian-style hostelry and has grown to encompass several adjoining buildings. Guests can choose between the antique motif or a contemporary room.

The dining choices vary with each season. Plentiful New England fare is served in the Founders Room and Stewart Library. Elegant candlelight buffets are frequent delights not to be missed. Also offered is a varied menu of fowl specials, nightly treats, with a sherbert course to cleanse your palate, and a finger bowl to help tidy up. During warmer weather, the wide sweeping porch is a natural setting for lunch or dinner while overseeing "goings on" on the green. A lighter fare menu is available in the Morgan Tavern. The tavern also provides the best in liquid refreshment, from the simplest drink to seasonal specials. The Country Peddler, a favorite with guests, is a unique combination of cafe, gifts, and New England crafts.

The Inn's staff is dedicated to gracious hospitality, which begins with the warm welcome. The Inn offers many different packages to choose from, whether it's skiing or just relaxing in front of the lobby fireplace reading a book. While enjoying central Vermont, stay at the Inn that has become a home away from home for many people, The Middlebury Inn.

Address: 14 Courthouse Square, Middlebury, VT 05753
Phone: 802-388-4961
Toll-Free: 800-842-4666
Fax: 802-388-4563
E-mail: midinnvt.@sover.net
Web site: http://www.MiddleburyInn.com
Room Rates: $
Credit Cards: Visa, Mc, AmEx, DS, DC
No. of Rooms: 75
Services and Amenities: Gift shop, Library, Card/game area, Checks accepted, Baby-sitting service, Cable TV, 2 telephones in each room, Clock radios, Complimentary toiletries, Packages available
Restrictions: Pets allowed (fee), 2 rooms equipped for handicapped, No minimum stay
Restaurant: Founders Room, 7:30 a.m.–9:30 p.m.
Bar: Morgan Tavern, 5:30 p.m.–10:00 p.m.
Business Facilities: Message center, Fax, Copier, Audio-Visual
Conference Rooms: 1 room, capacity 50
Sports Facilities: Nearby: Swimming, Hiking, Downhill and cross-country skiing, Health and fitness center, Tennis
Location: Historic college downtown, 35 miles to Burlington Airport
Attractions: The village green, Walking distance to boutique shops, Museums, Cinema, Magnificent waterfall, Festival-on-the-Green in July

THE WHITE HOUSE OF WILMINGTON

This Victorian mansion offers guests an elegant yet relaxed surrounding. Set on the crest of a high, rolling hill, and surrounded by towering hardwoods and formal gardens, it is readily obvious why the Boston Herald and New York Times selected this inn as "one of the ten most romantic places in the world." The magnificent structure, with fifteen fireplaces, crafted French doors and two-storied terraces supported by soaring pillars, is as timeless and lovely as the surrounding Green Mountains.

The inn's twenty-three guest rooms, each with private bath, are beautifully furnished with period pieces complimentary to a New England country inn. Beds are topped with oversized featherbeds for guest's comfort. All bathrooms have their original fixtures including deep tubs, many have whirlpools. Guesthouse accommodations are available for guests with younger children or simply for those who prefer additional space.

Guests have a plethora of activities to choose from ranging form skiing to lounging in the inn's extensive spa. With over thirty-eight kilometers of thoughtfully groomed trails on the premises, novice to expert skiiers have a wide range of scenic trails to explore. The inn also provides croquet facilities and two swimming pools. Other nearby activities include golf, tennis, boating, hiking, mountainbiking, antiquing, and outlet shopping.

The three intimate dining rooms continue the pronounced Victorian theme of the inn while providing guests with award-wining gourmet dining. Classical Continental dishes like baked brie and succulent duck are prepared by chef Fred Zinn. A sumptuous Brunch Buffet is served every Sunday from 11:00 a.m. to 2:30 p.m.

Address: 178 Route 9 East, Wilmington, Vermont 05363
Phone: 802-464-2135
Toll-Free: 800-541-2135
Fax: 802-464-5222
E-mail: whitehse@sover.net
Room Rates: $$
Suite Rates: $$$
Credit Cards: Most credit cards accepted
No. of Rooms: 24 **Suites:** 1
Services and Amenities: TV lounge, Card and Game area
Restrictions: Handicapped access, Children over 8 yrs. welcome at Inn & all ages in Guesthouse, No pets
Restaurant: In-house restaurant, 5:30 p.m.–9:00 p.m.
Bar: 5:30 p.m. -9:00 p.m.
Business Facilities: Copiers, Fax, Modems
Conference Rooms: 1 room, capacity 100
Sports Facilities: Indoor/Outdoor pool, Whirlpool, Sauna, Massage, Croquet, Golf, Tennis, Mountain Biking, Skiing, Hiking, Boating.
Location: North on 91, West on Route 9, 21 miles
Attractions: Nearby outlet and craft shopping, Antiquing, Formal garden, Mountain views, 10+ acre estate

BLUE BEARDS BEACH CLUB & VILLAS

The most popular, and most populated, of the Virgin Islands boasts the most beautiful beaches and some of the best sailing and fishing in the Caribbean. St. Thomas, called the "melting pot," is a blend of foreign influences, duty-free shops loaded with tourists searching out Gucci bags and French perfumes, and very friendly locals who will captivate you with their lilting West Indian-accented advice. The island isn't large: only 13 miles long and three miles wide, an easy day's trip around to see the countryside. Blue Beard's Beach Club & Villas is one of the better beaches on the south shore, and the hotel's main house, perched above the sugary-white stretch of sand, affords a magical view.

Rooms are oversized, some with sleeping lofts and all with air-conditioning, cable television and VCRs. Breakfast is included in the room rate. The Rogues Galley Restaurant offers a West Indian menu. You'll be in for a real treat if you sample the fungi (deep fried cornmeal dumplings) or the callaloo, a thick soup with greens and crab, spiced with pepper and okra. And who can resist the Cruzan rum? At night, you can hear calypso and steel band sounds while the dance floor is alive with swaying bodies.

Sunfish, Hobie Cats, and all sorts of boats are available, as well as charters and the day sails. You can even book a schooner. Other activities include scuba diving, tennis, and outstanding sport fishing. The best blue marlin months are between June and August, while wahoo, bonita, and allison tuna are caught year-round.

Address: P.O. Box 7480, St. Thomas, VI 00801
Phone: 809-776-4770
Fax: 809-693-2648
Room Rates: $$$
Credit Cards: Most credit cards accepted
No. of Rooms: 84
Services and Amenities: Valet service, Garage and parking, House doctor, Baby-sitting service, Cable TV, Radio, Individual air-conditioning, Complimentary newspaper, Non-smoking rooms
Restrictions: No pets allowed, No handicapped access
Restaurant: Rogues Galley, 7:30 a.m.–10:30 p.m., Formal attire
Bar: Restaurant Bar
Business Facilities: Copiers, Audio-Visual, Telex, Full-scale conference center
Conference Rooms: 1 room, capacity 150
Sports Facilities: Outdoor swimming pool, Tennis court, Sailing, Volleyball
Location: On the beach, Frenchman's Bay
Attractions: Government House built in 1867, Virgin Islands Museum in historic fort, Coral World, Ferry ride to Caneel Bay for buffet, Day trip to Tortola or St. Croix, Golf at Mahogany Run, Scuba diving excursions to shipwrecks

CLIFTON - THE COUNTRY INN

In an elegant federal style and colonial revival mansion just outside Charlottesville is a classic American Inn. Originally built in 1799 by Thomas Mann Randolph, Virginia Governor and son-in-law of Thomas Jefferson, and later expanded, Clifton is a haven of 14 rooms, each unique, with locally milled pine floors, exquisite antiques, romantic canopy beds and federal-style fireplaces (with firewood, of course).

An early morning Clifton plantation breakfast and afternoon tea can be taken on the terrace. In a paneled dining room, chef Craig Hartman—graduate of the Culinary Institute of America—serves sumptuous dinners ("beautifully prepared" wrote The New York Times, "with very fresh, local ingredients"), such as the provencal encrusted tenderloin of Virginia Angus Beef, stuffed with an exotic mushroom duxelle matched by Clifton's award-wining international wine cellar.

Clifton boasts a heated spa, spectacular pool with waterfall and 40 acres of manicured gardens and woods. Nearby Monticello, the University of Virginia and historic Charlottesville, The Inn is ideally located for guest's convenience. The Inn is available for catered receptions, weddings and small conferences by arrangement. "There are tens of thousands of hotels in the world" wrote International Living, "but just a few are themselves reasons to make the trip. Among these, Clifton ranks in the top three or four."

ddress: 1296 Clifton Inn Drive, Charlottesville, VA 22911
Phone: 804-971-1800
Toll-Free: 888-971-1800
Fax: 804-971-7098
E-mail: reserve@cstone.net
Web site: http://www.cliftoninn.com
Room Rates: $$$
Suite Rates: $$$$
Credit Cards: MC, Visa
No. of Rooms: 14 **Suites:** 7
Services and Amenities: Baby-sitting (with advanced arrangement), Card/game area, Library, Fireplaces, Radio, TV & Telephone available on request, Air-conditioning, Luxurious private bath, Robes, Complimentary toiletries & newspaper, Complimentary breakfast & afternoon tea
Restrictions: No pets allowed, 1 room with handicapped access
Restaurant: Clifton—The Country Inn, dining nightly
Bar: Open during dinner hours
Business Facilities: Audio-Visual facilities
Conference Rooms: 1 room, capacity 24
Sports Facilities: Swimming pool, Year-round heated spa, Whirlpool, Private lake for swimming and fishing, Clay tennis court, Croquet, Volleyball
Location: Shadwell
Attractions: Monticello (home of Thomas Jefferson), University of Virginia, Skyline Drive, Blue Ridge Parkway, 5 vineyards within 20 miles

TRILLIUM HOUSE AT WINTERGREEN

Named after the three-petaled wildflowers that grow profusely nearby, Trillium House is an English-style country inn in the heart of the 11,000 acre Wintergreen Mountain Resort. The striking stained cedar hostelry with 12 guest rooms was built in 1983 to the specifications of innkeepers Ed and Betty Dinwiddie.

Entering guests find themselves in the "great room," with its towering 22-foot ceiling, massive chimney and sun-catching Jefferson "sunburst" window. Persian rugs, stylish but comfortable furniture, and a large stone fireplace make this an inviting gathering place. There is a small bar off the great room, a TV room and a 2500-volume library.

All guest rooms and suites have private baths and individually controlled heat and cooling. Rooms are individually furnished in both layout and decor, with many furnishings, paintings and accessories from the Dinwiddies' own collection. Guests receive a full breakfast and afternoon coffee, tea, fruit and cheese. A prix fixe dinner is available in the dining room by advance reservation only.

Available to guests at preferred rates are two golf courses, four swimming pools, thirty tennis courts, 25 miles of mapped hiking trails, and downhill skiing in season. The entry gate to the Wintergreen Mountain Village is one mile from the Blue Ridge Parkway. Trillium also within driving distance of Jefferson's Monticello, Charlottesville, and many small country stores and wineries.

Address: 3421 Wintergreen Drive, P.O. Box 280, Nellysford, VA 22958
Phone: 804-325-9126
Toll-Free: 800-325-9126
Fax: 804-325-1099
Web site: http://www.trilliumhouse.com
Room Rates: $$
Suite Rates: $$
Credit Cards: MC, Visa
No. of Rooms: 12 **Suites:** 2
Services and Amenities: Television Lounge, Game area, Library, Cable TV, VCR, Telephone, Radio, Complimentary newspaper and toiletries, Complimentary afternoon coffee, tea, fruit and cheese, Complimentary breakfast
Restrictions: No pets allowed
Concierge: 8:00 a.m.–10:00 p.m.
Restaurant: Dining room, 8:00–9:00 a.m., 7:30 p.m. Friday-Saturday
Bar: Open by request
Business Facilities: Copier, Fax, Modem
Conference Rooms: 2 rooms, capacity 25 & 40
Sports Facilities: Indoor & outdoor pools, Sauna, Massage, Riding, Tennis, Golf at Wintergreen Resort, Skiing, Canoeing, 25 miles of trails nearby
Location: Wintergreen 4-season resort community, 1 hour from Charlottesville
Attractions: 1 hour to homes of Jefferson, Wilson, Monroe

THE BERKELEY HOTEL

First opened in 1988, The Berkeley Hotel's charm convinces many first-time guests that it's been around for ages. From the soft wood tones of the lobby, to the 30-foot vaulted ceilings of the Governor's Suite, the hotel embodies the gracious hospitality of a traditional Virginia hostelry.

Spacious guest rooms are decorated in deep hues of green and berry, with lovely botanical watercolors adorning the walls. Amenities include Krup coffee-maker, shower massage, complimentary valet parking and exercise facilities. The one-bedroom suite features two full baths, one with a jacuzzi, a luxurious king bed, large private terrace, and an elegant peaked ceiling living room with a panoramic view of Historic Shockoe Slip.

The Dining Room is decorated with watercolors, candlelit tables, and imported English china. The Chef's special homemade ice cream is among the many popular dishes he prepares. His medallions of Summerfield Farm Veal accompanied by corn and barley cakes and a twenty-four hour cooked tomato relish is high on the list of the "most favorites." After dinner relax in Nightingales Lounge and savor one of their specialty coffee drinks.

The hotel offers several inspired weekend packages, including "Romance," with champagne & chocolate truffles in your room, "A Civil War Experience" with 2 tickets to the Historic Richmond Tour, and "Berkeley Plantation," with tickets to tour Virginia's most historic planation. Not to be missed is a stroll down the cobblestone streets of Shockoe Slip, where renovated warehouses have been transformed into specialty boutiques and eateries.

Guests looking for the personalized attention of an elegant European hotel will be delighted to find The Berkeley Hotel waiting to greet them in the Capital of the Confederacy.

Address: 1200 East Cary Street, Richmond, VA 23219
Phone: 804-780-1300
Toll-Free: 888-780-4422
Fax: 804-343-1885
Room Rates: $$
Suite Rates: $$$$
Credit Cards: Visa, MC, AmEx, DC
No. of Rooms: 55 **Suites:** 1
Services and Amenities: Garage & parking, Laundry service, Babysitting service, Balconies, Cable TV, Radio, Individual heat & air-conditioning control, Robes, Complimentary newspaper
Restrictions: No pets allowed, Children free with parents
Concierge: 24 hours
Room Service: 7:00 a.m.–10:00 p.m.
Restaurant: The Dining Room at The Berkeley Hotel, 7:00 a.m.–10:00 p.m., Jacket requested for men
Bar: Nightingales, 5:30 p.m.–11:00 p.m.
Business Facilities: Copiers, Audio-Visual, Teleconferencing, Translators
Conference Rooms: 3 rooms, capacity 150
Sports Facilities: Handball/squash, Whirlpool, Sauna, Massage, Aerobics, Weight training
Location: Historic Shockoe Slip, Nearest airport is Richmond International
Attractions: Boutique shopping, Nearby Cary Town, Historic Berkeley Plantation

Washington Duke Inn & Golf Club, Durham, North Carolina. PAGE 167

Mayflower Park Hotel, Seattle, Washington. PAGE 211

The Country Inn at Walden, Aurora, Ohio. PAGE 169

THE INN AT GRISTMILL SQUARE

This colorful Virginia historic landmark conveys the romance and tradition of the Allegheny Mountains. Not just one but a whole complex of restored buildings around a small square, The Inn at Gristmill Square is a 19th-century country village with the modern convenience of private baths with bathrobes, hair dryers and toiletries, cable TV, and such special touches as fresh flowers, classic linens and a welcoming fruit and cheese platter.

Guestrooms are located throughout four of the five original turn-of-the-century buildings, previously a mill, blacksmith shop, hardware store and two private residences. The 17 rooms and suites are individually furnished in traditional decor with the feel of a country home. Many rooms have their own fireplace. A complimentary continental breakfast featuring fresh fruit and specialty breads still warm from the oven is served to each room.

Guests may enjoy fresh local trout at The Waterwheel restaurant, located in the restored gristmill. The ambiance here is rustic country, with fine prints and fresh wildflowers in season. Before dinner, patrons choose their own bottle from the wine cellar next to the mill stream.

For summer recreation, guests can utilize the outdoor pool, sauna and 3 tennis courts. The mineral-rich Warm Springs thermal pools are a mile away. Fishing, hiking and horseback riding are available at nearby George Washington National Forest. Also available are championship golf courses and an annual chamber music festival.

Address: P. O. Box 359, Warm Springs, VA 24484
Phone: 540-839-2231
Fax: 540-839-5770
E-mail: grist@va.tds.net
Room Rates: $
Suite Rates: $
Credit Cards: Visa, MC, Discover
No. of Rooms: 17 **Suites:** 5
Services and Amenities: Gift shop, Baby-sitting service, Cable TV, Telephones, Robes, Complimentary newspaper and toiletries, Complimentary breakfast
Restrictions: No pets allowed, Children welcome
Room Service: 7:00 a.m.–11:00 p.m.
Restaurant: The Waterwheel, 6:00 p.m.–10:00 p.m.
Bar: Simon Kenton Pub, 6:00 p.m.–10:00 p.m.
Business Facilities: Fax
Conference Rooms: 1 room, capacity 40
Sports Facilities: Outdoor swimming pool, Sauna, Tennis, Nearby golf, Skiing, Riding, Privileges at Homestead Resort
Location: Mountain-spa country
Attractions: Warm Springs thermal pools, 200 miles of hiking trails, Fly fishing, Driving tours of the Allegheny Mountains

L'AUBERGE PROVENCALE

Nestled in the Shenandoah Valley near the Blue Ridge Mountains, this stone farmhouse (built in 1753) is situated on eight acres and surrounded by six hundred acres of cattle, corn and soybean farms. Inside, the inn resembles a farmhouse from the South of France, with floral print fabrics, wine racks, antique sideboards and large fireplaces.

The staff is pleased to report that the *Washington Post* has name L'Auberge Provencale "One of the 20 most Romantic Places to stay in North America."

Each of the three guest rooms in the main house has a sitting area and fireplace. The most recent addition is the new suite Romantique which includes French Pine Antiques, Italian tiles, a whirlpool bath for two and a King Alcove bed. More private are the two newly built guest houses next door (one with four rooms, another with three), which feature either antique armoires and bureaus, Normandy floral wallpapers, white iron-and-brass beds or carved cypress oak headboards.

The main house has three dining rooms—one octagonal in shape with seven French doors, one decorated in Wedgewood blues—all with antiques, fine art, Provencale fabrics and an eclectic menagerie of hand-crafted animals. Using herbs and vegetables from his own garden and the freshest ingredients, many from local farmers, Chef Alain creates his special "cuisine moderne Provencale." Specialties include Smoked Rabbit Sausage with Wild Mushrooms, Pistachio Crust Venison Tournedos with Huckleberry Cabernet Sauce, Buffalo Carpaccio and Smoked Shrimp Salad. For dessert you may choose French Sweet Cream with Raspberries or Pecan-Apple Napoleon with Warm Banana Compote. Morning brings a breakfast that might include mixed fruit compote with champagne, fresh baked croissants and coffee cake, poached eggs or crepes, cottage fries and smoked trout.

Outside the inn, wander around the antique shops in the small towns of Berryville and Millwood, try wine tasting at several area vineyards, or enjoy the lush Fall scenery on nearby Skyline Drive.

Address: P.O. Box 190, White Post, VA 22663
Phone: 540-837-1375
Toll-Free: 800-638-1702
Fax: 540-837-2004
E-mail: cborel@shentel.net
Web site: http:// www.laubergeprovencale.com
Room Rates: $$
Suite Rates: $$$
Credit Cards: MC, Visa, AmEx, DC
No. of Rooms: 11 **Suites:** 3
Services and Amenities: Complimentary breakfast, Garage and parking, Laundry service, Baby-sitting service, Gift shop, Card/game area, Fireplaces (5), Balcony (1), Individual climate control, Whirlpool for two, Robes, Complimentary newspaper and toiletries
Restrictions: No pets allowed, Children over 10 only, 1 room equipped for handicappped
Room Service: 8:00 a.m.–9:00 p.m.
Restaurant: L'Auberge Provencale, 8:30–10:00 a.m., 6:00–10:30 p.m. Wednesday-Saturday, 4:00–9:00 p.m. Sunday, Dress code: jackets, dresses
Business Facilities: Copiers, Audio-Visual, Fax, Provide snacks for meetings
Conference Rooms: 1 room, capacity 20
Sports Facilities: In surrounding area: Tennis, Canoeing, Riding, Golf, Ballooning, Swimming, Hiking, Biking
Location: Rural, Nearest airport is Dulles International
Attractions: Antiquing, Wine tasting, Sky-line drive, Many outdoor activities

WILLIAMSBURG INN

The design of the Williamsburg Inn was inspired by founder John D. Rockefeller, Jr.'s desire that the palatial inn be a fit home away from home for its guests, including the many dignitaries, kings, queens and presidents who have stayed here over the years. In the lobby, subtle tones of beige with Regency-style furnishings create an atmosphere of warmth and elegance. Fireplaces flank each end of the lobby, which overlooks the terrace of this Georgian, country estate.

Guestrooms are also decorated in Regency style, with neutral color tones and rich accents. Silks and brocades add to the decor. In keeping with the desire for comfort and elegance, bathrooms are decorated in white marble with eyelet shower curtains and a luxurious array of toiletries.

Crystal chandeliers sparkle in the spacious Regency Dining Room. Tables are graciously set with white linen, custom made china, laurel wreaths, fresh flowers and silver. The most celebrated entree at The Regency is the Rack of Lamb and Salmon. A Chesapeake Seafood Platter may be ordered for a first course. As for the desserts, the Regency Ice Cream Cake is a must. Step into the Regency Lounge for a relaxing after-dinner drink as you are entertained by soothing piano and harp music.

Guests will want to allow ample time to explore the 173-acre capitol of colonial Virginia. It is alive with horsedrawn carriages, guides in colonial costume, and over 100 shops, taverns, homes and public buildings restored to their 18th century functions.

Address: 136 Francis Street, Williamsburg, VA 23185
Phone: 757-229-1000
Toll-Free: 800-447-8679
Fax: 757-221-8797
Room Rates: $$$$
Suite Rates: $$$$
Credit Cards: Most credit cards accepted
No. of Rooms: 135 **Suites:** 16
Services and Amenities: Valet service, Barber & Beauty shop, Gift shop, Laundry, Int'l currency exchange, Baby-sitting service, Library, Fireplaces, Balconies, Cable TV, Telephone, Radio, Individual heat/air-conditioning control, Complimentary shoeshine, newspaper, toiletries
Restrictions: 2 rooms with handicapped access, No pets allowed
Concierge: 8:00 a.m. -6:00 p.m.
Room Service: 7:00 a.m.–11:00 p.m.
Restaurant: Regency Room, 7:00 a.m. -10:00 p.m.
Bar: Lounge, 12:00 p.m.–11:30 p.m.
Business Facilities: Complete business service center, Translators
Conference Rooms: 3 rooms, capacity 40
Sports Facilities: Indoor & outdoor swimming pool, Whirlpool, Sauna, Message, Croquet, Aerobics, Weight training, 45-hole Golf Course, Tennis courts
Location: Historic Colonial Williamsburg
Attractions: Within walking distance to Historic Area, Museums, Shopping, and Sports facilities

HOTEL VINTAGE PARK

The Hotel Vintage Park, a vineyard-themed hotel, is located in the heart of Portland's thriving downtown. The hotel's decor of dark woods, comfortable furnishings, and large fireplace and hearth are complimented by rich fabrics to create an elegant atmosphere for guests to enjoy. While the hotel is a destination within itself, there are numerous other reasons to visit Seattle for business or pleasure. Attractions include fabulous skiing within minutes of downtown, excellent boutique and mall shopping, waterfront ferries, Pike Place Market, the Northwest's finest restaurants, the Space Needle, or simply the renowned coffee.

The 128 rooms are spacious and elegant with city, water and park views. Northwest color schemes create a tranquil, elegant atmosphere which offsets the busting city outside. Most rooms include a spacious sitting room featuring personal computers with the latest internet technology. The Grand Suite, featuring a large living room with computer station, elegant bedroom, large bathroom with whirlpool tub and terry cloth bathrobes, is perfect for honeymooners or small meetings.

Tulio, the hotel's 4-star bar and restaurant, is conveniently open for all meals. It's rich Northern Italian ambiance with Washington vintage wines lining cream walls and excellent cuisine, makes Tulio a truly unique dining experience. Chef Walter Pisano prepares such celebrated entrees as Pollo Arrosto with caramelized garlic and sage served with lemon risotto. Wood roasted asparagus hors d'oeuvres, tiramisu desserts and fine Washington wines will delight any palate. For special occasions, a private dining room is available.

The Hotel Vintage Park is known for its convenient, luxurious accommodations. Guests can expect personal service and attention to detail throughout their stay.

Address: 1100 Fifth Avenue, Seattle, WA 98101

Phone: 206-624-8000

Toll-Free: 800-624-4433

Fax: 206-623-0586

E-mail: hotelvintagepark.com

Web site: http://www.hotelvintagepark.com

Room Rates: $$$

Suite Rates: $$$

Credit Cards: Most credit cards accepted

No. of Rooms: 126 **Suites:** 28

Services and Amenities: Valet, Garage & parking, International currency exchange, Laundry service, Cable TV, Telephones, Radio, Plush terry cloth robes, Irons & boards, 30 rooms with computers at no charge, Individual heat & air-conditioning, Complimentary shoeshine & toiletries

Restrictions: 6 rooms with handicapped access, No pets allowed, Children free with parents

Concierge: 7:00 a.m.–11:00 p.m.

Room Service: 24 hours

Restaurant: Tulio, open for breakfast, lunch, and dinner

Bar: Tulio's Bar, 11:00 a.m.–2:00 p.m.

Business Facilities: E-mail, Copiers, Audio-Visual, Teleconferencing, Fax, Modems, Translators

Conference Rooms: Full-scale facilities available off-site

Sports Facilities: Skiing nearby, City attractions within close distance

Location: Downtown

Attractions: Boutique & mall shopping, 5 blocks from waterfront ferries, 10 blocks from world famous Pike Place Market, Close to Space Needle, Nearby all downtown businesses & attractions

MAYFLOWER PARK HOTEL

Located in the heart of downtown Seattle at Westlake Center, the Mayflower Park Hotel has retained the charm of yesterday with its crystal chandeliers, gleaming brass, and fresh flowers, while providing all the conveniences of today. Its beautiful lobby, accented with an oriental screen and period antique pieces, and its tastefully appointed rooms and suites, provide an elegant yet friendly atmosphere.

The beautifully appointed rooms with classically styled furniture, rich fabrics and individually selected art are air-conditioned and equipped with sound-insulated windows. Many top floor rooms offer views of the city or Puget Sound.

The Hotel's restaurant, Andaluca, features fresh seasonal Northwest foods influenced by the flavors of the Mediterranean. Oliver's is the Mayflower Park's popular and elegant bar serving your favorite cocktail along with their award-winning classic martini and complimentary hors d'oeuvres weeknights.

The Mayflower Park Hotel is ideally suited for conventions and meetings where personalized care and attention to detail are required. Eight attractive meeting rooms are available for groups from 12 to 200. The intimate setting of the Fireside Room is a favorite for weddings and receptions. Complete catering and banquet services are available.

Address: 405 Olive Way, Seattle, WA 98101
Phone: 206-623-8700
Toll-Free: 800-426-5100
Fax: 206-382-6996
E-mail: mayflowerpark@seanet.com
Room Rates: $$$
Suite Rates: $$$$
Credit Cards: Most credit cards accepted
No. of Rooms: 172 **Suites:** 20
Services and Amenities: Romance package available, Garage/parking, Valet, Laundry, Baby-sitting service, In-room heat/air-conditioning control, Cable TV, Radio, Voicemail, Data ports, Sound insulated windows, Some rooms have wet bars & views, Complimentary toiletries & newspaper
Restrictions: No pets allowed, Children 18 and under free in room with parent, 3 rooms equipped for handicapped
Concierge: 7:00 a.m. -5:00 p.m.
Room Service: 24 hours
Restaurant: Monday-Thursday 6:30 a.m.–10:00 p.m., Friday-Saturday 6:30 a.m.–11:00 p.m., Sunday 7:00 a.m.–Noon, 4:00–10:00 p.m.
Bar: Oliver's, 11:30a.m.–1:30a.m., Martini Award Winner
Business Facilities: Voicemail, Copiers, Audio-Visual, Fax, Modems, E-mail
Conference Rooms: 8 rooms, capacity 200, Complete catering/banquet facilities
Sports Facilities: Fitness room on premises
Location: Downtown shopping district, Nearest airport is Seattle-Tacoma
Attractions: Westlake Center; Walk five minutes to Pike Place Market and Seattle's Waterfront; Close to financial district, Convention Center, and Seattle Space Needle; Free bus to historic Pioneer Square and the Kingdome

PIONEER SQUARE HOTEL

This elegant, thoroughly restored turn-of-the-century hotel, conveniently situated on Seattle's Pioneer Square Historic District, takes guests back to a bygone era of style, grace and comfort.

The 75 romantic rooms and suites come in a variety of classic decor updated to the needs and comforts of today's guests. All rooms have individual heating and air-conditioning, direct dial, fax modem, data port telephones, remote control color cable TV, beautifully appointed individual bathrooms with hair dryers and for a good night's sleep, Serta Perfect Sleeper mattresses and soundproof double-pane wood windows. Some rooms have wrought iron New Orleans style balconies and French doors overlooking Yesler Way, while others overlook Puget Sound. Room rates include evening turndown service and a complimentary continental breakfast.

Fitness facilities are available nearby at the Valet Athletic Club. Al Boccalino's, located next door, is rated as the Best Italian restaurant in Seattle. The Pioneer Square Hotel is also the perfect location for wedding parties, receptions, meetings, and family reunions.

The many nearby attractions include Seattle's historic Pioneer Square, the Kingdome stadium, Pike Place Market, the Washington State Ferry system and Aquarium, the Underground Tour, shopping and art galleries, and Seattle's famous restaurants and night life.

Address: 77 Yesler Way, Seattle, WA 98104
Phone: 206-340-1234
Toll-Free: 800-800-5514
Fax: 206-467-9424
E-mail: info@pioneersquare.com
Room Rates: $
Suite Rates: $$
Credit Cards: Visa, MC, AmEx, Diners
No. of Rooms: 75 **Suites:** 3
Services and Amenities: Valet service, Car hire, Laundry service, House doctor, Baby-sitting service, Library, Fireplace, Balconies, Telephones, Radio Cable TV, Complimentary toiletries and breakfast
Restrictions: No pets allowed, 3 rooms handicapped-equipped
Concierge: Front desk
Room Service: Lunch and dinner
Restaurant: Al Boccalino, lunch and dinner
Bar: Pioneer Square Saloon, noon–2:00 a.m.
Business Facilities: Message center, Copiers, Fax, Modems
Conference Rooms: Board room
Sports Facilities: Whirlpool, Sauna, Massage, Aerobics, Weight training, Privileges at The Vault Club
Location: Seattle Waterfront, 12 miles from airport, Walk to Ferry Terminal & Amtrak
Attractions: Walk to Kingdome, Federal and County Courthouses, and Historic Pioneer Square's shopping, Restaurants, Nightlife and Tourist attractions

SORRENTO HOTEL

Seattle's oldest operating luxury hotel welcomes guests with a lighted Italianate fountain and a canopied carriage entrance, framed by palm trees nurtured by underground heating coils. In the lobby, one basks in the fireside glow of lovingly polished Honduras mahogany, amid fresh flowers. The message is clear: Someone at the Sorrento cares deeply about the details of the good life. The heart of the Sorrento is its superbly trained staff, subtly present and prepared to respond to any wish or requirement.

With custom furnishings and original artwork, no two guestrooms are alike. Yet each room pampers guests with goose down pillows, bathrobes, oversized towels and twice-daily maid service. A large desk, private fax machine and two-line phone with voice mail and data port make work easy. Evening turndown brings chocolate and—on chilly nights—a hot water bottle.

Almost half the guest accommodations are suites, the largest at 3,000 square feet boasting a baby grand piano, library and terrace overlooking Puget Sound.

Guests gather for afternoon tea in the Fireside Room. For dinner there is the award-winning Hunt Club, serving seafood with a continental touch in a romantic rose and salmon setting. Room service from the Hunt Club is also available.

Guests may elect to visit the fitness center or hair salon, or take advantage of the complimentary towncar service to vibrant downtown Seattle, to explore the waterfront or the many shops and theaters within a two-mile radius.

Address: 900 Madison Street, Seattle, WA 98104
Phone: 206-622-6400
Toll-Free: 800-426-1265
Fax: 206-343-6155
E-mail: sorrento@earthlink.net
Web site: http://usa.nia.com/sorrento
Room Rates: $$$
Suite Rates: $$$$
Credit Cards: AmEx, MC, Visa, DC
No. of Rooms: 76 **Suites:** 32
Services and Amenities: Valet service, Garage, Car hire, Laundry, Barber/beauty shop, Baby-sitting, Florist, Cable TV, Minibar, Audio cassette player, 2-line phone with voice mail & data port, Fax in room, Individual climate control, Complimentary shoeshine & toiletries
Restrictions: No pets allowed, No handicapped access
Concierge: 24 hours
Room Service: 6:00 a.m.–Midnight
Restaurant: The Hunt Club, breakfast, lunch and dinner
Bar: Hunt Club Lounge & Fireside Lounge, until 2:00 a.m
Business Facilities: Copiers, Translation & Secretarial services, Audio-Visual, Teleconferencing, Fax
Conference Rooms: Sorrento room, capacity 25; Top of the Town, capacity 125
Sports Facilities: Nautilus Fitness Center, Shiatsu massage
Location: Downtown, 15 miles n. of airport, I-5 to Madison
Attractions: Close to Seattle waterfront, Pike Place market, International district, Sports venues, Downtown shopping, One hour from Cascades, 1½ hours from Mt. Rainier

WASHINGTON HOUSE INN

The Washington House Inn was Cedarburg's first inn, built in 1846 on this site. In 1886 the original structure was replaced by the present Victorian cream city brick building. The Washington House existed as a hotel until the 1920's when it was converted into offices and apartments. In 1983 its ownership changed hands and renovation began to restore the Washington House to its original use as an inn. Presently, the building is listed on the National Register of Historic Places.

The romance of country Victorian style is captivating as one enters the Washington House Inn, the ultimate in bed and breakfast accommodations. A lovely collection of antique victorian furniture and marble trimmed fireplace offer a warm reception. Tastefully appointed, the comfortable, elegant guest rooms feature antiques, cozy down quilts, and fresh-cut flowers.

Each evening guests may join one another for a complimentary wine and cheese social hour, and relax in front of a cheery fire prior to dining at one of the excellent Cedarburg restaurants. The innkeeper will make dinner reservations at a restaurant of your choice.

A delicious continental breakfast is served each morning in the warm gathering room. Homemade muffins, cakes and breads are baked in the Inn's kitchen using recipes from an authentic turn of the century Cedarburg cookbook. Fresh fruit, cereal, freshly-squeezed juices, and a fine selection of tea and coffee are also offered.

The staff is friendly and helpful, with attention to detail their foremost concern.

Address: W62 N573 Washington Avenue, Cedarburg, WI 53012
Phone: 414-375-3550
Toll-Free: 800-554-4717
Fax: 414-375-9422
Web site: http://www.washingtonhouseinn.com
Room Rates: $
Suite Rates: $$
Credit Cards: Visa, MC, AmEx, Disc., Diners
No. of Rooms: 34 **Suites:** 3
Services and Amenities: Gathering room, Complimentary wine & cheese social hour each evening, In-room cable TV, Telephones, Radios, Individual heat & A/C control, Some rooms with whirlpool baths & fireplaces, Complimentary toiletries & newspaper, Gift Certificates available
Restrictions: No pets allowed, Handicapped facilities & elevator available
Concierge: Innkeeper
Restaurant: Walking distance to restaurants
Business Facilities: Copier, Audio-Visual, Fax
Conference Rooms: 1 room
Sports Facilities: Whirlpool, Sauna, Nearby golf, skiing and horseback riding
Location: Downtown Cedarburg, 20 miles north of Milwaukee, Nearest airport—Mitchell
Attractions: Unique shops, Many historic buildings, Cedar Creek Settlement, Cedar Creek Winery, Cedar Creek Park

THE AMERICAN CLUB

In 1918, Walter J. Kohler commissioned the American Club to be built as housing for the immigrant workers he employed in the Kohler Co. factory. At its dedication, Walter Kohler expressed his belief that workers should be given "roses as well as wages." His dedication to the Kohler Co. workers was unique in a time when workers at most factories were given little respect. To demonstrate his concern, he designed The American Club to be the finest in habitat for the Kohler Co. workers.

In 1978, new life was breathed into this historic edifice. Cultural values and the heritage of the past was married with modern conveniences to evolve to an epitome of hospitality and a home for gracious living. Listed on the National Registry of Historic Places, The American Club is the only AAA five-diamond resort hotel in the Midwest.

Each guestroom is appointed with fine furnishings, hand-crafted woodwork, and a Kohler whirlpool bath. Some rooms feature spas enclosed in private greenhouses, over-size whirlpool baths, or remarkable Kohler Habitats, environmental enclosures offering sun, steam, and rain. One and two-story suites offer separate living rooms with fireplaces, dining areas, wet bars and powder rooms.

Golf enthusiasts will find Pete Dye's Blackwolf Run and Whistling Straits Golf Courses to be spectacular and challenging with 72 holes of golf. Sports Core offers complete racquet, exercise and spa facilities.

The Kohler Design Center features 27 designer kitchens and bathrooms as well as a Kohler Museum. River Wildlife, a 500-acre wilderness preserve, offers hiking, canoeing, horseback riding, fishing and cross-country skiing. Nearby shops at Woodlake offer a full array of specialty shops and a unique home furnishing center.

Address: Highland Drive, Kohler, WI 53044
Phone: 920-457-8000
Toll-Free: 800-344-2838
Fax: 920-457-0299
Room Rates: $$$
Suite Rates: $$$$
Credit Cards: Most credit cards accepted
No. of Rooms: 234 **Suites:** 2
Services and Amenities: 24 hour security, Twice daily maid service, Laundry service, Gift shop, Valet parking, Doorman, Newstand, Currency exchange, Express checkout
Restrictions: No pets allowed
Concierge: 24 hours
Room Service: 24 hours
Restaurant: 9 restaurants and cafes: Immigrant, Wisconsin Room, Horse & Plow, The Greenhouse, Blackwolf Run, River Wildlife, Cucina, Jumpin' Jacks, and Woodlake Market Cafe
Bar: Horse and Plow, The Winery, Blackwolf Run, River Bar and Cucina
Business Facilities: Complete business service center, Full-service audio-visual department, Conference facilities
Conference Rooms: capacity 998
Sports Facilities: Blackwolf Run & Whistling Straits Golf Course, Sports Core—a complete fitness facility, health spa and racquet club
Location: East central Wisconsin, 60 miles north of Milwaukee, Near Mitchell Airport
Attractions: Kohler Design Center, Waelderhaus, Shops at Woodlake Kohler, John Michael Kohler Arts Center & the Old Wade House, River Wildlife game preserve with Hunting, Fishing, Canoeing, Horseback riding, Cross-country skiing, Crazy quail & International trap

THE GENEVA INN

There's more to The Geneva than a breathtaking view of Geneva Lake. It's charming, European elegance is inviting and comfortable. Maybe it's the presence of fine craftsmanship in every architectural detail. Or, the personal touches that make you feel extraordinary. Thick fluffy bathrobes, cognac and chocolates at evening turndown, oversized vintage or whirlpool baths, private balconies and more await the discerning traveler.

The Geneva Inn is the only property located directly on the shores of Geneva Lake—a premier recreation area in Wisconsin. Guests will find seclusion and uncommon comfort in the peaceful atmosphere of this traditional English Inn -fashioned after the grand old country-house hotels. Common areas of the Inn include a three-story atrium with raised hearth fireplace, piano lounge, landscaped terrace and patio. Boat owners can tie up at the Inn's private marina.

Guest rooms and suites are tastefully decorated in the best country manor, interspersed with antiques. Most rooms include a whirlpool or vintage bath and private balcony, many with outstanding lakeviews. Beds range from luxurious four-post kings to queens and doubles. Amenities include televisions with video players (complimentary classical videos), cable, fully stocked honor bar refrigerators, early morning coffee on each floor, and exclusive use of the Inn's exercise facility. Guests are treated to a complimentary, continental buffet breakfast, including fresh fruit and bakery items, flavored butters, delicious meats and cheeses, rich coffee and fragrant teas.

No matter how you spend your day, return to The Geneva Inn's renowned Grandview Restaurant for a romantic, candlelight dinner featuring distinct American Continental cuisine. Every table offers a scenic vista of Geneva Lake through large panoramic windows. Guests enjoy spectacular sunsets with quiet, unobtrusive service and softly played piano classics.

The Geneva Inn is a getaway unlike any other. Guests will find the beautiful surroundings mesmerizing and relaxing. Service and attention to detail stand out, creating an atmosphere which caters to guest's needs.

Address: N2009 State Road 120, Lake Geneva, WI 53147
Phone: 414-248-5680
Toll-Free: 800-441-5881
Fax: 414-248-5685
Room Rates: $$
Suite Rates: $$$$
Credit Cards: Most credit cards accepted
No. of Rooms: 33 **Suites:** 4
Services and Amenities: Valet service, Garage & parking, Gift shop, Laundry, Baby-sitting service, Balconies, Cable TV/VCR, Radio, Wet bar, Individual heat & air-conditioning control, Robes, Whirlpool, Complimentary Crabtree & Evelyn toiletries, newspaper, continental breakfast
Restrictions: No pets allowed, 4 rooms with handicapped access 24 hours
Restaurant: The Grandview Restaurant & Lounge, all meals including Sunday brunch and late afternoon dinner
Business Facilities: Full-scale conference facilities, Copiers, Audio-Visual
Conference Rooms: 2 rooms, capacity 40 & 80
Sports Facilities: Exercise Room, Individual whirlpools, Golf, Skiing, Riding, Tennis nearby
Location: Linn Township—residential
Attractions: Inland lake resort area, Boat excursions on lake, Quaint shops in downtown, Antiques

MANSION HILL INN

This landmark house was built in 1857-58 by pioneering Madison architects August Kutzbock and Samuel Hunter Donnel. It was restored to its original splendor by its present owners, who in 1985 opened the 11-room luxury hotel known today as the Mansion Hill Inn. Listed on the National Register of Historic Places and recipient of the distinctive AAA Four Diamond Award, the Inn is located just one block from Lake Mendota.

Selecting just the right suite in which to stay is a delightful chore. Each has a special decor and theme and some were named for individuals who had a history with the mansion. As guests check in, they are invited to partake of complimentary spirits and refreshments in the parlor. They are then guided by a helpful, informative valet up the spiral staircase to their rooms. Many of Mansion Hill's guest rooms feature sumptuous whirlpool baths and separate showers, four-poster beds, fireplaces, period antiques, and direct access to the veranda and the victorian garden.

Guests are pampered with complementary silver-service continental breakfast brought to their rooms with a daily newspaper. Afternoon spirits and refreshments are served in one of the Victorian parlors daily.

The Inn also provides special services for business travelers, such as the Executive Club Program which gives a discount, often at considerable savings, to those members who reserve rooms for at least 10 weeknights a year. The concierge, available with assistance for special events, has worked with the Greater Madison Convention and Visitors Bureau to help entertain prominent guests by serving cordials, packing a picnic basket and arranging for a horse-drawn carriage to carry them to the Capitol for an outdoor concert.

Address: 424 North Pinckney Street, Madison, WI 53703
Phone: 608-255-3999
Toll-Free: 800-798-9070
Fax: 608-255-2217
Web site: http://www.mansionhillinn.com
Room Rates: $$
Suite Rates: $$$$
Credit Cards: Visa, MC, AmEx
No. of Rooms: 11 **Suites:** 2
Services and Amenities: 24 hour valet and parking service, Minibars, Cable TV, VCR, Complimentary in-room continental breakfast, newspaper, afternoon spirits and refreshments
Restrictions: No pets allowed, Children over 12 only
Concierge: 24 hours
Room Service: 24 hours
Business Facilities: Message center, Copier, Fax, Data ports, Teleconferencing
Sports Facilities: Complimentary use of Madison Athletic Club
Location: Mansion Hill district, 4 blocks to State Capitol
Attractions: 3 blocks to restaurants, Boutique shopping, Area attractions, State Capitol, Lake Mendota, UW campus, State Historical Society, Geology Museum, Children's Museum

CHURCH HILL INN

Situated in the hub of Sister Bay, the Church Hill Inn is within easy walking distance of a fine sand beach, the public marina, and all of the amenities offered in the village. Elegant brick walks link the inn to Country Walk, a unique cluster of shops.

Designed in the English-country style, each guestroom is individually decorated with antiques. Most guest rooms exit directly to one of five cozy parlors, each with its own fireplace and four with wet bars.

A private pub provides a wide selection of domestic and imported beers. Each morning you will be treated to a full complimentary breakfast including three hot entrees, three freshly baked items, homemade granola, fresh fruit and beverages.

For those looking toward fitness as well as relaxation, the inn has an exercise room, spacious sauna and indoor whirlpool/spa. The outdoor pool is heated from late spring through early fall and features an elegant lattice-fenced sun bathing deck.

The Church Hill Inn is open year-round, but if you're lucky enough to be there in springtime you will see a showy bloom of wildflowers, cherry blossoms and an abundance of wildlife.

Address: 425 Gateway Drive, Sister Bay, WI 54234
Phone: 920-854-4885
Toll-Free: 800-422-4906
Fax: 920-854-4634
E-mail: churchhillinn@churchhillinn.com
Web site: http://www.churchhillinn.com
Room Rates: $
Credit Cards: Visa, MC
No. of Rooms: 35
Services and Amenities: Small shopping mall adjacent with barber, beauty & gift shop, TV lounge, Card/game area, Library, 5 rooms with fireplaces, Balconies, Cable TV, Radio, Individual climate control, Complimentary full breakfast, coffee, hors d'oeuvres, newspaper & toiletries
Restrictions: No pets, Minimum 2 night stay weekends Jun-Oct., 5 rooms handicapped-equipped, Children 10 & over
Restaurant: Hotel restaurant for guests only serves breakfast in season, dinner on Saturday (off-season)
Bar: Hotel bar, 8:00 a.m.–10:00 p.m., Honor bar for guests
Business Facilities: Audio-Visual
Conference Rooms: 1 room, capacity 15
Sports Facilities: Outdoor swimming pool, Croquet, Whirlpool, Sauna, Massage, Exercise room, Cross-country skiing, Sailing, Riding and Tennis nearby
Location: Door County, Nearest airport is Green Bay
Attractions: Boutique shopping, Several state parks, Hiking, Biking, Beaches, Golf, Tennis, 250 miles of shoreline

THE INTERNATIONAL HOTEL OF CALGARY

When Calgary takes off its cowboy boots and Olympic jackets, one finds a sleek, friendly city, proud enough of its heritage to preserve the pioneer architecture, willing to fund a spacious downtown performing arts center, and capable of producing an efficient twenty-first-century light-rail system.

Guests of the 27-year-old International Hotel find 250 recently remodeled suites, attractively decorated in light colors with contemporary furnishings. Each has a private bath, one or two bedrooms, a bar area, dining nook and living room.

Upon entering the atrium-style lobby, the impression is one of uncluttered calm with well-orchestrated hotel management. A knowledgeable concierge takes care of everything, and even knows the origins of the modern art.

The 4th Avenue Bar is actually a tri-level creation, with sports deck on the top, solarium and bar at mid-level, and an executive club room in the lower reaches. The 4th Avenue Cafe is "today" in feel, with peach, light blue, and gray hues dominating. Large bouquets of fresh flowers and splashes of color add to the informal atmosphere.

The location on 4th Avenue couldn't be better for walking to shopping, theaters, and the intriguing Glenbow Museum's collection of Eskimo and Indian artifacts. Any trip to Calgary should begin with the observation deck of the 626-foot Calgary Tower, below which Olympic sites and the panoramic mountains and prairies stretch out. Other attractions worth visiting are the Planetarium and Science Center, and the Calgary Zoo where you can watch polar bears swim underwater.

The International Hotel is a member of Sterling Hotels and Resorts.

Address: 220 4th Avenue Southwest, Calgary, Alberta T2P 0H5
Phone: 403-265-9600
Toll-Free: 800-223-0888
Fax: 403-265-6949
E-mail: book@intlhotel.com
Web site: http://www.intlhotel.com
Suite Rates: $$$ Canadian $
Credit Cards: AmEx, MC, Visa, CB, EnRoute,DC
No. of Suites: 250
Services and Amenities: Valet service, Garage and Parking, House doctor, Barber shop, Baby-sitting service, Cable TV, Radio, Coffeemakers, Complimentary newspaper, Complimentary soaps, shampoo, lotion and shoeshine mitt, Non-smoking rooms
Restrictions: No pets allowed, Handicapped access to 1 room
Concierge: 7:00 a.m.–11:00 p.m.
Room Service: 6:30 a.m.–1:00 a.m.
Restaurant: 4th Avenue Cafe, 6:30 a.m.–11:00 p.m., Dress code
Bar: 4th Avenue Bar, 11:00 a.m.–1:00 a.m.
Business Facilities: Message center, Copiers, Audio-Visual, Full-scale conference facilities
Conference Rooms: 9 rooms, capacity 150
Sports Facilities: Indoor swimming pool, Whirlpool, Sauna, Weight training, New health spa
Location: Downtown, 15 miles from Calgary International Airport
Attractions: Walking distance to: Shopping, Theaters, Financial Centers, Dining, Glenbow Museum, Calgary Tower, Chinatown, Olympic Plaza, Planetarium, Eau Claire Market

SOOKE HARBOUR HOUSE

The original Sooke Harbour House, overlooking the harbour, was built in 1920. It was renovated in 1982 by the present owners, who have since added to the new house and have restored and opened the Malahat Farm Cottage. Guests are invited to wander at leisure in the extensive gardens, where approximately 400 varieties of herbs, greens, vegetables, edible flowers and trees flourish.

All of the thirteen guest rooms are designed and decorated to reflect special aspects of West Coast life. Many rooms are furnished with antiques and original art. Each room has a balcony or terrace with ocean views. The three-bedroom one and a half bath Malahat Farm Cottage, located 7 miles north of the Sooke Harbour House on the picturesque acreage of a beautiful 19th century farm, is a ten minute walk from the beautiful Muir Creek Beach Estuary.

Complemented by an extensive award winning wine list, the a la carte menu in the four-star dining room changes daily, focusing on fresh organic ingredients. One might choose from the dinner menu the Pacific halibut filet baked with an apple cider vinegar, trout roe and spring herb butter served with a cabbage fennel ravioli, broccoli and banana squash, while enjoying a panoramic view of the gardens, the ocean and the Olympic Mountains.

Guests are pampered with complimentary breakfast brought to their rooms at the hour indicated the night before. Lunch in the dining room or packed for a picnic is also included in the room rate. Cookies and Port are replenished daily in the rooms.

Sooke Harbour House can accommodate up to twenty-six guests for seminars or for corporate retreats, with a wide variety of meeting and discussion rooms available. May through September the elegant Summer Pavilion is also available, accommodating business groups of up to seventy-five. For social events and weddings, the Marquise will accommodate 120 guests for dinner. Banquet events can be arranged to include dining, dancing, sitting area and stage.

Address: 1528 Whiffen Spit Road, Sooke, BC V0S 1N0
Phone: 250-642-3421
Toll-Free: 800-889-9688
Fax: 250-642-6988
E-mail: ssh@islandnet.com
Room Rates: $$$ Canadian $
Credit Cards: Most credit cards accepted
No. of Rooms: 13
Services and Amenities: Breakfast & lunch included in room rate, Continental breakfast in off season, Complimentary in-room fruit & baked goods, Gift shop, Baby-sitting, Wet bar, Radio, Fireplace, Iron, TV/VCR upon request, Robes, Hair dryer, Some rooms have hot tub/Jacuzzi tub
Restrictions: $20 pet charge, No smoking indoors, No charge for children under 12, Handicapped-equipped
Room Service: Daily
Restaurant: Sooke Harbour House dining room, Lunch and Dinner
Conference Rooms: 3 rooms, capacity 16-120, Full menu planning & catering
Sports Facilities: World class golf nearby, Hiking, Whale watching, Massage and reflexology by appointment
Location: Vancouver Island, 23 miles west of Victoria, 45 minutes—Victoria Airport
Attractions: Victoria, Beautiful beaches and cross-country skiing nearby, Salmon fishing charters

METROPOLITAN HOTEL

The Metropolitan Hotel welcomes you to discover the heart of downtown Vancouver, where exceptional service, sumptuous elegance, outstanding amenities, exquisite dining and remarkable pleasures reign—all at a superb value. You are within blocks of the high fashion district of Robson Street known for its trendy restaurants, shops and galleries. Entertainment abounds nearby at the Ford Center, BC Place and GM Place.

All 197 exquisite rooms feature wool carpets, solid oak cabinetry, marble countertops, and oversized beds with deluxe European down duvets and triple sheets. The baths offer deep soaker tubs and lush terry bathrobes. The 18 luxury suites offer unique furnishing and fine art in spacious entertainment areas. Indoor pool, full service health club and personal trainers are available to meet your fitness needs.

For special event, the Metropolitan's Grand Ballrooms provides elegant rooms with the perfect ambiance for that perfect event, with seating up to 400 and their experienced staff ready to assist you with every detail.

The Hotel makes dining a pleasure at Diva at the Met restaurant, known for its West Coast ambiance and delightfully inventive menus. Award-winning executive Chef Michael Noble takes center stage at the central open Waldorf-style kitchen here guests can find him preparing such contemporary dishes as smoked Alaskan black cod with leek whipped potatoes.

Metropolitan offers business travelers a full-service, expertly-trained staff whose behind-the-scenes planning anticipates every need. Fully equipped meeting rooms and all suites have state-of-the-art audio-visual displays and ISDN lines for rapid access to networks and video-teleconferencing world wide.

Address: 645 Howe Street, Vancouver, BC V6C 2Y9
Phone: 604-687-1122
Toll-Free: 800-668-6600
Fax: 604-689-7044
E-mail: reservations@metropolitan.com
Web site: http://www.metropolitan.com/
Room Rates: $$$
Suite Rates: $$$$
Credit Cards: Most credit cards accepted
No. of Rooms: 197 **Suites:** 18
Services and Amenities: Valet, Garage & parking, International currency exchange, House doctor, Baby-sitting service, Balconies off most rooms, Cable TV, VCR in suites, Telephones, Radio, Wet bar, Individual heat & air-conditioning, Robes, Complimentary shoeshine & toiletries
Restrictions: 2 rooms with handicapped access
Concierge: 24 hours
Room Service: 24 hours
Restaurant: "Diva at the Met," 6:30 a.m.–11:00 p.m.
Bar: Restaurant Bar, 11:30 a.m.–12:00 p.m.
Business Facilities: Business center—Secretarial service, E-mail, Fax, Modems, Teleconferencing, Copiers, Audio-Visual
Conference Rooms: 7 rooms, capacity 120
Sports Facilities: Indoor swimming pool, Whirlpool, Sauna, Massage, Weight training, Handball/Squash, Privileges to Signature Fitness Club
Location: Downtown
Attractions: Pacific Centre Mall, World Trade Centre, Vancouver Trade & Convention Centre, Robson Square Conference Centre, Stock Exchange, Gastown & Robson Streets, Art galleries, Queen Elizabeth Theatre, GM Place, Restaurants, Cafes, Stanley Park, Waterfront

WEDGEWOOD HOTEL

It's obvious upon entering Eleni Skalbania's Wedgewood Hotel that this local businesswoman is a collector of fine antiques and art. Her 89-room hostelry reflects her personal dedication to a project that involved gutting and rebuilding an old hotel in downtown Vancouver. Opened in 1984, the Wedgewood is like an elegant home, lovingly cared for yet stressing personal services such as complimentary shoeshine and morning newspaper at your door, in-room safety deposit box, as well as in-room coffee and tea. The gracious, inviting lobby is enhanced by a magnificent oriental rug, marble fireplace walls, a brass fire screen, and an assortment of period pieces.

Beyond the palladian windows of the Bacchus Restaurant and Lounge, diners find distinctive adaptations of regional Italian dishes—*nuovo cucina*. For an excellent opener with zest, try the House Smoked Salmon on Onion Bagel with Dill Cream Cheese and Caviar. There's a prodigious variety of wines from which to choose, ranging from gems from California's boutique wineries such as a Canyon Road Sauvignon, to such French treats as a Beaujolais Villages, Dubouef. You'll also find a nicely balanced representation from Italy, Spain, Germany, Australia, and Canada.

One-third of the accommodations here are suites, with tastefully coordinated furnishings. Flower-bedded balconies overlook gardens and waterfalls of Robson Square and the courthouse.

Though a small city by world standards, Vancouver is remarkably cosmopolitan and sophisticated, and elegant boutiques, fine restaurants, and cultural events are found nearby the hotel.

Address: 845 Hornby Street, Vancouver, BC V6Z 1V1
Phone: 604-689-7777
Toll-Free: 800-663-0666
Fax: 604-688-3074
Room Rates: $$$$ Canadian $
Suite Rates: $$$$ Canadian $
Credit Cards: Most credit cards accepted
No. of Rooms: 89 **Suites:** 38
Services and Amenities: Limo service from airport, Garage, Valet, Currency exchange, House doctor, Baby-sitting service, Laundry service, Cable TV, Radio, Iron, Some fireplaces & wetbars, Individual climate control, Complimentary shoeshine, newspaper, robes & coffee/tea
Restrictions: No pets allowed, Handicapped access to 1 room, Non-smoking rooms
Concierge: Available
Room Service: 24 hours
Restaurant: The Bacchus Restaurant
Bar: The Bacchus Lounge, Live entertainment Monday-Saturday, 6:30 a.m.–1:30 a.m.
Business Facilities: Complete business service center, Message center, Copiers, Audio-Visual, Fax, and more
Conference Rooms: capacity 80
Sports Facilities: Full health spa with stairclimbers, rowing machine, sauna
Location: Downtown Vancouver, Nearest airport: Vancouver International
Attractions: Elegant shops at Robson Street, Pacific Centre, Granville Island, Stanley Park, Robson Square, Vancouver Art Gallery

HOLLAND HOUSE INN

A charming Inn located only two blocks from Victoria's Inner Harbour and three blocks from the U. S. Ferry Terminals, the Holland House Inn boasts the best location in Victoria. A short walk to the Royal British Columbia Museum, Beacon Hill Park, downtown shopping, shuttle bus to Butchart Gardens, the Empress Hotel, whale watching expeditions and a variety of tours.

The Inn is decorated in an English Country motive. Each room is unique with warm colors, rich wallpapers, antique furniture, luxurious goose down duvet's and luxury linens. All rooms have a sitting area, private bathroom, TV and telephone. Most rooms have a balcony or patio. Special occasion suites are available with fireplaces and double soaker tubs. Some rooms have four poster beds, either King or Queen size, and twins for those who prefer to have their own bed.

An English country Inn with your comfort in mind. Guests are encouraged to enjoy the living room library where they can select a book and read by the fire.

Holland House Inn is renown for its breakfasts which are complimentary and are served each morning in the large plant-filled conservatory.

The Holland House Inn is a unique small hotel where fine art and unparalled comfort are combined to create an atmosphere of casual elegance for their guests enjoyment.

Address: 595 Michigan Street, Victoria, BC Canada V8V 1S7
Phone: 250-384-6644
Toll-Free: 800-335-3466
Fax: 250-384-6117
E-mail:
stay@hollandhouse.victoria.bc.ca
Web site: http://www.islandnet.com/~holndhus/
Room Rates: $$$
Suite Rates: $$$$
Credit Cards: Visa, MC, AmEx
No. of Rooms: 8 **Suites:** 6
Services and Amenities: Parking, Library, Fireplaces, Balconies, Cable TV, Telephones, Whirlpool bath, Complimentary: toiletries, breakfast in the conservatory amongst plants
Restrictions: One room equipped for handicapped, No pets allowed, Children over 10 years of age welcome
Location: 3 blocks from downtown, 20 kilometers from airport
Attractions: 2 blocks from Victoria Inner Harbour, Parliament Building and Royal B.C. Museum, Walking distance to U.S. Ferries, Major tourist attractions

OAK BAY BEACH HOTEL

Located in Victoria's oldest and most elegant residential district, this Tudor-style Inn overlooks the ocean and is surrounded by spectacular views of islands and mountains in the distance. Built in 1927, the Inn was intended to be a recreation of a British Country Inn. The hotel was rebuilt in 1930 and became the social center of Oak Bay, renowned for its service, elegant surroundings, fine dining and excellent views. The Inn's gracious ambience has transcended time and still remains warm and inviting.

The hotel is a wonderful collection of unexpected nooks and crannies. Rooms are furnished with antiques and period pieces, some of which are over two hundred years old. Each room is uniquely decorated creating a warm and inviting atmosphere. Many rooms feature balconies with sea or garden views. Their most celebrated suite, the Georgian Suite, features a king-size bed, quaint sitting room, luxurious bathroom, and exquisite dining room. The private balcony overlooks the ocean and is the perfect setting for a toast by sunset.

Known for its superior cuisine and beautiful decor, Bentley's On The Bay Dining Room, located within the hotel, offers culinary delights all year round. Overlooking the Haro Straits, the restaurant features a breathtaking seaview while boasting a relaxing atmosphere filled with warmth, charm, decor and ambiance. Chef Michael French is known for tempting even the most discerning palate with dishes such as Smoked Duck Breast and Rack of Lamb. For those guests who love chocolate, the chef has perfected his Chocolate Trilogy and White and Dark Chocolate Cannelloni on Bailey's Irish Cream Sauce.

The Inn's authentic English Pub, called the "Snug Lounge" is a warm, cozy Pub serving light lunches and dinner, as well as a wide array of beverages. Complimentary appetizers are offered daily (except Sunday) during cocktail hour.

Address: 1175 Beach Drive, Victoria, BC V8S 2N2
Phone: 250-598-4556
Toll-Free: 800-668-7758
Fax: 250-598-6180
E-mail: reservations@oakbaybeachhotel.bc.ca
Web site: http://www.bctravel.com/oakbay/beachhotel.html
Room Rates: $$ Canadian $
Suite Rates: $$$ Canadian $
Credit Cards: Most credit cards accepted
No. of Rooms: 50 **Suites:** 17
Services and Amenities: Valet & parking service, Car hire, Laundry service, Baby-sitting service, Card/Game area, Gift displays, Fireplaces, Balconies, Cable TV, Telephones, Radio, Robes in some rooms, Tubs for two, Complimentary toiletries, newspapers & evening snack
Restrictions: Children under 12 free in parents' room, No pets allowed
Concierge: 24 hours
Room Service: 7:00 a.m.–10:00 p.m.
Restaurant: Bentleys on the Bay, Open for breakfast & dinner
Bar: "The Snug" English Pub
Business Facilities: Message center, E-mail, Copiers, Audio-Visual, Fax
Conference Rooms: 4 rooms, capacity 130
Sports Facilities: Nearby to Oak Bay Recreation Center—Swimming pool, Squash, Massage, Golf, Sailing, as well as Whale watching & Sunset cruises
Location: Oak Bay, Residential district
Attractions: Nearby golf courses, Walking distance to shops & restaurants in Oak Bay Village, Marina nearby, Waterfront strolls, Butchart Gardens, 15 miles to downtown

VICTORIA REGENT HOTEL

The Victoria Regent Hotel offers a choice of recently redecorated spacious rooms with king-sized beds and a view of "Old Town" Victoria, or newly renovated large one- and two-bedroom luxury apartment-styled suites overlooking Victoria's picturesque Inner Harbour. The suites have fully-equipped kitchens, dining areas, gracious living rooms, balcony and separate bedroom(s) each with its own ensuite bathroom.

Complimentary services include in room coffee, morning newspaper, secured underground parking, passes to a nearby fitness centre, and movie and sports channels. Other services include coin operated laundry facilities, business centre, in suite modem hookups and valet service. Whale watching tours and regular float plane service to downtown Vancouver depart daily from the waterfront wharf. Discounted moorage rates are also available for Regent guests.

The Water's Edge Cafe offers a continental breakfast buffet daily. Enjoy a bowl of fresh fruit, assorted homemade muffins and pastries, coffee and juice while enjoying the friendly service and Inner Harbour activities at the waterfront cafe. For guests' dining pleasure, the Regent offers an innovative and creative selection of fresh seafood, meats and vegetarian cuisine.

The choice location allows guests to easily explore downtown Victoria. Shops, theatres, the world renowned Royal British Columbia Museum, the conference center and the city's year-round attractions are all within walking distance.

Address: 1234 Wharf Street, Victoria, BC V8W 3H9
Phone: 250-386-2211
Toll-Free: 800-663-7472
Fax: 250-386-2622
E-mail: regent@pinc.com
Web site: http://www.regent-hotel.victoria.bc.ca
Room Rates: $$
Suite Rates: $$$
Credit Cards: Visa, MC, AmEx, Disc., Diners
No. of Rooms: 11 **Suites:** 32
Services and Amenities: Valet service, Garage & parking, Laundry service, Baby-sitting service, Balconies, Cable TV, Telephones, Wet bar, Kitchen in suites, Some fireplaces & whirlpool baths, Sundries available at the front desk, Complimentary shoeshine & toiletries
Restrictions: No pets allowed, Children up to age sixteen free with parents, Two rooms equipped for handicapped
Concierge: 7:00 a.m.–11:00 p.m.
Room Service: 7:00 a.m.–10:00 p.m.
Restaurant: Water's Edge Cafe, 7:00 a.m.–10:00 p.m., Catered receptions for up to 40 people by prior arrangement
Business Facilities: Message center, Secretarial center, Copiers, Audio-Visual, Fax
Conference Rooms: 2 rooms, capacity 40, Theatre
Sports Facilities: Guest priviledges at the Y.M.C.A.
Location: On Vancouver Island in the heart of Downtown Victoria, Overlooking harbour
Attractions: Museums, Theatres, Shops, Conference Centre of downtown Victoria, Colorful landscaped gardens

HALF MOON GOLF, TENNIS & BEACH CLUB

Elegantly positioned on a 400-acre estate with a full mile of white sand beach, the Half Moon Club offers the upscale traveler the finest in accommodations, cuisine, and services. This tropical Caribbean jewel is consistently honored by Great Britain's "300 Best Hotels in the World," and is the deserved recipient of the American Automobile Association's Four Diamond Award.

Masterminded by acclaimed hotelier Heinz W. Simonitsch, the Club magically ties together 32 new Royal Villas into one splendid Jamaican Colonial showplace of suites, cottages and villas—the latter of which appeal to families and groups.

Elegance extends from the expansive columned dining veranda through the stunning mahogany-clad lobby. Ocean vistas and lush foliage are visual delights from every unit, patio, and balcony. Decor consists of crafted-in-Jamaica Queen Anne furnishings. All have lounge areas, bedrooms, baths and private bars, meticulously detailed villas boast their own kitchens, with cooks, maids, butlers and gardeners provided. Private gardens and swimming pools come with villas.

While many corporate guests find the suites suitable for meetings, larger groups may choose to assemble in our state of the art conference centre or in any of the thirteen fully detailed meeting rooms. A well-versed crew is on stand-by to assist. A kaleidoscope of sports activities is offered. Tee off at the 18-hole Robert Trent Jones-designed golf course, play tennis on 13 courts, or squash on four courts. Water sports on the crystal-clear bay and a fully equipped fitness center are among numerous diversions for the vacationer.

Both the Seagrape Terrace and Sugar Mill restaurants offer enticing local and international specialties. The Il Giardino offers exquisite Italian Cuisine in air-conditioned comfort or Alfresco on the Terrace. On the tree-framed Seagrape Terrace overlooking the wave-splashed beach, one might savor succulent Caribbean lobster tail accompanied by the choicest filet mignon, and served with fresh, home-grown vegetables. From the array of delectable desserts, the rum-sauced banana crêpes are particularly rewarding. Evening festivities include dancing, an Island-flavored floor show, and a sip of the Half Moon specialty (rum, Triple Sec and pineapple) in the handsome Cedar Bar.

Address: P.O. Box 80, Montego Bay, Jamaica, West Indies
Phone: 809-953-2211
Toll-Free: 800-626-0592
Fax: 809-953-2731
E-mail: hmoondat@infochan.com
Room Rates: $$$
Suite Rates: $$$$
Credit Cards: Most credit cards accepted
No. of Rooms: 220 **Suites:** 10
Services and Amenities: Car hire, Parking, Barber/beauty shops, Shopping arcade, Currency exchange, Laundry, Baby-sitting service, Ceiling fans, Individual air-conditioning, Maid/cook service available in apartments, Balconies/patios, Minibars in suites, Complimentary toiletries
Restrictions: No pets allowed, Children welcome
Concierge: 24 hours
Room Service: 7:00 a.m.–9:30 p.m.
Restaurant: Seagrape Terrace, 8:00 a.m.–3:00 p.m., 7:30 p.m.–9:30 p.m., Dress Code
Bar: Cedar Bar, 10:00 a.m.–closing
Business Facilities: Message center, Secretarial service, Translators, Copiers, Audio-Visual, Telex
Conference Rooms: 8 rooms, capacity 350
Sports Facilities: Robert Trent Jones designed 18-hole golf course, 13 Tennis courts, Swimming pools, Riding, Numerous water sports, Fitness Center
Location: Rose Hall area, 5 miles—airport, 7 miles—downtown, Adjacent to highway
Attractions: Dunns' River Falls, Rose Hall Great House, Bamboo rafting, Duty-free shopping

RONDEL VILLAGE

Located on Jamaica's romantic west coast, and offering private access to seven miles of white sand beach protected by offshore coral reefs, Rondel Village is a water-sports paradise with a wide array of recreational facilities close at hand. This is a small hotel specializing in personalized service from staff who are willing to go the extra mile to meet guests' needs.

Rondel Village's eight unusual octagonal villas are modeled on indigenous Negril architecture and set in tropical gardens. They feature an elegant marble floor living room with air-conditioned bedrooms, a kitchen and two bathrooms. Each villa has its own heated whirlpool spa enclosed in a Spanish style courtyard.

After a plunge in the pool or Jacuzzi or a sail on the tranquil jade-green sea, guests may enjoy the view while dining on the outdoor terrace of the Seaside Restaurant, also open for breakfast. The chicken and shrimp pasta come highly recommended.

Guests who venture forth from this private paradise may visit a nearby craft market and vendor's arcade or tour the Negril Point Lighthouse, built in 1894. Rondel Village is ideal for couples, singles and families. Wedding and honeymoon packages are available.

Address: Norman Manley Boulevard., P.O. Box 96, Negril, Jamaica
Phone: 876-957-4413
Fax: 876-957-4915
E-mail: wrightc@toj.com
Web site: http://www.negril.com/rondmain.htm
Room Rates: $
Suite Rates: $$
Credit Cards: Visa, AmEx, MC, JCB
No. of Rooms: 16 **Suites:** 8
Services and Amenities: Parking, Currency exchange, Laundry service, Baby-sitting service, Some kitchens, Balconies, Cable TV, Telephone, Complimentary Monday cocktail party
Restrictions: No pets allowed, Ramps for all units available, Children under 8 no charge, Cribs no charge
Room Service: Restaurant hours
Restaurant: Seaside Restaurant, 7:30–10:45 a.m., 6:30–9:30 p.m., Beach Snack Bar
Bar: Rondel Village Beach Bar, 11:00 a.m.–9:30 p.m.
Sports Facilities: Outdoor swimming pool, Whirlpool, Sailing
Location: Beachfront, 1½ miles from Negril
Attractions: Swimming, Snorkeling, Fishing, Sailing, 1½ miles from Craft market and Venders arcade, 10 miles from Negril Point Light House

TRIDENT VILLAS & RESORT

Strung along the coast between tropical greenery and sapphire sea, like a string of glowing pearls, the Trident lets you relax in warm soft breezes while in the care of a truly professional staff. The fresh white buildings are Old World Colonial English architecture with a Caribbean flavor. Covered verandas lead from antique-furnished villas, suites and rooms to manicured lawns that are worth a meander, possibly in the company of the peacock family elders, Oskar, Otto and Ophelia.

Fill your days ashore visiting waterfalls, caves, the towns, land and people of Jamaica, or spend your time on, over, or under the remarkably clear and gentle ocean off the shore.

Various meal plans are available while English afternoon tea is open to all, a nice break from the tennis courts, swimming pool, racquet ball and snorkeling.

For a very special visit, the Trident offers a wedding package, complete with marriage officer, cake, champagne, flowers and photos!

Dining completes the tropical luxury, with red and gold Terrace Restaurant, the waiters in white gloves, and service on Baccarat crystal and English silver. Several favorite menu items include hors d'oeuvres of bacon-wrapped banana, Duck a la Orange, and Chocolate Marquise with white and dark Chocolate for dessert. After a gourmet dinner, enjoy a tropical drink and the house Calypso band in the bar.

Tomorrow's yet another day of rafting, sunshine and relaxation.

Address: P.O. Box 119, Port Antonio, Jamaica
Phone: 876-993-2602
Fax: 876-993-2590
Room Rates: $$$
Suite Rates: $$$
Credit Cards: AmEx, MC, Visa
No. of Rooms: 26 **Suites:** 15
Services and Amenities: Several meal plans available, Parking, Laundry, Baby-sitting, Currency exchange, Gift shop, TV lounge, Card/game area, Balcony/veranda off each room, Telephones, Radios, Wet bar, Individual air-conditioning, Complimentary toiletries & afternoon tea
Restrictions: No minimum stay, No pets allowed
Room Service: 7:00 a.m.–10:00 p.m.
Restaurant: Terrace Restaurant, 7:00 a.m.–10:00 p.m., Jackets and Cocktail attire for dinner
Bar: 7:00–10:00 p.m.
Business Facilities: Secretarial services and business equipment available
Conference Rooms: 1 room, capacity 30
Sports Facilities: Ocean sports, Croquet, Massage, Aerobics, Horseback riding, 2 hard tennis courts
Location: On the ocean in the northeast, Port Antonio area, 2 hrs.—Kingston Airport
Attractions: Colonial Jamaica, The Victorian City of Port Antonio, Ocean sports galore, Rafting on the Rio Grande

HOTEL GUANAHANI

Hotel Guanahani consists of a series of bungalows set on 60 acres of attractively landscaped gardens. Rooms and suites are fully equipped with French Colonial style furniture, as well as king- size beds, ceiling fans and TVs. Suites have the added attraction of having sitting rooms, bedrooms, two baths and terraces overlooking the gardens. They resemble private houses in that there are no close neighbors.

There are two dining rooms - Indigo and Bartolomeo. Indigo overlooks the swimming pool, beach and lagoon and serves breakfast and lunch. Bartolomeo, the more formal one, is in a lovely setting which overlooks exotic gardens. It serves dinner which may include tartare salmon, lobster mousse and creme brulee.

The usual water sports are offered. In addition there are two night-lighted tennis courts, private beaches, and fabulous boutique shopping which is tax free.

The hotel promises its guests privacy, security and a beautiful location.

Address: Anse de Grand Cul de Sac, St. Barthelemy 97098 FWI
Phone: 590-27-66-60
Toll-Free: 800-223-1230
Fax: 590-27-70-70
Room Rates: $$$$
Suite Rates: $$$$
Credit Cards: Most credit cards accepted
No. of Rooms: 62 **Suites:** 15
Services and Amenities: Valet parking, Beauty/Barber shop, Car hire, Gift shop, International currency exchange, House Doctor, Laundry service, Baby-sitting service, Library, Game Area, Balconies, Cable TV, Robes, Complimentary toiletries and shoe shine
Restrictions: Small dogs only
Concierge: 24 hours
Room Service: 24 hours
Restaurant: Bartolomeo and Indigo, 11:00 a.m.–10:00 p.m.
Bar: 10:00 a.m.–11:00 p.m.
Business Facilities: Message service
Sports Facilities: Outdoor swimming pool, Whirlpool, Sailing, Riding, 2 night-lighted tennis courts, Watersports, Windsurfing rentals and school
Location: Island Paradise in the West Indies
Attractions: Luxury boutique shopping (tax free), 22 beaches, Mistral windsurfing rentals and school, Scuba diving center

SPICE ISLAND BEACH RESORT

Granada's elegant Spice Island Beach Resort is set along 1,600 feet of the world-renowned white sand Grand Anse Beach on the crystal-blue waters of the Caribbean. The natural beauty of Granada and the spectacular views of the lush surroundings provide the perfect setting for this world class resort.

Guests entering the Resort through the lobby, with its red clay tiles and brightly colored rattan furniture, are greeted by a view straight through to the sea. A complimentary welcome drink conveys the friendliness of the staff and their dedication to making every stay at the Resort enjoyable in every detail.

The suites are set in 8 acres of lush garden displays of local fruit trees and tropical flowers. Choose a garden-view whirlpool suite, a beach-front whirlpool suite just steps from the water, or a royal pool suite with private patio and pool. All are luxuriously furnished and air-conditioned, and each features a mini-bar and security safe.

With breakfast and dinner included in the room rate, fine dining is a long-standing tradition at Spice Island Beach Resort. Lavish buffets, elegant continental cuisine, and a wide selection of fine wines are served by a friendly and attentive staff and garnished with the beauty of Grand Anse Beach. Guests enjoy cool drinks in the spacious beachfront bar or on the breeze-cooled patio, where light meals are also served. Here the quiet murmur of the surf enhances the views of spectacular Grenadian sunsets.

Facilities include a lounge with cable TV and a boutique for shopping on-premises. Guests have complimentary use of a modern fitness center, tennis courts and racquets, bicycles, snorkeling equipment and sunfish for sailing. Also included in the room rate are golf green fees at the Grenada Golf Club's 9-hole course just a 10 minute cab ride away. A fresh-water pool and dining at La Belle Creole, one of Grenada's finest restaurants, are available at Blue Horizons, a sister resort just 100 yards away.

Spice Island Beach Resort is one of the most enjoyable and finest small hotels in the Caribbean.

Address: P.O. Box 6, Grand Anse Beach, St. Georges, Grenada
Phone: 473-444-4258
Fax: 473-444-4807
E-mail: spiceisl@caribsurf.com
Suite Rates: $$$$
Credit Cards: Most credit cards accepted
No. of Suites: 56
Services and Amenities: Parking, Modified American Plan (2 meals per day included), Gift shop, House doctor, Laundry service, Baby-sitting service, TV lounge, Card & game area, Balconies for all suites, Telephones, Radio, Wet bar, Individual air-conditioning control
Restrictions: No pets, 7 night minimum stay in season, Not appropriate for children under five in high season
Concierge: 9:00 a.m.–1:00 p.m.
Room Service: 7:45 a.m.–10:30 p.m.
Restaurant: Garden Restaurant, 7:30 a.m.–10:30 p.m., Dress code
Bar: Surf & Turf Bar, 11:00 a.m.–11:00 p.m.
Business Facilities: Audio-Visual equipment, TV, VCR, Microphone, Slide projector available, Fax
Conference Rooms: 1 room, capacity 75
Sports Facilities: 9-hole golf course, Water sports, Whirlpool, Sunfish sailing, Tennis, Bicycles, Fitness center
Location: On Grand Anse Beach, 3 miles—Point Salines Airport, 4 miles—St. Georges
Attractions: Banking facilities, Duty-free shops, Convenience stores & selection of Restaurants within walking distance

PETER ISLAND HOTEL

Checking into the tranquility of Peter Island means entering a world of unadulterated pampering in a tropical paradise. Since the resort owns nearly the entire island, you share your Eden with few others: maybe a hundred or so guests, and those who sailed over from Fallen Jerusalem or Prickly Pear. Beautiful palm-studded beaches, state-of-the-art furnishings in smart, contemporary villas, a harbor filled with yachts, and near- perfect sailing and fishing add up to the perfect hideaway.

Accommodations here include 30 Ocean View Rooms on Sprat Bay and 20 spacious Beach Front Rooms located on Deadman's Bay Beach. Three villas are also available, including the luxurious Crow's Nest Villa with four bedrooms, a private pool, a panoramic vista of the caribbean sea, private staff and an island vehicle for your convenience. Hawk's Nest Villa offers a beautiful view and a hot tub for the ultimate relaxation after an exhilarating day.

This private island paradise is just a 20 minute ride from Tortola on the resort's private yachts. Guests enjoy a full array of activities including deep-sea fishing, sailing, scuba diving, snorkeling, windsurfing, mountain-biking, tennis and island excursions including St.Thomas. Horticultural tours around the resort's private tropical gardens and bird-watching are also popular pass times.

The resort's friendly staff welcome your requests and look forward to providing you with their gracious island hospitality in either of our two restaurants featuring 5-star culinary specialties.

Address: P.O. Box 211, Road Town, Tortola, B.V.I.
Phone: 284-495-2000
Toll-Free: 800-346-4451
Fax: 284-776-6467
Room Rates: $$$$
Suite Rates: $$$$
Credit Cards: AmEx, Visa, MC, DC
No. of Rooms: 52 **Suites:** 3
Services and Amenities: Valet service, Mini-bars, Hair dryers, Robes, Complimentary toiletries
Restrictions: No pets allowed, No handicapped access
Concierge: 7:30 a.m.–7:00 p.m.
Room Service: 7:30 a.m.–7:00 p.m.
Restaurant: Tradewinds for breakfast and dinner, Deadman's Beach Bar and Grill for lunch and fun cookouts
Bar: Mian Bar, beach bar, 11:00 a.m.–11:00 p.m.
Business Facilities: Message center, Secretarial service, Copiers, Audio-Visual, Fax
Conference Rooms: 1 room, capacity 50
Sports Facilities: Freshwater pool, Tennis courts (2 lighted), Scuba diving, Sailing, Windsurfing, Deep-sea fishing, Mountain biking
Location: Private Island
Attractions: Island excursions to St. Thomas or Virgin Gorda, Daily scheduled ferry service to Tortola

PINK BEACH CLUB

Bermuda's premier south shore cottage colony is the perfect hideaway with elegant architecture, stunning views and exceptional service. The Gulf Stream meanders to the west of Bermuda, providing a subtropical climate. Any time of year guests can scuba dive and experience the wonders of marine life. Or if a gentle horseback ride across the sand sounds more appealing, then that too is available.

Whether honeymooners, golfers, families or business travellers, a mix of ocean view cottage deluxe suites and executive suites can provide accommodations for all needs. The junior suites feature a large living room/bedroom combination with private terrace. The spacious full suites have separate living and bedrooms plus private terraces. Both have high open beamed ceilings, soft tropical colors blending inside and out, and large sliding glass doors that open to the terraces and views of the Atlantic.

Breakfast is served in the main Club House or by one's own personal maid, either in suite or on the private terrace. Indulge in a before or after dinner drink in the bar or lounge, meeting old and new friends. Dine in the splendor of Pink Beach Club's oceanfront dining room. International dishes are prepared to perfection by European chefs. Entrees include ragout "Sir George" sauteed turkey, king prawns and champignons in lobstersauce combined with rice and spring onions. Guests may also dine at The Breakers ocean terrace cafe which offers such dishes as grilled Bermuda fish trio with jambalaya of tomato, okra and sweet potato. Entertainment is provided nightly on the pool terrace or in the bar.

European trained massage and beauty therapists offer guests in-room spa services. The newly appointed air-conditioned gym includes weight and cardiovascular rooms for guest use.

The friendly staff and spectacular surroundings will make guest's stays so memorable that guests will want to return year after year.

Address: 116 South Shore Road, Tuckers Town, Bermuda, FL06
Phone: 441-293-1666
Toll-Free: 800-355-6161
Fax: 441-293-8935
E-mail: pinkclub@bl.bm
Web site: http://www.pinkbeach.com
Suite Rates: $$$$
Credit Cards: Visa, MC, AmEx
No. of Suites: 91
Services and Amenities: Laundry service, Baby-sitting service, TV lounge in Club House, Card/game area, Library, Gift shop, Kitchen facilities in rooms, Balconies/decks, Telephone, Radio, Individual heat & air-conditioning control, Hair dryers, Complimentary toiletries
Restrictions: No pets allowed, 10 rooms handicapped-equipped, Children of all ages permitted
Concierge: 8:00 a.m.–11:00 p.m.
Room Service: 8:00 a.m.–10:00 a.m.
Restaurant: Club House Dining Room, 7:30—10:30 a.m., 7:00–9:30 p.m., Jacket required (tie optional)
Bar: Breakers Lounge, 11:00 a.m.–midnight with music and dancing nightly
Business Facilities: E-mail, Copiers, Audio-Visual, Teleconferencing
Conference Rooms: 2 rooms, capacity 85
Sports Facilities: Outdoor swimming pool, Massage, Weight training, 36 holes of golf nearby, 2 hard tennis courts, Snorkeling, Ping pong, Snooker
Location: Tuckers Town, South shore
Attractions: 5 minutes from Crystal Caves, Devil's Hole, Boa Aquarium, Spital Pond Nature Reserve

HOTEL VILLA DEL SOL

Villa del Sol, a member of the prestigious Relais & Chateaux and Small Luxury Hotels organizations, is located in a sheltered picturesque bay on the Mexican Pacific coast. Builder-owner Helmut Leins, an engineer from Munich, came under the spell of the sleepy fishing village of Zihuatenejo and its glistening ocean beach in 1969. Today his vision of an intimate beachfront inn, framed by lush tropical gardens, is a reality, and 47 tastefully appointed air-conditioned bungalow-suites now comprise Villa del Sol, including the newest addition: nine beautifully designed beach suites with a sweeping view of the ocean. The Mexican-style rooms feature large canopied beds and comfortable, attractive built-in sitting areas. Private terraces, fans and hammocks add to the relaxing Villa lifestyle, an ambience born of hospitality and a touch of romanticism.

Views from the rooms vary—from an elegant courtyard with its fountain, to an ornamental stream, to a miniature tropical island set in a shallow pool, to an eye-catching South Seas "palapa" (thatched roof) over the sunken dining and bar pavilion. Mexican and European chefs combine their talents to prepare the finest international cuisine for your enjoyment. Start with their famous margaritas. And then…feast! In the evening, Bach, Mozart and Beethoven will accompany you "mezzo voce" at dinner. (And, oh yes, Fridays, there's a Mexican Fiesta Buffet with fresh seafood.)

Be as energetic as you want and go for water sports, tennis, swimming, parasailing, fishing. Or simply relax on the beach and absorb the tranquil beauty of this Mexican paradise. Nothing will disturb your peace and quiet.

Address: Playa La Ropa S/N, Zihuatenejo, P.O. Box 84
Phone: 527-554-2239
Toll-Free: 888-389-2645
Fax: 527-554-2758
E-mail: villasoliwm.com.mx
Web site: http://www.villasol.com.mx
Room Rates: $$$
Suite Rates: $$$$
Credit Cards: Visa, MC, AmEx, Diners
No. of Rooms: 47
Services and Amenities: Valet service, Garage & parking, Car hire, Gift shop, Barber shop, Beauty shop, International currency exchange, Laundry, House doctor, Baby-sitting service, Card/game area, Library, Balconies in all rooms, Cable TV, Complimentary shoeshine & toiletries
Restrictions: 1 room with handicapped access, Only small pets allowed
Concierge: 9:00 a.m.–1:00 p.m.
Room Service: 8:00 a.m.–11:00 p.m.
Restaurant: Villa del Sol Restaurant, 8:00 a.m.–11:00 p.m.
Bar: Orlando's, 3:30 p.m.–11:00 p.m.
Business Facilities: Message & Secretarial center, E-mail, Copiers, Audio-Visual, Teleconferencing, Fax, Modems
Conference Rooms: 1 room, capacity 15
Sports Facilities: Outdoor swimming pool, Massage, Sailing, Tennis courts, Two 18-hole Golf Courses nearby, Water Activities also available nearby
Location: Only 2 kms from downtown & 10 kms from the airport
Attractions: Small boutique area in Ixtapa and Zihuantanejo, Magnificent beaches

Elegant Hotels of the Pacific Rim
by Pamela Lanier

In the spirit of *Elegant Small Hotels*, a guide to the finest lodging in the Pacific area—from California to Bangkok and points in between. Each of the 146 hotels described is highly rated by the world's top hoteliers. Most offer the finest cuisine to be found anywhere in the Pacific Basin. Each displays a special individuality that sets it apart.

THE COMPLETE GUIDE TO

BED & BREAKFASTS, INNS & GUESTHOUSES

IN THE UNITED STATES AND CANADA
—OVER 4,800 INNS AND ACCESS TO
  OVER 15,000 PRIVATE GUESTHOUSES

PAMELA LANIER

Complete Guide to Bed & Breakfasts, Inns & Guesthouses in the United States and Canada—A best-selling classic now in its twelfth fully revised edition. Over 10,000 inns listed and access to over 20,000 guesthouses. Includes specialty lists for interest ranging from bird watching to antiquing. "All necessary information about facilities, prices, pets, children amenities, credit cards and the like. Like France's Michelin ..." **New York Times**

Condo Vacations — The Complete Guide. The popularity of Condo Vacations has grown exponentially. In this first ever national guide, details are provided on over 3,000 Condo resorts in an easy to read format with valuable descriptive write-ups. The perfect vacation option for families and a great money saver!

All-Suite Hotel Guide—The Definitive Directory. The only guide to the all suite hotel industry features over 1,200 hotels nationwide and abroad. There is a special bonus list of temporary office facilities. A perfect choice for business travelers and much appreciated by families who enjoy the additional privacy provided by two rooms.

"They appeal to every segment—individual, corporate travellers, long time stays, and meetings**."– Corporate and Incentive Travel.**

"One of the hottest trends in the industry."
– Time

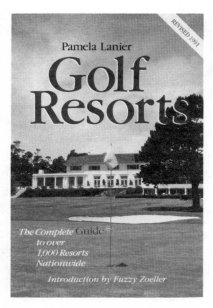

Golf Resorts—The Complete Guide. The first ever comprehensive guide to over 1,000 golf resorts coast to coast. Includes complete details of each resort facility and golf course particulars. Introduction by Fuzzy Zoeller.

Golf Courses—The Complete Guide. It's about time for a definitive directory and travel guide for the nation's 20 million avid golf players, 7 million of whom make golf vacations an annual event. This comprehensive guide includes over 8,000 golf courses in the United States that are open to the public. Complete details, greens fees, and information on the clubhouse facilities is augmented by a description of each of the golf courses' best features. A beautiful gift and companion to *Golf Resorts—The Complete Guide*. Introduction by Arthur Jack Snyder.

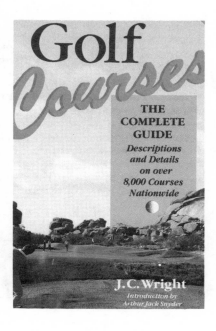

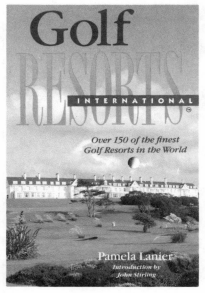

Golf Resorts International. A wish book and travel guide for the wandering golfer. This guide, written in much the same spirit as the bestselling *Elegant Small Hotels*, reviews the creme de la creme of golf resorts all over the world. Beautifully illustrated, it includes all pertinent details regarding hotel facilities and amenities. Wonderful narrative on each hotel's special charm, superb cuisine and most importantly, those fabulous golf courses. Written from a golfer's viewpoint, it looks at the challenges and pitfalls of each course.

For the non-golfer, there is ample information about other activities available in the area, such as on-site health spas, nearby extraordinary shopping, and more.

AVAILABLE AT BOOK STORES EVERYWHERE

Travel Books from
LANIER GUIDES
ORDER FORM

QTY	TITLE	EACH	TOTAL
	Golf Resorts—The Complete Guide	$14.95	
	Condo Vacations—The Complete Guide	$14.95	
	All-Suite Hotel Guide	$14.95	
	Golf Resorts International	$19.95	
	Golf Courses—The Complete Guide	$19.95	
	Elegant Small Hotels	$19.95	
	Elegant Hotels—Pacific Rim	$14.95	
	Complete Guide to Bed & Breakfasts, Inns & Guesthouses in the United States & Canada	$16.95	
	Family Travel—The Complete Guide	$19.95	
		Sub-Total	
		8% Sales Tax in California	
		U.S.A. Shipping International Shipping	$ 2.75 / 1 copy $ 5.75 / 1 copy (each additional book 50¢)
		TOTAL ENCLOSED	$

Send your order to:

LANIER PUBLISHING INTERNATIONAL, LTD.
Drawer D
Petaluma, CA 94953

Allow 3 to 4 weeks for delivery

NAME _____

ADDRESS _____

CITY _____ STATE _____ ZIP _____